# social psychology

*Prentice-Hall, Inc., Englewood Cliffs, New Jersey*

**JONATHAN L. FREEDMAN**
*Columbia University*

**J. MERRILL CARLSMITH**
*Stanford University*

**DAVID O. SEARS**
*University of California, Los Angeles*

# SOCIAL second edition
# PSYCHOLOGY

*Library of Congress Cataloging in Publication Data*

Freedman, Jonathan L.
   Social psychology.

   Bibliography: p.
   1. Social psychology.  I. Carlsmith, J. Merrill,
joint author.  II. Sears, David O., joint
author.  [DNLM: 1. Psychology, Social.  HM251
F853s 1974]
HM251.F68 1974     301.1     73–17142
ISBN  0–13–817833–X

Printed in the United States of America

10  9  8  7  6  5  4  3  2  1

Photo research for chapter opening photos
by *Gabriele Wunderlich*

Prentice-Hall International, Inc., London
Prentice-Hall of Australia, Pty. Ltd., Sydney
Prentice-Hall of Canada, Ltd., Toronto
Prentice-Hall of India Private Limited, New Delhi
Prentice-Hall of Japan, Inc., Tokyo

*No man is an Iland, intire of itselfe. . . .*
        *DONNE*

*I do not say it is good, I do not say it is bad,*
*I say it is the way it is.*
       *TALLEYRAND*

# contents

## eight

# attitudes: theoretical background 243

## nine

# changing attitudes 265

## ten

# attitude formation and change in real life 317

## eleven

# dissonance and attitude-discrepant behavior 341

x

# preface

The second edition of *Social Psychology* reflects change and progress in the field since the first edition was written. Although research continued on most problems that were of interest before, a number of new areas emerged. The burgeoning field of environmental psychology developed in response to growing concern about the population explosion, urban problems, pollution, and ecology in general. Attribution theory, while not a new idea, has become increasingly important in recent years. Research on social facilitation, mere exposure, risky shift, and altruism has either resolved or greatly clarified and extended our understanding of these phenomena. And there has been a gradual but substantial shift of locale from the experimental laboratory to more natural settings.

The new edition accordingly contains a totally new chapter on environmental psychology, covering the effects of crowding, personal space, and noise. Attribution theory, which was only alluded to in the first edition, is covered in depth in a chapter which relates it to other phenomena of social perception. Major sections are devoted to risky shift, altruism, bystander intervention, social facilitation, the relationship between attitudes and behavior, and mere exposure. The greater use of field research and applications is reflected in many more descriptions of this kind of research. In addition, the whole area of attitude change, which is often discussed only in terms of theory and laboratory studies, is given a new chapter devoted entirely to attitude change in the real world.

Naturally, more traditional areas have also been brought up to date. There are hundreds of new references to research that clarifies, refines, or even substantially redefines earlier findings. Some areas, such as affiliation, have been given relatively little attention during the past few years, while others, such as altruism have been investigated very actively. Our coverage reflects these differences in activity, some chapters changing much more than others. However, we have not included all new articles just because they were published. The revision concentrates on work that is not only new but also innovative and important.

As in the first edition, we have not tried to write an encyclopedia of social psychology. That may be useful for a professional, but it is not appropriate for an undergraduate course. As we said in the preface to the first edition, we have "attempted to present the knowledge that has been accumulated by social psychologists. This knowledge is based on the results of research. We have drawn on the findings of all kinds of research—experimental and correlational, laboratory and field, observational and archival, survey and individual. But throughout the book, our statements are based on hard data, on research findings, rather than on hypothetical notions about how something might work. We are firmly committed to the idea that social psychology is a scientific, not philosophic, field and that, as with any science, it must be firmly rooted in data. Thus, except when statements are labeled as speculations, the information presented is drawn from research.

However, we have not tried to present all the studies in detail. Our aim is to give the reader a clear, straightforward description of what is known, of what the research has found. Rather than burden the reader with descriptions of, say, ten studies that were conducted on a particular problem, we described one or two studies in detail to give a feeling for how the research on that problem was conducted and then presented our understanding of the pertinent findings in that area. Of course, there are times when results conflict. In these instances we tried to use our judgment, did not necessarily weight all the research equally, and sometimes drew conclusions for the reader. We feel that most students learn little from reading reports of conflicting studies and that we should bring order, if possible. Sometimes it is not possible—results are inconsistent and there is no rational way to choose between them. In these instances we described the inconsistencies and made it clear that the conflict is not yet resolved. Generally, however, we tried to present the best estimate of the truth at this time. Thus, the book is not an encyclopedia of studies nor is it a compendium of speculations—it is a description of the current state of knowledge of social psychology.

It should be made clear that we have not tried to oversimplify or present watered-down material. We feel that no useful purpose is served by presenting complexity and confusion when it is not necessary. Most social psychology textbooks have tended to disgorge numerous small, inconclusive studies that often leave the student confused and frustrated. Texts in other sciences present their discipline's knowledge as it exists at the time of writing. The introductory chemistry student, for example, is not assailed by contradictory and inconclusive experiments, even though they exist in that field as well as in ours. Instead, the student of chemistry is introduced to the field through the fundamental and important principles that have been established by research. Our goal in this text has been to do that for the student of social psychology.

The organization of the book is somewhat different from that of others. The book is organized around important behaviors and phenomena rather than around theories. Each chapter deals with a particular type of social behavior. We begin with affiliation, person perception, liking, and aggression, move to group behavior and conformity, and then to attitude change and compliance and finally to environmental psychology. Theoretical positions are described where they are appropriate. Thus, social comparison theory is discussed in the chapters on affiliation, liking, conformity, and so on—rather than in only one place. Theories of learning and of cognitive consistency appear in many chapters. And attribution is described in a chapter on social perception, but is referred to in many other sections. Similarly, concepts such as socialization are discussed in terms of aggression, affiliation, attitude formation, and other social phenomena. Socialization is thus incorporated throughout the book, rather than being considered only once. This organization, we feel, reflects the current research interests in the journals and the focus of attention within the field.

We are extremely grateful for the help we received from many sources. Friends and colleagues gave their time and thoughts generously while we were writing both the first edition and the second. We discussed aspects of the book with so many that it is impossible to list them all. We would like to give special thanks to Robert Krauss, Anthony Doob, Dennis and Judy Regan, Donald Kinder, and John McConohay for their contributions. And to Amy Midgley, Lorraine Mullaney, and Neale Sweet at Prentice-Hall who helped us with preparing, editing, designing, and illustrating the book.

Finally, let us note that we feel this revision is an improvement over the first edition. It incorporates more research, has two extra chapters, and has, we feel, benefited from the chance we had to rethink some of the major issues in the field. It is tighter, clearer, and in many places more sharply focused than the earlier version. The field has progressed and we hope this book adequately reflects that progress.

# social psychology

# one

# affiliation

**M**an is a gregarious animal. Although almost all animals spend much of their lives in close contact with other members of their species, human beings are probably the most social of the higher animals. The size and complexity of social groups vary considerably from species to species. Eagles live in solitary nests with just their mates and young. Timber wolves live with their immediate families, but hunt in packs. Lions live and hunt in prides consisting of a small number of males, females, and cubs. The great apes also live in groups of males, females, and young, with gorillas and chimpanzees having fairly small groups and baboons much larger ones. Burrowing animals, such as rats, often live in large communities, each family having a separate nest but sharing a network of paths, escape routes, and open space. And grazing animals such as deer and zebra sometimes live in huge herds.

## THE AFFILIATIVE TENDENCY

None of these social groups can compare in size or complexity to those of man. Most humans live in extremely complex societies consisting of a great many families that are combined and related in a vast array of personal and institutional groupings, with an almost unlimited variety of social ties, responsibilities, and dependencies. As far as we can tell, this tendency to live together has existed since the beginning of man's history and is one of the most basic facts of his life. In a sense, this tendency toward togetherness is the beginning of social psychology and therefore it is the first problem we shall consider. We all know that men associate with other men and that they appear to do this even when given the choice of being solitary. The question is: Why do men affiliate?

This is not a new question. It has been discussed, debated, written about for thousands of years. Philosophers, politicians, religious leaders, and poets argued that man *should* be gregarious. "It is not good that man should be alone" (Genesis 2:18); "Woe to him that is alone when he falleth, for he hath not another to help him up" (Ecclesiastes 14:10);

4

"Who can enjoy alone?" (Milton, *Paradise Lost*). And they have described the advantages of societies and tried to explain why men form them. "Man seeketh in society comfort, use and protection" (Bacon, *The Advancement of Learning*); "We do not by nature seek society for its own sake, but that we may receive some honor or profit from it. . . ." (Hobbes, *Philosophical Rudiments Concerning Government and Society*). Although not all agreed on the virtues of societies. "Society is always diseased, and the best is the most so" (Thoreau, *Excursions*); "Though the world contains many things which are thoroughly bad, the worst thing in it is society" (Schopenhauer, *Our Relations to Ourselves*).

Regardless of the points of view these statements express, they are primarily theoretical or philosophical. With a few exceptions, they are not so much concerned with why men affiliate as in outlining the good and bad aspects of existing societies. Social psychologists, in contrast, ask why. They want to know why men affiliate, not why they should affiliate. In other words, instead of attacking the phenomenon from a theoretical, conceptual, or philosophical point of view, social psychologists want to discover causes. There are two levels of answers to the question. First, there are fairly general basic explanations of the affiliative tendency in man, and second, there are particular factors that increase or decrease this tendency.

### Basic Explanations

**Instinct.** Early social psychologists such as McDougall believed that gregariousness is one of man's instincts. Just as ants collect in ant colonies by instinct, and baboons in the Amboseli Reserve in Africa build elaborate social structures, so man, *homo sapiens*, lives together in groups. He does this not because he thinks it is good or right or even useful; he does it without thinking, just as a baby sucks on a nipple or is afraid of heights.

Man is born with many genetically determined characteristics, and some social psychologists contend that among these characteristics is a tendency to seek out and to congregate with other human beings. If this were true, a child who had been raised in total isolation with a minimum of stimulation would be expected to affiliate with other human beings as soon as he was given the chance. It would not be necessary for a child to have any experiences after he was born in order for him to be an affiliative creature; he would affiliate even if he received no rewards or comfort from others. Although there may be considerable truth in this idea, it is almost impossible to test. One way to do so would be to raise a child in isolation and study his later behavior. Obviously we cannot and would not do this kind of experiment; and even if we could, it would not be a perfect test. Being raised in total isolation is not a normal environment for a human baby and it might have negative effects that would obscure any natural tendency to affiliate. Therefore, the explanation of affiliation in terms of instinct, although it must be kept in the back of our minds, cannot ordinarily be studied directly.

**Innate Determinant.**   A somewhat similar idea is that affiliation, though not innate or instinctive, is caused and made necessary by innate characteristics of human babies. The idea is that although there may be no instinctive drive or tendency to be gregarious, it is essential for humans to congregate in order to survive. Unlike most other animals, a human baby is virtually helpless for a long period of time. His early dependence on his mother for nurture and nutriments makes it necessary that he live with another *homo sapiens* for many years. Whereas most animals, even mammals, nurse for only a short time and can then forage for food on their own, the human baby is unable to feed itself for several years, at the very least. It is conceivable that in a mild, protected, rich environment a child could stay alive after he was one or two years old, but under normal circumstances this would not be possible. He needs food, he needs protection from predators, he needs some kind of shelter, etc. Similarly, a mother is extremely dependent on other humans for protection, particularly while she is taking care of her baby. Although it is possible for a solitary woman to survive even while nursing her child, under most circumstances she is dependent on at least one other human for protection and food.

Thus man is gregarious, by necessity, for the early years of his life. If the mother and child did not stay together, the child would die. In this sense man's innate characteristics, particularly his early helplessness, do cause him to affiliate. At a certain stage in life, however, man ceases to be absolutely dependent on others. He no longer needs them to give him food or protection. He could, in terms of his innate needs, become solitary. In our modern society a man could live in a penthouse apartment, have his food delivered, watch television, read newspapers that were delivered with the food, and lead a safe, secure, comfortable, solitary life for many years. Or he could live on an isolated farm and accomplish the same thing without any help from others.

Occasionally someone does. There are cases of people becoming hermits, living alone, and, as far as we can tell, surviving perfectly well. But these are unusual, deviant cases. There are very few voluntary hermits, and those that do exist are generally considered somewhat crazy, certainly eccentric, and objects of curiosity. They are rebelling against perhaps the most universal characteristic of man, the tendency to be gregarious. Solitary confinement is almost always considered a severe punishment. Although it seems that man's gregariousness is to some extent innately or instinctively determined, we are still left with the question of why men affiliate when they no longer need to.

**Learning.**   One answer is that men learn to affiliate just as they learn anything else. The child depends on others for essentials such as food, warmth, and protection, and each time one of these basic needs is satisfied by someone else, the child learns something. By the simple process of association, other people become connected with rewards and the child learns to consider people positive aspects of his environment. In addition, because the child is rewarded when he is with other people, the act of associating with people is reinforced. He learns that when he needs something, seeking out other people usually leads to satisfaction. Thus, he has learned to affiliate with others; it has become a customary part of his daily life.

This learning affects an individual's behavior throughout his life. As an adult, he no longer requires other people in order to survive, but he still associates with them because he has learned to. Thus, as children learn all sorts of habits that shape their lives, so they learn affiliation, and because all children in all cultures to some extent must learn to affiliate, it becomes a characteristic of all men.

**Satisfaction of Needs.**   It is also true that men have needs other than those that are necessary for personal survival—needs that only other people can satisfy. For example, although the solitary life leaves an individual with some means of sexual satisfaction, it denies him the outlet of sexual intercourse with other humans. In addition, the needs for achievement, love, appreciation, comfort, respect, and power, although not innate, are sought by most men, and these needs are extremely difficult to satisfy in isolation. Thus, although man could stay alive in isolation, he has acquired, through early social learning, many needs that can be satisfied only by other people.

### Specific Causes

Instinct, innate characteristics, learning, and the satisfaction of needs are all explanations of why men affiliate. They are, however, general answers that do not allow us to specify much about the forces that control affiliation. If we say that animals eat because they have a need to eat or because they have learned to eat, we are correct but we do not learn very much about eating. On the other hand, if we say that animals eat when they have been deprived of food for four hours or when their blood-sugar level is low, we have specific knowledge about hunger and eating and can control the amount an animal will eat.

This distinction between general and specific explanations is also applicable to affiliation. Social psychologists have tried to determine the factors that increase or decrease the tendency to affiliate. We want to discover specific conditions that produce more affiliation and those that produce less in order to gain a more detailed understanding of the nature and causes of affiliation. We begin with the premise that almost all men have a tendency to associate with other men. But we know there are times when this need is felt strongly, times when it is weak, and even times when people prefer to be alone. The question is: What factors increase and decrease affiliation?

Our general approach to answering questions in psychology is to collect data in controlled situations, rather than simply observing people and trying to guess why they behave as they do. In a controlled experiment on affiliation, one or more factors can be varied to determine how the tendency to affiliate is affected by each factor. We can expose one person to one condition, another to another condition, and see if their behavior differs. If it does, we can attribute the differences to the factor we varied. This is the basis of the experimental method and will be discussed in detail in Chapter 14.

**Anxiety and Affiliation.**  A report of the most systematic attempt to study the causes of affiliation was published in 1959 by Stanley Schachter. He began by noting that to ascertain the conditions under which the tendency to affiliate is strong, one should observe what happens when people are not allowed to affiliate. If affiliation is serving to satisfy a need, this need should become very salient when a person is denied the source of its satisfaction.

A study of case histories of people in total isolation—members of some religious orders, people who had been shipwrecked, volunteers for isolation experiments—did show some similarities. Almost all accounts of long-term isolation included descriptions of sudden fearfulness and feelings resembling anxiety attacks, and, within limits, longer isolation produced greater fear and anxiety. Although it is impossible to conclude anything definitive from this observed relationship because many other explanations are also plausible, it does suggest that fear and affiliation are closely linked. If isolation produces fear, affiliation may reduce fear. Thus, Schachter was led to the specific hypothesis that persons with high fear would affiliate more than those with low fear.

To test this hypothesis, one must examine individuals who differ in their amount of fear. One method of investigation would be to study individuals who differ in the amount of fear they are experiencing in life situations. However, such people almost certainly differ on dimensions other than their degree of fear. For example, although airplane pilots who are about to make their first solo flight are probably more afraid than pilots who have flown for years, they also differ in length of experience, probably in age, and certainly in attitude toward flying. Any differences found in affiliative tendencies might be due to factors other than the amount of fear they are experiencing. By using controlled situations, one can select people who are similar and then experimentally manipulate their degree of fear, making some more afraid than others. Then, when the subjects are given an opportunity to affiliate, the amount of affiliation they exhibit can be compared and any differences attributed to the degree of fear that had been aroused in them. This is what Schachter did, and his experiment has served as a model for almost all the subsequent work in this area.

**The Experimental Procedure.**   Each subject in Schachter's experiment entered a room to find an experimenter in a white laboratory coat, surrounded by electrical equipment of various sorts. The experimenter introduced himself as Dr. Gregor Zilstein of the department of neurology and psychiatry and explained that the experiment concerned the effects of electric shock. In order to make some subjects more afraid than others, the experimenter used two different descriptions of the electric shock.

Instructions designed to arouse a considerable amount of fear (high-fear condition) described the shocks in ominous terms. Subjects were told, "These shocks will hurt. . . . In research of this sort, if we're to learn anything at all that will really help humanity, it is necessary that our shocks be intense. . . . These shocks will be quite painful but, of course, they will do no permanent damage." By continuing at some length in this vein, the experimenter communicated the notion that the subject was in for a very frightening experience.

In the low-fear condition, by contrast, every attempt was made to make the subject feel relaxed and at ease, while communicating the same basic facts about the experiment. For example, the subjects were told, "I assure you that what you will feel [i.e., electric shock] will not in any way be painful. It will resemble a tickle or a tingle more than anything unpleasant." Thus, although both groups of subjects were told that the experiment would concern electric shock, one group expected a painful and frightening experience whereas the other group expected a mild and unthreatening experience. As shown by questioning the subjects, the result was that the former group was more afraid than the latter.

Following the arousal and measurement of fear, the experimenter told the subjects there would be a ten-minute delay while he prepared the equipment. He explained that there were a number of other rooms in which the subjects might wait—rooms that were comfortable, with armchairs, magazines, etc. The experimenter continued that it had occurred to him that perhaps some of the people would prefer to wait with other subjects in the experiment and for these, there was a classroom available. Each subject was asked to indicate whether he preferred to wait with others, alone, or had no preference. He was also asked to indicate the strength of his choice. In this and most subsequent experiments on this topic, the choice and rating of the intensity of subjects' desire to affiliate were the basic measures of the tendency.

The results of Schachter's study are shown in Table 1–1. The answer to the question of whether highly fearful subjects want to affiliate more than subjects with low fear is yes. The greater the fear, the greater the tendency to affiliate.

Now that we have found a relationship between fear and affiliation, the next step is to explain it. Why do fearful people affiliate more? There seem to be at least two explanations—fear reduction and social comparison.

**FEAR REDUCTION**

We have seen that isolation appears to increase fear, which, in turn, leads to an increase in affiliation. One probable explanation of this increase in affiliation is that people affiliate in order to reduce their fear.

Schachter's first experiment did not test this explanation directly, but some support for it was provided in a subsequent study (Schachter, 1959). Subjects were told that if they chose to wait with others they could either not talk at all or talk only about things unrelated to the experiment. The purpose of this restriction was to make it more difficult for the subjects to reduce fear by reassuring one another. To the extent that high-fear subjects were affiliating in order to reduce fear, there would be less preference for waiting together than there had been when

Table 1–1

*EFFECT OF FEAR ON AFFILIATION*

| | PERCENTAGE CHOOSING | | | |
|---|---|---|---|---|
| Condition | Together | Don't Care | Alone | Strength of Affiliation[a] |
| High fear | 62.5 | 28.1 | 9.4 | .88 |
| Low fear | 33.0 | 60.0 | 7.0 | .35 |

[a]Figures are ratings on a scale from −2 to +2.

Source: Adapted from Schachter (1959).

talking about the experiment was allowed. This was borne out by the study. Because it showed that being less able to reduce fear decreased affiliation, the study suggested that the desire to reduce fear is one factor producing affiliation.

### Birth Order

Even when high fear is aroused, some people have stronger needs to affiliate than others. Is there any systematic reason for this? An important, although supplementary, finding in Schachter's study of affiliation is that birth order is an important determinant of a person's desire to affiliate. First-born children and only children when afraid have a stronger tendency to affiliate than do later-born children. In fact, the tendency decreases progressively for the later-born children; those born second show a greater tendency to affiliate than do those born third, who, in turn, show a greater affiliative tendency than those born fourth, etc. As shown in Figure 1–1, this progression is maintained regardless of the size of the family. The affiliative tendency of someone born second

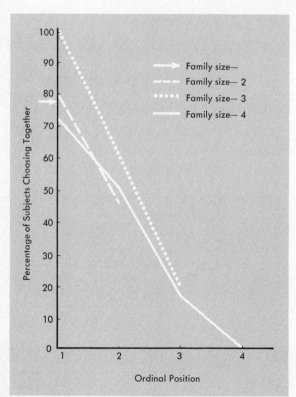

Figure 1–1

First borns, when afraid, affiliate more than second borns, who, in turn, affiliate more than third borns, and so on. This holds regardless of the size of family—order of birth, not number of siblings, determines affiliation. (Reprinted from *The Psychology of Affiliation* by Stanley Schachter with the permission of the publishers, Stanford University Press. © 1959 by the Board of Trustees of the Leland Stanford Junior University.)

in a family of six is about the same strength as that of someone born second in a family of two. In other words, the order of birth, not the size of the family, is the determinant. Why should birth order have this effect on affiliation?

Theoretically, the effect might be caused by some innate difference between first and later borns, but there is no evidence of such genetic differences. Most psychologists feel that the way children are brought up is crucial. One possible analysis is as follows. Parents are more concerned about their first child than about later children. When a first-born child falls, his mother runs to comfort him. Therefore, the first-born child soon learns that when he is uncomfortable, his mother is a marvelous source of comfort. So he learns to seek comfort from other people. With later children, parents become less concerned about the trials and tribulations of growing up. They learn that children are surprisingly resilient and their misery mostly transient. Moreover, the parents are a little tired of oohing and aahing over every scraped knee, and they now have two children to care for and not so much time for each. Therefore, the affiliative tendency of the second child is reinforced less than that of the first child—the second child learns less that other people are a source of comfort and thus he learns to depend less on other people. By the time the third child is born, the parents are quite calm about raising children. They have even less time for the third child so he learns even less, and so on. Thus, the earlier a child is in the birth order, the more he learns to depend on other people as sources of comfort when he is afraid.

To summarize: When people are afraid, they vary greatly in the extent to which they seek other people as a means of reducing their fear. One factor that affects this is their early exprience as children. First-born children are raised in such a way that they tend to seek others when they are worried, and the tendency decreases progressively for the later born.

This finding on the effect of birth order provides additional support for the conclusion that one cause of affiliation is the desire to reduce fear. Although the birth-order effect could be interpreted in other ways, it seems that first and later borns differ in their dependence on others in reducing fear. The first borns are more dependent and show the effect of fear on affiliation more strongly. Therefore, the reduction of fear is one of the motivations that increases affiliation.

### Fear Versus Anxiety

The situation is complicated somewhat by the distinction between *fear* and *anxiety*. Although people generally use the two terms more or less interchangeably, psychologists use them to refer to quite different feelings. Freud suggested that being afraid of a realistic object or source of injury is different from being afraid when there is no real danger. He called the former *realistic anxiety* or *object anxiety*, and we shall call it *fear*. He called the latter *neurotic anxiety*; today, it is generally called *anxiety* to distinguish it from fear.

A man being charged by a lion, advancing under enemy gunfire, or balancing on a narrow precipice while mountain climbing feels fear. He is in real danger and experiences the normal reaction to it. A man sitting in a room in which there is a mouse, walking through an unfamiliar but friendly neighborhood, or standing on a wide ledge with a high protective fence may also feel very uncomfortable. And there are times when he feels a sense of dread and becomes nervous and afraid but cannot connect the emotion to any specific object or situation. In all these instances there is no danger, he cannot be harmed, and yet he may experience a reaction similar to fear—this is anxiety.

According to Freud, anxiety is aroused by unconscious desires—sexual, aggressive, or otherwise—that people have but consider unacceptable. For example, men may unconsciously wish to be submissive, to act like children and be babied and taken care of by their mother. But modern society puts pressure on men to be assertive, dominant, independent. Most men assume the role society dictates and deny to themselves and others that they have the childish feelings. Then, when they are exposed to a situation that arouses these desires, men have a tendency to feel uncomfortable. However, because they are denying their needs, they do not know what is bothering them. Another example is the latent homosexual male who feels uncomfortable in a communal shower with other men. He is unaware of his homosexual feelings, but the situation arouses sexual feelings that he denies. He is, in a sense, afraid of his feelings, and it is this fear that we call anxiety. Stimuli that arouse hidden and/or unacceptable feelings produce anxiety.

Accepting this conceptual distinction, it is clear that Schachter's study of affiliation involved fear rather than anxiety. There was a real reason to be frightened—the painful electric shock. Thus, we have been careful to state the original finding as: High *fear* produces greater affiliation than low *fear*. This distinction is important because the reaction to anxiety is different.

Most people have learned that being with others usually reduces fear of something realistic. Other people reassure them, they realize that the others are going to experience the danger also, and there is strength in numbers.

When one's worry is unrealistic, however, associating with others is less likely to help and may even make things worse. The others pre-

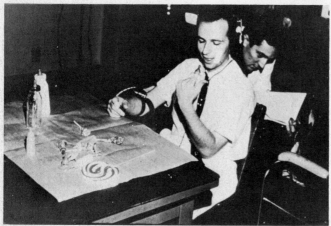

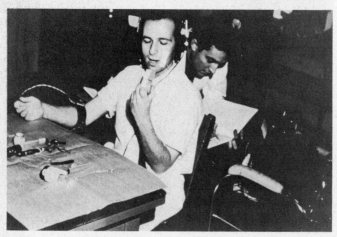

In the study investigating the effect of fear and anxiety on affiliation, fear was aroused (top) by telling the subject he was going to receive electric shocks. High anxiety was aroused by having the subject anticipate sucking on rubber nipples, baby bottles, and the other objects on the table (middle). Low anxiety was produced by telling him he would have to blow whistles and balloons and smoke toy pipes (bottom). (Courtesy of Irving Sarnoff and Philip Zimbardo.)

sumably are not feeling anxious, because there is really nothing to worry about; therefore, the anxious one cannot talk freely about his concerns. The others would be surprised at his feelings, he might be embarrassed, and the interaction might increase rather than decrease his anxiety. Even if he could talk to others, it would be more difficult for them to reassure him because they would not understand the real cause of his discomfort. Because associating might increase his anxiety by producing embarrassment, a high-anxious subject would try to conceal rather than reveal his feelings. Accordingly, he should want to be alone more than a low-anxious subject.

To test this hypothesis, Sarnoff and Zimbardo (1961) conducted a study similar to Schachter's but with one important difference—both fear and anxiety were tested. One group of subjects was told, as in Schachter's experiment, that they were going to receive electric shocks; some members of this group were told the shocks would be quite severe (high fear), whereas others were told the shocks would be mild (low fear). Another group was put in a situation designed to arouse anxiety involving unrealistic concerns. They were told they would have to suck on a variety of objects. Some in this group were told they would have to suck on breast shields, rubber nipples, and other emotionally laden objects. The subjects were undergraduate men who felt reasonably mature and adult. On the premise that being asked to suck on infantile, ludicrous objects would arouse a great deal of oral anxiety and would make them feel uncomfortable and foolish, these subjects were considered high anxious. Other subjects were told they would have to blow on relatively acceptable, innocuous objects such as whistles. This was expected to produce little or no discomfort, so these subjects were considered low anxious. The point was that neither anxiety group had anything realistic to be afraid of. All subjects were given the measure of affiliation described previously—they had to indicate their preference for being alone or with others while waiting to go through the expected procedure.

The results are shown in Figure 1–2. As before, those anticipating severe shocks (high fear) wanted to wait together more than did those expecting mild shocks (low fear). However, as predicted, anxiety produced the opposite effect. The high-anxious subjects wanted to wait alone more than did the low-anxious subjects. The higher the anxiety, the *less* the desire for affiliation.

We thus have two distinct findings: Fear leads to increased affiliation. Anxiety leads to decreased affiliation. In social psychology, making this kind of distinction aids in understanding a social phenomenon—in this case, affiliation. We can now make a more precise explanation of the relationships involved. Other people are a source of both comfort and

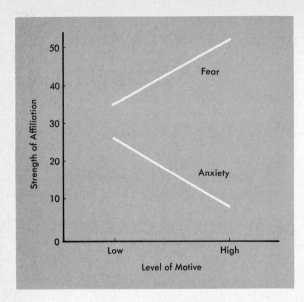

Figure 1-2

The desire to affiliate depends on the particular emotion that is aroused. High fear produces *more* affiliation than low fear; but high anxiety produces *less* affiliation than low anxiety. Note that the overall level of affiliation is higher under conditions involving fear than under those involving anxiety.

embarrassment. When one expects them to provide comfort, one seeks them out; when one expects embarrassment, one avoids them. Associating with others seems generally to decrease fear, so when fear is heightened, people seek others as a means of reducing it. But being around other people can increase anxiety, so when anxiety is heightened, people avoid affiliating.

**SOCIAL COMPARISON** The analysis of affiliation in terms of fear reduction is only a partial answer. Schachter's original finding can also be explained in terms of Leon Festinger's theory of social comparison (1954). The theory contains two basic ideas: People have a drive to evaluate themselves; and in the absence of objective nonsocial means, they will evaluate themselves by comparison with other people.

Everyone wants to know how good he is at whatever he does—is he a good tennis player, a fast runner, a good marksman, a talented writer, a graceful dancer? Sometimes there is a fairly obvious objective criterion of self-evaluation. For example, a marksman who shoots a perfect score knows he is doing as well as he can and that he is very good. But most of the time there is no such convenient criterion. How does a runner know if he is fast? Is a five-minute mile good? How about a mile in four minutes, ten seconds? Twenty years ago a four-ten mile would have been superb; today, because others are running faster, it is only fair. Is a man 5 feet, 10 inches in height tall or short? In the United States he is about average; in Japan he would be tall; among the Watusi in Africa he would be short.

16

An example of self-evaluation by comparison with others can be seen in the experiences of high school students who enter college. In high school they were the brightest ones around and they and everyone else considered them quite exceptional. But in college many of the freshman class had been outstanding high school students. Each must now compare himself to an essentially all-star high school group. Most discover that they are not so outstanding after all, that in this new group they are just average. Their own intelligence has not changed—the comparison group by which they evaluate their intelligence has. They feel that they adequately evaluate their abilities only by comparing themselves to the people around them. When these people change, their evaluations of themselves change.

This is especially true when feelings and emotions are involved. Because there are rarely objective criteria to indicate if one's feelings are appropriate to a situation, other people are the only source of information. In fact, to a large extent individuals define an appropriate reaction as the one most people have. Should one be afraid of a huge but harmless snake? By any realistic standard, the answer is no. But most people probably are somewhat frightened of a five-foot snake, regardless of its potential danger. Because the typical reaction is fear, most people would consider feeling fear to be more appropriate than not feeling fear. In fact, someone who was not frightened by such a snake would generally be considered rather odd. Thus, the so-called normative response is considered correct; anything else is, in a sense, wrong.

The appropriateness of any emotional reaction, therefore, can be ascertained only by seeing what others are feeling. This can apply to the type of emotion and also to the strength of the emotion. People clarify and evaluate their reactions by comparing them with others' reactions. Therefore, when an individual is uncertain about his feelings, he seeks to clarify them. When other people are the only useful source of information, he compares himself to them. Thus we have another explanation for the effect of fear on affiliation. The more uncertain an individual is about his feelings, the more he will want to affiliate with others in order to reduce the uncertainty.

When subjects are told they are going to be given a severe electric shock, they naturally become frightened; we have seen that this leads to greater affiliation than if they were less afraid. One reason for this heightened affiliation is the subject's desire to reduce his fear and his expectation that being with other subjects will accomplish this. However, though they know it is appropriate to be afraid, they are not sure how afraid they should be. Should they be terrified? Or should they not be terribly worried? They are in a state of some uncertainty as to what the appropriate emotional reaction is. According to the theory of social comparison, they should have strong needs to affiliate in order to find out what others are feeling and thereby to evaluate and clarify their own reactions.

## Hunger

The arousal of needs other than fear reduction can also increase affiliation. Whenever someone has a strong need, he tends to be uncertain about how he should be feeling. This uncertainty leads to a desire for social comparison and thus to affiliation. For example, one experiment (Schachter, 1959) demonstrated that a high degree of hunger causes people to want to affiliate more than a low degree of hunger. Subjects were called the night before they were to take part in the experiment and told that it would involve the effects of particular kinds of food deprivation on sensations. One group of subjects (classified as high hunger) were asked to fast for approximately twenty hours by omitting breakfast and lunch on the following day, and one group (medium hunger) were asked to fast for six hours by omitting lunch. A third group were also asked to omit breakfast and lunch but when they arrived for the experiment, they were presented with an array of foods and told to eat as much as they wished. The subjects in this group, who were then not at all hungry, were classified as low hunger.

All the subjects were put in individual rooms. The experimenter explained that the study actually involved four different tests—named, respectively, binocular redundancy, visual diplacity, auditory peripherality, and aural angular displacement—but that each subject would take part in only one. Two of the tests, the first and third, would be taken with another subject; the second and fourth tests would be taken alone.

Table 1–2

*EFFECT OF HUNGER ON AFFILIATION*

| Condition | PERCENTAGE OF SUBJECTS CHOOSING | |
| --- | --- | --- |
| | *Together* | *Alone* |
| High hunger | 67 | 33 |
| Medium hunger | 35 | 65 |
| Low hunger | 30 | 70 |

Source: Adapted from Schachter (1959).

In addition, before each test there would be an adaptation period during which the subjects would be waiting either with the other subject, if they chose the first or third test, or alone. The subjects then ranked the tests in the order in which they would like to take them. Thus, if they wanted to wait with another subject, they could choose test one or three; if they wanted to wait alone, they could choose test two or four.

The results are shown in Table 1–2. They indicate that high hunger increased the tendency to want to be with another subject. Of the subjects in the high-hunger condition, 67 percent chose a test in which they would wait with another subject; only 35 percent in the medium-hunger condition and 30 percent in the low-hunger condition chose one of those tests. Because moderate hunger is not a particularly unusual experience, it did not produce great uncertainty and did not lead to strong pressures toward affiliation for social comparison. By contrast, twenty hours of hunger, being unusual for these subjects, led to considerable uncertainty about feelings and therefore produced strong pressures toward affiliation for the purpose of social comparison.

### Affiliation with Whom?

A more direct effect of the drive for social comparison can be seen when we examine with whom the subjects want to affiliate. One of the basic hypotheses of the theory is that people wish to compare themselves with others similar to them. The more similar they are, the stronger the drive for social comparison. For example, if a student is worried about a test and feels the need to find out how worried it is appropriate to be, does he want to talk to another student or the teacher? In most cases, another student. It would not help at all to find out that the teacher is not worried, because the teacher does not have to take the test. Moreover, the student wants to compare himself to others who are similar in ability to him. A better student may not be worried, but that would tell the poorer student very little about what is appropriate for himself. In comparing, he prefers someone as close as possible to himself in ability, diligence, concern for grades, and so on. Such a student would give him the best information about how he should be feeling.

This leads to a clear prediction in terms of affiliation. To the extent that people affiliate for reasons of social comparison, they should have a stronger desire to affiliate with people who are similar to them than with people who are dissimilar. When they are concerned about evaluating their own emotions, they should particularly desire to affiliate with someone who is in their own situation.

Several studies have tested this prediction. Schachter (1959) used his standard procedure in which subjects were threatened with severe shock and then asked whether they would like to wait alone or with others. But for this experiment, the people with whom the subjects could wait were either other subjects who were waiting to take part in the study or students who had nothing to do with the experiment but who were waiting to talk to their advisers. In other words, one group of subjects was given a choice of waiting alone or with people who were similar to them; the other group was given a choice of waiting alone or with subjects who were quite different from them.

The results strongly supported the prediction from the theory of social comparison. Under high fear, subjects showed a strong preference for waiting with other subjects who were similar to them but did not want to wait with subjects who were different from them. However, in some sense the choice the subjects were given was not really fair. After all, there could have been considerable reluctance to walk into a room of students who were waiting to talk to their advisers, who may have known one another, and who certainly knew nothing about what the subject was doing.

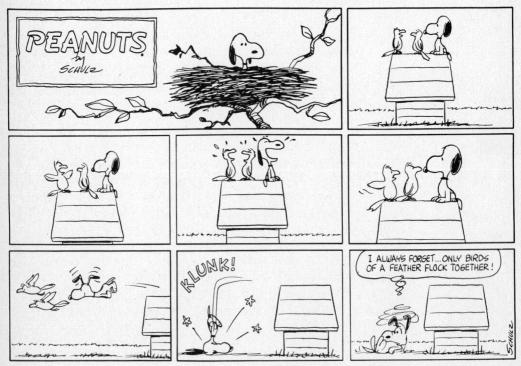

Drawing by Charles Schulz; © 1965 United Feature Syndicate, Inc.

A better test of the hypothesis was provided in a study by Zimbardo and Formica (1963), in which subjects were given the choice of waiting either with people who, like themselves, were about to take part in the study or with others who had just completed the study. The results of this test are more convincing because the people with whom the subject could wait were identical in both conditions, except that those who were about to take part in the study were presumably in the same emotional state as the subject making the choice whereas the others were in a different emotional state. Once again, the results supported the social-comparison hypothesis. Subjects showed a greater preference for waiting with those who were about to take part in the study than they did for waiting with those who had already been through the procedure. The more similar the others, the stronger was the drive to affiliate. Schachter has summarized these results: "Misery doesn't love just any company, it loves only miserable company."

### The Role of Uncertainty

The central assumption of the social comparison analysis is that uncertainty produces a need for comparing oneself to others. The more uncertain people feel about their reactions, the stronger should be this need for social comparison. Because the need for comparison leads to affiliation, the implication is that increasing uncertainty increases one's desire to affiliate. A series of studies by Harold Gerard investigated this relationship between uncertainty and affiliation.

Gerard argued that merely arousing fear, as Schachter did, is not a very powerful way to make people want to compare themselves with others. The subjects in Schachter's experiment may not have been sure how frightened they should be, but they must have been sure that what they were feeling was appropriate (assuming they were frightened). In terms of the theory, the important factor influencing the strength of the desire for social comparison and consequently the drive toward affiliation should be the degree of uncertainty as to the appropriateness of one's feelings. When one is extremely uncertain as to how he should be feeling, the drive for social comparison should be very high; the more certain he is that what he is feeling is appropriate, the weaker should be the drive for social comparison and the less the tendency to affiliate.

One critical factor affecting the degree of uncertainty is how much one knows about his own feelings and the feelings of others. Thus, the more information one has about these feelings, the less the need for social comparison and, accordingly, the less the desire to affiliate.

Gerard and Rabbie (1961) tested this hypothesis. The basic design of their experiment was similar to Schachter's. However, before the subjects made the choice of waiting either alone or with others, some of them were given information about their reactions and those of the other subjects and some were not. In this way, the subjects' degree of uncertainty was manipulated directly, so that its effect could be clearly observed.

The procedure for informing the subjects of their reactions was quite ingenious. Each subject was seated in a separate cubicle, and electrodes were attached to his ring finger and forehead. The experimenter explained that these measuring devices gave an accurate picture of the subject's "emotionality," that is, recorded how afraid he was. Subjects in one condition were shown four dials, supposedly corresponding to the subject being tested and three others. The subject saw that he registered 82 on a 100-point scale and that the other subjects were registering 79, 80, and 81, respectively. Thus, he learned what he and the others were feeling and that they were all feeling about the same amount of fear. In another condition, the subjects were shown only their own rating, and in a third condition, they were given no information. Then all the subjects were asked to state their preference for waiting alone or with others.

The analysis of uncertainty in terms of social comparison implies that the desire to affiliate should be affected by the degree of uncertainty people feel about the appropriateness of their own reactions. Because they are concerned about how they compare with others, when they know their own and others' reactions and also that they all are experiencing about the same amount of fear, there should be little uncertainty.

Table 1–3

INFORMATION, FEAR, AND STRENGTH OF DESIRE TO AFFILIATE

| Condition | STRENGTH OF DESIRE TO AFFILIATE | |
| --- | --- | --- |
| | High Fear | Low Fear |
| No information | 66.80 | 54.53 |
| Information about self | 70.50 | 64.12 |
| Information about self and others | 55.09 | 47.67 |

Note: Figures are ratings on a scale from 0 to 100.

Source: Adapted from Gerard and Rabbie (1961).

When they have either no information or information about only their own reaction, there should be considerable uncertainty. As shown in Table 1–3, the results agreed with these expectations. The subjects who had been given information about themselves and others showed the least preference for waiting together, whereas the other groups did not differ appreciably in their desire to affiliate. In other words, removing uncertainty—and therefore the need for social comparison—reduced the tendency to affiliate. This finding strongly supports the theory that one reason for affiliating is social comparison.

Uncertainty is also affected by the ambiguity of the information one has about his own feelings and those of others. We have seen that the amount of information is an important determinant of affiliation. In addition, the more difficult it is to understand the information, the more uncertain one should be and the greater should be his tendency to affiliate in order to reduce this uncertainty. In another study by Gerard (1963), subjects were shown dials that either wavered wildly or remained steady. Thus they had either clear or ambiguous information about fear levels. If one knows how afraid he is and how afraid others are there is little to be gained by social comparison and therefore little need to affiliate. If the information is vague (and a rapidly oscillating needle on a meter is vague), there is good reason to affiliate—to find out what this vague information means. The study showed that with steady dials, subjects who knew their own and others' scores had little desire to affiliate; with wavering dials, however, even subjects who knew their own and others' scores had a strong need to affiliate.

The effect of uncertainty on affiliation was demonstrated in a particularly elegant way in a recent study by Mills and Mintz (1972). The idea was to produce a physiological arousal by the use of a drug and to tell some subjects what had caused the arousal and not to tell others. Presumably those who knew that they had been aroused by the drug would feel little or no uncertainty about their emotional state, but those who did not know would feel uncertain as to what they were feeling and why. Therefore, those who knew that the drug had caused the arousal should feel little uncertainty and should not have a strong tendency to affiliate; whereas those who were aroused and did not know why should be quite uncertain and should have strong tendencies to affiliate. As you can see in Table 1–4, this is exactly what was found, once more supporting the notion that uncertainty is a major cause of the desire to affiliate.

All this evidence indicates that the need for social comparison is one reason why people affiliate. The major factor affecting the strength

Table 1–4

*DESIRE TO AFFILIATE RELATED TO AROUSAL AND
KNOWLEDGE ABOUT THE AROUSAL*

| Condition | Strength of Affiliative Tendency |
|---|---|
| Placebo—no arousal | 4.7 |
| Caffeine—informed (Aroused and told what produced it) | 4.5 |
| Caffeine—misinformed (Aroused but not told what produced it) | 5.4 |

Source: Adapted from Mills and Mintz (1972).

of this need seems to be the individual's degree of uncertainty about his feelings. The more uncertain he is, the more he can gain by comparing himself to others and, consequently, the greater the desire to affiliate.

**THE EFFECT OF AFFILIATING** We have explained the effect of fear on affiliation in terms of two quite different mechanisms: the frightened person wants to affiliate in order to reduce his fear; he also wants to affiliate in order to compare his feelings with those of other people so as to discover if his feelings are appropriate. A somewhat separate, but obviously related question is whether or not these two processes actually occur when affiliation is permitted. That is, does the individual become less afraid and does he compare his emotions?

If fear reduction is a rational reason for affiliating, waiting with other people should reduce fear even if the others are also afraid. If social comparison is a strong motive for affiliating, we would expect subjects to notice what others are feeling and to be concerned about the appropriateness of their own feelings. To the extent that their own feelings are different from those of the others (i.e., are inappropriate), subjects should tend to modify their feelings so as to make them less different. If everyone in the group does this, the feelings of the various members of the group should become more similar.

An experiment designed to test these two hypotheses was conducted by Wrightsman (1960). People who were very frightened were allowed to wait together or were forced to wait alone, and measures of fear level were taken before and after the waiting period. It was found that waiting in a group reduced fear more than waiting alone, with this applying particularly to first-born subjects. The group also showed a strong tendency toward uniformity of feeling.

McDonald (1970) also demonstrated the fear-reducing effect of waiting with others. However, this occurred primarily for first-born subjects and surprisingly was most strong for those first-borns who said that they would prefer to wait alone but were forced to wait with others. Despite these somewhat perplexing findings, this study does provide more evidence that, in general, highly fearful subjects who wait in groups become less fearful. Thus both fear reduction and social comparison apparently do operate when people affiliate under conditions of high fear.

To summarize, people affiliate for many reasons. The desire may be partly instinctive; it is certainly the result of innate characteristics that make man dependent on others during his early years. In part because of this forced association in childhood, men learn that affiliation is a way of satisfying needs, and it becomes a learned behavior that continues into adulthood. Throughout life, other people are the only or primary means of satisfying certain needs, and men therefore affiliate in order to obtain this satisfaction.

Within this general framework, there are a number of more specific factors that increase or decrease the desire to associate in a particular situation. Fear, anxiety, uncertainty, similarity of other people, possibility of verbal communication—all affect the amount of affiliation. Explanations of these effects in terms of fear reduction and social comparison provide us with more detailed understanding of the phenomenon of affiliation.

## CHAPTER REVIEW

The chapter reviews at the end of each chapter are brief statements of the issues, facts, and ideas discussed in the chapter. They are not summaries but should serve as starting points for your own summary or review of the material. After reading a chapter, you should know something about and be able to discuss all the topics mentioned in the review.

1. Man as a gregarious animal. Some of the underlying causes of his tendency to affiliate.
2. Experimental approach to the study of affiliation.

3. Fear as one factor that affects the amount of affiliation.

4. One explanation of the effect of fear on affiliation is that people affiliate with the hopes of reducing their fear.

5. The distinction between fear and anxiety.

6. Birth order affects affiliation.

7. Another explanation of the effects of fear on affiliation, in terms of social comparison.

8. Hunger also affects affiliation.

9. The theory of social comparison.

10. The consequences of affiliation when frightened.

## APPLICATIONS AND SPECULATIONS

1. There is considerable evidence from World War II and the war in Vietnam that intensive bombing does not demoralize a population. Why do you think this is so?

2. We have seen that uncertainty about emotional reactions tends to lead to affiliation. In a Darwinian sense, what is the survival value of this tendency?

3. Astronauts, fighter pilots, and alcoholics tend to be later borns; college students and people listed in *Who's Who* tend to be first borns. How would you explain this?

4. It has been suggested that one important characteristic of the nuclear age is uncertainty about both personal and species survival. Does this kind of uncertainty lead to affiliation? What phenomena of current life might be explained in these terms?

## SUGGESTIONS FOR ADDITIONAL READING

### Articles

Gerard, H. B. Emotional uncertainty and social comparison. *Journal of Abnormal and Social Psychology*, 1963, *66*, 568–73.

Mills, J. and Mintz, P. M. Effect of unexplained arousal on affiliation. *Journal of Personality and Social Psychology*, 1972, *24*, 11–13.

Sarnoff, I., and Zimbardo, P. G. Anxiety, fear, and social affiliation. *Journal of Abnormal and Social Psychology*, 1961, *62*, 356–63.

*Books and Longer Discussions*

Harlow, H. F. The nature of love. *American Psychologist*, 1958, *13*, 673–85.

Schachter, S. *The psychology of affiliation.* Stanford, Calif.: Stanford, 1959.

# two

# social perception
# and attribution

Affiliation is determined to some extent by one's expectations about interactions with other people and by one's knowledge of them. As we have seen, high anxiety reduces affiliation because one expects the interaction to be embarrassing and high fear increases affiliation only if the other people are in a similar emotional state. Since our knowledge of and expectations about others are determined in part by impressions we form of them, it is appropriate now to consider the phenomenon of person perception. A glance at someone's portrait or at someone passing on the street gives us some ideas about the kind of person he is; even hearing a name tends to conjure up pictures of what its owner is like. And when two people meet, if only for an instant, they form impressions of each other. With more contact, they form fuller and richer impressions that pervade their entire relationship. These impressions determine how they behave toward each other, how much they like each other, whether the two associate often, and so on. First impressions are not only the beginning of social interaction, they are one of its major determinants. Consider the following situations.

A murder trial hinges on the testimony of one witness. The jury's belief in this witness, which will determine their decision, depends almost entirely on the impression they form of him in his brief time on the witness stand. They examine his face, his features, his clothes, the quality of his voice, and his answers and try to decide what kind of person he is.

Two freshmen who are destined to be roommates arrive at college and meet for the first time. Each one's personality—how easy he is to get along with, how nice he is—will have an enormous effect on the other's life. In the first few minutes of their meeting, they try to form an impression of each other, because they know they will be spending a great deal of time together during the year. They try to find out as much about each other as they can so they can behave accordingly.

People use whatever information is available to form impressions of

30

others—to make judgments about their personalities, to adopt hypotheses about the kind of persons they are. This chapter deals with this process of social perception—with the kinds of information on which it is based, with the factors that affect it, and with the question of whether or not it is accurate.

**FORMING IMPRESSIONS**

One important and apparently universal tendency is that people form extensive impressions of others on the basis of very limited information. Having seen someone or even his picture for only a few minutes, people tend to make judgments on a large number of his characteristics. Although ordinarily individuals are not overly confident of opinions formed in this way, they are generally willing to estimate the other's intelligence, age, background, race, religion, educational level, honesty, warmth, and so on. They would also tell us how much they thought they would like the other person if they could get to know him better and how much they like him at the moment. We shall discuss the accuracy of these impressions below; for the present, it is important merely to note that people quickly form impressions on the basis of very little information.

### Consistency

Moreover, given a few pieces of information, people tend to form consistent characterizations of others. In this respect, person perception is different from other kinds of perception. When people look at a house, a car, or any other complex object, they usually get a mixed impression. A house is large, is attractive, needs painting, has a nice dining room, is cold and unfriendly, and so on. In viewing a house, they do not force themselves to conclude that the whole house is warm or attractive. Objects do not have to be consistent. But when another person is the object of this kind of judgment, there is a tendency to view him as consistent, especially in an evaluative sense. A person is not seen as both good and bad, honest and dishonest, warm and frightening, considerate and sadistic. Even when there is contradictory information about someone, he usually will be perceived as consistent. The perceivers distort or rearrange the information to minimize or eliminate the inconsistency. This may also happen to some extent when people perceive objects, but it is particularly strong in person perception.

Naturally people do not always form consistent impressions of another's personality. There are times when two pieces of information about an individual are so contradictory that most people are unable to fit them into a consistent pattern. In such a situation, they may try to form a consistent pattern and some may succeed. Others, being unable to resolve the inconsistencies between the contradictory qualities, end up with an impression that is relatively unintegrated. However, there are strong tendencies toward forming a unified impression of another person even though the attempt to do so is not always successful.

### The Centrality of Evaluation

Work by Osgood, Suci, and Tannenbaum (1957) on the so-called semantic differential showed the overwhelming importance of basic dimensions and, in particular, of the evaluative dimension. Subjects were given a list of pairs of words denoting opposite ends of various dimensions and were asked to indicate where on these dimensions they felt particular concepts, persons, objects, and ideas fell. The list consisted of such dimensions as happy-sad, hot-cold, and red-blue, and the items the subjects had to place consisted of all sorts of things from mother to boulder.

When the subjects' responses were collected, Osgood and his associates analyzed them to see if any clusters of adjectives emerged that could be considered basic dimensions on which all things had been described. They found that three dimensions accounted for a large percentage of the variation in all descriptions. By determining where subjects had placed a particular item on the dimensions of *evaluation* (good-bad), *potency* (strong-weak), and *activity* (active-passive), the experimenters needed little additional information in order to describe that item fully. To a large extent, all other dimensions (e.g., brave-scared, polite-blunt) were aspects of these major dimensions rather than separate attributes.

This phenomenon is most dramatic when applied to the perception of people. Impressions of people can also be described in terms of the three basic dimensions, but one dimension—evaluation—accounts for a huge amount of the variance in them and appears to be the main distinction made. Once we place someone on this dimension, we never add much else to our impression of him. A favorable or unfavorable impression in one context, at one meeting, extends to all other situations and to other seemingly unrelated characteristics.

Later research has used much more sophisticated mathematical techniques, but has mainly served to emphasize these early results: evaluation is by far the most important underlying dimension of person perception (cf. Rosenberg and Olshan, 1970).

One interesting implication of this centrality of evaluation is that certain traits imply more about an individual than others. For example, the pair of traits *warm-cold* appears to be associated with a great number of other characteristics, whereas the pair *polite-blunt*, under most circumstances, is associated with fewer. Traits that are highly associated with many other characteristics have been called *central traits*. In a classic demonstration of their importance, Asch (1946) gave subjects a description of an individual that contained seven traits—intelligent, skillful, industrious, warm, determined, practical, and cautious. Other subjects were given exactly the same list except that *cold* was substituted for *warm*. Both groups of subjects were then asked to describe the individual and also to indicate which of various pairs of traits he would most likely possess. The portraits elicited from the two groups were extremely different—substituting *cold* for *warm* made a substantial change in the subjects' impression of the other person. In another condition, instead of the warm-cold pair, Asch used polite-blunt. He found that substituting *polite* for *blunt* made considerably less difference in the overall picture formed by the subjects.

A later study by Kelley (1950) replicated this result in a more realistic setting. Students in psychology courses were given descriptions of a guest lecturer before he spoke. The descriptions included seven adjectives similar to those Asch used: half the students received a description containing the word *warm*, and the other half were told the speaker was *cold*; in all other respects their lists were identical. The lecturer then came into the class and led a discussion for about twenty minutes, after which the students were asked to give their impressions of him. The results are shown in Table 2–1. As in the Asch study, there were big differences between the impressions formed by students who were told he was warm and those who were told he was cold. In addition, it was found that those students who expected the speaker to be warm tended

Table 2–1

EFFECT OF "WARM" AND "COLD" DESCRIPTIONS ON
RATINGS OF OTHER QUALITIES

| Qualities | INSTRUCTIONS[a] | |
| --- | --- | --- |
| | Warm | Cold |
| Self-centered | 6.3 | 9.6 |
| Unsociable | 5.6 | 10.4 |
| Unpopular | 4.0 | 7.4 |
| Formal | 6.3 | 9.6 |
| Irritable | 9.4 | 12.0 |
| Humorless | 8.3 | 11.7 |
| Ruthless | 8.6 | 11.0 |

[a]The higher the rating, the more the person was perceived as having the quality.

Source: Adapted from Kelley (1950).

to interact with him more freely and to initiate more conversations with him. Thus, the different descriptions affected not only the students' impressions of the other person but also their behavior toward him.

Since Kelley's study, there have been various criticisms of the notion of central traits. Careful work has shown that the centrality of a particular trait depends to some extent on the context in which it is used. When someone is described as obedient, weak, shallow, unambitious, and vain, it does not matter much whether he is warm or cold—warmth does not affect these other characteristics. Similarly, *polite* or *blunt* can have a considerable effect on the significance of certain other qualities even though generally it is not important. The significance of a particular dimension also depends to some extent on the characteristics the judges are supposed to determine. If they were asked to decide how sociable or popular an individual is from a list of other traits, the dimension of warmth would be important because warmth is highly related to sociability and popularity. But warmth has relatively little effect on other qualities and would be less central if the judges were asked to rate the individual on these.

This work gives us more detailed knowledge of the factors that determine the centrality of a particular characteristic. The dimension warm-cold is still considered central, but we now understand that centrality depends on the context and the responses required. When a dimension is called central, we mean it has a considerable effect in a large number of contexts and on a large number of responses.

Centrality is closely related to the tendency discussed earlier of people to form consistent impressions. Good traits go together. Someone who is warm is also seen as positive in other respects, thus producing a consistent picture. In fact, perceivers sometimes modify the meaning of a trait so that it will fit in with other information they have about the stimulus person. Such *context effects* cause a person's traits to be distorted to produce consistency within an impression (Kaplan, 1971).

### Averaging Model versus Additive Model

How do people form an impression of someone when they have many pieces of information about him? One basic issue is whether they tend to add or average the facts they know. As we shall discuss in more detail in Chapter 3, traits can be rated in terms of how positive they are. For example, sincerity is considered an extremely favorable quality and, accordingly, is assigned the maximum value ($+3$); determination is considered only moderately favorable ($+1$) and dishonesty very unfavorable ($-3$). The question is how traits are combined to form an overall evaluation. If an individual is known to have one highly positive trait and one slightly positive trait, how positively is he rated? The averaging model suggests that someone who is sincere (rated +3) and also determined (+1) would receive an evaluation that was approximately an average of the two traits, that is, he would be considered moderately positive (+2). Thus learning of a slightly positive trait in someone about whom we already know a highly positive trait reduces the overall evaluation, even though both pieces of information are positive. In contrast, an additive model suggests that the two pieces of information would be summed and the final evaluation would be higher (+4) than an evaluation based on either one by itself.

Some sample predictions of the two models are shown in Table 2–2. The first trait set includes three highly positive traits. The second adds three moderately positive ones. According to the averaging model, this should reduce the overall evaluation; according to the additive model, it should increase it. The evidence indicates that in such situations most people average. The third set adds three highly positive traits to the original three. Averaging would result in the same evaluation as that with the original set; adding would result in a higher evaluation. In this kind of situation, the evidence slightly favors adding, but the addition does not have as large an effect as the model suggests.

Although there has been a considerable amount of research on this problem, a final answer is not yet available. Norman Anderson, in a

Table 2–2

*AVERAGING VERSUS ADDING IN IMPRESSION FORMATION*

| | PREDICTIONS OF RELATIVE LIKING | |
|---|---|---|
| *Trait Sets* | *Averaging Model* | *Adding Model* |
| Sincere (+3), intelligent (+3), warm (+3) | +3 | +3 |
| Sincere (+3), intelligent (+3), warm (+3), persistent (+1), cautious (+1), perfectionist (+1) | +2 | +4 |
| Sincere (+3), intelligent (+3), warm (+3), friendly (+3), humorous (+3), loyal (+3) | +3 | +6 |

Note: All predictions are in relative rather than absolute terms. Thus to make the models comparable, the adding model's prediction for the first situation is +3 rather than +9, for the second situation, +4 rather than +12, and so on. The important point is that the averaging model predicts, for example, that the first and third situations would produce equal evaluations, whereas the adding model predicts that the third situation would produce an evaluation twice as positive as the first.

series of careful and precise experiments (1959, 1965, etc.), produced strong evidence to support the averaging model. He found that when a piece of information that is only moderately favorable is combined with a previous evaluation that had been based on very favorable information, the overall evaluation did not increase and could even decrease. Similarly, two strongly negative traits produced a more negative evaluation than two strongly negative plus two moderately negative traits. On the other hand, there is some evidence (Fishbein and Hunter, 1964) that one's knowing five strongly positive characteristics about another individual makes him somewhat more positive than knowing only two positive characteristics about him. Anderson (1968, etc.) has proposed a resolution of this contradictory evidence in terms of a weighted averaging model. He presented data showing that people form an overall impression by averaging all traits but giving more weight to polarized (highly positive or highly negative) traits. This model appears to explain most situations, although under some circumstances adding does occur. It also seems to account for activity judgments, but neither works particularly well for potency (Hamilton and Huffman, 1971). Thus, one's overall impression seems to be determined by a combination of adding and averaging, with averaging explaining most situations.

**Accuracy of Judgments**

Most people assume they can determine other people's emotions and know what their personalities are like. But how accurate is person perception? One argument is that people must be reasonably accurate in their perception of others in order for society to function as smoothly as it does. After all, we interact with other people hundreds of times every day and most of these interactions seem to require accurate judgments of others. Since the interactions proceed without serious conflict or mistake, person perception must be fairly accurate.

It is generally no more difficult to judge the height of a man than it is to judge the height of a bookcase, a car, or a camel. The same is true of weight, color, and even attractiveness. We make these kinds of judgments of all objects and we make them fairly accurately. The characteristic that distinguishes person perception from all other kinds is that we infer that individuals have internal states—feelings, emotions, and personalities. The bookcase obviously has none of these; the car has them only in advertisements and fantasies; perhaps the camel has them, but we usually do not worry about camels. However, we do attempt to make judgments of the internal states of human beings. We look at people and perceive them as being angry, happy, sad, or frightened. We form an impression of another person and think of him as warm, honest, and sincere. We also make judgments about such internal characteristics as a person's attitudes toward various issues. We guess whether he is a Republican or a Democrat, religious or nonreligious, promiscuous or not promiscuous.

As long as the appropriate cues are provided, it is fairly easy to make judgments about somebody's role. We recognize that the girl standing behind a counter in a clothing store is a salesgirl and we ask her how much a particular item costs. The man in the blue suit with the gun strapped to his side is a policeman and we treat him accordingly. The man rushing down a platform toward a train is obviously in a hurry and we get out of his way to make it easier for him to catch the train. The contexts in which we see the people enable us to make accurate assumptions about their roles and sometimes even their emotions and feelings. But under most circumstances, judgments of internal states are extremely difficult. The internal state cannot be observed directly— it must be inferred from whatever cues are available. Therefore, we must restate our aim in studying the accuracy of judgments and the cues on which they are based. We are interested primarily in determining the kinds of judgments individuals can make of internal states and the cues on which these judgments of emotion, personality, and attitude are based.

How a person is feeling—whether he is happy or afraid, horrified or disgusted—is a type of judgment we often make. Therefore, much of the work on the accuracy of person perception has focused on the recognition of emotions. It began in 1872 when Darwin asserted, on the basis of this evolutionary theory, that facial expressions universally conveyed the same emotional states. Since then, experimenters have been studying how accurately people can make inferences about emotional states. The basic procedure is to present a subject with a stimulus representing another person and ask the subject to identify the other's emotion. For some studies, trained actors made their faces portray a number of different emotions and pictures were taken of their expressions. One picture was chosen for each emotion and these were then shown to subjects, who were asked to indicate what emotion was depicted. Some of these pictures are shown in Figure 2–1.

Other studies used different kinds of stimuli. In some (e.g., Boring and Titchener, 1923), subjects were simply shown drawings of a person's face, each of which was supposed to represent an emotion. Other experiments have employed motion pictures (Cline, 1964) and, occasionally, real people (Sherman, 1927). Subjects have also been presented with disembodied voices (Davitz, 1964) and voices from which the content has been removed and the emotion supposedly left in (Starkweather, 1956).

In addition, the emotions the stimuli were supposed to portray were produced in a variety of ways. In one study (Langfeld, 1918), they

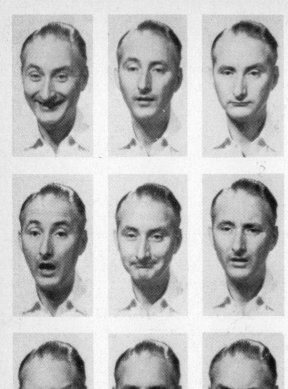

Figure 2–1

Examples of stimuli used in the study of the perception of emotions. The photographs illustrate expressions posed to portray the emotions listed. (You might try to identify them before looking at the key below.)

Top (left to right): glee, passive adoration, complacency. Middle: amazement, optimistic determination, dismay. Bottom: rage, mild repugnance, puzzlement. (From Hastorf et al., 1966.)

were drawn by an artist who was trying to represent faces showing particular emotions. In other studies, actors posed emotions (Ruckmick, 1921), emotions were produced in the laboratory by exposing people to situations designed to arouse them (Sherman, 1927), or emotions were produced in actual situations (Munn, 1940).

Given this wide range of techniques, it is perhaps not surprising that the results also have been varied. A number of studies (e.g., Guilford, 1929; Sherman, 1927) indicated that people cannot judge emotions any better than they would by chance. But other studies (Langfeld, 1918; Munn, 1940; Thompson and Meltzer, 1964) have shown that subjects label emotions consistently and accurately.

Which emotions people are asked to determine is an important variable—some are extremely difficult whereas others are relatively easy. Although individuals may not be able to discriminate perfectly among all emotions, they can discriminate among groups of emotions. Woodworth (1938) suggested that emotions can be arranged on a six-point continuum, with confusion between any two emotions being inversely related to the distance they are from each other. The six groups of emotions are

1. love, happiness, mirth
2. surprise
3. fear, suffering
4. anger, determination
5. disgust
6. contempt

Apparently people are quite adept at distinguishing emotions in categories that are three, four, or five points apart—they rarely confuse happiness with disgust or contempt with surprise. But they are much poorer at discriminating emotions that are closer on the continuum and find it almost impossible to discriminate emotions in the same category or only one group away. There is also some evidence, collected by Thompson and Meltzer (1964), that even on this continuum some emotions are more consistently identified than others. Happiness, love, fear, and determination tend to be relatively easy to discriminate, whereas disgust, contempt, and suffering are much more difficult.

The lack of consistency in the results of work on the accuracy of person perception is due in part to the methodology used in the research and in part to confusion about the issue. The central issue is whether there is a particular facial expression or body posture for each emotion. Does everyone who is feeling a particular emotion have the same expression on his face or are there great variations among people in how they manifest emotions? Is it possible, for example, that one person's expression of disgust is another person's expression of contentment?

The more general question concerns the determination of a correct identification. When an artist tries to draw someone experiencing disgust or an actor tries to portray disgust, is it appropriate to say that disgust is

The people pictured here have very different expressions on their faces and appear to be experiencing different emotions. Yet they were all in the same photograph, which was taken while they were witnessing a rally. They may, in fact, be feeling different emotions. On the other hand, they may simply be expressing the same emotion in different ways.

the correct identification? Perhaps the artist or the actor did not do a good job. Or perhaps their impression of what disgust looks like is different from other people's. In a study by Langfeld (1918), subjects were shown an artist's drawings of various emotions and only 32 percent of the subjects agreed with the artist's labels. However, other subjects were shown what the artist had called the picture; when they were asked whether they agreed or disagreed, 75 percent accepted the artist's labels. Thus, the artist's picture could represent, say, disgust, but it could also represent other emotions. When subjects were told it was supposed to represent disgust, most of them agreed that it could; however, when they were asked for their own label, most chose other emotions.

Nevertheless, it appears that Darwin was approximately correct after all: A given facial expression appears to convey approximately the same emotion throughout the world. Ekman, Sorenson, and Friesen (1969) found that college educated subjects in Brazil, the United States, Argentina, Chile, and Japan labeled the same faces with the same emotion words. However, all these subjects might have simply been exposed to a common set of television portrayals of facial expression from which they might all have learned a common set of Hollywood conventions for how best to communicate emotions through facial expressions.

Thus, Ekman and Friesen (1971) repeated the study with natives of New Guinea who had seen no movies, understood neither English nor Pidgin, had not lived in any of the Western settlement or government towns, and had never worked for a Caucasian. Presumably these subjects had had no visual contact with conventional Western facial expression of emotions. Each of these subjects was given a brief story depicting an emotion, such as, for "sadness," "His child has died, and he feels very sad." Then he was given one photograph supposedly depicting that emotion, and two pictures depicting other emotions. On the average, they found that adults chose the correct picture more than 80 percent of the time. Children were only asked to choose between one correct and one incorrect picture, and they averaged almost 90 percent correct. This does not prove there are no cultural differences in the facial expression of emotion, but it does provide evidence of universals that transcend cultural boundaries.

**FACTORS AFFECTING JUDGMENTS**

Although there has been a great deal of work on the judgment of personality and emotions, it has not provided a definitive answer to the question of whether people can make accurate judgments of others. Instead, this research has demonstrated forcefully that in making these judgments people are influenced by a wide variety of factors relating to themselves, the person being judged, and the situation in which the judgment is made.

### The State of the Judges

A series of studies has demonstrated that how judges are feeling and their current life situation influence their judgment of others to some extent. As early as 1932, Bartlett showed that men who were liable to be drafted into the military rated pictures of military officers as more threatening and indicating greater command ability than did men who were not draftable. Murray (1933) had girls judge photographs of faces after some had played a frightening game. Those who had played the game judged the photographs to be more menacing than those who had not played the game. And in 1957, Feshbach and Singer found that subjects who were frightened because they were expecting electric shocks perceived other people as more fearful than did subjects who were not frightened. Thus, as might be expected, a judge's needs and feelings greatly influence his perception of other people—he tends to project his own feelings onto others and to be more sensitive to particular characteristics because of his own emotional state.

### Perceptual Biases

**Halo Effect.** Several biases seem to influence impression formation for most people most of the time. As we said earlier, most judgments of other people are made primarily in terms of good and bad. Then all their other qualities are deduced from this decision. This is called the *halo effect* because one who is labeled *good* is surrounded with a positive aura and all good qualities are attributed to him. The converse (what should be called a "negative halo" or "forked-tail" effect) is that one who is labeled *bad* is seen as having all bad qualities.

A good illustration of these effects is provided in a study by Dion, Berscheid, and Walster (1972). Subjects were given pictures of people who were either physically attractive, unattractive, or average. They then rated each of the people on a number of characteristics that have nothing to do with attractiveness. As you can see in Table 2–3 (p. 42), the attractive person was rated highest and the unattractive person lowest on all characteristics. Just because they looked good and therefore had one positive trait, they were perceived as having other positive traits (conversely those who looked bad were perceived as having other bad traits).

**Logical Error.** There is a strong tendency for people to infer from the presence of one trait in an individual that he has various other traits. Knowing someone is intelligent causes most people to expect him also to

Table 2–3

THE "HALO" AND "FORKED-TRAIL" EFFECTS ILLUSTRATED BY RATINGS OF ATTRACTIVE, UNATTRACTIVE, AND AVERAGE PERSONS

| Trait Ascription[a] | Unattractive Stimulus person | Average Stimulus person | Attractive Stimulus person |
|---|---|---|---|
| Social desirability of the stimulus person's personality | 56.31 | 62.42 | 65.39 |
| Occupational status of the stimulus person | 1.70 | 2.02 | 2.25 |
| Marital competence of the stimulus person | .37 | .71 | 1.70 |
| Parental competence of the stimulus person | 3.91 | 4.55 | 3.54 |
| Social and professional happiness of the stimulus person | 5.28 | 6.34 | 6.37 |
| Total happiness of the stimulus person | 8.83 | 11.60 | 11.60 |
| Likelihood of marriage | 1.52 | 1.82 | 2.17 |

[a]The higher the number, the more socially desirable, the more prestigious an occupation, etc., the stimulus person is expected to possess.

Source: Dion et al., "Title of Article to Come," *Journal of Personality and Social Psychology*, 1972, *24*, 285–90. Reprinted by permission of the publisher.

be imaginative, clever, active, conscientious, deliberate, and reliable. Knowing someone is inconsiderate leads most people to expect him also to be irritable, boastful, cold, hypocritical, etc. As Bruner, Shapiro, and Tagiuri (1958), who collected these data, point out, these inferences are not derived logically from the given trait; they are based on the individual's assumptions about personality. Intelligence does not necessarily denote activity, nor does inconsiderateness denote irritability. The tendency to make these assumptions is sometimes called the _logical error_, because people see certain traits as going together and assume that someone who has one of them also has the others.

This tendency has been explained in terms of implicit personality theories. We all categorize people into a limited number of types, and when we meet anyone we do not know, we try to fit him into one of these molds. If we discover that he has some of the traits supposedly characteristic of a particular type, we assign him to that type. Once he is so stereotyped, of course, he is assumed to have all the other traits belonging to that type. In this way, our implicit theories about personality influence our perceptions of others.

**Positivity Bias.** Finally, there is a general tendency to express positive evaluations of people more often than negative evaluations. This has been called the *leniency effect* or sometimes the *positivity bias* (Bruner and Taguiri, 1954; Sears and Whitney, 1973). Ratings of stimulus persons in laboratory studies are consistently positive, on the average, whether the subject knows the person or not. Similarly, public opinion polls show that political leaders are consistently rated positively more often than they are evaluated negatively. Reference groups such as political parties, civil rights groups, and so on, also receive positive evaluations more often than they receive negative ones (Sears, 1969). Positive evaluations of other people are rated as more pleasant, are learned more readily, are expected in the absence of any specific information about them, and are expected to result from any changes in interpersonal relationships. When change in an impression does occur, it generally occurs toward more positive evaluations, everything else being equal. There are exceptions, of course. For example, political figures tend not to be evaluated so positively by college educated people as they are by less educated persons (Sears and Whitney, 1973).

**Assumed Similarity.**    There is a strong tendency for people to assume that others are similar to them. This is particularly true when they are known to be similar in demographic features such as age, race, national origin, and socioeconomic status, but also occurs when they differ considerably on these characteristics. If one likes large parties, he tends to assume that other people like large parties; if he is aggressive, he assumes other people are also aggressive; and so on. In Freud's terminology, this would be called *projection*—individuals attribute their own characteristics to others.

There are two related results of this phenomenon. First, the individual rates another more similar to himself than he actually is; he distorts the other's personality to make it more like his own. And second, this distortion usually is so great that his rating of the other person corresponds more to his own personality (as he sees it) than to the other's personality (as the other sees it). As we shall discuss in more detail below, this means that perception of another person is influenced more by what the rater is like than by what the person being rated is like.

Another result of this tendency to project is that people are more accurate in rating others who are similar to them, not because they are more perceptive with such people, but because they always rate people similar to themselves so when they finally find one who is, they are naturally correct. Paradoxically, perhaps the most interesting implication of this phenomenon is that one's rating of others may be as good a measure of his own personality as it is of the other person's—or even a better one. It may actually be a better measure of his personality than is his own self-rating, because he is less likely to be concerned about concealing faults or exaggerating strengths. Therefore, if we want to find out what someone is like, the best procedure may be to ask him to rate other people.

### Knowledge of the Other

A factor that increases the accuracy of judgments of personality and behavior but seems to have little to do with person perception is one's knowledge of the group or subculture to which the person to be judged belongs. Members of subcultures (e.g., jazz musicians, baseball players, college students) share, to some extent, certain characteristics, values, and behaviors. If one knows the characteristics shared by a group, he is better able to make an accurate guess as to a member's responses. A rating of a person in terms of the stereotype for his group will be accurate insofar as the stereotype is accurate and the person judged conforms to that stereotype. Thus, knowledge of a person's group increases accuracy but this increase may have nothing to do with person perception.

To demonstrate this phenomenon, Gage (1952) had subjects rate people whom they had never seen but who were identified as college students. Then he let the subjects see the students and rate them again. He found that the ratings made before the subjects saw the students were more accurate than those made afterward. Evidently, the subjects' stereotype of college students provided a better estimate of the students than did their visual impressions.

### Prejudice and Accuracy of Perception

For some time, a controversy raged as to whether or not some people were better than others at identifying ethnic groups. In particular, some anti-Semites claimed to have an unerring eye for a Jewish face. And an American pilot in Vietnam thought he could tell a Vietcong from a loyal South Vietnamese from 5,000 feet in the air. The same kind of confidence seems to imbue people having other prejudices—they all feel they are specially adept at identifying members of the group toward which they are prejudiced. Recent research indicates that prejudiced people, while not much better at picking out members of the group in question, have a great deal more *confidence* in their judgments than do nonprejudiced persons! (Dorfman, Keeve, and Saslow, 1971.)

In terms of our discussion, their confidence is not entirely misplaced. We have seen that to the extent that a stereotype is accurate and the person to be judged is characteristic of his group, knowledge of the stereotype does increase accuracy of judgment. It is theoretically possible for this to work in reverse. If one is familiar with the stereo-type of a particular ethnic group and if the stereotype is accurate, one's accuracy in identifying members of that group should increase. Thus, anti-Semites, who presumably are concerned about Jews and have strong stereotypes about them, could be better at identifying them. However, it would seem that members of the ethnic group would be even more familiar with the group characteristics (if any existed) and, therefore, would be even better at this kind of identification.

But accuracy does not depend primarily on knowledge of a stereo-type—the critical factor is the validity of the stereotype. Since most stereotypes tend to be somewhat inaccurate, they are usually of doubtful help in identifying members of particular groups. If one believes that most Swedes have blonde hair, it will probably help him identify Swedes because this is a fairly accurate picture—although not all Swedes are blonde, a high percentage are. But, believing that all Jews wear glasses will be little help because Jews and non-Jews do not differ appreciably

Drawing by Chas. Addams; © 1936, 1964
The New Yorker Magazine, Inc.

*"You are trustworthy, loyal, helpful, friendly, courteous, kind, obedient, cheerful, thrifty, brave, clean, reverent."*

in this respect. Obviously, knowing anything correct about someone or some group tends to make our perceptions more accurate, but having false information or misconceptions does not.

Although this distinction between accurate and false stereotypes may seem evident, it is often obscured. Many people feel that all stereotypes are bad, that they automatically indicate prejudice and produce inaccuracies. Of course, it is true that people should not be treated in accordance with a stereotype just because they belong to a particular group; as much as possible we should treat people as individuals. However, if we have no knowledge about a person, knowledge of the groups he belongs to often helps us perceive him more accurately. If we know that someone is a twenty-year-old male college student, we are probably correct in assuming that he would prefer a football game to a horticultural exhibit and rock and roll to revival music. We might be wrong in these assumptions because not all twenty-year-old male college students have these tastes, but we are more likely to be right because most of them do. Often we must interact with someone before getting to know him, and these interactions can be smoother if we rely to some extent on what we know about the groups to which he belongs. The danger with such reliance is that the individual may be atypical, the stereotype may be wrong in general, and we may never bother to find out what the person is like as an individual simply because our superficial knowledge enables us to interact with him reasonably well.

### Anticipated Interaction

We have seen that person perception is affected by many factors in the situations in which judgments are made, but it is also affected by one's previous expectations regarding the other person. One of the most interesting findings is that our perception of someone is affected by whether or not we expect to interact with him in the future. If further interaction is anticipated, there is a tendency to reduce negative perceptions and give greater weight to positive ones—the impression of the other is altered to make the upcoming interaction seem more desirable. As we shall see in the next chapter, this kind of distortion may play an important role in liking.

This was shown in an experiment by Darley and Berscheid (1967). Each of their subjects—girls in an introductory psychology class—was presented with information about two other girls in introductory classes. They expected to meet with one of them and talk about dating and sex behavior, and not to meet the other at all. Then the subject rated both girls, without ever meeting either one. Much more positive evaluations were made of the girl whom the subject expected to meet. Anticipated interaction led to more positive evaluations.

Other research suggests, however, that this effect only holds with stimulus persons that are fairly positive to begin with, and with whom the subject expects generally to agree. Sears (1967) found no increase in liking due to anticipation of interaction with a highly critical person with whom the subject disagreed on the discussion topic. Aderman (1969) found that anticipated interaction increased liking only under conditions of prior liking and of initial agreement.

There is also evidence that expectations about another's personality affect how we treat him and how we ourselves behave. For example, if someone is told that his partner in a discussion is a dominant person, he tends to be passive. Similarly, if he thinks the other is passive, he tends to be dominant. Moreover, these effects tend to produce the anticipated behavior. Being dominant causes the other person to appear submissive; being submissive makes the other relatively dominant. Therefore, not only does the expectation affect behavior, it also tends to be self-ful-filling, at least in a limited situation.

**THE PERCEIVER AND THE PERCEIVED**

Although, as we have said, the three basic dimensions of the semantic differential explain a great deal of the variance in person perception (with the evaluative dimension accounting for most of the variance), there are obviously more than three dimensions. We also care about specific qualities of individuals, such as whether they have a good sense of humor, whether they are good athletes, and whether they are beautiful. In order to give a complete description of anyone, we would want to use many such dimensions.

One of the interesting aspects of person perception is that different people organize their perceptions of others along different dimensions. For example, one person might always describe others in terms of their sense of humor, their physical attractiveness, their warmth, their honesty, and their intelligence. Someone else might consider these characteristics to be relatively unimportant and instead would emphasize the individual's diligence, aggressiveness, religiosity, and athletic prowess. This was illustrated in a study by Dornbusch et al. (1965), in which each child at a camp was asked to describe, in his own words, every other child. The children were provided with no scales or specific questions but were simply asked to give free descriptions of the others. These descriptions were then analyzed in two ways—in terms of the characteristics on which each child was described and in terms of the characteristics each child used in making his own descriptions. The experimenters could then examine the characteristics in terms of those used in each perception or in terms of those used by each perceiver.

When the data were examined in this way, a clear pattern emerged. It might have been thought that some children would have a particularly outstanding characteristic, such as a sense of humor or aggressiveness, and that everyone would describe them in these terms. This was not the case. There was no agreement among the descriptions on which dimensions were important for a particular child. Many different characteristics were used to describe each child, and those used to describe one did not differ from those used to describe everyone else. But the situation was entirely different for the children writing the descriptions. Here great consistency emerged. Each child tended to use the same characteristics no matter whom he was describing. The children differed among themselves as to which characteristics they used, but each of them had his favorites or those he considered important and used them for virtually all his descriptions. So it was found that the dimensions used depended much more on who was perceiving than on who was being perceived.

This is a further indication that each person has his own view of personality and of the qualities that are important in other people. Each of us tends to organize the world and, in particular, other humans in our own terms and to use these terms for all our perceptions. Whenever we meet someone, we form an impression of him in terms of the characteristics we consider important. Regardless of what the other person is really like, our impression tends to be organized along the same dimensions of personality.

One implication of this is that it is difficult to get accurate or meaningful descriptions of someone unless we allow the person giving the description to provide his own terminology. Although it is always more convenient to provide subjects with a series of scales on which to make ratings, the subjects may do poorly because they are not accustomed to using the chosen scales so the scales have little meaning for them. Or perhaps the scales are similar to those used by one subject but not by another. The first subject would be able to use them comfortably and well whereas the second one would be handicapped. Letting subjects use their own scales avoids this problem but, unfortunately, makes their judgments virtually impossible to evaluate and compare.

A more profound implication of this phenomenon is that people do not see the world in the same way; they emphasize different aspects of other people, notice and focus on different qualities. Sometimes this is merely the result of using different terminology for essentially the same characteristic. When one person talks about another's warmth and sense of humor and someone else talks about his kindness and good-naturedness, the only disagreement may be one of semantics. On the other hand, people do differ on the personality qualities they consider important and their impressions of others are based on their own standards.

**ATTRIBUTION THEORY**

As we indicated above, the perception of people differs from the perception of inanimate objects because it often involves inferences about internal states. When we are thinking about a person, we are concerned about his motives, personality, feelings, and attitudes. We must make such inferences on the basis of limited information, because we have access only to such external cues as facial expressions, gestures, what the person says about his internal state, what we remember about his behavior in the past, and so forth. In other words, we have only the indirect information given by external cues, and we must make inferences about his internal state from these. The study of these inferences has become one of the most active areas of social psychological research. It has been organized by several theoretical approaches which have been designated *attribution theory*. An "attribution" is the inference that an observer makes about the internal state of an actor or of himself on the basis of overt behavior.

Theorizing about attributions began with Heider (1958), whose concern was with phenomenal causality. That is, he was interested in how people in everyday life figure out what causes what. He postulated that the search for causal explanations was a central motive in human beings (not just psychologists!). We stated previously that a unique aspect of person perception is that people are assumed to have internal states—emotions, feelings, personality. A related facet is that people, unlike inanimate objects, are perceived to have intent. When explaining why a particular event occurs, we usually do not consider the motivation of objects. Aristotle believed that rocks fall because they wanted to or because they were heavy—it was their nature to fall. This animistic notion of nature was dominant for some time and still persists in some cultures, religions, and superstitions. Galileo and Newton changed this by introducing a new concept: rocks fall because of gravity; they have no internal need or motivation. Nonliving things behave in accordance with physical laws and are controlled by forces outside themselves. We assume that people are different from objects, that people have needs and motives that cause them to seek out certain goals. When someone does something, we assume that he has acted intentionally unless it is obvious that his actions were accidental or forced; we also assume that he had a reason for acting as he did. There seems to be a tendency to perceive people as free agents. Physical events happen for mechanical or accidental reasons or perhaps in line with some great external plan, but when people act it is because they want to. Therefore, when we observe someone's behavior, we not only see what he did but try to see why he did it.

The central issue in perceptions of causality is whether to attribute a given act or event to *internal* states, or to *external* forces. A person is perceived as acting either because of some internal motivation or need or because of some external force. Behavior is generally motivated at least in part by internal considerations, but the extent to which the motivation is perceived to be external is an important factor in person perception. If a man is trying to seduce a girl, she wants to know whether he is motivated primarily by an overwhelming and undiscriminating internal sexuality (he would go to bed with anything that wore skirts), or by the uniqueness of her, an external object. A student who is failing a course wants to know whether it is because he is not smart enough or doesn't work hard enough (internal causality), or because the professor's lectures are ambiguous, the text is set at a level too difficult for the class's background, or the tests are unfair (external causality). Debates rage in school board meetings, academic conventions, courtrooms, and legislative halls about whether black children do less well in school than white children because of inferior native endowment and low motivation (internal causality) or because of racial discrimination, insensitive middle class white teachers, inferior facilities, and unstimulating peer groups (external causality).

**Psychological Epistemology.** Kelley (1967) has offered a theory of how people make such causal judgments. Since this theory essentially deals with the question "How do people know what they know," it is analogous to the philosopher's concern with the basis of knowledge in general (i.e., with epistemology).

Kelley's main proposition is that people assess causality for a particular act or event by using four different criteria, more or less automatically and simultaneously. They check across (1) entities: was the response made uniquely to this entity and not to others? (2) persons: was it made uniquely by this person, or was it a consensus across persons; (3) time: was it made consistently over time? and (4) modalities of interaction with the entity: was it made consistently across different modalities of interaction with the entity?

A simple example is the dilemma of whether or not to believe our friend's report that he has seen the new local movie four times, that it is terrific, and that we should go see it ourselves. What caused that report? In particular, was the report caused by a truly terrific movie? According to this model, our automatic response would be to ask ourselves: (1) Does he always say *any* movie is good, or is this report unique to *this* movie? (2) Have we heard the same report from *others*, or is it just something peculiar to *him* and his weird taste in movies? (3)

Did he like the movie *consistently* over the four times he saw it, or did he like it some times and not other times? (4) Was it just that he had eaten well, or was with an especially exciting girl, or had unusually good seats, or got in free? Or did he like it no matter whom he went with, when he went, or where he sat?

If the movie passes all four tests (uniqueness, consensus, consistency over time, and consistency over modalities), then we attribute the report to the goodness of the movie, rather than to something else. This, then, is the process Kelley hypothesizes to occur, however implicitly and automatically, as we attempt to attribute a given effect to a given cause.

**Attribution of Causality to Others' Acts.**   As indicated above, one important area of causal inference is the question of whether others' behavior is caused by their internal states or by external forces acting upon them. A series of studies by Jones and his associates (Jones et al., 1968; Jones and Harris, 1967; Nisbett et al., 1971) demonstrated a general tendency for people to assume that others' behavior is internally controlled. Although this assumption can be affected by the situation, other things being equal we perceive others as acting for internal reasons. In contrast, people tend to exaggerate the extent to which their *own* behavior is *externally* determined.

The debate over internal versus external causality is perhaps hottest these days regarding children's performance in school. If children do poorly, is it because they have no ability or are not trying hard enough (internal causality), or because they have a bad teacher, are victims of racial discrimination, or have a poor family background (external causality)? Since these attributions are political dynamite, it would be useful to know what inspires one set rather than the other.

Weiner and his colleagues have tried to test the simple hypothesis that such attributions are a function of success or failure. They presented subjects with a hypothetical person who had just either succeeded or failed at a particular task. Then the subjects were asked to indicate why this had occurred. The data are shown in Figure 2–2. In this case, failure was externally attributed to a difficult task, while success tended to be attributed primarily internally to effort and ability (Frieze and Weiner, 1973). It would appear that in this experiment the subjects were giving rather generous explanations for the stimulus person's actions. One wonders if they would be so generous with a member of a social group against which they were prejudiced.

One simple demonstration of how the attribution of causality can be varied is provided in an experiment by Hastorf et al. (1965). In an earlier line of research (as we shall discuss in chapter 6) it had been shown that a group member's rate of talking in a group discussion could be significantly increased by giving him private reinforcements each

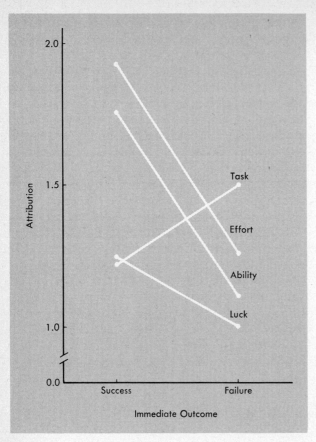

Figure 2–2

Attributions to ability, effort, task difficulty, and luck as a function of the immediate outcome (success or failure).

time he talked. Indeed it was found that the least talkative group member could be transformed into the most talkative. In the Hastorf experiment, tape recordings of these sessions were played to a new set of subjects under two conditions: either they were informed of the reinforcement procedure, or they were not. Subjects who were informed of the reinforcement procedure (i.e., of the systematic external forces) interpreted the rise in talking as being caused by *external* forces, while those unaware of the reinforcements tended to revise their estimates of the talker's *internal* attributes (e.g., they saw him as having more leadership skill).

One of the most straightforward findings about the perception of causality is its relationship to the perception of power. The more power a person is seen to have, the more internally caused his acts are seen to be. Conversely, if he is perceived as being weak, there is a tendency to perceive his behavior as being externally caused. This relationship also holds in reverse—someone whose behavior is seen to be internally caused is perceived as being more powerful than someone whose behavior is externally caused.

Two studies by Thibaut and Riecken (1955) provide a clear demonstration of this relationship. In one experiment, three people were at each session of the experiment, but only one, a student in an introductory course in psychology, was a genuine subject—the other two were confederates. One confederate (the high-status person) was neatly and formally dressed and was described as having just received his Ph.D. and as currently being on the teaching staff of the university. The other (the low-status person) was in shirtsleeves, was somewhat messy, and was described as an undergraduate in the freshman class. The experimenter explained that one of the three was to serve as a communicator to attempt to influence the other two to donate blood for a Red Cross blood drive. The true subjects always served as the communicators. They presented their persuasive talk to both confederates and, at the end, both of them indicated that they had been considerably influenced. The experimenter then examined the subjects' perception of the two confederates.

When the subjects were asked to indicate why they thought the confederates had been influenced, in almost all cases they reported that the high-status confederate had "wanted to anyway" but that the low-status confederate had yielded because of the pressure put on him. Thus the locus of causality was internal for the high-status person and external for the low-status one.

A second finding from this study illustrates another effect of perceived causality. The subjects were also asked, at the beginning and at the end of the experiment, how much they accepted or liked the two confederates. It was found that there was a strong tendency for them to become more favorable toward the high-status person during the course of the experiment than toward the low-status person. This suggests that someone who agrees with us for reasons of his own is liked and accepted more than someone who agrees with us because we put pressure on him.

The other study by Thibaut and Riecken provided supporting evidence for this finding. It showed that a strong person who performs a helpful act is seen as nicer and as a better person than a weak person who performs the same act. Being helpful when strong portrays more internal causality than being helpful when weak, and the more internally caused good behavior is, the more credit one receives for it.

**Inference of Other's Attitude.** Another causal problem we sometimes face is figuring out what another person's true attitude is toward something. A black person interviewing for a job would like to know something about his prospective employer's true racial prejudices, regardless of how much he smiles and how liberal he says he is. A girl on the verge of losing her virginity would like to know something about her prospective lover's intentions.

What has generally been found is that when external forces upon another person are strong, his stated opinion is not necessarily perceived as an accurate reflection of his true underlying attitude. On the other hand, when external forces are weak, the expressed opinion tends to be trusted as reflecting the internal attitude. Jones and Harris (1967), for example, presented subjects with essays written by other students, in several conditions: the essays either supported Fidel Castro or opposed him (at a time when most college students and other Americans opposed Castro), and were supposedly written in some cases on an assigned side, and in other cases with free choice of position.

With free choice, of course, the observers readily inferred that the writer's expressed opinion was the same as his true underlying attitude. Even when the writer was described as having no choice of position (i.e., strong external forces), the observers still generally felt the written position reflected the underlying attitude. However, they were much less confident this was so, especially when the assigned position deviated sharply from that expected from most college students (i.e., when the writer had been assigned to write a pro-Castro essay).

In other experiments, people giving speeches are perceived as more sincere, impartial, and influential when the speech opposes the audience's interests (Mills and Jellison, 1968). Generally it appears that people are in doubt about the sincerity of a persuasive appeal when it can be interpreted as self-serving, ingratiatory, or otherwise made in response to strong external instrumental demands.

**Self-Perception of Attitudes.**　Conventionally, psychologists have assumed that people determine their own attitudes by reviewing the various cognitions and affects in their consciousness, then expressing the result. Bem (1965) has made the interesting argument that people know their own attitudes not by inspecting their insides, but by inferring from their own external behavior. In other words, people infer their own attitudes in the same way that they infer other people's attitudes: by inspecting whatever external cues are available, and then making the appropriate attribution.

Bem does not hold that people never use internal evidence to infer their own true attitudes, but his work does suggest that to a surprising degree people rely upon the external evidence of their overt behavior, and the conditions under which it occurs, as evidence for inferring their own attitudes.

We shall discuss research related to this idea in the chapter on cognitive dissonance. For the moment, the important point is that even attitudes, which are usually considered to be internally determined, may to some extent be affected by attributions based on overt behavior.

**Self-Perception of Ability.**　The same process has been thought to account for how people come to causal explanations for their own performance. Essentially, they use an attribution process to make internal or external attributions about their successes and failures.

In one experiment, Fitch (1970) tested the straightforward hypothesis that high self-esteem people would be likely to attribute their success to internal factors, such as ability or effort, more than would low self-esteem people. A high self-esteem person enters the situation already believing that internal causes predispose one to success. On the other hand, he predicted that failure would be attributed to external factors—chance or the person's mood or temporary physical state—more by high self-esteem people than by low self-esteem people. The same reasoning applies; a low self-esteem person is going to believe that failure follows from his chronic inadequacy and laziness, while a high self-esteem person will believe it must be some accidental outcome from temporary conditions.

He tested these ideas by presenting subjects with slides depicting large numbers of dots spread randomly over the screen. After the subject had seen the slide for 3 seconds, he was asked to estimate how many dots there were. This of course was rather ambiguous, so it was easy to provide false feedback about the subject's performance. Half the subjects, selected at random, were told they did very well (at the 83rd percentile of all subjects), and the other half very poorly (at the 23rd percentile). Then subjects were asked to provide causal explanations for their performances. As expected, the high self-esteem subjects more often used internal explanations (ability and effort) for their successes than did low self-esteem subjects, and more often used external explanations (chance, mood, temporary physical state) for their failures than did low self-esteem subjects.

**Self-Perception of Emotions.**   Attribution theorists have worked on the notion that people infer their emotions and other internal states related to physiological arousal on the basis of external cues. Traditional theories of emotion proposed that we recognize what we feel by considering our physiological state, our mental state, and the external stimulus causing these states. But recent evidence indicates that many, if not all, emotional reactions are biochemically similar—perhaps identical. That is, their internal physiological characteristics are indistinguishable. This emphasizes the importance of external cues. It suggests that without them, the individual might be unable to identify the emotion he is feeling.

The simplest form of the attribution hypothesis runs like this. When a person believes his internal physiological arousal is due to a clear and present external stimulus, he will (1) make an external attribution (i.e., infer that he feels strongly about the stimulus), (2) display appropriate overt emotion toward it, and (3) label his emotion accordingly. If, on the other hand, he believes his arousal is due to circumstances irrelevant to the stimulus, he will not make an external attribution, nor will he be likely to become emotional in relation to it. With this as a starting point, Stanley Schachter conducted a series of studies on the interrelationship between physiological and social factors in emotion. Schachter and Singer (1962) produced a state of physiological arousal in subjects without providing any cues specific to one emotion by injecting the subjects with the drug epinephrine. In appropriate quantities, this drug produces the kind of physiological arousal that is generally associated with emotions but that does not resemble any particular emotion. Some of these subjects were told that the drug would produce physiological arousal—others were not. Thus, some of the aroused people could attribute their internal state to the drug while others were unable to. A final group of subjects was not given epinephrine so was less aroused physiologically. Both the aroused and unaroused subjects were then placed in a situation in which a confederate of the experimenter pretended to be experiencing a particular emotion. Half the subjects were exposed to someone behaving in a euphoric, elated way; half were exposed to someone acting very angry. The euphoric confederate made paper planes and flew them around, instigated a small game of basketball using crumpled papers and an old wastebasket, sang, danced, hopped around, and in general presented a zany, light-headed attitude. The angry confederate made nasty remarks, had an unpleasant expression on his face, muttered to himself, and generally presented a disgruntled, annoyed picture. The question was, how did the subjects react to these two conditions.

Those who had been aroused by the drug and *not* informed of this became more euphoric in the euphoria condition and more angry in the anger condition than the other groups. When there was arousal and no irrelevant cause to which to attribute it, the subjects interpreted their arousal in terms of the other person's behavior. When he was happy, they became happy; when he was angry, so were they. But, when aroused subjects could attribute their arousal to the drug, they were relatively unaffected by the other person's behavior. They knew that their physiological state was due to the drug and therefore did not interpret it as emotional arousal.

Other experiments have varied the availability of an internal attribution for physiological arousal, hypothesizing that when no internal attribution was available, arousal would be attributed to the external situation. In one experiment, Nisbett and Schachter (1966) gave all subjects a placebo pill, and then administered some painful electric shock to them. In between, experimental subjects were told the pill would produce physiological symptoms, such as hand tremors and palpitations, while control subjects were told it would produce only nonphysiological symptoms. The hypothesis was that the experimental subjects would attribute their physiological reactions after the shock not to the shock itself, but to the pill. The control subjects, having no basis for an internal attribution, would blame their reactions on the shock itself. Indeed it was found that these control subjects found the shock more painful than did the experimental subjects.

In a related experiment, Storms and Nisbett (1970) gave insomniac patients placebo pills before going to bed. In the arousal condition, they were told the pills would cause physiological arousal, while in the relaxation condition they were told it would actually reduce arousal. Table 2–4 presents the results. As expected, arousal subjects got to sleep more quickly, because they attributed their jumpiness and restlessness to the pills rather than to any emotional preoccupations. On the other hand, the relaxation subjects actually got to sleep later than usual, because they were still jumpy and restless after taking a supposedly relaxing pill. They could only infer that their emotional problems and worries were even worse than usual.

Another demonstration of the same point, by Dienstbier and Smith (1971), involved giving all subjects a placebo pill, and telling some to expect arousal and others not to. Then all subjects were given an opportunity to cheat on a vocabulary test. Subjects who expected arousal from the pill cheated more, presumably because they interpreted their feelings as caused by the pill rather than from fear or guilt associated with cheating. Subjects who expected no effects from the pill associated their emotionality with guilt about the temptation to cheat, and thus refrained from cheating.

One demonstration that people infer their feelings about external stimuli on the basis of their physiological arousal is provided by Valins (1966). He presented male subjects with slides of nude females, and after each slide provided faked feedback to the subject about his rate of heartbeat. Each subject was wired to fake electrodes, and told that his own heartbeat was played into his earphones. After each slide, some subjects heard increased heartbeats, which they thought were their own, and

Table 2–4

TIME TO GET TO SLEEP PER NIGHT, IN MINUTES, AS A
FUNCTION OF EXPERIMENTAL CONDITION

| Statistic | Arousal | Control | Sedation |
|---|---|---|---|
| Average of preexperimental nights | 53.22 | 38.40 | 36.09 |
| Average of experimental nights | 41.52 | 36.96 | 51.24 |
| Mean change | 11.70 | 1.44 | −15.15 |

Source: After Storms and Nisbett (1970).

others heard what they thought were irrelevant sounds. Valins found that subjects rated nudes as more attractive when they had been accompanied by their own supposedly increased heartbeat. Also, after the experiment was over, subjects were allowed to take some slides home. They mostly took slides that had been associated with increased heartbeat. This was evidence that people infer their own internal subjective states (in this case, sexual attraction to a particular girl) on the basis of what their body tells them, and not necessarily on their perceptions of the external stimulus itself.

This work on attribution demonstrates the importance of people's perception or interpretation of a situation. Judgments of the intentions, beliefs, attitudes, values, and emotions of others and ourselves depend in part on assumptions we make about causality. In particular, the difference between internal and external causality is crucial. The decision as to where to attribute causality affects virtually all aspects of person perception, as well as our evaluations of our own feelings and behavior.

## CHAPTER REVIEW

1. People form consistent impressions of others, even with little information.
2. The recognition of emotions from minimal cues.
3. Averaging and adding models of impression formation.
4. Emotions divided into six categories.
5. The criterion problem in the perception of emotions and personalities.
6. Some traits as more central than others.
7. The importance of the evaluative dimension in the perception of people.
8. Halo effects and positivity biases.
9. Knowledge, stereotypes, and prejudice as they affect accuracy.
10. Internal vs. external attributions.
11. Perceiving causality in other people's actions.
12. Making causal attributions about ourselves.

## APPLICATIONS AND SPECULATIONS

1. Programs for aiding people in urban ghettos and other disadvantaged people are usually administered in part by people from inside the

ghetto and in part by people from outside. This dual administration often leads to tensions between the inside and outside administrators. What do you think are the advantages and disadvantages of having administration from either inside or outside?

2. Candidates for political office almost always overestimate their chance of winning and also misperceive the citizenry as being closer to them on the issues than they actually are. In addition, the candidates overemphasize the importance of the issues, whereas the people are generally ignorant of particular issues. How would you explain these tendencies and what are their implications for the candidates' behavior?

3. Scientists, philosophers, and others engage in a continuing discussion of free will and determinism. Most people appear to avoid accepting a belief in determinism; they like to think of themselves as free. Why do you think this is so?

## SUGGESTIONS FOR ADDITIONAL READING

### Articles

Anderson, N. H. Application of a linear-serial model to a personality-impression task using special presentation. *Journal of Personality and Social Psychology*, 1968, *10*, 354–62.

Dornbusch, S. M., Hastorf, A. H., Richardson, S. A., Muzzy, R. E., and Vreeland, R. S. The perceiver and the perceived: their relative influence on the categories of interpersonal cognition. *Journal of Personality and Social Psychology*, 1965, *1*, 434–40.

Kelley, H. H. The warm-cold variable in the first impressions of person, *Journal of Personality*, 1950, *18*, 431–39.

Schachter, S. and Singer, J. E. Cognitive, social and psychological determinants of emotional state. *Psychological Review*, 1962, *69*, 379–99.

Valins, S. Cognitive effects of false heart-rate feed-back. *Journal of Personality and Social Psychology*, 1966, *4*, 400–408.

### Books and Longer Discussions

Hastorf, A. H., Schneider, D., and Polefka, J. *Person Perception*. Reading, Mass.: Addison-Wesley, 1970.

Jones, E. E., Kanouse, D., Kelley, H. H., Nisbett, R. E., Valins, S., and Weiner, B. (Eds.). *Attribution: Perceiving the Causes of Behavior*. Morristown, N.J.: General Learning Press, 1972.

# three

# liking

In the previous chapter we discussed how people perceive other people. Now we turn to a consideration of a basic dimension of interpersonal perception and interpersonal relations, that is, how much people like one another. In our discussion of the semantic differential, we saw that the evaluative dimension explains a great deal of the variance in one's attitudes and perceptions. When one rates anything, whether a book, a house, or the president of the United States, how positive he feels toward the object is a key factor in his rating. This is particularly important when other people are involved, because the extent to which two people like each other is a fundamental determinant of their interaction. It affects practically every phase of their relationship—how much they choose to see each other, how close they stand, what they say to each other, how they treat each other, how much they are influenced by each other, and on and on. Among the first questions one asks himself when he meets somebody else are: Will he like me? Will I like him?

It should be noted that we have used the word *like* rather than a more technical or neutral term such as *positively evaluate*. The reason is that we are concerned with something more than a positive evaluation of another person. One may positively evaluate a candidate for the presidency of the United States or a movie actress, but he is not friends with them. We are concerned with the factors that lead to friendship and liking in the more personal sense. The distinction is, of course, not clear, for most of the factors that affect positive evaluation also affect more personal liking. However, we shall use *liking* because we are dealing not only with the question of why someone evaluates another person positively but also with why someone tends to like and become friends with another person.

Liking is not unique to human relationships; other animals also seem to have relationships that can be characterized only as friendships. Research by Frank Beach (1969) has shown that beagle dogs have definite preferences among other beagles, at least for mating. A number of these dogs were given a spacious home, with nice pens and big runs, in the hills above the University of California at Berkeley. They were allowed to run free much of the time, and their behavior was observed. Definite patterns of associations developed among the dogs. When they ran free, each dog spent most of its time with certain other dogs. In particular, each male had preferences for specific females and the females had preferences for specific males. These preferences were usually reciprocal, but not always.

The preferences were very clear when a male and a sexually receptive female were put together with no other dogs around. The males attempted to mate with some females but not others (or at least showed more enthusiasm for some than for others). Even when no mating could occur because the females were in a pen, the males continued to show preferences. They stood at the fence, sniffed, and in other ways showed interest in some females but not others. And the females' behavior was even clearer. Some males they welcomed, encouraged, and generally did all they could to help. Other, equally interested males received a colder reception; the females growled menacingly, kept turning to face them, snapped at them, and even attacked if the males tried to get romantic.

It could be argued that this study simply shows that some dogs are more attractive sexually than others. But the preferences are not consistent. Some males preferred certain females, other males preferred different ones. Although this could still be interpreted as simply a difference in sexual preferences, it does seem quite similar to the behavior we associate with liking in a general sense.

Our main purpose in discussing this work on animal friendships is to put human liking in a somewhat broader context so we can see that liking is not a uniquely human characteristic. The major difference between animal and human liking is that for humans it is an important determinant of almost all interactions. Nevertheless, many of the factors that determine animal likes probably also apply to humans. In this chapter we shall consider three major determinants of liking—proximity, rewardingness, and similarity. In each case, we shall describe the general effect of the variable but shall concentrate most of our attention on trying to explain why it operates as it does and on specifying situations that magnify or minimize its effect.

**PROXIMITY**     Probably the best single predictor of whether two people are friends is how far apart they live. If one of them lives in Brazil and the other in China, it is almost certain they are not friends. If one lives in New York City and the other in Los Angeles, or even if they live on opposite sides of the same city, it is unlikely they are friends. In fact, if two people live

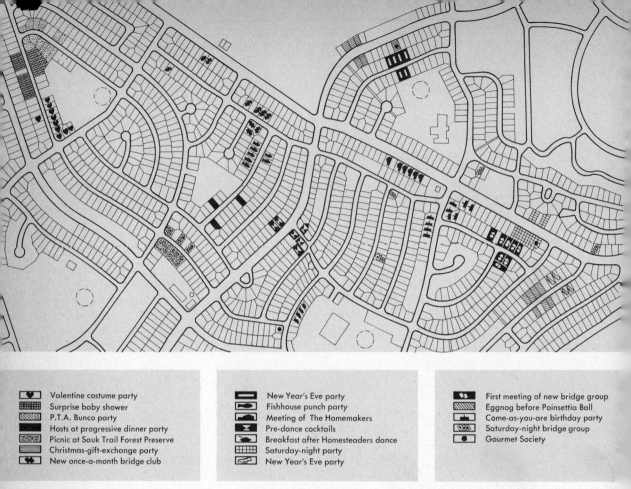

| | Valentine costume party | | New Year's Eve party | | First meeting of new bridge group |
|---|---|---|---|---|---|
| | Surprise baby shower | | Fishhouse punch party | | Eggnog before Poinsettia Ball |
| | P.T.A. Bunco party | | Meeting of The Homemakers | | Come-as-you-are birthday party |
| | Hosts at progressive dinner party | | Pre-dance cocktails | | Saturday-night bridge group |
| | Picnic at Sauk Trail Forest Preserve | | Breakfast after Homesteaders dance | | Gourmet Society |
| | Christmas-gift-exchange party | | Saturday-night party | | |
| | New once-a-month bridge club | | New Year's Eve party | | |

### Figure 3–1

Attendance at various social gatherings in Park Forest. Proximity was the dominant factor operating in the friendship patterns in this community—almost all the people who attended each party lived near each other. However, similarity of interests also caused people to be friends, as shown by the Saturday-night bridge group and the Gourmet Society. (Copyright © 1956 by William H. Whyte. Reprinted by permission of Simon & Schuster, Inc., and Jonathan Cape Limited.)

only ten blocks apart, it is considerably less likely that they are friends than if they live next door to each other.

W. H. Whyte (1956) conducted a study of friendship patterns in Park Forest, a suburban residential community. Almost everyone had moved into Park Forest at about the same time, and, because all the houses were similar, the residents had chosen their homes and neighborhoods pretty much by chance. There were no "better" areas, no cheap houses—nothing in particular to distinguish the various parts of the town. Thus, the possibility was minimized that people in one area were in some way different from those in another before they moved into the community. It was almost as though a large group of people had been assigned randomly to houses.

For some time Whyte read the social column in the newspaper and kept a careful check on who gave parties, who was invited by whom, and, in general, who was friendly with whom. The diagram in Figure 3–1 illustrates the patterns of association he found. Note the clustering. Almost everyone at the baby shower lived within a few blocks of one another, and almost everyone who lived within the area was there. The same was true on the other side of town at the eggnog party. In the whole town there were practically no friends who did not live near one another. Similarly, there was a remarkable occurrence of friendships among people who lived close together.

This same kind of effect occurs in much smaller units than a whole town. A study by Festinger, Schachter, and Back (1950) investigated the patterns of friendships in a large housing development called Westgate West, which consisted of seventeen separate two-story buildings, each containing ten apartments (five on a floor). The layout is shown in Figure 3–2. This housing development was similar to Park Forest in certain

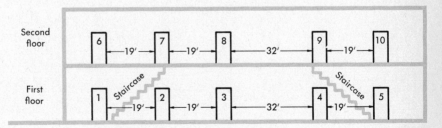

Figure 3–2

Floor plan of Westgate West. All the buildings in the housing development had the same layout. In the study, functional distance was defined simply as the number of doors away two people lived—the differences in distance measured by feet were ignored. (Adapted from Festinger, Schachter, and Back, 1950.)

respects. For one thing, the apartments were almost identical. More important, however, residents did not choose where they were to live; they were given apartments as the apartments became vacant. In other words, like Park Forest, Westgate West came close to being a field experiment—the residents were randomly assigned to a condition.

All the residents were asked, "Which three people in Westgate West do you see socially most often?" The results are shown in the graph in Figure 3–3. It is clear that residents were most friendly with those who lived near them. People on the same floor (top line) mentioned their next-door neighbor more often than their neighbor two doors away and their neighbor two doors away more often than their neighbor at the other end of the hall. Of next-door neighbors, 41 percent were chosen, whereas only 22 percent of those two doors away and 10 percent of those at the end of the hall were. Moreover, it should be noted that the distances were very small. People who lived next door were 19 feet apart (in the case of the two middle apartments, 32 feet apart), and the maximum distance between two apartments on one floor was only 88 feet. But these differences, which would necessitate only a few extra seconds in walking time, were important factors in determining friendships.

In addition, people who lived on different floors (the bottom line of the graph) were mentioned much less than those on the same floor even when the physical distance between them was roughly the same. This was probably because it takes more effort to go up or down stairs than to walk down a hall. Thus, people on different floors were in a sense far-

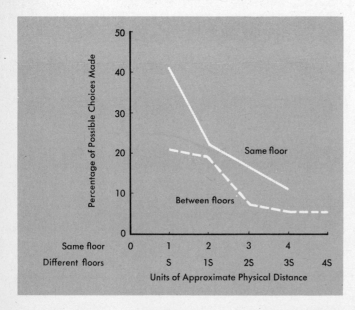

Figure 3–3

The relationship between functional distance and liking. The distance between people on the same floor and on different floors was closely related to friendship patterns—the closer two individuals lived, the more likely they were to be friends. Living on different floors (bottom line) reduced the likelihood of friendship because functional distance was increased. (Festinger, Schachter, and Back, 1950.)

ther away than those on the same floor. The investigators referred to this phenomenon as *functional distance*, meaning that the probability people would meet was determined by the design of the apartment house plus actual distance. The closer people lived, as measured by either physical or functional distance, the more likely they were to be friends.

This phenomenon is so strong and ubiquitous that it is one of the easiest to demonstrate. Every year in our social psychology class we ask a student to make a map of the friendships in his dormitory; and every

Drawing by Claude; © 1959
The New Yorker Magazine, Inc.

*"Do you really love me, Anthony, or is it just because I
live on the thirty-eighth floor?"*

year this map shows that those who live near each other are much more likely to be friends than those who live far apart. Thus, proximity generally produces increased liking. Why does proximity have this effect?

### Availability

The simplest explanation of the effect of proximity is that people who are close are more available than those who are farther away. One cannot like or be friends with someone he does not know, and it is difficult to remain friends with someone he does not see fairly often. Obviously, we choose our friends from people we know; we also choose our enemies this way. Close relationships, either positive or negative, are generally with people we see regularly—and certainly with people we know. At this level, the phenomenon does not sound very exciting. Naturally, we are not going to become friends (or enemies) with someone we do not know and the closer another person lives to us, the more likely it is that we would know him well enough to become friends.

However, it is a mistake to explain the effect of proximity entirely on the grounds of availability. Residents of Westgate West liked people who lived 19 feet away more than those who lived 38 feet away. Although it is true that they were somewhat more likely to see the people who lived closer, in terms of availability they would certainly get to know quite well people who lived only 38 feet away—the people who lived two doors down the hall were assuredly available as friends. The people downstairs were also available; it certainly was not beyond the strength of these people to walk downstairs if they wanted to make friends with somebody. Yet, there was a strong effect of proximity. Why did sheer physical closeness or likelihood of seeing someone make such a difference in patterns of liking, even when other people were readily available as friends? Also, why did proximity lead primarily to positive, rather than negative, relationships? After all, one has to know someone to hate him just as one has to know someone to like him.

### Continued Interaction

When an individual knows he is going to be in a particular situation, he generally tries to convince himself that it will be pleasant or, at least, not too unpleasant. Similarly, one who expects to interact with someone else in the future tends to exaggerate the other person's positive traits and ignore or, at least, play down his negative ones. Presumably people try to convince themselves that interactions will be pleasant. When one decides ahead of time that another person is nice, he probably will like the other person when they actually meet. If the other person lives next door, one anticipates a great deal of contact with him and wants this contact to be pleasant. Accordingly, people are strongly motivated to perceive their neighbors in positive terms.

Studies by Darley and Berscheid (1967) and by Mirels and Mills (1964) have demonstrated this effect. The subjects in Darley and Berscheid's study were given information about two other persons and told that they would interact with one of them. When the subjects evaluated the two other people, their evaluation of the one with whom they expected to interact was more positive than that of the other person. The Mirels and Mills study was quite similar. It showed that subjects minimize the negative characteristics of someone with whom they expect to deal.

This tendency to accentuate the positive characteristics of persons one must interact with is clearly associated with the effect of proximity. An individual is not forced to have much contact with a neighbor four doors away and can probably avoid him most of the time if he is unpleasant. Thus, there is less motivation to develop a pleasant picture of him. The farther away someone lives and the less contact with him one anticipates, the weaker is this motivation. Conversely, the closer the neighbor, the more one distorts his perceptions in a positive direction and the more probable it is that one will end up liking him.

Anticipated interaction also has other effects. In addition to deciding that the other person is very pleasant, one will go out of his way to be pleasant himself. In first meetings, knowing there will be many others, an individual will try to be especially nice, to avoid conflict, to promote a friendly relationship. As we shall discuss at greater length below, being nice to someone is a good way to make him like us. Thus, two people who are anticipating future interactions and therefore behaving nicely are likely to be friends.

### Predictability

Another possible explanation of the effect of proximity involves how predictable the other person's behavior becomes. Presumably, the more one sees someone else, the more one learns about him and the better one can predict how the other person will behave in a variety of situations. When someone knows fairly well how another will act or react to what he does, he is less likely to do something to annoy the other person—and vice versa. Each learns how to act to make their interaction free of unpleasantness and, therefore, does not cause unpleasantness unintentionally. Of course, two people can still annoy each other, but generally they can avoid conflict. Although this does not necessarily make people friends, it does make it easier for them to be friends. At least they have primarily pleasant interactions, which lay the groundwork for friendship.

**Familiarity**

Some recent studies have produced results that suggest a particularly fascinating explanation of the effect of proximity on liking. To begin with, when a quality continuum in the English language has both negative and positive poles (e.g., good-bad, right-wrong, tall-short, beautiful-ugly), the word describing the positive pole is almost always used more frequently. Thus, *good* appears in books and newspapers more frequently than *bad*, *right* more frequently than *wrong*, and so on. This finding, by itself, is just a curiosity. Without additional research, there would be no way of knowing whether familiarity made the words positive, or vice versa. But the finding does suggest that familiar things may be or become more positive than unfamiliar things. In some way, familiarity is associated with being good.

Zajonc conducted several experiments (1968) to demonstrate that

Drawing by Bob Zahn; © 1967.

*"I've decided that maybe you are my type after all."*

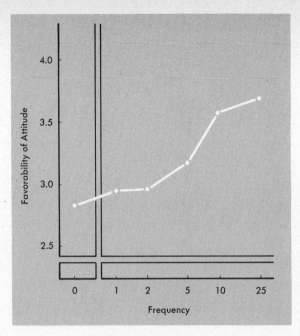

Figure 3–4

The relationship between frequency of exposure and liking. Subjects were shown photographs of different faces and the number of times each face was shown was varied. The more often the subjects saw a particular face, the more they said they liked the person pictured. (Zajonc, R. B., "Attitudinal effects of mere exposure," *Journal of Personality and Social Psychology*, 1968, *8*, p. 18. Copyright 1968 by the American Psychological Association, and reproduced by permission.)

familiarity does lead to a positive reaction. In one study, subjects were shown a number of Turkish words, and some of the words were shown many more times than others. (In other studies, nonsense syllables and Chinese words were used.) Afterward, the subjects were asked to guess the meanings of the words. There was a strong tendency for them to give positive meanings to the words they had seen more often. This result may have been due simply to the fact that the subjects were used to English, in which frequent words have more positive meanings; on the other hand, it may have been due to a more basic phenomenon.

In another study by Zajonc that is directly relevant to our current concern, subjects were shown pictures of faces. Some of the faces were shown as many as twenty-five times, others only one or two times. Afterward, the subjects were asked how much they liked each face and how much they thought they would like the person pictured. The results are shown in Figure 3–4. Familiarity appeared to have the same effect with faces as it had with words. The more often the subjects had seen a face, the more they said they liked it and that they thought they would like the person pictured.

Finally, an experiment by Freedman, Carlsmith, and Suomi (1967) studied the effect of familiarity with actual people. Each pair of subjects met either three, six, or twelve times. At each meeting, they sat across from each other without talking. At the end of the series of meetings, the subjects were asked how much they liked each of the other subjects. The more often they had met, the more they said they liked each other. Similar findings were reported by Saegert, Swap, and Zajonc (1973).

Although the findings from these studies are not conclusive, there does seem to be considerable evidence that familiarity leads not to contempt but to liking.

### Reinforcement Explanation

A number of experimenters (e.g., Burgess and Sales, 1971) have offered an explanation of the familiarity effect in terms of simple reinforcement principles. They argue that in all of the studies performed so far, the stimuli were presented in a predominantly positive situation. If this were true, the familiarity effect could be due merely to a greater number of positive reinforcements for those stimuli that were presented more often. Although the simplicity of this explanation is appealing, there is little reason to accept it at the present time. It is hard to see why the situations were particularly positive. In most of them a subject is sitting in a psychological experiment watching a screen or memory drum on which various words or pictures appear. Watching a long series of words or faces does not seem to be an especially pleasant way of spending time. Certainly it would be easy to find a large number of subjects who would tell you that this is the kind of experiment they find unpleasant and boring.

Two experiments by Saegert, Swap, and Zajonc (1973) provide strong evidence that the familiarity effect is not dependent on positive situations. In these studies, the amount of exposure to other people was varied as in previous work, and the exposures occurred in either pleasant or unpleasant circumstances. The subjects were all tasting a variety of substances, but for half of them the tastes were pleasant while for half they were quite unpleasant. The results of their first experiment are shown in Figure 3–5. As you can see, for both pleasant and noxious taste conditions, the people liked each other more when they had seen each other more. The second experiment produced almost identical findings. Thus, it seems clear that the reinforcement explanation of the familiarity effect is not correct. Exposure increases liking regardless of whether the situation is positive or negative.

### Exceptions to the Positive Effects of Proximity

Although increased contact with other people usually makes one like them more, it does not always have this effect. The simplest exception occurs when there are strongly anchored initial antagonisms. If one forms a strong dislike for another person at the first contact, there is evidence that additional contacts do not increase liking.

A study by Freedman and Suomi (1967) investigated the effect of varying both familiarity and initial evaluation. Three subjects were escorted by a secretary to the experimental room, where they found another "subject" (actually, a confederate of the experimenter) waiting.

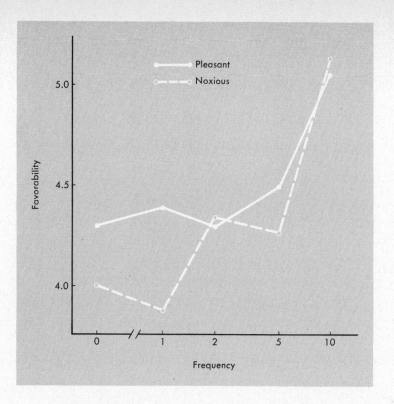

Figure 3–5

Favorability as a function of the number of exposures and the pleasantness of taste of the solutions. (Saevert, Swap, and Zajonc, "Exposure, context, and interpersonal attraction," *Journal of Personality and Social Psychology*, 1973, *25*, p. 237. Copyright 1973 by the American Psychological Association, and reproduced by permission.)

At this point before the experimenter appeared, the confederate went through a short act designed to make him seem either nice or extremely unpleasant.

In the pleasant condition, he asked the secretary where the experimenter was, explaining that he (the confederate) had been waiting for some time and was getting concerned. The secretary answered that the experimenter had been slightly delayed and would be there shortly. The confederate said fine, he had just been wondering whether everything was all right, thanked the secretary, and sat down to wait. This conversation was spoken in a pleasant tone of voice, and the confederate showed interest and concern rather than anger. The experimenter arrived immediately afterward and the study began.

In the unpleasant condition, the interaction was entirely different. The confederate spoke in an extremely belligerent tone of voice. He demanded to know where the experimenter was and why he was not there on time. He said he had been waiting for a long time and was not going to waste his time on some stupid experiment. He uttered a few mild epithets and, when the secretary tried to explain, cut her off by saying, in a demanding, vicious tone of voice, "You go and get the experimenter right now." The secretary acted flustered and rushed off. Once again, the experimenter appeared immediately afterward and the study began. The skits had the desired effect—all the subjects tended to dislike the unpleasant confederate and to like the pleasant confederate.

Subjects then saw the confederate three, six, or twelve times and indicated at the end of the sessions how much they liked him. As with the other research on familiarity, the more often the pleasant confederate was seen, the more he was liked. In contrast, the ratings of the unpleasant confederate were not affected by the number of contacts. Those who had seen him twelve times liked him no more than those who had seen him only six or three times. In other words, familiarity produced increased liking for somebody who initially was neutral or slightly liked but had no effect on attitudes toward someone who was strongly disliked. It may be, of course, that more extensive contact eventually would have produced increased liking even for the unpleasant confederate.

It should be noted that if an initial rating is only mildly negative, increased familiarity does have a strong effect. For example, in Zajonc's studies, many of the initial ratings were on the negative side of neutral and he did get the familiarity effect. Thus, it appears that only a strongly negative initial evaluation or perhaps one that is anchored in some actual occurrence is immune to the familiarity phenomenon.

Another exception to the general tendency of contact leading to liking occurs when people have conflicting interests, needs, or personalities. As long as they see little of each other the conflicts are minimized. They may not particularly like each other but they have little reason to dislike each other. When contact is increased, however, the conflicts are exaggerated and aggravated. Under these circumstances, they may sometimes dislike each other more as a result of closer contact.

### Proximity and Prejudice

Unfortunately, increased dislike seems to occur on some occasions when blacks and whites are placed in closer contact then they had been. It is true that under these conditions, various prejudices and stereotypes are decreased because the groups get to know each other better. When they learn more about each other, they realize they are more similar than they had thought and unrealistic biases decrease. This is particularly true when there are no basic economic conflicts between the groups. Then increased contact leads to increased liking. In World War II, when black and white soldiers fought together, racial prejudice decreased and so did antagonisms (Stouffer et al., 1949). There were no realistic conflicts between the groups because they were fighting a common enemy and were not competing. With this lack of conflict, the unrealistic stereotypes decreased markedly because of the greater knowledge gained by the increased familiarity. But if the two groups have somewhat different values and are competing (for jobs, housing, etc.), the increased contact may increase the conflicts between them, which, in turn, makes the groups dislike each other more than they did before. We thus may have the paradoxical situation of prejudice and bias decreasing but antagonisms increasing.

The evidence on the effects of closer contact between blacks and whites is somewhat inconsistent. At least one study (Kramer, 1950) has shown that the short-term effect of integration may not be entirely positive. In this study, the increased contact resulted in less bias but more antagonism.

In contrast, most of the other research on this problem indicates that increased contact reduces antagonism as well as prejudice and stereotypes. Studies on public housing (Deutsch and Collins, 1951; Jahoda and West, 1951; Works, 1961) have found less antagonism in both blacks and whites in integrated areas than in segregated areas. Similar results have been reported in studies that concerned integrated working conditions. When blacks were hired to work in department stores in New York City, white clerks became progressively more accepting of their black coworkers (Harding and Hogrefe, 1952). The white customers had similar positive reactions (Saenger and Gilbert, 1950). Comparable results have been found in the Army (Stouffer et al., 1949) and the Merchant Marines (Brophy, 1946) and among policemen( Kephart, 1957) and government workers (MacKenzie, 1948). Thus, although there are some indications that increased contact could actually increase antagonism, most of the research indicates that greater familiarity, even under trying conditions, leads to less antagonism.

Although we do not yet know enough about the effects of contact on prejudice to draw definite conclusions, it seems likely that the crucial factor is the type of contact. It is overly simple to conclude that more contact is always good. However, it is probably correct that more *appropriate* contact, which has been called *equal-status contact*, reduces both bias and antagonism. Contact of this type, which means simply that the two groups meet on equal terms, generally occurs in the armed forces, where blacks and whites fight together with more or less equal rank (at least among enlisted men), and in factories and stores in which members of the two races hold comparable jobs. But in housing developments and many businesses, interracial contact is between people of different status. Sometimes relatively poor blacks move into white neighborhoods and the whites are afraid that the value of their homes will be reduced; sometimes integration occurs in business only by giving the least desirable jobs to blacks, who then have to interact with whites who outrank them; and so on. Under these circumstances, increased contact seems less likely to have a positive effect and may even have a negative effect on relations between blacks and whites. Thus, those who expect that integration of any kind or on only one level will reduce racial tensions may be disappointed, at least in the short run. But integration that is backed up by programs of equal jobs, education, and housing will have the desired effect.

The results of the research cited above indicate that, in general, increased contact has a positive effect. Proximity leads to liking, which effect appears to be due to several different mechanisms. In the first place, proximity makes people available, and, of necessity, friends are chosen from those one knows. In addition, proximity implies continual interactions and greater predictability. And finally, proximity leads to greater familiarity with the other person, which in itself leads to greater liking.

### Other Factors Affecting Liking

Of course, proximity is not the only factor affecting liking. People do not always like their next-door neighbors, even roommates do not always like each other. One's best friend can live down the hall or on the other side of town. Friends and marriage partners must be chosen from those available, from those one knows; but among those who are available, one has a considerable amount of choice and this choice is affected by a number of other important factors.

We have already noted, in Figure 3–1, page 65, that almost all the parties and friendship patterns in Park Forest showed a strong effect of proximity. Everyone at the baby shower and the eggnog party lived close together. However it should be noted that not everyone at all the parties lived close together and that all the people who lived close were not invited to any single party. In other words, all those we see often do not become our friends and, similarly, not all our friends are people who live near us. Most people have some friends who live fairly far away, and almost everyone dislikes or is neutral toward some of the people he sees a great deal.

We can all name a number of qualities that, at least in our society, tend to make people like other people. Other things being equal, there is a tendency to like people more if they are honest rather than dishonest, helpful rather than harmful, friendly rather than unfriendly, kind rather than cruel, and so on.

Norman Anderson (1968) compiled a list of 555 adjectives that are used to describe people. He then asked college students to indicate how much they would like a person who had each of these characteristics. (A

Table 3-1

*LIKABLENESS OF PERSONALITY TRAITS*

| Highly Likable | Slightly Positive to Slightly Negative | Highly Dislikable |
|---|---|---|
| Sincere | Persistent | Ill-mannered |
| Honest | Conventional | Unfriendly |
| Understanding | Bold | Hostile |
| Loyal | Cautious | Loud-mouthed |
| Truthful | Perfectionistic | Selfish |
| Trustworthy | Excitable | Narrow-minded |
| Intelligent | Quiet | Rude |
| Dependable | Impulsive | Conceited |
| Thoughtful | Aggressive | Greedy |
| Considerate | Shy | Insincere |
| Reliable | Unpredictable | Unkind |
| Warm | Emotional | Untrustworthy |
| Kind | Bashful | Malicious |
| Friendly | Naive | Obnoxious |
| Happy | Restless | Untruthful |
| Unselfish | Daydreamer | Dishonest |
| Humorous | Materialistic | Cruel |
| Responsible | Rebellious | Mean |
| Cheerful | Lonely | Phony |
| Trustful | Dependent | Liar |

Source: Adapted from Anderson (1968).

sample of the adjectives is listed in Table 3–1.) One of the most striking results of the study was that apparently the trait most valued by college students in the 1960s was sincerity. Of the eight top adjectives, six—sincere, honest, loyal, truthful, trustworthy, and dependable—related to sincerity in one way or another. Similarly, the adjectives rated lowest were liar and phony, with dishonest being close to the bottom. There seemed to be agreement among the subjects on which characteristics are desirable and which undesirable. Presumably, possessing the highly rated qualities increases the probability that one will be liked, whereas possessing those rated low reduces this probability.

Another simple but potent factor that affects liking is physical attractiveness. Other things being equal, people considered attractive are liked more than people not considered attractive. If, for example, students are assigned partners for dates at random, knowing how attractive each student is would make it possible to predict with some accuracy how much his partner will report liking him (Walster et al., 1966). Both girls and boys who are considered attractive are liked more.

It is hardly surprising that physical attractiveness plays an important role in determining choices for dates and even for marriage partners. Almost by definition we would expect that a man would prefer to date or marry a woman he considered attractive to one he considered less attractive; and that the same would hold for a woman picking a man. A number of studies (Walster, 1970; Berscheid et al., 1971; Stroebe, 1971) have provided evidence that supports this common sense expectation. This research also indicates that physical attractiveness is more important to men than to women. In making choices both for dates and for marriage partners, men are more influenced by the physical attractiveness of women than the women are by the physical attractiveness of the men. The last study listed also found not surprisingly but somewhat reassuringly that physical attractiveness is less important when a marriage partner is being chosen than in simply dating. Apparently for long-term relationships, other factors play a relatively more important role.

Although there is a general tendency for all people to prefer dates who are as attractive as possible, there is some evidence that people do not always choose the most attractive possible person to ask for a date. Walster (1970) suggests that people tend to match their own attractiveness with that of the person they choose. The less attractive someone thinks he is, the less attractive will be the person he chooses for a date. In other words, unattractive people will tend to choose unattractive people; moderately attractive will choose moderately attractive, and highly attractive will choose highly attractive. This is a plausible notion but by and large it has not been supported by the research. Two experiments reported in Berscheid et al. (1971) did find some evidence of this kind of matching, but both Walster (1970) and Stroebe (1971) found very little matching. It may be that only when the subject feels that he is likely to be rejected by the person he chooses will he tend to minimize that likelihood by picking somebody of his own attractiveness level. Except for special circumstances, it now appears that everyone, given the chance, will choose the most attractive person available.

All the traits we have listed, including physical attractiveness, are value judgments. Therefore, it is almost redundant to say we like people who have "good" traits. Naturally, we like them more because, by definition, they are better, more likable, more attractive than people who do not have these traits. Thus, the listing of the traits is, in a sense, simply a listing of the qualities we value in our society. But we should be able to point to general principles underlying these specific characteristics, and it is these general principles that really explain why people like each other.

**REWARDING-NESS** People like others who reward them or who are associated with pleasant experiences. Most of the characteristics mentioned above can be classified accordingly. We like beautiful women or handsome men because we enjoy looking at them. Kind people reward others constantly and are therefore liked more—the same is true of people who are friendly, sincere, trustworthy, warm, and so on. Someone with these qualities is nicer to be with than somebody without them.

The effect of rewardingness can be explained in terms of simple learning principles. If somebody rewards us or we share a rewarding experience with him, the positive aspects of the experience or the reward are linked with the other person. He thus becomes more positive and we like him more.

A particularly important application of this principle is that we like people whom we know like us. If the only information we have about someone is that he likes us, we are predisposed to like him also. If he dislikes us, this feeling also will be reciprocated.

This effect has been illustrated in an experiment by Aronson and Linder (1965). They had subjects go through a series of brief interactions with a confederate who was posing as another subject. After each interaction the subject overheard an interview between the confederate and the experimenter in which the confederate gave his impressions of the subject. In one condition, the confederate was quite flattering and said at the beginning that he liked the subject. He continued to make positive statements about the subject after each of the interviews. In another condition, the confederate was critical. He said he was not sure that he liked the subject much and gave fairly negative descriptions of him. He continued being negative throughout the study. Afterward, the subjects were asked how much they liked the confederate. The results are shown in Table 3–2. (The third condition will be discussed later.) As expected, the subjects reciprocated the confederate's evaluation of them, liking him when he liked them and disliking him when he disliked them.

Of course, this does not mean that *all* likes and dislikes are reciprocal. Sometimes we like someone who dislikes us, and vice versa. But

Table 3–2

*LIKING IN RESPONSE TO ANOTHER'S EVALUATION*

| Condition | Liking[a] |
| --- | --- |
| Positive evaluation throughout | 6.42 |
| Negative evaluation throughout | 2.52 |
| Negative-positive evaluation | 7.67 |

[a]Figures are ratings on a scale from —10 to +10.

Source: Adapted from Aronson and Linder (1965).

other things being equal, there is a strong tendency to like others who like us. Although there are various explanations for this phenomenon, as we shall see below, probably the main reason for it is that the nicest thing anyone can tell us is that he likes us; it is extremely rewarding, and we like others who give us this reward.

## Ingratiation

Rewardingness may seem like a simple principle, but actually it has many complexities. Let us consider a simple case of rewardingness—a person who says nice things about us or to us. In general, this is rewarding and there is a tendency for us to like him more as a result of his comments. However, his behavior affects our liking for him more at some times than at others. Having someone say something nice is more rewarding under some circumstances than under others, and the more rewarding it is, the more we like him.

A large fuel corporation was planning to construct a gas station in a residential neighborhood. They sent representatives to try to convince the residents that the station would be attractive and would not need a wall to screen it from neighboring houses. The company representatives all took a hard line and were quite unpleasant. At one meeting, however, a company public relations man appeared. Whereas the other company men acted normal throughout the meetings—scowling when angry, smiling when pleased—the PR man smiled all the time. He particularly smiled and nodded when any of the residents said anything. He listened very hard, agreed with everything in principle, and was generally very rewarding. It is always nice to have someone listen intently to what one is saying, all the while smiling and nodding understanding and agreement. At the same meeting there was a homeowner who had recently moved into the neighborhood and was therefore a stranger. He was as concerned as the other residents about the ugliness of the station but throughout the meeting behaved much like the company PR man—he also listened carefully and nodded agreement. How did the other residents feel about the two men?

There are two answers. The first is that they liked the PR man more than the company men who were scowling and arguing. After all, as we have said, one likes people who reward him and this person was certainly being rewarding. Even though the residents knew he was acting and actually disagreed with them, they could not help liking him a little. In other words, regardless of the situation, there is a strong tendency to like people who say nice things to us.

The second answer, however, is that the residents liked the smiling neighbor more than they liked the PR man—not because the neighbor was such a fine person but because the PR man was being nice on order, as an act. Despite his smiles and agreeable behavior, it was obvious that he actually disagreed with almost everything the residents said. He was being agreeable for public relations—so that no one would get angry, so the irate residents would be less irate. In contrast, the neighbor was being honest—he smiled and nodded because he did agree with the residents.

This illustrates an important distinction between saying something nice to or about somebody and behaving in a so-called ingratiating way. E. E. Jones (1964) has conducted a series of studies on this phenomenon. In one experiment, female subjects were given a standard interview in which they were asked about their background, values, and personal opinions. While they were answering these questions, they knew they were being observed by somebody sitting behind a one-way mirror, who was presumably recording her impression of the subjects. After the interviews, the observer told the subjects her impression of them. Regardless of the manner in which the subjects had acted, the observer always responded in one of three set ways—she gave either neutral responses, responses that were as similar as possible to a subject's own self-concept, or positive evaluations.

In addition, subjects were given two different types of information about the observer. In what was called the accuracy condition, the subjects were told that the purpose of the experiment was to discover how accurately people form impressions of others. The observer in this condition was supposed to be a first-year graduate student in clinical psychology who was participating as part of her training. It was mentioned that clinical psychology students received special training designed to enable them to be objective and to prevent their own feelings from influencing their judgments.

Subjects in what was called the ulterior-motive condition were told that the observer was a graduate student who had asked to take the place of the regular assistant just for the day, because she was hoping to use the subjects in her own experiment in exchange for serving as the observer. The experimenter remarked that the observer would be very grateful for the subject's cooperation but that the decision was up to the subject. In this condition no mention was made of the importance of accuracy, nor was anything said about special training in being objective. In other words, in one case the observer was an objective, disinterested judge; in the other case she was someone who wanted a favor from the subjects and was under no special pressures to be objective.

After hearing the observer's judgments of her, each subject was asked to rate the observer. It was made clear that these ratings would be confidential and would not be shown to the observer. The subjects rated the observer on a variety of scales, all designed to indicate how much they liked her.

To begin with, the findings showed a strong effect of reinforcement. The more favorable rating the observer had made of the subject, the more the subject liked the observer. As stated before, we like someone who likes us.

The effect of the different instructions was very interesting. Regardless of the type of remarks the observer had made, the observer who had an ulterior motive was liked less than the one who was trying to be objective and accurate. Most important, the largest difference in liking between the accuracy and ulterior-motive conditions and the only one in which there was an appreciable effect occurred when the observer made consistently positive evaluations of the subject. Under these circumstances, it probably appeared that the observer who had the ulterior motive was not being honest but was making the statements in order to get the subject to agree to take part in her experiment. Therefore, she was rated lower than the objective observer.

Apparently it is nice to receive favorable comments from somebody even if we suspect the person's motives. But we will like the other person less if we do have suspicions than if we do not. When a person has something to gain from us, when we are in a superior position, there is a tendency to perceive his behavior as ingratiating rather than honest. And then, the nice things he says do not have the same effect. In general, flattery does not make us like others as much as honest compliments do. Under some circumstances it may actually make us dislike them, presumably because we feel they are being dishonest and are trying to take advantage of us. In other words, although there is a general tendency to like someone who says nice things, the effect is not as strong when his compliments are seen as ingratiation.

### Self-Evaluation

Another important factor determining our attitude toward someone is the degree to which our perception of ourselves coincides with the nice things the other person says about us. Suppose, for example, that one knows he is unable to sing on key and that after he has completed a song, somebody tells him how good a job he did. This is different from a situation in which a person who thinks he is a good singer is complimented. Under most circumstances we like the person who compliments us even if we do not think we deserve it and perhaps even if we think he is deliberately lying. It seems that hearing something nice said about us is so pleasant that it overcomes the potential negative effect of hearing something we do not believe. However, Deutsch and Solomon (1959) did find that a compliment had less effect when the person felt that he did not deserve it than when it was deserved, but in both cases the person giving the compliment was liked more than if a compliment was not offered. And a more recent study by Skolnick (1971) found that under some circumstances a positive statement might produce an even greater increase in liking when the person felt he did not deserve it than when he did. This may be due to the fact that someone who feels that he is not good at something needs a compliment more and appreciates it more than someone who is confident of his ability.

One reason why undeserved compliments may sometimes be ineffective is the ingratiation phenomenon. When we receive an entirely undeserved compliment there is a tendency to suspect the motivation behind it. The other person may have any one of a number of ulterior motives—he may be trying to get something from us, he may be flattering us because he is sorry for us, etc.—but his intentions are suspect and the compliment may not have its usual rewarding value. It will then be less rewarding and may sometimes be negative if we suspect some sort of negative intention.

Another factor determining the effect of compliments is illustrated in the experiment by Aronson and Linder (1965) described earlier. In that study, subjects heard a confederate making either positive or negative statements about them and the subjects generally reciprocated the confederate's evaluations. The experiment included one other interesting variation—a condition in which the confederate began by making negative statements about the subjects and became more and more positive in his descriptions throughout the course of the experiment. By the last few interviews, he was making as positive statements about the subjects in this condition as he did in the condition in which he was positive throughout. In other words, some subjects heard a confederate who liked them at the beginning and continued to like them, whereas other subjects heard a confederate who did not like them at the beginning but ended up liking them.

Although in both these conditions the subjects liked the confederate, they liked him even more when he began critically and ended positively than when he was positive throughout (see Table 3–2, page 79). Note that this seems to run counter to a simple reinforcement or reward theory, because the confederate delivered more total reinforcements when he was nice all through the experiment than when he was positive only toward the end.

Aronson and Linder explained this result in terms of a "gain-loss" effect. The initial negative statements caused the subjects some anxiety, self-doubt, etc., all of which are painful feelings. When the statements gradually became more positive, they not only were rewarding in themselves but they also reduced these previously produced negative feelings. Thus, the later positive statements were more rewarding than they would have been without the initial negative evaluations. Essentially, the negative statements increased the need for positive evaluations and this made them more rewarding when they finally came.

Another explanation offered by the authors concerned the manner in which the subjects perceived the confederate. When the confederate liked them immediately and continued to like them, there may have been some doubt in the subjects' minds as to how honest or how discriminating the confederate was. They may have said to themselves, "This guy likes everybody." On the other hand, when the confederate began in a negative way, he must have impressed the subjects as being the type of person who could say unpleasant things about others and who takes time to make up his mind about them. That is, the critic appeared more discriminating and perhaps more reliable. Then, when he said nice things about the subjects, his opinion carried more weight and was therefore more rewarding. The subjects might have thought, "This guy is pretty careful about making up his mind about people, but he likes me." The determining factor in the subjects' liking the confederate was how much they were rewarded by the nice things he said—and it is more rewarding to be praised by a careful, discriminating person.

This explanation has been supported in two studies by Mettee (1971a, 1971b) in which the discernment of the person making the positive or negative statements was explicitly varied. In one case he appeared to be quite discerning, made some negative statements and some positive ones, and generally gave the impression of someone who made careful, deliberate discriminations. When the discerning person made positive statements about the subject, he was liked more than was someone who seemed less discerning.

Thus we can see that saying something nice about someone is almost always rewarding. The more he believes us and values our judgment, the more it is rewarding; to the extent that he distrusts us and does not value our opinion, it is less rewarding. We like people who say or do nice things for us, but the strength of our liking is determined by how much we trust the motivation behind the action and how much we value the action itself.

An important implication of this research is that how much you like someone will greatly affect how much he likes you. Naturally there is a strong tendency to be nicer to someone whom you like. You are more likely to say nice things about him, to spend more time with him, and generally to behave in such a way that he will tend to like you. Every factor that affects liking is to some extent under the individual's control and will also be affected by his liking of the other. Thus it becomes a circular phenomenon—the more you like somebody, the more you will behave in such a way as to make him like you, which will in turn cause him to be nicer to you, which will make you like him more and so on. This is one reason why initial attitudes are so important. Once you form a positive impression of someone, it makes it much more likely that the two of you will end up liking each other; whereas if you form a negative impression, obviously the reverse is true.

A particular instance of this circular phenomenon occurs when you simply think that someone else likes you. If, for example, you have never met somebody and you hear that he likes you, it predisposes you to like him. Accordingly you treat him better and that in turn causes him to like you more (even if, in fact, he did not particularly like you in the first place). Jones and Panitch (1971) demonstrated that simply telling one member of a team that his partner likes him will result in both of them liking each other more than if he is told that his partner dislikes him. In other words, going into an encounter expecting to be liked will produce what has been called a "self-fulfilling prophecy" in that it will greatly increase the chance that you really will be liked. Conversely, if you enter the encounter expecting to be disliked, that too will probably come true.

SIMILARITY     In our discussion of the Park Forest study (pages 64 to 65), we paid most attention to the effect of proximity. The study also brings to light another factor that determines friendship and liking patterns. In the diagram in Figure 3–1, notice the Gourmet Society and the Saturday-night bridge group. The members of these groups come from all parts of the town, and no two live within even a few blocks of each other. Yet they all are members of the same society and presumably are friends. Why? They share a common interest—they like good food or bridge—and this interest brings them together. This is one example of how similarity leads to liking.

The influence of similarity on friendship patterns is pervasive and important—in friendships or marriages or even simple likes and dislikes there is a strong tendency for people to like others who are similar to them. Moreover, society generally assumes this to be true. The current vogue of computer dating is based almost entirely on this idea. In applying for a date, people list their interests and characteristics and the computer matches them with someone of the opposite sex who has similar interests and characteristics. Presumably this would lead to a better date than one chosen at random or one that does not take into account the importance of similarity.

The effect of similarity is seen most clearly with people who share gross cultural and demographic characteristics, attitudes, beliefs, interests, and backgrounds. Frenchmen like Frenchmen and Americans like Americans; elderly people tend to like other elderly people and young people like other young people. Such characteristics as national background, religion, politics, social class, educational level, age, sophistication, and skin color influence friendship patterns. Also influential are one's profession, intelligence level, talent in a given field, and probably

Drawing by Saxon; © 1970 The New Yorker Magazine, Inc.

*"There's really not much to tell. I just grew up and married the girl next door."*

even height, weight, physical agility, and strength. In fact, on practically every dimension except perhaps personality characteristics (which we shall discuss at greater length below), people who are similar tend to like each other more.

Theodore Newcomb conducted an extensive study of friendship (1961) by taking over a large house at the University of Michigan and running it on an experimental basis. Students lived there just as they would have in any other dormitory except that they agreed to take part in the study and were questioned at periodic intervals. Newcomb had control over room assignments, and on the basis of information from tests and questionnaires, he assigned some boys who were similar to each other to be roommates and others who were dissimilar to be roommates. He then intervened very little in their affairs. Under these circumstances, the effect of similarity proved to be powerful. Those roommates who were selected as being similar generally liked each other and ended up as friends; those who were chosen to be dissimilar tended to dislike each other and not to be friends. Thus, this study gave evidence that the computer dating services are correct in assuming that putting similar people together usually leads to a more successful, friendlier relationship than putting dissimilar people together.

The same effect has been observed in even more closely controlled situations. In laboratory experiments (Byrne, 1961; Byrne and Nelson, 1964), subjects were given a description of another person and asked how much they thought they would like him. The descriptions included his attitudes, opinions, and almost any other characteristics. The important variation was that some descriptions made the other person seem very similar to the subject (with the same characteristics), whereas others made him seem very different. The results indicate that the similarity of the description determined how much the subjects thought they would like the other person. The more similar he was described, the more they liked him.

A series of studies (Byrne and Wong, 1962; Rokeach and Mezei, 1966; Stein et al., 1965) has compared the relative importance of racial and attitudinal similarity. In most of this work, subjects were given a description of another person who was either similar to them in attitudes and dissimilar racially or the reverse. Each subject was then asked how much he thought he would like the other person. The typical, although not unanimous, finding was that similarity of attitudes was more important in determining liking than was belonging to the same racial group. These findings have been interpreted as showing that racial differences are relatively unimportant when compared to differences in attitude.

It would be nice to believe that this is true when real contacts are involved, for it would indicate that getting to know someone of another race and discovering that his attitudes are similar to one's own would make one like him regardless of the racial difference. The logical projection would be that a simple program of educating people about other races would reduce racial conflicts. However, the findings held only for relatively nonintimate relationships such as working together. Race was considerably more important when closer relationships, such as dating or marriage, were concerned. In addition, we think it is a mistake to put too much weight on these particular studies. The subjects were given written descriptions and asked to make a decision about the other person. Under these circumstances, there were strong pressures against weighting race very high and toward being rational and objective. In actual situations, there is much less pressure toward the rational, objective approach—biases and prejudices become more important than in the experimental situation. Nevertheless, these sudies do hold out some hope that under appropriate circumstances people will weight attitude similarity more heavily than racial similarity and that, in the long run, prejudice can be reduced by learning about members of other races.

The work on similarity demonstrates that it is one of the most important factors affecting liking. In fact, if two people who do not know each other should meet, probably the single most important factor determining whether or not they will like each other is how similar they are.

### Common Behavior and Taste

The simplest explanation of the effect of similarity on liking is that the kinds of characteristics we have described are important in determining how people think and act, and people who think and act similarly find it easier to get along. If, on a date, one wishes to go horseback riding and the other wants to go dancing, the evening probably will not be very pleasant. Or, if one values and has good table manners and the other is messy, neither would enjoy having dinner together. Or if one goes to church every Sunday and the other would prefer to go for a drive, the chance that the two people would have an argument and would dislike each other is greatly increased. Of course, people can be dissimilar on many dimensions and still get along, but each dimension on which they are alike increases their compatibility. The more alike they are, the more probable it would be that they enjoy the same things and each other's company. In other words, similarity increases the possibility that two people will reward and reinforce each other directly and will share rewarding experiences. Similar values and behavior also enable them to avoid conflict and reduce the possibility that they will upset or annoy each other. Thus, similar people reinforce each other, share pleasant ex-

Drawing by Gallagher; courtesy
Cartoon Features Syndicate.

*"You're the kind of man we need around here!"*

periences, and avoid conflicts and unpleasantness, which means that people who are similar tend to like each other.

A closely related but generally less important consideration is that someone who is similar to us will usually be more acceptable to our other friends and our family. There is a tendency for other people we value to find fault with a person who is dissimilar to us, to find it hard to get along with him, and so on. In contrast, the people we value would probably find it easy to get along with one who is similar to us and would accept him more readily. These tendencies accentuate our own feelings and strengthen the process described above.

### The Balance Model

Partly as an attempt to explain the relationship between similarity and liking, Fritz Heider, Theodore Newcomb, and others have proposed a theory of cognitive balance or, as it is commonly referred to, the balance model. The basic assumption behind this model (and other similar models which are discussed in Chapter 8) is that people tend to prefer consistency. They want things to fit together and to be logical and harmonious, and this holds for their own beliefs, cognitions, thoughts, and feelings. In particular, people want their feelings about other people and objects to be consistent.

The simplest situation to illustrate consistency in this context is one person's feelings about another person and both their feelings about an object. For example, consider a student's attitude toward a teacher and both their feelings about a radical student group such as the SDS. If we limit ourselves to simple positive-negative feelings, there are a limited number of combinations of these elements. They are diagrammed in Figure 3–6, with the initials S, T, and R standing for the student, teacher, and radical group, respectively. The arrows indicate the direction of the feel-

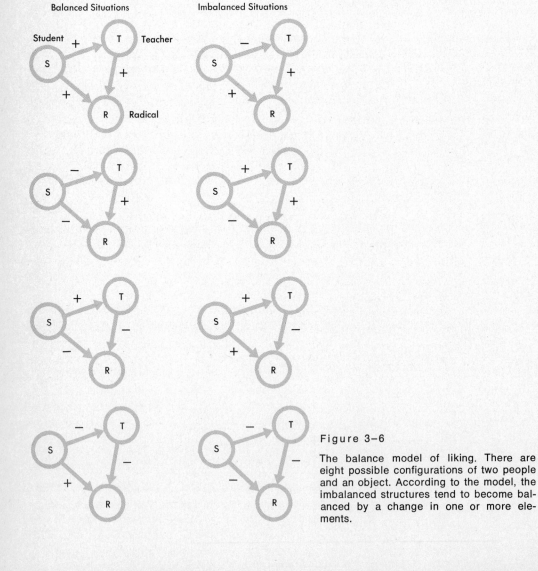

Figure 3–6

The balance model of liking. There are eight possible configurations of two people and an object. According to the model, the imbalanced structures tend to become balanced by a change in one or more elements.

ings, a plus sign means a positive emotion, and a minus sign means a negative one. Thus, the first diagram shows that the student likes the teacher and they both like the radical group.

Shown on the left side of the diagram are four possible balanced situations—situations in which the relations among the elements are consistent with each other, that is, in which the elements are in harmony. When the student likes the teacher and they both like the radical group, the structure is balanced. It is certainly consistent when two people who like each other like the same things—their relationship is harmonious because they both agree with what the group is doing. If the student likes the teacher and they both dislike the radical group, balance (harmony) also exists—neither likes what the group is doing and neither would join it. Finally, if the student dislikes the teacher and likes the radical group while the teacher dislikes it, or if the student dislikes the teacher and dislikes the radical group while the teacher likes it, balance exists. In either case, they disagree about the radical group, but the student dislikes and would not want to have much to do with the teacher anyway, so there is no conflict. For convenience, notice that each of the four balanced structures contains an even number of minus signs (negative relations). Whenever there is one negative relation, another is necessary to balance it.

The unbalanced structures have an odd number of negative relations. They occur when the student and the teacher like each other but disagree about the radical group or dislike each other and agree about the radical group. The imbalance of these situations may be less obvious; the inconsistency lies in the fact that we expect those we like to have similar likes and dislikes to ours and those we dislike to have different likes and dislikes from ours.

The second assumption of the balance model is that imbalanced configurations tend to shift toward balanced ones—it is this assumption that gives the model its importance. Unstable systems produce pressures toward change and continue this pressure until they are balanced; that is, the structures on the right side of the diagram will shift toward those on the left.

The change from imbalance to balance can occur in many ways. Any of the relations may be altered to produce balance. For example, the situation in which the student likes the radical group and dislikes the teacher, who also likes the radical group, could be balanced by any one of the following changes. The student could decide that he really does like the teacher or that he actually dislikes the radical group, or he could convince himself that the teacher actually dislikes the radical group. Which change occurs depends on the degree of difficulty of each one and

Drawing by Charles Barsotti: © 1968.

*"Oh dear! I knew we should have invited another tall
person for Mr. Harrelson."*

probably also on the desirability of the final structure from other points of view. We shall discuss this in more detail in Chapter 8. For the moment, the important point is that the various possibilities do exist and that one of them is for the student to change his evaluation of the teacher.

Moreover, the student could produce the changes in a variety of ways. He could seek out information or experiences that would convince him, for example, that he really likes the teacher—he might get very involved in the teacher's course, invite him to a party, and make every effort to have a good relationship with him so that he will seem nicer than the student had thought. Alternatively, he might distort reality by believing that the teacher is antagonistic to radical groups. Or he might simply change his opinion of the teacher under pressure from the imbalanced system. Which mechanism is chosen depends on the ease of using it and on the individual doing the changing. (Again, we shall discuss this in more detail in Chapter 8.)

One implication of the tendency to seek balance is that people like others who are similar to them. The student who likes the radical group but dislikes the teacher who also likes the radical group is faced with a conflict that might cause him to change his opinion and end up liking him. Similarly, if the student likes radical groups and the teacher dislikes them, the student will tend to dislike the teacher. Thus, if we meet someone about whom we know nothing except that he shares our love of skiing, or radical groups, or anything else, we will tend to like him.

This discussion is, of course, greatly simplified. We have considered a simple system with only two people and one object and have ignored the multitude of other objects that are involved in any such structure, as well as the feelings of the teacher toward the student. But the basic principles work in more complex and realistic systems also. Instead of only radical groups, we could include hundreds of things ranging from books to music, religion, politics, drugs, and law. Each item on which the student and teacher agree tends to make them like each other more; each item on which they disagree has the opposite effect. They may both like music, drugs, and law and dislike religion and books; but one may like the Democrats and the other the Republicans. Thus, they agree on five and disagree on one. Assuming for the moment that the topics are equally important and ignoring the possibility that their strength of liking and disliking for them may differ, this structure of items should tend to make them like each other. If their agreement were split four-two, the effect would be weaker; if they agreed on only one and disagreed on five, they would dislike each other. The more items they agree on, the more they should like each other.

This is a cognitive explanation of what is basically an affective rather than a cognitive phenomenon. In essence, the balance model states that similar people like each other because liking makes their cognitive systems more balanced. It could be said that the model simply restates, in other terms, the idea described above that people with similar attitudes have less conflict. However, the balance model does take a somewhat different position. The model states that an individual's simply knowing that someone disagrees with him on something is in itself unpleasant and that therefore he avoids this kind of relationship.

A final point in our analysis of the balance model is that the effect of similarity on liking is further strengthened by the fact that we tend to exaggerate the similarity between ourselves and someone similar to us and the dissimilarity between ourselves and someone different from us. (Chapter 2 discusses perception of other people in greater detail.) Moreover, if we like someone we tend to exaggerate how similar he is to us, and if we dislike someone we tend to exaggerate how different he is from us. Thus, two tendencies work in the same direction—we tend to like someone similar to us and we tend to perceive someone we like as being more similar to us than he is. In addition, we tend to exaggerate the similarity that does exist, which makes us like the person more. In other words, when someone is similar to us, we exaggerate this similarity, it makes us like him, which makes us think he is more similar than he really is, which makes us like him more, which makes us see him as more similar, and so on. In contrast, those who are dissimilar and whom we dislike are seen as even more dissimilar and are disliked even more. The result is that those we like are seen eventually as extremely similar to us and those we dislike as extremely dissimilar. So, the already strong effect of similarity on liking or disliking is greatly enhanced.

The balance model also predicts that liking is affected by how we treat other people. We have seen that we tend to like someone who does nice things to us, who treats us well; and we have explained this primarily in terms of a simple reinforcement principle. It is also true that when we tend to like someone else or when we do something nice for someone else, we tend to like him more because of it. If we say something nice about another person, we like him more than if we say something unpleasant about him (even when we do not know him). Similarly, if we hurt another person or do something unpleasant to him, such as reporting that he was cheating on a test, we tend to like him less. This seems to hold even when, instead of hurting the other person ourselves, we simply watch him being hurt. These tendencies do not fit into a reinforcement paradigm but do fit quite nicely into a balance model. If we do something nice to someone, it should follow that we like him; if we mistreat him, we should dislike him. We treat our friends well and our enemies badly. Thus, someone we treat well must be our friend, whereas someone we treat badly should be our enemy.

### Social Comparison

The effect of similarity on liking may also be due to the need for social comparison. We saw earlier (in Chapter 1) that when people are unsure whether their feelings are appropriate to a situation, they want to affiliate with others so they can compare them. This kind of social comparison occurs not only for emotions but for all sorts of characteristics—abilities, interests, opinions, attitudes, physical characteristics, and so on. It seems likely that individuals compare themselves to others on virtually every attribute of importance to them.

Social comparison is not, however, entirely indiscriminate. The theory states explicitly and the research has shown that people prefer to compare themselves to others whom they know are similar to them. Thus, someone similar to us in terms of, say, age, religion, national background, and educational level would be a good person with whom to compare ourselves on other dimensions, such as political opinions. To the extent that he is similar to us, we would like to compare ourselves with him; to the extent that he is different from us, we would not want to compare ourselves with him. And knowing that someone would be a good person with whom to compare ourselves may, by itself, make us like him; since we want to compare ourselves and he satisfies this need, we should tend to like him.

In addition to satisfying the need for comparison, comparing oneself to somebody who is similar should be a rewarding experience because we are assured that what we are feeling or doing or believing is correct. Since we are similar, we agree on most things. This agreement is naturally reassuring and reinforcing and makes us like the person who provides it.

Thus, our analysis of the effect of similarity in terms of social comparison leads to the expectation that we will like others who are similar to us. First, we seek out people who are similar in order to compare ourselves to them, and then, because the similarity makes our comparison reinforcing, we have a strong tendency to like the other people.

**COMPLE-MENTARITY**     We have seen that there are a number of reasons why people like others who are similar to them. Thus far, however, we have omitted discussing one important characteristic—personality. Is it also true that people tend to like others whose personalities are like theirs? This issue has created some controversy in the literature. Many studies of friendship and marriage have indicated that people tend to like and marry those who are similar to them in terms of personality. On the other hand, some studies have shown that there is a tendency for people to seek out those whose personalities complement theirs, that is, those who have qualities opposite rather than similar to theirs. For example, a dominant person may prefer a submissive person to another dominant one. The question of whether similarity or complementarity is the critical factor is quite complicated—the answer seems to be that both are important determinants.

As our discussion has demonstrated, under almost all circumstances similarity is an important consideration in liking and marriage. This applies to personality characteristics as well as to the factors discussed above. Under most circumstances, a quiet, thoughtful, introverted person likes somebody similar to himself more than he does a loud and flighty extrovert. And the same is probably true of most important personality dimensions—aggressive-nonaggressive, stable-unstable, neurotic-nonneurotic, and so on. There is good reason to believe that friends tend to be similar on these types of dimensions.

But what kind of woman does a man who is extremely assertive, aggressive, and domineering marry? It would seem that if he married a woman who was similar to him, there might be an explosion. Fortunately, there is evidence that marriage partners seem to be complementary rather than similar on these kinds of dimensions. A domineering man tends to marry a passive woman; a talkative woman probably marries a quiet man; and, in general, a masculine man tends to marry a feminine woman. In other words, on certain kinds of personality dimensions, opposites do seem to attract.

Although at first glance the effect of complementarity seems to contradict the principle of similarity, the two are sometimes consistent. The domineering male and the dominated female actually are similar in one sense—they share similar attitudes and values as to the role of the man and the woman in marriage. They both agree that the male should be dominant and the female submissive. This is not simply playing with words in order to disguise the contradiction. There is an important similarity in this kind of marriage. If they were both domineering, they might seem to be more similar because they behaved similarly, but their views as to their individual roles would necessarily be different. So if we consider basic values and attitudes the most important aspects of personality, the similarity principle continues to hold in this situation because the man and woman define their respective roles in the same way.

On the other hand, there are times when real complementarity is important in determining liking. When the needs of one person satisfy the needs of another, the two tend to like each other. A dominant and a submissive person have complementary personalities, for the need of one (to dominate) satisfies the need of the other (to be dominated), and vice versa. Thus, they can form a stable relationship and should tend to like each other. The same is true of a sadist and masochist, a person who likes to talk and one who likes to listen, and so on. In these instances, the complementarity should lead to liking. The situation is probably quite different when complementary attitudes do not satisfy each other. A person who likes to talk would probably not be friendly with a person who dislikes discussions; a person who enjoys activity would probably not like a person who enjoys being quiet; a music lover would probably not like a music hater; and so on. In these cases, complementarity does not lead to mutual reinforcement and, therefore, does not lead to liking.

Our original question—of the relative importance of similarity and complementarity to liking—can be resolved as follows. When two people have similar roles, as in most friendships, the dominant determinant of liking is generally similarity. When two people have different roles, as in marriage, some friendships, and professional relationships in which one is superior to the other, complementarity is important. In these cases, people tend to like others whose behavior fits their role; and since their roles are different, their behaviors tend to be complementary rather than similar. However, even with differing roles, the major determinant of liking in most relationships is similarity on dimensions such as cultural characteristics, socioeconomic class, and so on.

We have described a number of important determinants of liking —proximity, rewardingness, similarity, and complementarity. Of course, not all our friends live next door, are identical to us, and constantly say nice things about us. Conceivably we may be very friendly with someone who lives a thousand miles away, is very different from us in many ways, and constantly criticizes us. But the factors we have discussed are important. Although someone who fits all these criteria may not become a friend, the chances are he will; similarly, someone who does not meet them may become a friend, but the chances are he will not.

*CHAPTER REVIEW*

1. Functional proximity as a major determinant of liking.
2. Availability and familiarity as explanatory mechanisms.
3. The "mere" exposure effect.
4. Physical attractiveness, sincerity, and other specific qualities affect liking.
5. People like others who reward them; they like others who like them.
6. Ingratiation and other limits on rewardingness.
7. Similarity, complementarity, and liking.
8. The balance model as an explanation of the effect of similarity.

*APPLICATIONS AND SPECULATIONS*

1. It has been remarked that people who get divorced often remarry someone who is similar to their first spouse. Why do you think this might be true?

2. Even when there is little or no prejudice, it seems that friendships between whites and blacks are relatively rare. Why is this true and what might be done to counter this tendency?

3. Freud has argued that taboos against incest are essential because the attractions within the family are so strong. Why might this be true?

4. Colleges that have dormitories on the campus often must decide between allowing students to choose where they want to live or randomly assigning them to living units. What differential effects might this have on friendship patterns, exposure to different and new ideas, and polarization on the campus?

5. Many people have very strong feelings about their pets. The old saying that dogs are man's best friends is perhaps overstated, but people do become very attached to their dogs. How would you explain this?

*SUGGESTIONS FOR ADDITIONAL READING*

*Articles*

Aronson, E., and Linder, D. Gain and loss of esteem as determinants of interpersonal attractiveness. *Journal of Experimental Social Psychology*, 1965, *1*, 156–71.

Saegert, S., Swap, W., and Zajonc, R. B. Exposure, context, and interpersonal attraction. *Journal of Personality and Social Psychology*, 1973, *25*, 234–42.

Stein, D. D., Hardyck, J. A., and Smith, M. B. Race and belief: an open and shut case. *Journal of Personality and Social Psychology*, 1965, *1*, 281–89.

Zajonc, R. B. Attitudinal effects of mere exposure. *Journal of Personality and Social Psychology*, 1968, *8*, Monograph, 1–29.

*Books and Longer Discussions*

Festinger, L., Schachter, S., and Back, K. *Social pressures in informal groups: a study of human factors in housing.* New York: Harper & Row, 1950. Chapter 3.

Jones, E. E. *Ingratiation.* New York: Appleton-Century-Crofts, 1964.

Pettigrew, T. F. Racially separate or together? *Journal of Social Issues,* 1969, *25,* 43–69.

four

aggression

In the previous chapter, we discussed the factors that cause people to like or dislike others. Clearly, liking is one of the most important aspects of interpersonal relationships. A closely related factor is how well we treat others. In a sense this is the behavioral counterpart of our feelings toward them. Although it is true that treatment of others can range from very negative to very positive, most of the research and interest have centered on aggression.

Although it might seem that everybody understands what aggression is, there is considerable disagreement as to what behavior should be considered aggressive. The simplest definition and the one favored by those with a behaviorist or learning approach is that aggression is any behavior that hurts or could hurt others. The advantage of this definition is that the behavior itself determines whether or not a particular act is aggressive. One merely has to ascertain whether an act was potentially harmful.

Unfortunately, this definition is not satisfactory because it ignores the intention of the perpetrator of the act—and this factor is critical. If one tries to hurt someone, we ordinarily consider him to be aggressive; if he is not trying to cause harm, he is not being aggressive. Thus, the definition of aggression should be any action that is *designed* to hurt others. This conception is more difficult to apply, because it does not depend solely on observable behavior. Often it is difficult to know someone's intention, and thus we cannot judge whether he is being aggressive. But we must accept this limitation, for only by including intent can we define aggression meaningfully.

If we used the behavioral definition, some actions that most people consider aggressive would not be labeled as such, because, for one reason or another, they are actually harmless. Suppose someone fires a gun at someone else, but the gun turns out to be either unloaded or loaded with blanks. The shooter was trying to cause harm, but in fact his act was harmless. It could not have hurt anyone because firing an unloaded gun or one loaded with blanks is not dangerous. Despite the fact that he was enraged and was trying to kill someone, by the behavioral definition, he was not being aggressive.

Ignoring intention also forces us to call some acts aggressive that are not, by the usual meaning of the term. If a golfer's ball accidentally hits a spectator, has the golfer committed an aggressive act? He has certainly done something that could cause harm. A golf ball travelling over 100 miles an hour is a dangerous object. In addition, he has in fact caused somebody a great deal of pain. Thus, the act fits one of the popular definitions of aggression: a response that delivers noxious stimuli to another organism. But surely no one would believe that the golfer was being aggressive. He was playing a game that, of all popular games, involves perhaps the least aggression.

Another category of pain-causing acts that should not be considered aggressive are those in which the ultimate goal is to help another person. Consider a dentist who gives his patient an injection of Novocain. Although an injection is painful, most patients are grateful for it because it prevents them from feeling the pain caused by drilling. Therefore, they would not consider the dentist to be acting aggressively when he provides them with the pain-killer. Moreover, if the Novocain did not work for some reason, they would still not consider its administration an aggressive act, because the dentist was trying to ease their pain even though he was unsuccessful. We can see that ignoring intent forces us to call acts aggressive that, by common sense and any reasonable criteria, are not. We must therefore define aggression as behavior that is designed to hurt others.

Our basic goal is to explain why people are aggressive, and as usual we shall answer the question in terms of the factors that increase or decrease the effect. However, our discussion of aggression is somewhat more complicated than that of other subjects, such as affiliation, because it must consider two distinct phenomena, namely, aggressive feelings and aggressive behavior. Generally when one feels like affiliating with others, he does so if others are available and they do not reject his company. The desire to affiliate usually leads to affiliation. But with aggression, as with certain other behaviors (e.g., sex), internal feelings are not always expressed openly. Whereas society welcomes and encourages affiliation, it discourages and condemns most forms of aggression. Society can exist only if people control their aggressive feelings most of the time. We cannot have people hitting other people, breaking windows, or acting violently whenever they feel like it. Society places strong restraints on such expression and most people, even those who feel angry much of the time, rarely act aggressively. Therefore, specifying the factors that increase aggressive feelings does not completely answer the question of what produces aggressive behavior. It provides part of the answer because people rarely act aggressively if they do not feel that way, but it does not tell us when people will or will not turn their aggressive feelings into action. We thus have two questions—what produces aggressive feelings and what produces aggressive behavior.

**AROUSAL OF AGGRESSIVE IMPULSES**

An aggressive impulse or feeling is an internal state that cannot be observed directly. We all experience anger, and virtually everyone at one time or another would like to hurt someone else. But these feelings are not necessarily expressed openly, and therefore aggressive impulses must be studied largely by asking individuals how they are feeling or by inferring the existence of their internal state from physiological measures or behavior, neither of which is a reliable indicator. Nevertheless, there has been a considerable amount of research on the factors that arouse aggressive feelings. In discussing the question we shall consider three major factors—instinct, frustration, and annoyance or attack.

### Instinct

It has been proposed, by Freud, McDougall, Lorenz, and others, that men have an innate drive or instinct to fight. Just as they feel hungry, thirsty, or sexually aroused, so they feel aggressive. Although there are no known physiological mechanisms connected with aggressive feelings, as there are for the other drives, aggression is considered a basic drive that all men feel.

Freud argued that there were only two basic drives in man—the *libido,* which is constructive, sexual energy, and *thanatos,* which is destructive, aggressive energy. He suggested that all men have within them strong self-destructive impulses—death wishes, he called them—which sometimes are turned inward and sometimes outward. When these impulses are turned inward, they cause men to restrict their energies, to punish themselves, to become masochistic, and, in the extreme case, to commit suicide. When the impulses are turned outward, they are manifested in aggressive, warlike behavior.

As with other explanations in terms of instinct, the instinctual theory of aggression is difficult to evaluate. The ideal test would be to raise someone in complete isolation, being careful to eliminate all external stimuli that might arouse aggressive feelings. Then, if the individual acted aggressively when first given the chance, the indication would be that aggression is, at least in part, instinctive. Since we cannot conduct this type of experiment, we rely heavily on investigations of aggressiveness among nonhumans.

Animals certainly do a great deal of fighting. They fight for food, to protect their territory, to defend their young, and so on. But one of the difficulties in evaluating this evidence is that our definition of aggressiveness may not be appropriate to much of this behavior. A lion that chases and kills a zebra obviously intends to harm the zebra. On the other hand, as far as we know, the killing is not done in response to anger or with intent to cause suffering. The lion must hunt for food and the zebra happens to be its natural prey. Even if we do consider this aggression, it does not indicate the presence of an instinctive aggressive drive. The lion is hungry and kills in order to get food with which to satisfy the hunger. The instinctive drive is hunger, not aggression.

The same argument holds for fighting among members of the same species. They fight for mates, for territory, and for dominance. The first type of fight is motivated by sexual drives; the second, by the need for sufficient food supply. Battles for dominance are more complicated. Sex and hunger may be involved, because the dominant male usually has his choice of mates and the most desirable bits of food. Also, demonstrating dominance avoids unnecessary fights in the future, because the less dominant animals always give way before the more dominant. They fight only once to establish their positions and from then on coexist peacefully. Establishing dominance also facilitates the protection of the group, because it determines which animals will play what roles in defense. Thus, fighting for dominance serves many purposes and cannot be interpreted as evidence of instinctive aggressive impulses.

However, the instinct notion does make one prediction that most other formulations would not—that aggressive impulses build up within the animals regardless of the external environment. If these impulses are not expressed, they continue to build up and the animals feel increasingly aggressive. According to the theory, a tropical fish swimming alone in an aquarium should feel gradually more aggressive, even if all its basic needs are satisfied. After, say, a week, the fish should be more likely to attack than it would have previously. On the other hand, if aggression is aroused only by external factors, the fish should not be especially aggressive, because it has spent a week swimming in a comfortable pool.

Although this ideal experiment has never been performed, Konrad Lorenz (1963) observed tropical fish under a variety of circumstances similar to those just described. He reported that certain male fish normally attack other males of the same species but ignore other fish. If, however, all the males of the same species except one are removed from the aquarium, the one remaining attacks fish of other species he had previously left alone. And if all fish are removed except a female of his own species, he will eventually attack and kill her. Lorenz interpreted this behavior as showing that fish have instinctive needs to be aggressive and that when the ordinary targets are removed, these needs cause them to attack whatever target is available.

Lorenz bases much of his argument for an aggressive instinct on the response to crowding. He claims that animals who are put in small spaces with many other animals of the same species will inevitably become aggressive. This response to a lack of space, often called territoriality, seems to suggest an instinctive aggressive response to a common life situation. However, as we discuss in detail in Chapter 13, the evidence for territoriality and for this aggressive response to crowding is questionable. There is some suggestion that this phenomenon occurs among some species, but it is almost certain that it does not occur among humans. People do not consistently respond aggressively to a lack of space. Thus responses to crowding should not be considered evidence for an aggressive instinct in humans.

The work by ethologists such as Lorenz and Tinbergen is fascinating. It indicates that many species respond instinctively to specific cues and have many instinctive drives. It does not, however, provide evidence concerning humans. The research relevant to humans has generally been done under less than ideal conditions and definitive experiments have not yet been performed. Although some ethologists continue to be convinced that all animals have instinctive aggressive drives, most psychologists would now dispute this. Among animals relatively low on the phylogenetic scale, instinct plays an important role in producing aggression, but as one ascends the ladder, instinct probably becomes less and less important. In particular, there seems little reason to believe that humans have any instinctive impulses toward aggressiveness.

### Frustration

Frustration is the interference with or blocking of the attainment of a goal. If one wants to go somewhere, perform some act, or obtain something and is prevented, we say he is frustrated. One of the basic tenets in psychology is that frustration tends to arouse aggressive feelings.

In a study by Funkenstein et al. (1954), subjects were given a difficult digit-span test and their efforts were repeatedly criticized by the experimenter, who made sarcastic comments and generally annoyed the subjects while they were trying to perform. In a second task, subjects were required to speak as rapidly as possible but were given acoustical feedback that confused their speech, caused them to stutter, and made rapid speech almost impossible. Moreover, electric shocks were administered whenever the subjects spoke slowly. These frustrating procedures produced a variety of physiological reactions, including a marked increase in systolic and diastolic blood pressure. In addition, whereas the subjects were quite calm and relaxed beforehand, afterward they were highly aroused and reported feeling angry and aggressive.

The behavioral effects of frustration were demonstrated in a classic study by Barker, Dembo, and Lewin (1941). Children were shown a room full of attractive toys but were not allowed to enter it. They stood outside looking at the toys, wanting to play with them, but unable to reach them. After they had waited for some time, they were allowed to play with them. Other children were given the toys without first being prevented from playing with them. The children who had been frustrated smashed the toys on the floor, threw them against the wall, and generally behaved very destructively. The children who had not been frustrated were much quieter and less destructive.

Holmes (1972) produced frustration by causing the subjects to sit around waiting because one subject (actually a confederate) arrived late for the experiment. No explanation for his tardiness was given. In another condition, all of the subjects arrived on time. The participants were subsequently given an opportunity to behave aggressively toward the latecomer or toward an innocent member of the group. Holmes found that subjects who had been frustrated by having to wait were more aggressive toward both the latecomer and the innocent bystander.

This effect of frustration may be seen in broader perspective in society at large. Economic depressions produce frustration that affects almost everyone. People cannot get jobs or buy things they need and are greatly restricted in all phases of their lives. The consequence is that all forms of aggression become more common. Evidence of this was presented by Hovland and Sears (1940) and confirmed by Mintz (1946). They found a strong relationship between the price of cotton and the number of lynchings in the South during the years 1882 to 1930. When cotton prices were high, there were few lynchings; when prices were low, the number of lynchings was relatively high. A drop in the price of cotton signified a depressed period economically, and this depression produced frustration, which, in turn, led to more aggression. An extreme manifestation of the increased aggression was the increase in lynchings.

These examples illustrate the typical effect of frustration, but the original statement of the relationship between frustration and aggression was in more absolute terms. Dollard, Doob, and others at Yale were the social psychologists who began the work on this problem. They asserted, "This study takes as its point of departure the assumption that aggression is always a consequence of frustration. More specifically, the proposition is that the occurrence of aggressive behavior always presupposes the existence of frustration and, contrariwise, the existence of frustration always leads to some form of aggression" [Dollard et al., 1939, p. 1]. It appears now that neither *always* in these assumptions is correct. Although frustration usually arouses aggression, there are circumstances when it does not, and, as we shall discuss below, factors other than frustration can also produce aggression.

Whether or not frustration arouses aggressive feelings depends in part on how arbitrary is the frustration. The more arbitrary the frustration, the more aggression is aroused. A hitchhiker on a cold, windy night feels frustrated when a car whizzes past him, but he feels different if the car is a large sedan with only one occupant than if it is an ambulance rushing to a hospital. Although he is frustrated in both cases, he is angrier and more aggressive if it is the car that passes him than if it is the ambulance. A teacher who prevents her class from taking a trip to the zoo is frustrating their wishes. If she explains that the trip is a bad idea because rain is expected and because many of the animals are ill and will not be on view, less aggression will be aroused than if she offers no explanation or a poor one. A good reason for frustration minimizes aggressive feelings.

Thus, an individual's understanding of a situation influences his reaction to frustrations. This tendency for cognitive factors to affect the arousal of emotions is similar to phenomena we discussed in relation to affiliation and liking—how the environment determines the emotion a person feels when he is physiologically aroused, and how the individual's perception of another's motives is a major factor in how much he likes someone who compliments him. In both these cases and in the present case involving frustration and aggression, one's cognitive interpretation of the situation has a major effect on his motives and emotions. The interaction between cognitive and emotional factors occurs continually and is an important thread running through much of social psychology.

### Annoyance and Attack

When we are bothered or assaulted by someone, we tend to feel aggressive toward him. Imagine the reaction of a driver who is waiting for a traffic light to change from red to green when, before it does, the driver of the car behind him starts blowing his horn. Or that of someone peacefully reading the newspaper when somebody pours a glass of water down his neck. Or, finally, imagine a student's reaction when he expresses an opinion in a class and someone else disagrees with him and says he is stupid to hold such an opinion. In all these cases, someone has done something unpleasant to someone else. Depending on how the injured person takes it, he has been annoyed or attacked. He has not, in any normal sense of the word, been frustrated. It is extremely likely that he would become angry and feel aggressive toward the source of the attack. Although no goal has been blocked, except perhaps that of living peacefully, aggression has been aroused.

**AGGRESSIVE BEHAVIOR**   Frustration, annoyance, and attack all tend to make people feel aggressive, and these aggressive feelings constitute one important element producing aggressive behavior. Ordinarily, the more aggressive a person feels, the more likely it is that he will act aggressively. But people often feel aggressive and behave peacefully or, at least, are not overtly aggressive; and it is also possible for people to be aggressive without feeling aggressive. Thus, the factors that conrol the expression of aggression are as important as those that arouse it in the first place.

### Instinctive Responses

Many animals respond aggressively to certain stimuli whenever they appear. These responses appear to be instinctive. If two male Siamese fighting fish are put in the same tank, they immediately attack each other and fight until one is badly mauled or dead. The presence of another male is sufficient to produce this aggressive behavior in each one. Konrad Lorenz described an aggressive response by jackdaws—black birds closely related to the crow and starling—that was triggered by a different kind of stimulus. Lorenz described jackdaws as intelligent, reasonably peaceful, and somewhat playful. He kept a number of them for some time, and they learned to recognize him after a while and usually reacted calmly to his presence. But one day when he entered the room carrying a black rag in his hand, the birds flew at him, pecked at his hand, fluttered about his head, and in general did what they could to attack him—an animal much larger than themselves. After experimenting for a while, Lorenz discovered that the rag was the stimulus. The birds attacked anything that was holding a small, black object. This could be interpreted as an attack on an animal who was stealing a young jackdaw and, therefore, as a useful defensive maneuver. For our purposes the important point is that it was triggered seemingly automatically by the black object and was obviously not learned. There are countless other examples of similar reactions. Many animals have instinctive aggressive responses to particular stimuli—the presence of these stimuli immediately sets off a specific aggressive reaction. When the stimuli are removed, the aggressive behavior ceases.

There is, however, little evidence that humans have this kind of instinctive response to external cues. Leonard Berkowitz of the University of Wisconsin produced evidence that under some circumstances the presence of certain stimuli would cause people to be more aggressive than they would if these stimuli were not present. In one study (Berkowitz and LePage, 1967) some subjects were made angry by being shocked by a confederate and some were not angry. They were then all given the opportunity to deliver shocks to the confederate. When the subjects sat down at a table to deliver the shocks, they noticed a gun or a badminton racket lying near by. The measure of aggression was how many shocks the subjects delivered, and the experiments found that angered subjects gave more shocks when the gun rather than the badminton racket was present.

Although this is a fascinating effect, later research has not confirmed it. Page and Sheit (1971) found that the effect occurred only when subjects were aware of what the experimenters were trying to demonstrate and were also cooperative. More impressively Buss, Booker, and Buss (1972) repeated the study almost exactly and did not get more aggression when the gun was present. In four different experiments they tested the effect of having subjects fire a weapon before delivering shocks. They argued that if the presence of a gun should increase aggression, surely actually firing a gun would have an even greater effect. Yet they found that subjects who fired a gun were no more aggressive subsequently than subjects who had not fired a weapon.

It is always difficult to come to a definite conclusion when there is conflicting evidence of this sort. One study apparently did get a clear effect of cues in arousing aggression, but most of the other work has not been able to produce this result. It seems likely that under most circumstances humans do not respond to the mere presence of an aggression-arousing cue. Simply having a gun or a boxing glove or a knife present does not ordinarily increase the amount of aggression that is expressed. These objects are not "triggers" of aggression the way some stimuli are for other animals. On the other hand, appropriate cues can probably increase aggressiveness when they alter the subject's perception of the situation. If they cause the subject to feel that aggressiveness is more appropriate or more expected, this would certainly increase aggression. Also if the cue causes the subject to feel that the other person is a more aggressive person or more deserving of being aggressed against, that too would tend to increase aggression. For example, in the Berkowitz and LePage study the subjects were told that the gun belonged to the confederate who was using it in another experiment. This may have suggested to the subject that the confederate was a violent person, lowered his estimation of the confederate, and therefore caused him to be more aggressive. In contrast, Buss et al. (1972) described the gun as belonging to the confederate who was lending it to a friend, not using it himself. This apparently was a crucial difference, probably because it did not make the confederate seem as violent a person. Thus, we would conclude that humans tend to be relatively unaffected by the presence of aggression-arousing cues except in those circumstances in which the cues produced a marked change in the perception of the situation.

### Learning

Although man's aggressiveness is only minimally controlled by instinctive responses, it is greatly influenced by what he learns. A newborn infant expresses his aggressive feelings in an entirely uncontrolled manner. Whenever he is the least bit frustrated, whenever he is denied anything he wants, he cries in outrage, flails his arms, and strikes out at anything within range. In the earliest days of life, an infant does not realize that other people exist and therefore cannot be deliberately trying to harm them. When he does discover the existence of others, he continues to vent his rage and probably directs much of it toward these people. But by the time he is an adult, this savage, uncontrolled animal has his aggressive impulses under firm control and aggresses only under certain circumstances, if at all. This development is primarily due to learning. Anything that teaches a child that aggression is acceptable will increase his overall level of aggressiveness; anything that teaches him that aggression is wrong will have the opposite effect. However, most learning related to aggression is more specific than this. Individuals learn to aggress in one situation and not in another, against one person and not against another, and in response to one kind of frustration and not to another.

A few people take the position that aggression is never justified. Most people agree, however, that there are times when it is not only acceptable but even essential. When a person is attacked, we expect him to defend himself even if this means hurting the attacker. In certain situations, such as football or formal debates, individuals are expected to attack their opponents. Also, aggression that does not involve physical violence, such as literary criticism or political campaigning, is much more acceptable than an attack that might cause bodily harm. Although these distinctions are sometimes quite subtle, individuals must learn them in order to function effectively in society. Those who never control their aggression will not be allowed to remain free; those who never use aggression are probably worse off than those who use it at appropriate times. Therefore, the critical problem in socialization is not how to teach a child never to aggress but how to teach him when aggression is appropriate and when it is inappropriate.

The first mechanism by which this learning occurs is reinforcement. When a particular behavior is rewarded, an individual is more likely to repeat that behavior in the future; when it is punished, he is less likely to repeat it. Just as a child learns not to track mud onto a rug, so he learns not to express aggression. He is punished when he punches his

Drawing by Charles Schulz; © 1965 United Feature Syndicate, Inc.

brother, throws stones at the girl next door, or bites his mother, and he learns not to do these things. He is rewarded when he restrains himself despite frustrations, and he learns this also.

Imitation is another mechanism that plays an important role in shaping a child's behavior. All people, and children in particular, have a strong tendency to imitate others. A child watches people eat with a fork or listens to them talking and tries to do the same. After a while, he also uses a fork and talks. This imitation extends to virually every kind of behavior, including aggression. A child observes other people being aggressive and controlling their aggression, and he copies them. He learns to aggress verbally—to shout at people, to curse, and to criticize—and not to resort to violence—not to punch people or throw stones or blow up buildings. He also learns when, if ever, each of these behaviors is permissible. At certain times he should not aggress even verbally (e.g., when he disagrees with his parents), but at others, any kind of aggression is not only allowable but even necessary (e.g., when he is being attacked). Thus his own aggressive behavior is shaped and determined by what he observes others doing.

An experiment by Albert Bandura (Bandura, Ross, and Ross, 1961) illustrated the effect of witnessing aggression. Children watched an adult play with tinker toys and a Bobo doll (a 5-foot, inflated plastic doll). In one condition, the adult began by assembling the tinker toys for about a minute and then turned his attention to the doll. He approached the doll, punched it, sat on it, hit it with a mallet, tossed it in the air, and kicked it about the room, all the while shouting such things as "Sock him in the nose," "Hit him down," "Pow." He continued in this way for nine minutes, with the child watching. In the other condition, the adult worked quietly with the tinker toys and ignored the doll.

Some time later, each child was left alone for twenty minutes with a number of toys, including a 3-foot Bobo doll. The children's behavior was rated as shown in Table 4–1. They tended to imitate many of the actions of the adult. Those who had seen the adult act aggressively were much more aggressive toward the doll than those who had witnessed the adult working quietly on the tinker toys. The first group punched, kicked, and hammered the doll and uttered aggressive comments similar to those expressed by the aggressive adult.

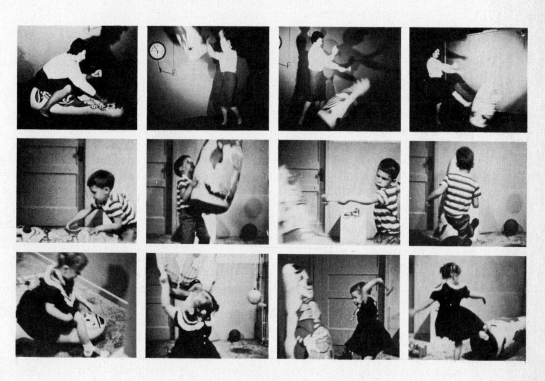

The children who witnessed an adult model kick and punch a Bobo doll imitate her behavior closely. Children who witnessed a less aggressive model are themselves less aggressive.

Table 4–1

*AGGRESSION BY CHILDREN WITNESSING VIOLENT OR NEUTRAL MODEL*

| Condition | AMOUNT OF AGGRESSION | |
| --- | --- | --- |
| | *Physical* | *Verbal* |
| Violent model | 12.73 | 8.18 |
| Neutral model | 1.05 | 0.35 |

Source: Based on Bandura, Ross, and Ross (1961).

The children in this situation learned to attack a certain type of doll. It is highly likely that they would attack the same kind of doll in a different situation. They would also probably attack a different kind of doll. Just how far this would extend—whether or not they would also punch their sisters—is not clear; but it is clear that they would be somewhat more likely to attack some things than they were before. Through the process of imitation, these children became more aggressive.

Two studies (Baron and Kepner, 1970; Baron, 1971) demonstrate that modeling can not only increase but also decrease the amount of aggression. In both studies some subjects observed a model who gave a great many shocks to a confederate while other subjects observed a model who gave very few shocks. There was also a condition in which there was no model. Subjects who observed the aggressive model gave more shocks and those who observed the unaggressive model gave fewer shocks than when there was no model present.

Children do not imitate indiscriminately—they imitate some people more than others. The more important, powerful, successful, and liked the other people are, the more a child will imitate them. Also, the people he sees most often are the ones he imitates most. Parents, who fit all these criteria, are the primary models for a child during his early years.

Since parents are both the major source of reinforcement and the chief object of imitation, a child's future aggressive behavior depends greatly on how his parents treat him and on how they themselves behave. This joint dependence on the parents for reinforcement and imitation produces an interesting consequence. Punishing a child for acting aggressively might be considered an effective method of teaching him not to be aggressive, but it often produces the opposite effect. Punishment should make the aggressive behavior less likely in the future. The child learns that he will be punished if he hits his sister, so he avoids the punishment by not hitting her. More generally, he will not be aggressive whenever he expects to suffer for it. He will not ordinarily start a fight with someone who is certain to beat him; he will not start a fight, even

114

if he can win it, if he expects to be severely punished for it afterward. Parents are aware of this simple relationship and employ it to stop children from fighting. In order to teach their children not to be aggressive, they punish them for fighting and other forms of aggression.

As far as the parents are concerned, this tends to have the desired effect. A child who is punished for fighting does tend to be less aggressive—at home. Home is where the risk of punishment is greatest and therefore where the threat of punishment has the strongest inhibiting effect on his aggression. Unfortunately, the situation is quite different when this child is out of the home. A child who is punished severely for being aggressive at home tends to be more aggressive outside the home than does a child who is punished less severely (Sears, Whiting, Nowlis, and Sears, 1953). The punishment inhibits aggression in the home but seems to encourage it outside the home.

The explanation for this effect is that the child imitates his parents' aggressive behavior. When he is in a situation in which he has the upper hand, he acts the way his parents do toward him. They are aggressive and so is he. Thus, the punishment teaches him not to be aggressive at

Drawing by Stanley Stamaty;
© 1951 The Saturday Review Associates, Inc.

*"This will teach you not to hit people."*

*"Oh, for heaven's sake, pat him! **He** doesn't know it's
Lindsay you're mad at, and not him."*

home, but it also teaches him that aggression is acceptable if he can get away with it. Regardless of what parents hope, children will continue to do what their parents do as well as what they say.

### Displacement of Aggression

This brings us to a discussion of what happens to aggressive feelings when, for one reason or another, they cannot be expressed against the cause of the feelings. People are often frustrated or annoyed by someone but unable to retaliate against that person—he may be too powerful or just not available. In such a situation, they can satisfy themselves in several other ways, one of which is called displacement, that is, expressing aggression against a substitute for the original source.

For example, in the experiment by Holmes (1972) which we discussed earlier, some of the frustrated subjects were allowed to behave aggressively toward the person who had caused their frustration by appearing late for the experiment. Other subjects, however, were not given this opportunity but instead were allowed to aggress against someone else who had nothing to do with the frustration. It was found that frustration increased aggressiveness toward the innocent person just as it did toward the guilty party.

Displacement of aggression tends to follow certain patterns and has been demonstrated dramatically with nonhumans. A rat was trained to attack another rat when it received an electric shock. When, instead of another rat, a toy rat was placed in the cage, it too was attacked, although not so forcefully. This displacement extended to plastic dolls, other toys, and even rags, but as the object became less similar to a rat, the amount of expressed aggression decreased. However, in all cases, when the frustration was severe enough, the rat attacked the other object.

The same phenomenon occurs with people. When a man forbids his son to go to the movies, the boy feels angry and aggressive. He cannot attack his father because his father is too strong and because there are social inhibitions against it. Also, doing so would probably make it less likely that he would be permitted to go to the movies in the future. So he vents his rage on someone else.

He has available a wide range of people. There is his mother, his older brother, his older sister, his younger brother, and a boy his own age who lives next door. All these people can be placed on a continuum in terms of their similarity to the boy's original source of frustration— his father. Although this similarity depends primarily on the boy's own view of the situation, let us suppose that he ranks them in the order listed, ranging from his mother to the boy next door. The question is, what determines which of these people he will select and how much aggression he will express against them.

The basic principle of displacement is that the more similar a person is to the original source of frustration, the stronger will be the individual's aggressive impulses toward him. Thus, as shown by the solid line in Figure 4–1, the boy's aggressive impulse is strongest toward his father and gets weaker as the person toward whom it is directed becomes less similar to his father.

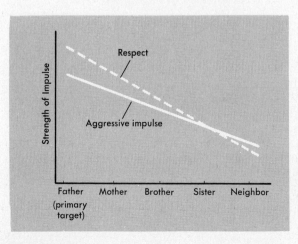

Figure 4–1

Feelings of aggression and respect are strongest toward the primary target. The strength of the aggressive impulse and of the respect decreases as the distance from the primary target increases. Since respect declines faster, at some point the aggressive impulse is stronger. It is then that the child expresses his anger. The height at which the two emotions cross determines the strength of the aggression expressed.

When the only reason for not aggressing against the primary source of frustration is that he is not available, the aggression will be directed toward the next best person. Thus, if the boy cannot express his aggressive feelings toward his father simply because he left town, he would aggress against his mother—the person most similar to his father. Next would come his older brother, then his sister, and so on. The anger he feels toward his father is displaced to these people in the order listed.

The more complicated and probably more common situation is one in which aggression is not expressed because the victim has some reason for restraining himself. If, for example, he feels so much respect for his father that he cannot attack him, his respect operates in much the same way as does his aggressive impulse. Just as his impulse to hurt the source of frustration generalizes to other people, so does his respect for the source. And as with the aggression, the more similar the person is to this source, the stronger is the respect felt for him. This is shown by the dotted line in Figure 4–1. The boy is most respectful of his father, less respectful of his mother, still less of his sister, and not at all respectful of the boy next door.

An important characteristic of the situation is that the respect declines faster than does the aggressive impulse, which means that eventually the two lines must cross. As long as the respect is stronger than the aggressive impulse, the individual will restrain himself; when the tendency to aggress becomes stronger than the respect, the individual will express his aggression. Thus, in our diagram, the boy would not attack his mother or his older brother because his respect for them is stronger than his aggressive impulse. But his sister is just dissimilar enough to his father that there is relatively little respect for her and similar enough that the aggressive impulse is still quite strong. So because the boy is unwilling to hit his father, he makes a nasty comment to his sister.

Note that the relative strengths of the two tendencies (respect and aggression) determine who will be the target of aggression and how much aggression will be expressed. When the aggressive response is almost as strong as the respect, the two gradients will cross quickly, the target of aggression will be very similar to the primary target, and the amount of aggression will be great. When the respect is much stronger than the aggressive feelings, the target will be quite different from the primary object and there will be relatively little aggression expressed.

It should be pointed out that the dimension along which similarity is determined need not be as simple as the one in our example. Much of the aggression in society may be due to displacement along complex and subtle continua. For example, almost all adolescents tend to have feelings of anger against their parents. Parents are the source of power in the family, they are the authority, and they must inevitably frustrate their children's wishes to some extent. Thus they arouse feelings of anger. In some cases, this anger is expressed directly against the parents in adolescent rebellion and breaks with the family. In many cases, however, it is displaced to other people who represent authority. Adolescents need not select those who are related to their parents by family ties or friendship. School administrators, trustees, teachers, the government, and so on fit the criterion and become likely objects for aggression. Thus, it is typical for adolescents and college students to feel angry toward all figures of authority and to express aggression toward them. This may explain some of the student unrest in our country and the fact that in all countries young people tend to be the major source of the criticism directed against the government.

This is not to say that government and school authorities do not also produce frustrations that arouse anger, but it is possible that the strength of feeling is at times due to the fact that it was originally aroused by strong and deep-seated frustrations within the family rather than by frustrations in the specific situations.

The same argument holds, of course, for many other forms of aggression within our society. Prejudice toward and persecution of minorities are due in part to displaced aggression. School administrators who punish students for having long hair or liberal attitudes and regents who punish students, teachers, and even administrators for similar "offenses" are almost certainly expressing more aggression than the situations warrant. Their overreaction is due in part to aggressive feelings that they are displacing to the relatively vulnerable students and teachers. Thus, the tendency to displace aggression is exceedingly important and should be taken into account when one attempts to explain why somebody acts aggressively or violently with apparently insufficient provocation.

### Scapegoating

Displacement occurs when the source of frustration or annoyance cannot be attacked. There are some occasions, however, when there is no visible, identifiable source of frustration. Lightning hits a man's home, he gets a flat tire on the highway, there is a depression and he loses his job. The man feels angry and aggressive, but there is no obvious person at fault. Under these circumstances, there appears to be a tendency to find someone upon whom to vent aggressive feelings. People look for a scapegoat whom they can blame for their difficulties and whom they accordingly can attack.

The choice of a scapegoat is determined by a number of factors. Children learn that it is more acceptable or safer to be aggressive toward some people than toward others. They probably discover early in life that they should not fight someone who is bigger or stronger than they are—whenever they engage in a fight with such a person, it turns out badly. Thus, they learn that ideal scapegoats should be weak and unable to retaliate.

In addition, children learn that there are certain groups in society who are relatively acceptable targets of aggression. These "socially approved" targets depend on which subculture the children are members of. In the white middle-class subculture of Cicero, Illinois, or Little Rock, Arkansas, blacks seem to be favorite objects of aggression. In a similar subculture in San Jose, California, it might be Mexicans or Orientals. Elsewhere, Catholics, Jews, Okies, Poles, or Yankees would be targets of aggression. And in black subcultures, it appears that whites, in general, are now accepted objects of aggression. It is likely that children learn to express more aggression toward whomever their parents and the rest of the subculture choose for this role than against others.

It is difficult to pick someone at random from the general population to attack—after all, he has done nothing to justify it. If, however, a scapegoat has some distinguishing characteristic that sets him off from he rest of the population, the problem is less acute. He is not like everyone else; he is distinctly different. Then when he, or his entire subgroup, is chosen for attack, people do not feel they are blaming the whole world for their ills—they are blaming one specific, distinguishable group.

Another more important reason why scapegoats typically have a distinguishable characteristic is that people are generally suspicious of and somewhat antagonistic toward those who are different from themselves. The mere fact of the difference, regardless of how they are different, seems to produce a negative reaction. Group members treat other members better than they do nonmembers because they feel closer to the other members, know more about them, feel more loyal to them, and so on. But the suspiciousness and aggressiveness that is displayed toward people who are different seems to be more than a reaction to group loyalty. There seems to be a general tendency to mistreat people who are different.

An experiment by Freedman and Doob (1968) exemplified this phenomenon. Six subjects took a long, complex personality test that was described to them as being an extremely good indicator of their personalities. Afterward, each subject was given a sheet of paper on which the test scores of everyone in the group were indicated as well as the distribution of scores of a large sample of subjects similar to themselves. On these sheets, half the subjects were told that their scores were different from those of the rest of the group, and also from most of the people in the larger sample. Scores were given on five scales, and they received deviant scores on all five. The other half of the subjects received scores at or near the middle of the scale. The purpose was to make some subjects feel deviant and others nondeviant. In addition, all the subjects were led to believe that one of the others was extremely deviant. His scores were consistently extreme. Thus, each subject saw the group as consisting of himself, four nondeviants, and one deviant. The scores were indicated by a code letter and the subjects knew only their own letter; they did not know which score belonged to whom.

The experimenter then explained that the second part of the study consisted of a learning test. One of the subjects would serve as a learner while the rest of them would act as judges. The learner would try to give good responses to an originality test, and the others would decide whether his responses were good. Whenever they judged a particular response to be not good, the learner would receive a severe electric shock. The experimenter said he did not care which subject served as the learner and that it was customary to let the group decide this for themselves. He then asked each subject to rank the others in the order that they wanted each of them to be the learner. In other words, the subjects were given an opportunity to select one of their number for an extremely unpleasant, painful task. The data appear in Table 4–2.

Almost all the nondeviants chose the one deviant subject in the group for the unpleasant task. The deviant subjects showed the opposite tendency; they chose a nondeviant for the painful role. Thus, all the subjects picked someone who was different from themselves—despite the fact that they had no idea how the one they chose differed from them.

It might be noted that this tendency to pick out people who are different is not entirely indiscriminate. When subjects in this same situation were asked to pick somebody for a good role (one in which he would earn money), they tended to pick someone who was similar to themselves rather than someone who was different. Thus, not only did

Table 4–2

DEVIANT AND NONDEVIANT SUBJECTS' CHOICE OF DEVIANT
FOR SHOCK AND REWARD

| Subject Choosing | For Shock | For Reward |
|---|---|---|
| Deviant | 2.18 | 3.73 |
| Nondeviant | 3.91 | 2.82 |

Note: Figures are the mean rankings for the deviant on a scale from 1 to 4; the higher the number, the more the deviant was chosen.

Source: Adapted from Freedman and Doob (1968).

they choose deviants for an unpleasant task, they avoided choosing them for a pleasant one.

We can now see why scapegoating might be one of the bases of prejudice. Ideal scapegoats are weak, different, and easily distinguishable —qualities that seem to be characteristic of the groups that are the major targets of prejudice, at least in the United States. American blacks share all of these characteristics. They are in a relatively weak position in society because they are poor and less well educated than whites. They are also noticeably different from the white majority. Catholics and Jews are not distinguishable from the Protestant majority by anything as noticeable as skin color, but they do tend to have different names, different national backgrounds, and, most important, different religious practices. We are not stating that scapegoating is the only or even the major cause of prejudice, but it is one of the mechanisms that produces it. As we mentioned above, learning the appropriate targets of aggression from parents or peers is a major factor that keeps prejudice alive from generation to generation. However, scapegoating may be one explanation of how it began in the first place.

### Catharsis

Whether or not somebody aggresses in a particular situation is determined by two variables—the strength of his aggressive impulses and the degree to which he has learned to express aggression in the given situation. As described above, the strength of the impulse is determined partly by the degree of frustration or annoyance that produced it and partly by the extent to which the individual, because of learning or personality characteristics, tends to react to this frustration with feelings of aggression. The tendency to express this aggression is determined by what he has learned about aggressiveness in general and the situation in particular.

When one feels aggressive and cannot attack the source of this feeling, another possible way for him to reduce his aggressive feeling is to find a nonaggressive or more socially acceptable outlet for his anger. He may play football. Or he can simply witness someone else being aggressive—he can go to a movie that has a lot of violence in it, watch a friend scold his secretary, or even read about a war in the newspaper. This vicarious aggression often serves to lessen anger that cannot be expressed openly. A final possibility is that he can sublimate his anger, that is, channel it into relatively constructive behavior. He can throw himself into his work, pound away at a typewriter, write a critical essay, or do anything that is a socially acceptable form of behavior but that uses a lot of energy. The idea that any of these behaviors—socially acceptable aggression, vicarious aggression, or sublimation—will reduce feelings of anger and therefore reduce subsequent aggression is called *catharsis.*

Aristotle originated the idea of catharsis in his discussion of the purpose and effect of Greek tragedy. Members of an audience experience a variety of emotions while viewing a play. For example, although they are not in danger themselves when the hero is threatened, they experience fear. This fear does not affect their behavior directly—they do not run from the theater. Instead, they express their fear through the actions of the play's hero. According to Aristotle, this arousal and expression of emotion results in a purging, or catharsis, of the emotion, by which he meant that the viewers are less likely to experience this emotion in the future.

Freud's conception of catharsis was somewhat different—he emphasized the expression of the feeling. His basic idea was that expressing a particular impulse reduces its strength. If one is sexually aroused, expressing that feeling in behavior reduces this sexual impulse; if he is angry, acting aggressively makes him less angry.

Although the most effective way of producing this catharsis is for the individual to express the impulse himself, indirect expression also reduces the strength of the feeling. If the boy who was forbidden to go to the movies and is angry at his father sees his father scolded by an irate neighbor, this vicarious aggression reduces his anger. Also, yelling at his sister makes him less angry at his father. In other words, any expression of aggression—direct, displaced, or vicarious—should produce some catharsis.

The major implication of the catharsis notion is that expressing aggressive impulses tends to reduce subsequent aggression. If a person feels aggressive, committing an aggressive act should reduce the intensity of his aggressive feelings. This, in turn, should make him less likely to act aggressively afterward. The idea is that aggressing is very much like eating. Whether or not someone eats is determined partly by how hungry he is and partly by the situation in which he finds himself. If he eats something when he is hungry, he reduces his hunger and will eat less later. If someone annoys us by honking his horn at us, we feel aggressive. If, at the next traffic light, we find ourselves behind his car and honk at him, this should reduce our aggressive feelings toward him. Or if we see a policeman giving him a ticket, this also should reduce our aggressiveness because our annoyer has been punished by someone else. Finally, if instead of honking at our annoyer we honk at someone else, this venting of aggressive feelings should also reduce our annoyance, although probably not as effectively.

Under many circumstances, catharsis probably does operate in this way. Committing an aggressive act or seeing the source of one's frustra-

Drawing by Jack Tippit; reprinted
by permission, *Parade Magazine*.

*"Go ahead, Dad . . . release all that hatred and resent-
ment. It's good to get it out of your system."*

tion punished makes one feel less aggressive toward the other person
and less likely to hurt him. It would be a serious mistake, however, to
conclude that allowing someone to express aggression necessarily makes
him less aggressive. On the contrary, allowing aggression often has the
opposite effect—it increases aggressive behavior.

The explanation of these different effects lies in the extremely complex determination of aggressiveness. As we have said, an aggressive act
is ordinarily produced by a combination of two circumstances: the individual feels aggressive and the situation is one in which he is willing
or able to express that aggression. The act will occur only when the
strength of his aggressive impulse is great enough to overcome whatever
inhibitions he feels because of the situation. Thus anything that reduces
the aggressive impulses or increases the inhibitions will reduce the likelihood that he will behave aggressively; and conversely anything that increases aggressive impulses or decreases the inhibitions will increase the
likelihood of an aggressive act.

It is important to distinguish between two types of catharsis situations: One in which the individual himself behaves aggressively and one
in which he witnesses aggression. The traditional notion of catharsis was
that either of these would reduce subsequent aggression, but we know
now that the factors involved are somewhat different. Committing an

124

aggressive act should reduce the individual's aggressive impulses and thereby reduce the tendency to be aggressive. But being allowed to commit the hostile act without punishment teaches the individual that it is appropriate or acceptable to be aggressive in this particular situation; this of course would make him more likely to be aggressive again when he gets the chance.

Witnessing aggression also should affect both the aggressive drive and the assessment of the situation, but in somewhat different ways. Observing aggressiveness, violence, and hostile acts seems to arouse most people rather than soothe them. Watching a violent movie excites people and may even make them feel aggressive. Watching a professional football game causes people to yell out "kill them, get them, tackle them" and far from soothing their savage impulses, it arouses them. In addition, just as in the other situation, observing aggressiveness teaches the individual that it is acceptable or appropriate in the situation. Thus both factors should tend to produce an increase in subsequent aggressive behavior. The individual who observes violence will feel more aroused himself and will also learn that aggressive behavior is acceptable.

This analysis leads us to make several predictions about the effects of behaving aggressively or witnessing aggression on subsequent agressiveness.

1. If the individual is very angry, acting aggressively or witnessing the source of his anger being hurt will reduce his aggressive impulse and reduce subsequent aggression.

2. If the individual is not very angry to begin with, the major effect will be on his assessment of the situation rather than on his own aggressive impulses. That is, someone who is not particularly angry to begin with will be more likely to behave aggressively after witnessing aggression or behaving aggressively himself.

3. Witnessing aggression that is not related to the source of anger should increase aggressive feelings and also teach the individual that aggression is appropriate; therefore, it should not reduce the amount of subsequent aggression but rather should almost always increase it.

Most of the research is consistent with this analysis and these predictions. To begin with, two studies (Hokanson, 1961; Hokanson and Burgess, 1962) provide evidence that expressing aggression decreases anger. In these studies, subjects were insulted by a low-status person, with the immediate effect being to increase their systolic blood pressure, indicating that the annoyance had increased physiological tension. We can in-

Table 4–3

*EFFECT OF FANTASY ON AGGRESSION*

| Condition | Aggression |
|---|---|
| Angered: | |
| With fantasy task | 21.17 |
| Without fantasy task | 23.09 |
| Not angered | 14.92 |

Note: Figures indicate the amount of aggression on a scale from 0 to 36.

Source: Adapted from Feshbach (1955).

terpret this as evidence that the subjects were made angry. Some of the subjects were then given an opportunity to deliver shocks to the experimenter who had annoyed them; some were not given this opportunity. Physiological measures showed that being allowed to express aggression resulted in lower systolic blood pressure—evidence that subjects who are originally angry will be less angry if they are allowed to express some aggression toward the source of their annoyance.

Seymour Feshbach (1955) conducted an important study of catharsis in which half of a group of subjects who had been angered by being insulted in class by their instructor was allowed to express aggression on a fantasy task—responding to four TAT cards (cards showing ambiguous pictures for which the subjects were to make up a story). The other half of this group did not respond to the cards, but all the subjects in an uninsulted group did. Afterward, there was another measure of aggression, the results of which are shown in Table 4–3. The insulted subjects who were given the opportunity to express aggression on the fantasy task were less aggressive on the final measure than were the insulted subjects who did not take the fantasy task.

Studies by Doob illustrate the two possible effects of expressing or witnessing aggression. In one (1967), subjects were made angry by a confederate who insulted them, disagreed with everything they said, and were generally obnoxious. Other subjects talked to the confederate but were not made angry in this way. Then some of the subjects in each condition witnessed the confederate losing money in a game. When the confederate suffered a loss, the aggressive feelings of the angered subjects should have been satisfied to some extent. They should have felt less angry and, if given a chance, been less aggressive. In contrast if the subjects were not angry to begin with, witnessing the confederate's loss should have no effect on their level of aggressive feelings. That is what the experiment showed. Angry subjects who witnessed the loss were less aggressive than angry subjects who did not witness it; but nonangry subjects expressed the same amount of aggression whether or not the person had lost money.

The second study (Doob and Wood, 1972) makes this point even more clearly. Once again subjects were either angry or not angry. Some of the subjects in each condition then gave electric shocks to the confederate; other subjects merely witnessed the confederate receive the electric shocks; and still other subjects neither witnessed nor gave shocks to the confederate. When the subjects were then allowed to give shocks themselves, the result fell into a nice pattern that is shown in Table 4–4. The angry subjects gave fewer shocks when they either had shocked the confederate previously or had witnessed him getting shocked. The subjects who were not angry, however, gave more shocks in both of those conditions than they did when no shocks had been given in the first place. In other words when the subjects were angered, catharsis resulted from giving or witnessing shocks to the confederate; when the subjects were not angered, the opposite occurred with more shocks being given than otherwise. In addition, an experiment by Konecni and Doob (1972) showed that angry subjects gave fewer shocks to their tormenter when they had been given an opportunity to shock either their tormenter or somebody entirely different than when they were not given this opportunity. Apparently, behaving aggressively to anyone reduces their aggressive feelings somewhat and thereby reduces subsequent aggressive behavior. Once again there was no catharsis effect with subjects who were not initially angry.

Thus, this work quite consistently demonstrates that angry people who express aggression become less angry and are then less aggressive, while people who are not angry to begin with are either unaffected by acting aggressively or actually become more aggressive. Although this

Table 4–4

NUMBER OF SHOCKS GIVEN BY ANNOYED AND NOT ANNOYED SUBJECTS WHO FIRST GAVE SHOCKS THEMSELVES, WITNESSED SHOCKS BEING GIVEN, OR SAW NO SHOCKS

| Condition | Subject Shocks | Experimenter Shocks | No Shocks Given |
|---|---|---|---|
| Subject Annoyed | 6.80 | 7.60 | 10.67 |
| Subject Not Annoyed | 8.07 | 9.73 | 6.60 |

Source: Adapted from Doob and Wood (1972).

provides support for the original notion of catharsis, the situations involved are limited to those in which the individual himself behaves aggressively or observes his tormentor suffering.

By far the bulk of the research on catharsis has involved the other kind of situation—one in which the individual neither expresses aggression himself nor witnesses aggression expressed against the source of his anger. Instead he watches a violent film or some other form of aggression not particularly relevant to his current situation. This research has produced results that are almost unanimous in demonstrating that witnessing aggression in this way does not reduce subsequent aggression but instead tends to increase it. Perhaps the only exception is a famous study by Feshbach (1961) in which angered and not angered subjects were shown either a violent boxing film or a neutral film. Measures of aggression taken after the film showed that watching the prize fighting film lowered the aggressiveness of angry subjects and slightly increased the aggressiveness of subjects who were not initially angry. With this one exception practically all of the other studies have shown that watching violent films actually increases aggressiveness. For example, Hartmann (1969) had angered and not angered subjects watch a fight film with emphasis on the person doing the hitting, a fight film with the emphasis on the pain cues of the person being hit, and a control film. He found that for angered and not angered subjects both fight films produced more aggression than the control film.

Berkowitz and Geen (1966) had subjects watch a clip from the film *Champion* in which a boxer is badly mauled. Other subjects watched a track film. Some of the subjects in each condition had been angered and others had not. When subjects were subsequently given the opportunity of delivering shocks, those who had witnessed the fight film tended to give more shocks than those who had witnessed the track film, although this was stronger for the angered subjects than for those who were not angered. A second study (Geen and Berkowitz, 1966) produced similar results using only angered subjects.

A study by Doob and Climie (1972) indicates that part of the effect of observing aggression is due to increased arousal of aggressive impulses. They demonstrated this by allowing the subject to behave aggressively either immediately after observing an aggressive film or twenty minutes later. They found that subjects who watched an aggressive film gave many more shocks immediately afterwards than did subjects who watched a neutral film, but the difference was much smaller twenty minutes later.

This effect of arousal has been studied in a very interesting way in a series of experiments by Zilman. He argues that any kind of arousal will increase aggressiveness and that it need not be specifically the arousal of anger or aggression. Just as subjects who are excited might eat more or run faster, so they will be more aggressive if given the opportunity. In one study (Zilman, 1971) subjects watched either a neutral film, an aggressive film, or a sexually arousing film and were then given the opportunity to behave aggressively. As shown in Table 4–5, it was found that both the erotic and aggressive films produced more aggression than the neutral film. In a second study (Zilman, Katcher, and Milavsky, 1972) subjects were angered or not angered and half of each group also exercised. Those subjects who were angry and exercised subsequently behaved more aggressively than when the exercise was not included. Thus even arousal that is apparently irrelevant to aggressiveness or anger produces an increase in aggressive behavior. It seems, as we have discussed in previous chapters, that individuals have considerable difficulty labeling the emotions they are feeling and the relationship between one emotion and behavior is not always specific. Arousing any kind of drive or emotion may increase the performance of a behavior even if it is irrelevant. This would explain why witnessing exciting, violent, or even erotic films will lead to increased aggressiveness rather than produce a cathartic effect.

The research by Bandura and others demonstrated that children who witness an adult behaving aggressively will be more aggressive than those who watch an unaggressive adult. The same kind of phenomenon occurred when adults or children watched films in which violence occurred. In addition to the effect of arousal which we just discussed, the films teach the person to behave aggressively. This has been amply demonstrated in research on modeling by Bandura, 1965; Walters and Willows, 1968; and many others. But as we mentioned earlier, imitation is not entirely indiscriminate. When the person in the film is punished for behaving aggressively the amount of aggression actually decreases. For example Baron (1972) showed that a model who was censured for behaving aggressively had less influence than one who was not criti-

Table 4–5

THE EFFECTS OF NEUTRAL, AGGRESSIVE, AND EROTIC FILMS ON
SUBSEQUENT AGGRESSIVENESS

|  | TYPE OF FILM | | |
| --- | --- | --- | --- |
|  | Neutral | Aggressive | Erotic |
| Intensity of Shocks | 3.07 | 3.95 | 5.07 |

Source: Adapted from Zilman (1971).

cized. Meyer (1972) showed that unjustified aggression did not necessarily produce an increase in aggressive behavior although justified aggression clearly did. And Berkowitz and Rowlings (1963) and Berkowitz and Geen (1967) also showed that witnessing justified aggression produced a greater increase in subsequent aggressiveness than did unjustified aggression.

Thus the work on catharsis seems to fit into a fairly neat pattern. When an individual is angry, expressing aggression or witnessing the source of his anger suffering reduces his aggressive feelings and makes it less likely that he will behave aggressively immediately afterward. On the other hand, if he is not angry to begin with or if he witnesses but does not engage in aggressiveness toward someone other than the source of his anger, the opposite effect will occur. In both cases he will probably become more aroused as a result of witnessing the aggression and this will cause him to be more aggressive in the future. In addition he will learn that it is appropriate to be aggressive and this too will increase aggression. Berkowitz, Buss, and Feshbach—three of the men who have done the most work in this area—appear to agree with at least the first part of this analysis. Berkowitz summarized his opinion as follows: "Providing an opportunity to express hostility may lessen the frustration-engendered instigation to aggression (anger) but could also evoke and/or strengthen a person's habitual hostile tendencies (1962, p. 203)." Buss stated "When aggression occurs in the absence of anger there is an increase in the tendency to aggress. When aggression occurs in the presence of anger, there is a cathartic effect, i.e., a decrease in the tendency to aggress (1961, p. 89)." By now, Berkowitz and Buss would also add that under most circumstances witnessing aggression but not actually engaging in it will tend to increase subsequent aggressiveness whether or not the individual was angered in the first place.

## Television Violence

It is an understatement to say that current movies portray a great deal of violence. Fighting, beating, killing, and murder have always been common in Westerns and gangster movies. But recent movies have escalated the amount of carnage as well as its vividness. It might be said that *Bonnie and Clyde* and *The Wild Bunch* made blood red for the first time in American movies. People did not just die at a distance or clutch their stomachs and fall slowly to the ground. In these movies they actually bled and suffered; the bullet wounds gaped; people were not only killed, they were actually hurt. *Straw Dogs*, *The Getaway*, and *Clockwork Orange*, three popular movies of recent vintage, show every conceivable kind of violence in great detail and largely without any kind of censure or punishment of the offenders. Even a clearly antiwar movie such as *M\*A\*S\*H\** seemed to revel in blood and gore although, of course, making fun of it and condemning the violence.

Perhaps because it is not yet allowed to show much sex, television is even more dependent upon violence for its programming. With the exception of talk, variety, doctor, and comedy shows, virtually all original programming for prime time television, as well as shows designed specifically for children, involves violence in one form or another. Westerns, police, gangster, spy, and most television movies include a full complement of fighting, shooting, and killing. Although the violence on television is much less explicit and vivid than that in the movies, it is remarkably pervasive. All of which leads to the question of how this constant exposure to violence affects behavior.

A presidential commission spent a great deal of time trying to answer this question. The commission included some eminent psychologists and it listened to testimony from many others. The final conclusion of the commission was that all of the violence was probably not good for the viewers, that it tended to foster immoral and antisocial values about violence, and perhaps caused some individuals to be more aggressive. As soon as the report was issued, some of the members of the commission claimed that the conclusion was too moderate—that actually television had much more severe effects than the commission had admitted.

This disagreement is understandable since much of the evidence is contradictory. As we have discussed in some detail, the experimental evidence and the theoretical explanations would suggest that viewing violence would, if anything, make the individual more violent himself. The child who watches someone get beaten up will probably be aroused somewhat himself and will also learn that this kind of aggression is acceptable and even desirable in society (particularly if it is the hero who wins the fight). Both of these reactions should tend to increase the child's tendency to behave aggressively in the future. Viewing violence might possibly decrease his aggressiveness if it allowed him to express aggressive feelings vicariously and thus produce a cathartic effect. But all of the laboratory evidence suggests that only by behaving aggressively himself or by watching the source of his anger get punished will the individual's aggressive feelings be reduced. Since this ordinarily does not happen on television, whatever aggressive feelings the child has should not be reduced and thus his aggressiveness should not decline.

Yet these conclusions are based largely on laboratory studies and ignore some important considerations. The major counterargument is that television programs show nothing that children are not exposed to anyway. We live in a violent society and a violent world, and almost all children know this. Their parents talk about muggings and murder and war; the newspapers and magazines tell about these phenomena; and unfortunately many children witness it themselves. Children are mugged on the way to school, beaten up in class, and even witness their teachers being robbed right in the classroom. As a famous quote puts it: "Why teach a child to read 'See Jane run' when they've seen Jane raped?" And even if children have been sheltered from violence in their own lives, they surely know about it from television news programs which necessarily show a great deal of violence that occurs in the world.

If children already know about violence and are exposed to it regularly, it is less likely that witnessing it on television will have any appreciable effect. They do not need television to demonstrate that violence occurs in society, nor that often people who are violent are not punished. Thus it is difficult to generalize directly from the laboratory studies to this real life situation. In the laboratory, subjects learn that aggression is more acceptable in this given situation. But in the real world, children already know that violence is part of our society and television may have little effect on their attitudes toward aggressiveness.

The only major study attempting to investigate this problem in a realistic situation was conducted by Feshbach and Singer (1970). Boys in private boarding or state residential schools were randomly assigned to two groups: One group watched largely aggressive television programs such as "Gunsmoke" and "The FBI" while the other group was limited to nonaggressive programs such as the "Ed Sullivan Variety Show" and "Bachelor Father." The boys watched only shows on the designated lists and could watch as much as they wanted as long as they spent at least six hours a week watching television. Various measures of aggressiveness were given before and after the six-week viewing period, and both peers and adult supervisors also rated the boys' aggressiveness.

The results showed that particularly in the state schools boys who watched aggressive programs were actually less aggressive themselves. They engaged in fewer fights and argued less with their peers. The effect was the same but somewhat weaker for the boys in the private schools. This impressive study thus indicates that, at least under some conditions, observing television violence might actually decrease aggressive behavior. The explanation for this effect might be that the children identified with both the heros and the villains in the programs, and thus did vicariously express some of their aggressive feelings through the violence on television. On the other hand it must be noted that the effect could be due to the fact that boys who were limited to the nonaggressive programs might have been annoyed because they were not allowed to watch their favorite television shows. Despite this possible alternative explanation, the study is the one attempt to establish how television affects aggressiveness, and it does suggest that the effect may not be negative.

As with the issue of catharsis in general, there is no definitive answer to this question. The few well-controlled studies that have been conducted have not produced consistent results. Although there is a great deal of violence in our society, it may be that television, because of its vividness and the great amount of time children spend watching it, does play a special role in shaping children's attitudes. If so, the violence on TV may have the generally negative effect described above. It may cause children—and adults—to become so accustomed to violence that they are less likely to restrain their aggressive impulses and no longer object as strongly to violence in others. Even if this is not the effect on most viewers, it may be the effect on enough of them to have serious results for our society. On the other hand, it should be noted that the current generation of college and high school students were raised during the height of television violence but that this generation is as strongly, perhaps more strongly, opposed to war than their parents. True, some

© 1969 Newspaper Enterprise Association, Inc.

among them use violence to fight for their causes, but this may be the minority whom TV caused to be more accepting of violence as a way of life. Perhaps, then, under appropriate circumstances, watching violence on television can cause people to understand violence better and to have more healthy attitudes toward it. However, this is all speculative at the moment. It seems likely that the answer will be that the effect of observing violence on television is more dependent on how it is presented than on its quantity.

CHAPTER REVIEW

1. Aggression must be defined, at least in part, in terms of intent.
2. Aggressive impulses distinguished from aggressive behavior.
3. Instinct, frustration, and annoyance are possible causes of aggressive impulses.
4. Specific cues may trigger aggressive behavior.
5. Learning and imitation affect aggressive behavior.
6. Aggression may be displaced from the primary target.
7. Scapegoating as an example of displacement; its relation to prejudice.
8. Catharsis of aggression.

APPLICATIONS AND SPECULATIONS

1. Of all mammals only man systematically kills other members of his species. Why?
2. Many college campuses have experienced disruptions in the past few years. How would you explain this in terms of the material covered in this chapter?
3. Perhaps related to the previous question is the observation that until recently adolescent rebellion seemed to play almost no role in United States politics. Do you think this is changing, and if so, why?
4. The United States is one of the few industrialized countries that allows almost anyone to own a gun. The United States also has a much higher rate of murder than comparable countries. (With a population of 200 million, the United States had over 3000 homicides by gunfire in 1968, whereas Japan, with 100 million people, had only 50 such homicides.) It has been argued that this high rate of homicide is due

at least in part to the presence of guns. Think about this in terms of the concepts described in the chapter.

## SUGGESTIONS FOR ADDITIONAL READING

### Articles

Bandura, A., Ross, D., and Ross, S. A. Transmission of aggression through imitation and aggressive models. *Journal of Abnormal and Social Psychology*, 1961, *63*, 575–82.

Berkowitz, L., and Green, J. A. The stimulus qualities of the scapegoat. *Journal of Abnormal and Social Psychology*, 1962, *64*, 293–301.

Doob, A. N., and Wood, L. E. Catharsis and aggression: effects of annoyance and retaliation on aggressive behavior. *Journal of Personality and Social Psychology*, 1972, *22*, 156–62.

Zilman, D. Excitation transfer in communication-mediated aggressive behavior. *Journal of Experimental Social Psychology*, 1971, *7*, 419–34.

### Books and Longer Discussions

Berkowitz, L. *Aggression: a social psychological analysis*. New York: McGraw-Hill, 1962.

Buss, A. H. *The psychology of aggression*. New York: John Wiley, 1961.

Feshbach, S., and Singer, R. D. *Television and aggression*. San Francisco: Jossey-Bass, 1970.

Lorenz, K. *On aggression*. New York: Harcourt, Brace & World, 1966. Especially Chapters 1–3.

# five

# group structure
# and leadership

Thus far we have been discussing primarily how individuals function in social situations. Now we shall shift our attention to the group. In a complex society, groups range from small, intimate ones such as a family or a bridge club to large, complex ones such as the Teamsters' Union, white Protestants, the United States Army, or even all United States citizens. The activities and interactions within and between these large groups are very important and interesting, but traditionally, social psychologists have tended to concentrate on the smaller groups, in which the members are in face-to-face contact, and sociologists and political scientists have tended to study the big groups. However, because all large groups are composed of a number of smaller ones, understanding how small groups operate and behave should also enable us to understand a great deal about the more complex, larger ones.

When a number of people are brought together in a group, they do not remain entirely undifferentiated. They develop patterns of behavior, divide tasks, adopt different roles, and so on; these *structural aspects* of the group have a profound effect on how it functions. Therefore, we shall begin our discussion of groups with two questions: What kinds of organization and structure appear in groups? How does a structure that is imposed on a group affect other aspects of its organization?

**COMMUNI-CATION PATTERNS**

When people are gathered together in a room and allowed to talk, an almost universal phenomenon occurs—some people talk a great deal and others say very little. The circumstances of the situation have relatively little effect on this pattern. The group can be structured or unstructured, the problem they are discussing specific or general, the members friends or strangers. In a seminar with a permissive instructor, for example, there always seems to be one or two people who monopolize the discussion, regardless of the topic. They do most of the talking, and the rest say only an occasional word or two. And to the talkers it must seem that no one else has anything to say. Regardless of the size of the group, if discussion is not restricted artificially, some people do most of the talking.

Moreover, communication follows a fairly regular pattern, one that can be well represented by a logarithmic function. Figure 5–1 illustrates this pattern for groups of four, six, and eight. Note that in all cases one person does a great deal of talking, the next most talkative person does considerably less, and so on—the amount of talking done by each person drops at a logarithmic rate. In an eight-member group, two people contribute 60 percent of the conversation, one other contributes 14 percent, and the other five contribute only 26 percent among them. This type of pattern seems to hold in all sorts of groups—whether they are highly structured or unstructured, are new or old, or are composed of friends or strangers, young or old persons. It is probably reflected even in an institutionalized group such as the United States Senate, despite the restrictions imposed on communication by the complexity of its rules and structure; it is almost certainly true of the British Cabinet and Parliament; and it is true of classroom seminars and informal discussion

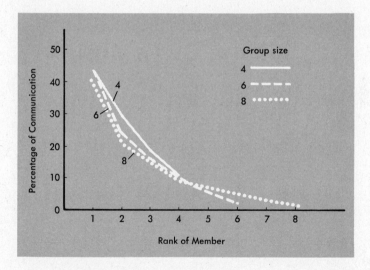

Figure 5–1

The amount of communication by members of a group follows a logarithmic or exponential curve. Regardless of the size of the group, the most talkative member does about 40 percent of the communicating and the amount of the other members' communication drops off sharply. The difference between the amount of communication of the first and second most talkative people increases as the size of the group increases. (Based on Stephan and Mishler, 1952.)

sessions in dormitories. That one person does most of the talking seems to be a virtually universal characteristic of groups.

Other patterns also emerge within groups before a formal structure develops. For one thing, they adopt various habits and traditions. Merei (1949) noted that after three or more meetings, groups of young children formed traditions—where each member would sit in the room, who would play with which toy, what sequence of activities would be followed, and so on. Strong patterns of this type have also been observed in mental hospitals. Particular patients sit in particular chairs and follow certain sequences of action. For example, someone sitting in one spot might always have his cigarette lighted by another patient standing near him but might also lend cigarettes to someone else. Or the whole group might shift places at a particular time and in a set pattern. These examples are probably more extreme than those occurring in most situations, but one can also notice that college students tend to take the same seat at each meeting of a class—even if they selected a poor one at the beginning of the term. This kind of organization of activity appears in all groups, although few members are consciously aware of it and most might be surprised if it were pointed out. Moreover, although the patterns are informal and unverbalized, they are generally firmly held and highly resistant to change.

The differentiation of communication and development of habits are the beginnings of structure. Each member has a somewhat separate function, some participate more than others, some perform acts that others do not, etc. It is a minimal type of structure but is important as the forerunner of a more explicit type. The communication pattern is particularly crucial, because it is one of the key elements in the formation and identification of leadership in the group.

**LEADERSHIP**  One of the most striking and universal facts about groups is that they almost always have a leader. Groups of sled dogs, baboons, lions, elephants, and chickens all have leaders. Usually the strongest male asserts his dominance and then has the rights and responsibilities of leadership. He gets his pick of mates, food, and position but also must make decisions—such as where to find food—and must lead the defense of the group when necessary. Examples from nonhuman societies could be multiplied indefinitely—virtually all animals that live in groups appear to have leaders.

This is also true of human groups. Teen-agers standing on a street corner, men in a foxhole, a work gang, the United States Senate, and subjects gathered in a room to discuss a problem would all have one thing in common. Despite the fact that the purposes, structure, and memberships of these groups are entirely different, they would all have a leader. In a sense, some kind of leadership is probably a necessary condition for an assemblage to operate as a group.

Although the terms *leader* and *leadership* are commonly used and everyone probably has similar notions as to their meaning, there are two different ways of identifying the leader of a group. A straightforward approach, and in many ways the most reasonable one, is to ask the group members. If everyone agrees that a particular person is the leader (and they usually do in a group that has existed for any length of time), they must believe it and must look to him when they want leadership; thus, in a sense, he is the leader. This method avoids the tricky problem of constructing a formal definition, with which not everyone would agree entirely. True, the members of the group may disagree among themselves as to what they mean by leader, but as long as they agree on who the leader is, this is no problem. In fact, it is an advantage, because the person chosen fits all the implicit definitions that the different group members hold. The method does run into difficulties when there is some disagreement as to who the leader is, but even then it is quite useful.

Although this makes good sense, to some extent it avoids the issue. We really want to say what we think makes a person a leader; we want to be able to tell someone how to identify the leader of a group by himself. If we watch a juvenile gang, the United States Senate, or any other group, we want to be able to identify the leader ourselves without asking for a poll. This is partly because it is often quite an undertaking to ask a group who their leader is. A more basic problem, however, is that we want to be certain we know what we are talking about when we say someone is a leader.

The central attribute of leadership is influence—the leader is generally the person in the group who has the most influence on its activities and beliefs. He is the one who initiates action, gives orders, makes decisions, settles disputes between members, and makes judgments. He is also the one who dispenses approval and disapproval, offers encouragement, serves as inspiration, and is in the forefront of any activity. These functions are merely examples of the general influence the leader exerts over the group; any particular leader may not perform all of them, but to be a leader, he must perform many. The members do, think, and feel what he wants them to and what he tells them to a greater extent than for any other member of the group.

Thus, there are two ways of defining a leader. He is the person who the group says is the leader and/or the person who has the most influence on the group. Both these definitions are workable and will almost always result in the same person's being selected. When they do not, there is probably more than one real leader, a situation that will be discussed below.

**FACTORS PRODUCING LEADERSHIP**

The rules governing dominance in animals are apparently quite simple compared to those in human groups. In virtually all animal groups, the males who have aspirations toward leadership fight, and the winner—the strongest—becomes most dominant. There is also some evidence that occasionally leadership or dominance can be achieved by two animals cooperating so that they are stronger than any other single animal. Two male baboons might cooperate to achieve dominance even though neither of them is as big and strong as a single other male. Somewhat similar cooperation occurs among jackdaws (birds resembling crows), so presumably this behavior is not limited to primates. But even in these circumstances, leadership depends, to a large extent, on strength, which is determined in more or less open competition. Determinants of human leadership are considerably more complex.

Why do particular people become leaders? There are two facets to this question. The first deals with the kinds of situations, procedures, or other factors that make a person a leader; the second deals with the kinds of people who become leaders. That is, we can answer the question in terms of properties more or less external to the individual or in terms of personality or other characteristics of the individual.

### Appointment

One way to become the leader in a human group is to be appointed by someone outside the group rather than being selected by the group itself. An Army lieutenant is the official leader of his company, and the man who happens to be selected as the first juror and is therefore the jury foreman tends to lead the jury. Simply being in a position of authority or being the person who is *supposed* to be the leader tends to make one the leader. This is obvious in the case of the Army lieutenant, because he can give orders to the others and no one can give orders to him—almost automatically he is the leader. It is less obvious and more interesting in the case of the jury foreman—he has no more authority than any other juror, yet he tends to lead the discussion and act as the leader of the group. In general, regardless of his qualifications, someone who has the formal position of leader performs the functions of the leader.

It should be pointed out, however, that there are often important differences between leaders who have been appointed and those who have earned their position. In many cases, a group will not think an appointed leader deserves his position; they will not think he is the legitimate leader. This notion of legitimacy can be extremely important. In a study by Raven and French (1958), leaders were either appointed by an outside agency or elected by the group. The elected leaders had considerably more influence and power than the appointed ones. Presum-

Drawing by Handelsman; © 1972 The New Yorker Magazine, Inc.

*"This daily metamorphosis never fails to amaze me.*
*Around the house, I'm a perfect idiot. I come to court,*
*put on a black robe, and, by God, I'm **it**!"*

ably, this was due to the fact that the elected leaders were seen as more legitimate and their power to lead was therefore recognized by the rest of the group.

In recent years, the question of legitimacy of leadership has been continually raised in American universities and colleges. Even though the trustees and administrators have the legal right to run a school, students and faculty have begun to question the legitimacy of that right. The basis of the argument is that the trustees generally are not elected by the people at the institution. They are either self-perpetuating (electing their own successors) or elected by alumni, who are no longer intimately involved with the school. Similarly, presidents of colleges are usually appointed by the trustees with little or no consultation with faculty and even less with students. The students and faculty do not feel involved in the choices of trustees and administrators and, consequently, accord them little legitimacy.

This problem is even more severe in public universities, which tend to be governed by boards of regents whose appointment is usually political and is almost always out of the control of the school concerned. The regents are seen as being imposed on the school by outside forces, and therefore have even less legitimacy than trustees of private schools.

There is no easy solution to this problem, but many schools are moving in a direction that is likely to increase the legitimacy of their governing bodies. They are giving those who are intimately involved with a school more voice in electing its leaders. In particular, schools that have had self-elected boards of trustees are moving toward more open elections. They are also setting up nominating committees with student and faculty members, consulting with elected representatives of both groups before appointing administrators, and generally trying to get the support of the whole school for new appointments. Similar changes are being made throughout the university structure, with students serving on more committees and many schools having powerful committees composed of equal numbers of administrators, faculty, and students. Of course, increasing the legitimacy of college presidents and trustees does not guarantee that their decisions will always be popular, but it does increase the likelihood that even unpopular decisions will be accepted.

It is clear that being appointed leader does not guarantee that one has the power that normally accrues to a leader. It does give one the nominal position, but only by legitimizing that position in some way can he guarantee that the group will follow his lead and that he will be effective. An appointed leader should do what he can to gain the support of the group—by demonstrating his ability, by becoming popular, or by using any means at his disposal to convince the members that he deserves to be their leader.

### Amount of Communication

The most active member in terms of communication is also usually the leader of the group. At the simplest level, the most active person is the leader because he has the most influence on the group. He determines the course of conversation (most of what is said comes from him), he initiates interactions by asking questions, he receives the most replies, and he makes the most suggestions and gives the most orders. Whatever the group is doing, he plays a central role. An outside observer would consider him the group's leader—and the group concurs in this opinion. Usually the person who talks the most is perceived as the leader by the rest of the group. Thus, amount of communication is a critical determinant of leadership.

This suggests that one way of influencing leadership is to influence communication. To make someone a leader, perhaps all that is necessary is to make him talk more. An experiment by Bavelas, Hastorf, Gross, and Kite (1965) demonstrated this effect. Subjects from industrial engineering classes, who did not know each other well, were recruited to participate in group discussions. They were divided into four-man groups, given a problem to discuss for ten minutes, and told that their discussions would be observed through a one-way mirror. An observer recorded the amount of time each subject talked and the number of times he talked. After the discussion session, all subjects filled out questionnaires in which they were asked to rank the other subjects on general leadership ability and a few other dimensions. Three such sessions were held.

Each subject had in front of him a small box containing a red and a green light, and only he could see his own lights. Before the second discussion session, some subjects were told they would receive feedback on their performance. If the red light went on, it would indicate that they had been hindering or interfering with the discussion; if the green light went on, it would indicate that their contribution was helpful. In other words, they would be negatively or positively reinforced for what they said.

One subject who was at or near the bottom on both verbal output and others' rankings of his leadership potential was selected from each group. During the succeeding discussion period, he was positively reinforced (his green light was flashed) whenever he spoke, whereas the rest of the group was negatively reinforced (with their red lights) for most of their speeches. In control groups, members did not receive reinforcements of either kind. When the discussion period was over, all subjects filled out the rating forms again. Finally, a third discussion session was held without reinforcement and a third rating filled out.

Thus, after one session in which the subjects' normal behavior was observed, one subject was encouraged to talk while the others were discouraged. This was followed by a third session, in which no reinforcements were given. In this way, the experimenters could see how positive reinforcement affected the performance of the chosen subject and whether or not the effect lasted.

The results are shown in Table 5-1. During the second session, as one might expect, the positively reinforced subject began to talk more; conversely, the others talked less. After a while, the chosen subject was doing a much greater percentage of the talking than he had to begin with. Moreover, this effect persisted during the third (nonreinforced) session, even though he was receiving no special encouragement.

At one level, it would be easy to say that the reinforced subject was more of a leader than he was before simply because he talked more. Impartial observers would see that he was taking an active, even dominant, role in the group and would rate him more of a leader than he was at the beginning. Another and perhaps more important test was the group's opinion of him. The striking result was that the group also rated him

Table 5-1

EFFECT OF REINFORCEMENT ON VERBAL OUTPUT AND READING AS LEADER

| Discussion Period | Verbal Output[a] | Ranking as Leader[b] |
| --- | --- | --- |
| First (no lights) | 15.7 | 1.77 |
| Second (reinforcement) | 37.0 | 3.30 |
| Third (no light) | 26.9 | 2.70 |

[a]Figures are percentages of total group output.
[b]Figures are rankings on a scale from 1 (lowest) to 4 (highest).

Source: Based on Bavelas, Hastorf, Gross, and Kite (1965).

much higher on the leadership scale. In fact, he went from very low to very high.

For our purposes, the main point is that simple verbal activity appears to be a critical factor in determining leadership. The more active a part one takes, the more likely he is to be the leader.

It should be noted that this research was done in discussion groups, in which one might expect verbal activity to be particularly important. It may be that other kinds of activity are equally or more important in other kinds of groups. For example, the strong, silent athlete may be the captain of his team. We do know, however, that verbal behavior is extremely important in many situations and that one who talks a lot is for that reason alone perceived as a leader by the group.

### Type of Communication

Although the amount of an individual's communication is one determinant of leadership, the type of his communication is also important. Just as members of a group differ in the amount of talking they do, so they differ in the kinds of things they say. Analyzing the content of communications in a group is obviously much more complicated than measuring the quantity. The latter can be done by simply recording how often and how long each person talks. The communications themselves can be recorded on tape or witnessed by trained observers. But separating communications into discrete categories is more difficult. Fortunately, Robert Bales has devised a system that makes it possible to analyze a complex communication in terms of a relatively small number of categories, and thereby to describe the interaction with a manageable number of quantitative measures.

Every communication—indeed, every interaction whether or not it is verbal—is placed into one of twelve broad categories: showing disagreement or agreement, tension or tension release, solidarity or antagonism; and giving or asking for suggestions, opinions, information. Note that the first six categories are emotional or reactive, whereas the latter six are cognitive. Each communication is broken down into distinct parts, and each part is scored separately. For example, consider the following interaction and its scoring of a group trying to build a model airplane. Member A: Where is the scotch tape? (Asks for information.) I think we need it. (Gives opinion.) Member B: Right. (Shows agreement.) Put it on the tail. (Gives suggestion.) Member C: Clumsy oaf. (Shows antagonism.) Member A laughs nervously (shows tension), and member B then tells a joke (shows tension release). Of course, this interaction is simple and most of the scoring is straightforward. But even in complex interactions, trained observers can use Bales' system with a high degree of reliability.

One point that should be made clear is that the system is designed to score only overt behavior. No attempt is made to deduce an individual's inner feelings during interaction. If someone says, "I agree with you," it is scored *shows agreement*, even if the individual appears to be angry at the other person. Although emotions are important elements in group interaction, they could not be scored accurately simply by observing the interaction. Therefore, the system deals with them only insofar as they are expressed openly. Despite this limitation, the system does allow a specification of the kinds of interactions taking place and the role each member is playing in the group.

Analyses of this kind indicate that there is a marked difference in the communications of the two people who do the most talking in a group. One of these people tends to make supportive, encouraging, conciliatory, friendly statements. He says such things as "This is a great group," "We're doing fine," "How do you think we should do this?" He is also the one who would tell a joke in order to release tension or amuse the group. In Bales' terms, this person initiates more interactions that fall into the categories of showing solidarity, tension release, and agreement than anyone else. He also asks more questions than the others—seeking information, opinions, or suggestions. The other talkative person comes to the fore when a task is being carried out. His communications fall into the categories of giving suggestions, opinions, and information; and he is somewhat high on disagreements. He says such things as "Do it this way," "You work on that," "Let's get going," "That's the wrong way to do it." In general, one person concentrates more on the social aspects of the situation, keeping the group running smoothly and happily, whereas the other concentrates on getting the work done. Accordingly, the two have been labeled the *social*, or *socioemotional*, and *task leaders*, respectively.

The difference in function is most apparent when the group is working on a specific task or toward some goal, but it appears in other circumstances as well. One distinction is that the same person tends to be the social leader throughout the existence of the group, whereas the task leader can change according to the requirements of a particular task —when special skills are needed, someone who has them may assume this role temporarily. Generally, however, one person retains the role of task leader in most situations.

The emergence of the task leader during task-oriented activity and the difference in the types of communications made by the two active people make it seem as if groups actually have two different leaders. The social leader fulfills most of the roles we have described as being the job of the leader—he is the true leader, the one about whom the group revolves. But he may not have the particular skills necessary for a given task and may lack the general organizing skills necessary for carrying it out. If these skills reside in someone else, this person will take over certain aspects of leadership when the group is working. However, this task leader usually has a limited role—he controls, shapes, directs, and organizes the group in carrying out a specific task. Although he may have more influence than the social leader during the activity, his influence is limited to the particular job being done.

The qualities necessary for the two types of leaders are antithetical to some extent. The social leader must be agreeable, conciliatory, concerned about the members' well-being and personal feelings, and generally socially oriented. The task leader must be firm, directive, efficient, and generally concerned about getting the job done. It is not probable for one person to have all these qualities; someone who is conciliatory and agreeable ordinarily would not be firm and directive. One who has the characteristics necessary to be a social leader usually would not make a good task leader, and vice versa. The task leader would have to be particularly good in the area the group was working on; he would need special talents and abilities that the social leader would not. Thus, one personal attribute that often produces leadership is outstanding ability in the area of primary concern to the group. But the major effect of this special talent is the determination of the task leader only. He may sometimes be the social leader also, but that would be determined by other factors.

Therefore, most groups do have two leaders, with their relative importance depending on the kind of group, its goals, its degree of task orientation, and the degree to which specific skills are necessary for completion of its task. A group might be extremely task oriented, but if its task does not require special skills and needs a leader merely as a guide and decision maker, the social leader probably would be dominant. For example, the task might be agreeing on a beauty contest winner, deciding on a movie to see, or simply choosing a topic and holding a meaningful and interesting discussion on it. On the other hand, if the task were to build a clubhouse or defeat a filibuster in the Senate, the man who had the necessary skills for the job would emerge as leader until the task was completed. In an extremely task-oriented group, the task leader might be quite dominant; his skills might be so important that he essentially would become the true leader. But the usual situation is for both leaders to coexist and cooperate with each other—the skills of one complement those of the other, with the relative dominance of the two depending on the group's situation at any particular time.

### Communication Networks

We have been discussing groups as though they were entirely undifferentiated to begin with. In particular, we have assumed that everyone is free to communicate with everyone else. Although this is true in a discussion group, there are many groups in which communications are limited, and this limitation constitutes another important aspect of group structure that is intimately related to leadership. A series of experiments have studied groups having a variety of so-called communication networks. The basic idea is that communication is essential for leadership and that the person who can communicate most freely tends to be the leader.

The importance of communication has not escaped the notice of the revolutionaries of the world. One of the highest priority targets of any coup d'état is a nation's radio stations. It is not uncommon to read that the rebellious forces of some general are fighting the premier's loyal troops for control of a country's radio stations or that the stations have been occupied and are broadcasting the news that the coup is successful despite the fact that well-informed sources report that fighting continues. The aim is to take over the stations, tell everybody the coup has succeeded, and prevent the other side from saying it has won and from getting in touch with its troops. If one side can hold the stations long enough and assert its victory often enough, perhaps everyone will believe it and then it becomes true. The side that controls communication is not only in a strong position tactically but also has the evidence that it is the victor—the one who can communicate is, or is seen as, the leader. This is what strategists believe and the research indicates that, at least in small groups, it is true.

The typical study in this area consists of forming a group to work on some problem and imposing limits on the communication permitted among the members. This is accomplished by putting the subjects in separate rooms or booths and allowing them to communicate with each other only by written messages or an intercom system. In this way, the experimenters are able to control who can talk with whom, and a large number of different communication patterns can be imposed. By examining Figure 5–2, in which some of these patterns are represented for groups of five people, one can see that the structures determine the members' freedom of communication. In the circle, all the members are equal—each of them can talk to his two neighbors and to no one else. In the chain, two of the members can each talk to only one person—obviously, in terms of communication, it is not advantageous to be at the end of a chain. The three other members are equal in terms of the number of persons they can talk to; but the man in the middle is only one person away from everyone, whereas the two intermediate people are somewhat isolated from the opposite end. This progression is carried a step farther in the Y-shaped structure—with three end members, only one of the others is able to talk to two people and the fifth member is able to talk to three. Finally, in the wheel, one member can talk to everyone else, but all the other members can talk only to the central one.

A study by Leavitt (1951) provides information on what happens

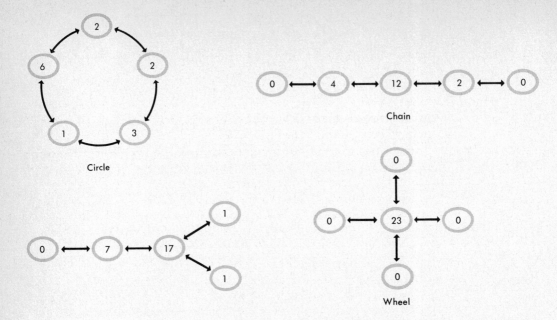

**Figure 5-2**

Communication networks and choice of leaders. The positions connected by a line can communicate directly to each other. The networks range in centrality of communication from the circle (least central, least restricted) to the wheel. The number at each position indicates the number of times the member at that position was considered the leader of the group. (Leavitt, 1951.)

when these types of groups are given a problem to work on—a problem that requires communication in order for a solution to be reached. The more freedom the members had to talk, the more satisfied they were. One who could talk to everyone was the most content, whereas those on the end of the chain, who could talk to only one other person, were the least content. The networks also played a crucial role in producing a leader. When the members of all the groups were asked if there was a group leader and to name him if there was one, the various groups differed markedly in their responses. There was a clear progression from circle to wheel in terms of the number of times a leader was named and in the agreement among members as to who the leader was. The number shown at each position in Figure 5-2 is the number of times the person at that position was named leader. Only half the members of circles named any leader at all and there was little agreement among them, whereas virtually all the wheel members named the central person as the leader. The other two structures fell in between on both counts. It appears that simply being in a position to control communication makes a person a leader.

An interesting sidelight on this type of analysis can be seen by examining the structures in Figure 5–3. As Alex Bavelas has pointed out, type B looks to many people to be an autocratic set-up, whereas type A appears to be a typical business or hierarchical structure. A second look, however, reveals that the structures are identical, with one person able to talk to everyone else and the rest able to talk only to him.

The initial (mistaken) impression is caused by the fact that one man is on top in type A, and we assume that he communicates down much easier than the others communicate up to him. The leader communicates primarily through a subordinate, and this seems to make it easy for him to communicate to the others and relatively difficult for them to communicate to him. Thus, he is assumed to be in a stronger position in terms of communication than they are.

Actually, the intermediary is the freest of all in terms of communication. He corresponds to the top figure in type B, because he can talk to everyone, including the leader. He controls who sees the leader and, to some extent, whom the leader sees. Every communication must be relayed through him; not only does he pass on the leader's orders, he also controls communication up to the leader. A General Motors vice-president who wants to talk to the president has to ask the president's secretary. And, although theoretically the leader can communicate with anyone, he too must usually use the intermediary. This description immediately brings to mind the secretary who seems to run every department. Everyone fears her but is careful to remain on her good side, because she dispenses everything from paper clips to new typewriters. She is a very important and powerful person around an office.

What can happen under these circumstances is that the leader relinquishes some authority to his assistant. Since the latter knows the subordinates better and communicates with them more often, it is easier for him to give the orders. The leader can often give an able assistant considerable autonomy and let him make the routine decisions. After a while, the assistant knows more about what is going on and is considered

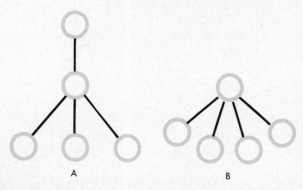

Figure 5–3

Hierarchical and autocratic communication networks. These structures are identical in terms of who can communicate to whom, as long as the direction of communication is ignored. The pattern on the left looks like a hierarchical structure, because we assume the man on top can communicate down easier than the others can communicate up.

A        B

*"Oh, I don't know—I just feel sort of **out** of things."*

by many of the subordinates to be the one in charge. Once this happens, he, in fact, does have considerable power. Unless the titular leader is able to reassert his own authority, the assistant will emerge as the real leader. In extreme cases, the "boss" may actually lose power completely.

Of course, this picture is somewhat exaggerated. Most of the time the top man retains leadership. Although formally his communications are restricted, actually he can communicate with anyone whenever he wants to. The intermediary merely saves him the trouble by relaying his messages. If the president of General Motors wanted to talk to anyone in the organization, he would pick up the nearest phone and tell whomever answered to connect him with the person he wanted. It is difficult to imagine the president's assistant saying that he could not reach this person. As long as a leader remains the duly constituted authority, he can ordinarily exercise that authority whenever he desires, including communicating freely with anyone subordinate to him.

However, the situation discussed above, in which the leader's assistant gradually takes over the leadership, is not merely a theoretical possibility that never occurs; it happens even in important positions. For example, observers have suggested that for many months after President Eisenhower had his heart attack while in office, his assistant Sherman Adams was making most of the decisions in the White House. And at times it seemed as if Kissinger, who talked to the press and met with many other political figures, had more power than Nixon who often kept himself isolated. One cannot lead unless he can communicate with his followers and they can communicate with him. Thus, one who can communicate freely, particularly when others cannot, is in a strong position to become the leader—and often does.

### Personal Characteristics of Leaders

Thus far in our discussion of the determination of leaders, we have been dealing with factors more or less external to the leader himself. What can we say about the personal characteristics of people who become leaders?

**Verbal Activity Level.** We have seen that people who talk freely and easily tend to be leaders. If we think of this ability as a personality factor, we could say that this is one of the most important qualities of a leader. A leader should not be shy—he must participate actively in the group. At least in small groups, extraversion, garrulousness (perhaps even glibness), high activity level, and assertiveness tend to characterize the leader.

**Status.** Some people are by nature more active than others in any circumstance. However, there are factors other than personality that tend to make someone more or less active and talkative. There is strong evidence, for example, that people of higher status talk more and have more influence than those of lower status. Strodtbeck, Simon, and Hawkins (1958) demonstrated this in a study in which people were selected from regular jury pools and asked to take part in mock trials. The participants listened to a recorded trial, debated, and returned a verdict—very much as in a real trial. After hearing the case, each jury chose a foreman. The members were given no criteria on which to base this choice—they were completely free to pick whomever they pleased.

For our purposes, the major results are the effects of the members' occupational status on the selection of the jury foremen and the amount of participation in the deliberations of high- and low-status people. As shown in Table 5–2, there was a strong tendency to select as foremen people of relatively high status. Proprietors (i.e., professionals, man-

Table 5-2

OCCUPATIONAL STATUS, PARTICIPATION, AND LEADERSHIP

| | PARTICIPATION[b] | | |
| Occupation | Elected Foreman[a] | Including Foreman | Omitting Foreman |
| --- | --- | --- | --- |
| Proprietor | 185 | 11.8 | 8.9 |
| Clerical | 100 | 9.2 | 7.0 |
| Skilled | 84 | 7.1 | 6.3 |
| Labor | 54 | 6.4 | 5.9 |

[a]Figures are the percentage of the expected value. A number greater than 100 indicates that members with that occupation were elected more than would be expected by chance.
[b]Figures are percentages of the total group participation. The figure expected by chance was 8.3.

Source: Adapted from Strodtbeck et al. (1958).

agers, officials, engineers, etc.) were chosen almost twice as often as would be expected by chance, whereas laborers (i.e., semiskilled workers, servants, nonfarm laborers, etc.) were chosen half as often as would be expected by chance. In addition, high-status jurors participated considerably more than low-status jurors. Proprietors had a participation score of 11.8, laborers of only 6.4, and the other groups fell in between. This finding holds even when the amount of participation by the foremen is eliminated—proprietors still score highest and laborers lowest. Even in a democratic situation such as a jury, socioeconomic status is an almost perfect predictor of participation in discussions.

Although it is somewhat difficult to separate the effects of status and personality because a person's personality may affect his choice of job, and vice versa, it appears that status is an important determinant of leadership. A high-status person is likely to become a leader even though his status derives from factors entirely extraneous to the group.

**Relation to the Rest of the Group.** Although a leader must be active and assertive, there is good reason to believe that he must also be not too different from the group. Particularly in small groups, members prefer their leader to be one of them—but the best of them. He may have higher status—but probably not much higher. In street corner gangs, the leaders apparently must share most of the values of the rest of the group—they must not take too independent a stand on anything; they must not be deviates. When they make decisions (and they often do), they must make the choices that most of the group would have made. They can have somewhat different ideas from the rest of the group and can lead the members into new activities and attitudes, but the ideas must not be too different nor the new activities too sudden. If they cease to be "one of the gang," they risk losing their leadership and may, in fact, cease to be a member of the group.

A group rarely chooses a leader who holds deviant views. In a study by Schachter (1951), groups were set up to discuss a variety of problems and several confederates were included in each group. One of the confederates (deviate) took a position on the first issue different from that taken by the rest of the group; another confederate (deviate-agreer) also took a deviant position but eventually changed so that he agreed with the group; and a third (agreer) agreed throughout. After the discussion, each group nominated members for the executive, steering, and correspondence committees, which varied in importance in that order. The executive committee was, in essence, the leadership branch of the government. The nominations for the deviate, deviate-agreer, and agreer are shown in Table 5–3. The confederate who took a consistently deviant position was nominated less often for the executive committee than anyone else. The confederate who began deviant and ended by agreeing was treated the same as the one who agreed all along. Thus, the group avoided making the deviate its leader but was willing to accept someone whom it could convince.

The tendency for a deviate not to be chosen as leader applies to characteristics other than opinions. People generally do not pick the one who is most outstanding or who is so independent that he would revolutionize the group. They tend to choose someone who would maintain the status quo and communicate easily with the rest of the group because he shares their values. However, the members do make distinctions among themselves and choose as leader someone who is outstanding.

Table 5–3

LIKING AND TREATMENT OF DEVIATE, CHANGER, AND NONDEVIATE

| Confederate | Liking[a] | Election to Executive Committee (Good)[b] | Election to Correspondence Committee (Bad)[b] |
|---|---|---|---|
| Deviate | 3.89 | −9.46 | 14.43 |
| Changer | 5.24 | 1.70 | 1.30 |
| Nondeviate | 5.53 | −2.69 | −6.92 |

[a]Figures are rankings of the confederate by the group members on a scale from 1 (lowest) to 9 (highest).
[b]Figures are percentages above and below expected by chance.

Source: Adapted from Schachter (1951).

Thus, the group does not want their leader to be too different from them, but neither do they want him to be an average group member.

The study conducted by Merei that we mentioned earlier provides some interesting insights into the relationship between the leader and the group. Merei formed groups of young boys and girls and let each group meet for thirty or forty minutes on several successive days. At the end of this time, all the groups had adopted various habits and traditions, as described on page 139. At this point, a somewhat older child who had previously shown evidence of being quite dominant, of having initiative, and of tending to be a leader was introduced into each group. The question was whether he would assume leadership of the already established group and, if so, how he would accomplish it.

The first finding was that, by and large, the new member was unable to change the traditions of the group. Many tried, but eventually they had to accept these traditions themselves. In this sense, the new member proved weaker than the group. This does not mean that no one can ever enter a group and change it to fit his own values—this does occur sometimes with strong leaders and relatively weak groups. But in most cases, once a group has established some norms, these norms are resistant to change; someone who wishes to become the leader of such a group must, to some extent, accept the established system.

Despite this, most of the new members did manage to become the leaders of their respective groups. They were, after all, older and stronger than any of the individual members and therefore would be expected to play somewhat central roles in the groups. Although they were not able to change existing patterns or initiate many new activities, they were looked to as leaders, did make some decisions, and were more influential than any other single member. One way they attained their positions was to give orders that were in line with the traditions of the group. Instead of telling the members to do something new or different, the new leaders ordered them to do what they would have done anyway. If they knew at some point that the groups would begin playing with blocks, they said, "Okay, let's play with blocks now." Then, when the groups were about to stop, they said, "Let's stop now." And so on. Since these orders were consistent with what the groups wanted to do, they obeyed them. After a while, they looked to the new leader to see what they should do. He became their spokesman. He still continued to give orders consistent with group traditions in order to maintain his position, but in a sense he had become the leader.

Many leaders operate this way. Certainly successful politicians often attempt to discover what the people want and then come out in favor of it. In one sense, this seems dishonest since the politician is saying what he thinks the people want to hear rather than what he believes. In another sense, leaders are supposed to represent their constituency and this is one way to do it. The key point is that any leader must agree with his followers on most issues if he is to have any lasting power. Once he has achieved support he can express some deviant views and perhaps then influence the opinions of the others. Ideally, of course, the leader's attitudes should generally agree with the group's so that he can be honest and still be an effective leader.

Other than these relatively few pieces of information, we know little about the personality of leaders. There is some suggestion that leaders are more intelligent, more flexible, better adjusted, and perhaps more interpersonally sensitive than other members of groups. These variables, however, have relatively small effects. Someone who had them all would be somewhat more likely to be a leader than someone who had none of them, but they do not make a big difference. Some other factors we have mentioned seem to be more important. Leaders usually are more active, more talkative, more assertive, and not too different from the groups they lead.

Psychologists are still puzzled about the quality that is often described in the literature and elsewhere as "the ability to lead" or, more forcefully, as "charisma." Just what, if anything, this consists of is yet to be detailed by controlled research. It does seem that some people make outstanding, forceful leaders and that the few qualities we have mentioned do not fully account for their ability. It may be that they simply have all the right qualities in large amounts, or it may be something additional. At the moment, we do not know.

**EFFECTS OF STRUCTURE ON GROUP PERFORM- ANCE**

Let us now consider the effects of various aspects of a group's organization and structure on how it functions. As discussed above, many groups are so structured that there are certain limitations on communication. These limitations can take the form of poor communication—members are free to talk to each other but what they say may not get through—or actual restrictions—certain members are unable to talk to others. Both types of limitation affect a group's performance. In addition, there are different types of leaders. The style of leadership in a particular group is a major determinant of its performance.

### Communication and Performance

As might be expected, the ability to communicate plays an important role in determining the performance of a group. To begin with, it seems clear that anything that interferes with communication among group members would hurt group performance. As we shall see below, it is not always necessary or even desirable for all group members to be able to communicate directly with one another. But if communication between two members is permitted, any ambiguities or restrictions in that communication—irrelevant noises, static, etc.—have serious interfering effects. Obviously, if two members are trying to talk to each other and have trouble understanding each other's messages, they are unable to operate effectively.

Furthermore, if there is static in the system, it is crucial for the member who is sending a message to be able to get feedback from the recipient. Without feedback, member A can never be sure his message got through—he can only hope that B received it intact. Thus, A does not know whether he should repeat the message or go on to others. If the first message did get through, repeating it might confuse the situation. But if it did not get through and A does not repeat it, that piece of information is not available to B. If B can respond to A, this ambiguity is immediately removed—A can repeat the message until he is sure B understands it. When the lines of communication are freer, feedback is considerably less important, because A can be quite confident his message was received even without it. Thus, both clarity of message and the possibility of feedback are important, and feedback is particularly crucial when the messages themselves are not clear.

Knowledge that the other person has heard and understood is sometimes called *secondary information*, because it is data about the transmission of other data. An example of the importance of secondary information is provided by the "hot line" between Washington and Moscow, by which the President of the United States and the Premier of the Soviet Union can call each other directly. One of the primary purposes of these calls is for each to make clear to the other what he is planning to do. For example, during the June, 1967, war between Israel and the Arabs, many such calls were supposedly made, with both men making it clear that they were not planning to intervene in the war. At one point, the United States scrambled some planes to protect an American ship, and the President immediately called the Russian Premier to explain why the planes were in the air and to assure him that they were not engaged in the war.

Thus, the "hot line" is a fast, efficient means of communication that enables each side to know what the other is doing. But one of the problems in setting it up was that the President and the Premier speak different languages and must communicate through interpreters. This introduced difficulty in ascertaining that the messages got through as intended. Clear feedback was needed—it was provided by allowing the two interpreters to hear each other's translations. If the President said, for example. "Our planes are not attacking Cairo," the American translator would listen to the Russian translation so that he would know exactly what the Premier heard. If the American thought the translation was incorrect, he could ask the President to clarify his statement to avoid the wrong meaning, innuendo, or connotation. The critical aspect of the "hot line" is that each man knows when the other has misunderstood him or heard the wrong message and is free to correct the communication until it is understood. In this way, possibly fatal misunderstandings can be avoided, or at least minimized.

The importance of secondary information can also be seen in confrontations between groups in our society, such as school administrators and students, or blacks and whites. In a typical situation, black students might ask administrators of a university to admit more minority group students. What the blacks are really asking for, however, is more complicated—they want a minority group member to be involved in admissions and they want to have a part in running the university. But the white administrators think that all the students want is for more blacks to be admitted. Both the blacks and the administrators think the administrators have understood. Then, when a program for admitting more black students through the normal admissions procedure is inaugurated, the administrators are surprised and upset that the black students feel they have been tricked because the old admissions procedures were used. Actually, neither side fully understood the other and did not know that they misunderstood. If either side had known, they could have asked for clarification and avoided unnecessary conflicts.

### Communication Networks and Performance

As we have noted, various kinds of communication patterns produce corresponding patterns of power and decision-making ability. The person at the center of the wheel, for example, is generally considered to be the leader of the group, and he is obviously in the best position to make decisions and see that the rest of the group agrees with them. Conversely, the circle structure, in which each person can talk only to his two neighbors, has decentralized communication and leadership. Thus, a highly centralized communication network produces a group with strong centralized leadership and power.

The evidence on how these different kinds of networks affect group performance is not entirely consistent, but most of the data suggests that centralized groups are more effective when the group is working on simple problems, whereas decentralized groups are effective with more complex problems. In some studies, each member of a group was given a card with a number of geometric symbols written on it, and the group's task was to discover which symbol was on all the cards. The solution was essentially trivial—the problem was to get all the information in one place as quickly as possible. This problem is ideally suited to groups with highly centralized communication networks, in which all the information can be quickly given to one person. And as might be expected, they did better than decentralized groups on this type of problem. The leader simply collected the messages from the group members and discovered which symbol they all had.

In other studies, groups were given problems requiring a series of fairly complicated arithmetic manipulations. In order to solve this kind of problem efficiently, each group member should work on part of the problem by himself, at least one other member should check his solution, and all the information should be combined. The evidence suggests that decentralized groups are more effective on this kind of problem than are centralized groups.

The findings can be seen to be due to several different effects of decentralization. On one hand, the more decentralized a group is, the less efficient it is in distributing information. The centralized group can quickly transmit all the information to the leader, who can then, if necessary, redistribute it to the members, also quite efficiently. The decentralized group is less well organized for distribution of information; it must expend more effort and almost always must send more messages than the centralized group. Thus, because the centralized group provides more efficient, faster, and clearer communications, to the extent that transmission of information is necessary to arrive at a solution, the centralized group should be superior.

The centralized group also has fewer distractions. As we shall see in Chapter 6, one of the characteristics of almost all groups is that they tend to be distracting. Since ordinarily not everyone need know everything in order for a group to solve a problem, many of the communications in decentralized groups are unnecessary distractions. The less free the communications, the fewer there are; and the fewer the people involved in decisions, the less distractions there are. The centralized group has less total communication and fewer members participating in decisions. Thus, it has the additional advantage of being less distracting, so to the extent that concentration is important, it should be superior to a decentralized group.

On the other hand, the motivation of the group members is also critical. Members of decentralized groups tend to be happier and more satisfied with their positions and to like the group more. As we noted earlier, satisfaction and morale are directly related to an individual's freedom of communication and his sense of participating actively in group decisions. Members who can communicate freely (e.g., the central member in the wheel or any member of the circle) are more satisfied; those who can communicate least tend to be least happy in the group. Therefore, the structure of the wheel produces the least overall satisfaction and the decentralized structure of the circle produces the most. The lower morale in the centralized groups tends to result in less production because the members work less hard. Thus, from this point of view, the decentralized group should be more effective.

The relative effectiveness of the various types of groups depends, therefore, on how important each of these factors is in a particular context. When a group is faced with a simple problem that primarily involves passing information from one member to another and performing easy operations on it, efficiency of communication and lack of distractions are normally the most important factors. In such cases, the centralized group is superior. When the problem is more complex and involves difficult operations or requires more intimate cooperation among group members, the morale of the individuals and their ability to communicate freely are more important, so the decentralized group performs better.

A somewhat different interpretation of the data is that the critical factor underlying the performance differences among groups with the various kinds of communication networks is the relative difficulty of organization. A group that is disorganized and has not yet worked out an efficient operating procedure obviously would do less well than one that is organized. And the simpler the group's communication structure, the simpler it is to organize. For example, the wheel is an exceedingly simple structure that allows only one reasonable organization. A group with this structure should find its organization easy to determine. In contrast, the circle and a group with no restrictions on communication (usually called an all-channel structure) are more complex and allow a variety of organizations. These groups have greater difficulties in setting up organizations. The effect of organization is most marked with simple problems for which a solution depends almost exclusively on the efficient passing of information, whereas group organization is relatively unimportant in solving complex problems for which a solution depends on considerable individual effort and a more creative combination of information.

Evidence for the organizational interpretation of the effect of communication networks on group performance comes from a study by Guetzkow and Simon (1955). The first and most important finding is that group differences in performance on simple tasks tend to disappear with time. After twenty trials the all-channel and wheel groups no longer differed; and although the circle groups continued to be somewhat less productive, the difference declined. Detailed analysis of the group organizations showed that by twenty trials, the all-channel groups had worked out an organization but the circle groups had not yet settled on one.

Another piece of relevant evidence is that the degree of organization was highly correlated with group performance. The groups that had organized satisfactorily did not differ in performance, regardless of their original structure. Well-organized wheel groups were no faster than well-organized all-channel or circle groups. The only difference was that most of the all-channel groups had not become well organized until after at least ten trials and very few of the circle groups had produced a good organization even after twenty trials. Presumably, with more time, all the groups would settle on a good organization and then none would differ in performance. Nevertheless, the circle groups were harder to organize than the wheel groups; under many circumstances, circles might never achieve good centralized organization. Thus, although the structure of the groups did not fully determine their final organization, it did have an important effect. The more centralized the communication network, the more centralized was the final organization. This means that a group can overcome a particular structure, but there will still be some tendency for groups with less centralized structures to remain less centralized. Although the effect of communication networks is most apparent at the beginning of a group's meetings, to some extent it continues throughout the life of a group—unless for some reason the group overcomes the initial structure and imposes a different organization on itself.

Although most of the research on communication networks has been conducted in the laboratory, where communication has been artificially restricted, these kinds of communication networks often play an important role in real groups in our society. For example, university communities vary greatly in their freedom of communication. Some have highly restricted communication networks, which might be called wheel-within-wheel structures. The top members of the administration talk only to one another and to their immediate subordinates, who, in turn, talk only to one another and their subordinates, and so on. In addition, the administration talks only to the most senior faculty members, who talk to the junior faculty, who talk to the students. Thus, the junior faculty forms the only link with the students. The students, in turn, are free to talk only to one another and to the junior faculty but not to senior faculty or administrators. This structure is probably quite efficient in certain respects, but morale is low and dissatisfaction is high. At present, however, most universities are moving toward less centralized structures, in which everyone is relatively free to talk to everyone else. This seems to lead to higher morale and to the feeling that everyone is participating in running the university, but it produces more distractions and is probably less efficient in handling straightforward problems. When everyone can take part in making simple decisions, it is difficult to make them quickly. Thus, this change to a more open communication structure has resulted in somewhat slower action on minor problems but increased satisfaction and more creative solutions to complex, important problems.

### Type of Leader and Performance

There has been a considerable amount of discussion in the literature about the relative effectiveness of different types of leadership. In particular, psychologists have tried to compare the so-called democratic and authoritarian types of leadership. A democratic leader allows the group as a whole to make decisions, to choose the jobs they want to do; he generally issues few orders and serves primarily as a guide or chairman. In contrast, the authoritarian leader makes most of the decisions himself, issues a great many orders, and is generally a commander of the group.

Part of the interest in the effectiveness of these two types of leaders stems from their correspondence to democratic and nondemocratic political organizations and societies. Of course, the effectiveness of leaders is also important in maximizing the efficiency of any group—in business, in government, and so on.

In a well known study, Lippitt and White (1943) assigned adult leaders, who behaved in either a democratic or an authoritarian manner, to groups of ten-year-old boys. The authoritarian leaders determined all policy, dictated the techniques and activities of the groups in such a way that future steps were uncertain, often assigned the particular work task and work companion of each member, tended to be personal in their praise and criticism of the work of each member, and remained aloof from active group participation. With democratic leadership, all policies were discussed by the group, the complete plan of action was detailed in advance, members were free to work with whomever they chose and on the task they desired, and the leaders were objective in their praise and criticism and tried to be regular group members in spirit. In a third condition, there were laissez-faire leaders, who allowed the group complete freedom and did not really act as leaders at all.

The findings of this study are somewhat mixed. There was some tendency for the quantity of work to be greatest in the autocratic groups and least in the laissez-faire groups. The motivation to work, however, seemed to be stronger in the democratic groups than in either of the other types. There was more aggression as well as more discontent expressed in the autocratic groups, and the members of the democratic groups seemed to be happier and more self-reliant than those in the autocratic groups.

It should be noted that this study has many important limitations. The leaders were imposed on the groups rather than elected by them and, perhaps more important, were adults whereas the group members were children. The groups were informal and not designed primarily to work on specific problems. In addition, the leaders were not free to provide the best possible kind of authoritarian or democratic leadership— they had to follow fairly strict patterns, which may or may not have been the most efficient for the given kind of leadership. For these and other reasons, the results are interesting but can be considered only suggestive.

An extensive series of studies by Fred Fiedler (1958, 1964) provided additional information on the effects of differing styles of leadership. He distinguished between two kinds of leaders on the basis of a personality test, in which the essential element was the individual's feelings toward the other members of the group. The key factor was how much esteem the leader felt for the group member he liked least. Stated somewhat differently, the test measured the minimum amount of esteem he felt for anyone in the group. Thus, the test was called the least preferred coworker, or LPC, scale.

Someone high on this scale tends, in Fiedler's words, "to see even a poorer coworker in a relatively favorable manner." A low LPC leader, on the other hand, perceives "his least preferred coworker in a highly unfavorable, rejecting manner." More generally, high LPC leaders are permissive, passive, and considerate; they are more relaxed, friendlier, more compliant, less directive, and tend to reduce the group members' anxiety. Low LPC leaders are controlling, active, and structuring; they are less tolerant of irrelevant comments, produce less pleasant relationships within the group, are highly directive, and tend to induce anxiety. It can be seen that high and low LPC leaders tend to correspond to certain aspects of democratic and authoritarian leadership respectively.

A concerted attempt has been made to specify in detail the kinds of situations in which each type of leader is most effective. Although the research has not yet produced definitive answers, there are some findings in which we can have considerable confidence. Under most circumstances, a low LPC leader is more effective when the task is highly structured. With such a task, it is important to assign roles to individual members, to divide the work, and, in general, to organize efficiently. Interactions among the members, discussions, and interchange of ideas are relatively unimportant because the problem is straightforward. The low LPC leader is successful because he knows what has to be done and the main problem is getting it done. Moreover, the rest of the group tends not to resent this kind of leader in this case, because his instructions increase efficiency and make the task easier for everyone. The one instance in which the situation does not hold is when the prior relationship between the leader and the group members is poor. Then, the group seems to react negatively to being ordered around and tends to be less efficient than it would be with the relatively warm, high LPC leader.

With unstructured tasks, the relationship is somewhat less clear. The strong, assertive, low LPC leaders also seem to do well in many unstructured situations. The exception is when the initial relations between the group and the leader are good but the leader's position is weak. This could be caused by a variety of factors, such as rotating leadership or the fact that the appointed leader was of lower status than the rest of the members. Under these conditions, a low LPC leader does quite poorly, for although the group likes him, they are unwilling to accept strong leadership from someone in a weak position.

These studies demonstrate that the most effective kind of leadership depends on a variety of factors in the situation. The relations between the group and the leader, the degree of structure in the task, and the strength of the leader's position play vital roles. Although the low LPC leader does tend to be more effective in a majority of the situations, there are some in which he is less effective. Thus, no overall statement can be made about the kind of leadership that is best. Future research may enable us to determine exactly which situations favor each kind of leadership, and it is likely that many other aspects of the leader's personality will also be important.

*CHAPTER REVIEW*

1. Communication patterns within groups.
2. The emergence of a leader as a crucial and almost universal factor in groups.
3. The distinction between a social leader and a task leader.
4. A leader's legitimacy affects his power.
5. Communication as an important determinant of leadership.
6. Personal determinants of leadership.
7. The performance of the group as affected by communication patterns and group structure.
8. Type of leadership affects group behavior.

*APPLICATIONS AND SPECULATIONS*

1. Radical groups in our society such as the "new left," SDS, etc., seem to favor decisions made in town meetings, in which everyone has a voice, rather than leadership by elected officers. It has been suggested that this emphasis on participation is to some extent due to feelings of powerlessness that are one of the motivations for the formation of the radical groups in the first place. Why might this be so?
2. "Leaders are born, not made." Discuss this in light of the current phenomenon of American politics that actors, astronauts, and athletic stars are elected to important public offices and in light of the observation that in baseball, infielders are more likely than outfielders to become managers.
3. Although the American and English governments are often considered quite similar, they do differ in important respects. The United States President is elected directly and has essentially all the power in the

executive branch of government. In contrast, the English Prime Minister runs for Parliament just as any other member and is then elected by his party. In addition, the other members of the English cabinet have a great deal of power on their own that is to some extent independent of the Prime Minister. Finally, party discipline (i.e., pressure on the party members to go along with the leadership) is much greater in England than in the United States. How would all or any of these differences affect the governments of the two countries?

## SUGGESTIONS FOR ADDITIONAL READING

### Articles

Bavelas, A., Hastorf, A. H., Gross, A. E., and Kite, W. R. Experiments on the alteration of group structure. *Journal of Experimental Social Psychology*, 1965, *1*, 55–70.

Leavitt, H. J. Some effects of certain communication patterns on group performance. *Journal of Abnormal and Social Psychology*, 1951, *46*, 38–50.

### Books and Longer Discussions

Fiedler, F. E. A contingency model of leadership effectiveness. In L. Berkowitz (Ed.), *Advances in experimental social psychology*. Vol. 1. New York: Academic, 1964. Pp. 150–90.

Machiavelli, N. *The prince*. Originally published in 1513, many paperback editions are currently available.

Whyte, W. H., Jr. *The organization man*. New York: Simon & Schuster, 1956.

# group dynamics

Someone is sitting alone in a room working on simple mathematical problems. He works steadily and makes a reasonable amount of progress. Then someone else comes into the room and begins to work on similar problems. The two people do not know each other; they do not talk to each other; they have little or nothing in common. Yet the presence of the second person has a profound effect on the first one—he begins to work harder, to solve the problems more quickly, and, in general, to be more productive. Merely having someone else in the room has increased the effectiveness of his work.

Three hundred people are having dinner in a restaurant. Suddenly there are cries of fire, and smoke begins pouring out of the kitchen. The crowd rushes for the exits and the first lucky few escape. But there are too many people trying to get through the narrow doorways. They block one another's progress so that no one can get through. The bodies pile up at the doorways within easy reach of safety.

A young black man is in a Southern jail, accused of raping a white girl. There is no evidence against him except that he was in the general vicinity of the crime. A crowd gathers outside the jail, builds up, and gets more and more excited and enraged. Members of the crowd start talk of lynching and before long the crowd has turned into an angry mob. It rushes the jail, breaks down the doors, and drags the prisoner from his cell. He is tortured and killed in a sadistic orgy of violence.

A large advertising company is trying to devise a new campaign for selling soap. The eight executives working on the account have been thinking about the problem separately for several weeks. Then they decide to have a brainstorming session. They all get together in a big, comfortable office to discuss their ideas. No one criticizes anyone, everyone is urged to say anything that could be helpful. They all talk freely and accumulate a large number of ideas. Afterward they feel they have accomplished a great deal they could not have done alone.

These examples are representative of the kinds of effects groups have on their members. People are stimulated and distracted by being in a group. They respond to a wide variety of group norms and pressures. Being in a group or just in the presence of other people causes an individual to behave and think differently from when he is alone. This chapter concerns the effects of groups and the processes by which they are produced.

**SOCIAL FACILITATION IN A MINIMAL SOCIAL SITUATION**　For a long time it has been reported that people perform tasks better when they are in the presence of others than when they are alone. Although, as we shall see, not every kind of performance is improved, this effect—so-called social facilitation—occurs on a wide variety of tasks. A number of studies conducted at Harvard by Allport (1920, 1924) used five different tasks ranging from simple and trivial (crossing out all the vowels in a newspaper column) to somewhat more difficult (performing easy multiplications) and finally to fairly complex (writing refutations of a logical argument). On all of these, performance was better when there were five people in the room than when there was only one, even though in all cases the participants worked individually. Dashiell (1930) replicated these results; Travis (1925) found facilitation on a pursuit-rotor task; and many recent experiments (e.g., Zajonc and Sales, 1966; Martens, 1969; etc.) have demonstrated the social facilitation effect.

Remarkably, the phenomenon is not limited to humans. Chen (1937) compared the amount of sand dug by ants when they were alone or in pairs or in groups of three. He found that groups of two and three did not differ appreciably but in both conditions the ants dug more than three times as much sand per ant as they did when the animals were alone. It is also worth noting that pairs of rats copulated less when there was a single pair in the cage than when there were three pairs (Larsson, 1956). Thus for many different species and a number of different behaviors, the presence of another member of the species has been shown to improve performance over that which occurs when an individual is alone.

Despite these impressive findings, it has become clear that under some circumstances the social facilitation effect does not occur and in fact the presence of others can interfere with performance. In Allport's study (1924), subjects in the group condition wrote more refutations of the logical argument, but the quality of these refutations was lower than when the individuals were alone. Pessin (1933) found that the presence of a spectator reduced performance on a memory task, and Dashiell (1930) showed that there were more errors made in simple multiplications when there was an audience. Recent research has also found that subjects in groups perform less well on certain kinds of tasks (which we will discuss in a moment) than they do when they are alone (e.g., Cottrell, Rittle, and Wack, 1967). This same inconsistent pattern holds for other animals. Cockroaches (Gates and Allee, 1933), parakeets (Allee and Masure, 1936), and green finches (Klopfer, 1958) all performed less well in groups than when alone. Thus, although the majority of the findings do demonstrate a social facilitation effect, there is a substantial body of evidence indicating that under some circumstances the presence of others can actually interfere with performance. How can these diverse results be explained?

Zajonc (1965, 1966) made a very interesting proposal which accounted for virtually all of these diverse results. He suggested that being in the presence of another individual causes a person's drive or motivation to be increased, and this increased drive should sometimes facilitate performance and sometimes interfere with it. It is well established that high drive tends to improve performance on simple tasks in which the correct response is well known and dominant, but tends to hurt performance on more complex tasks for which the correct response is not dominant, or on learning tasks. Cancelling the vowels in a newspaper, doing simple arithmetic, learning a simple list of words, or performing any other easy, repetitive tasks should be facilitated by an increase in drive level. In contrast, difficult arithmetic problems, complex logical deductions, memorizing a difficult list of words, or performing any other complicated tasks should be inhibited by increased drive. Although it is sometimes difficult to determine which group a particular task falls into, most of the findings seem to fit this formulation quite well. Allport's tasks were relatively simple and he found a social facilitation effect. The one exception was the quality of the logical refutations, which is presumably a very complex task and should be performed less well with an audience. Digging sand and copulating are both fairly simple tasks for ants and rats respectively and are also highly dominant behaviors. Both were facilitated by the presence of other members of the species. Learning a maze is a difficult task for cockroaches and parakeets, and they did less well in the presence of others.

More recent research has been designed specifically to test this explanation. In an experiment by Cottrell, Rittle, and Wack (1967), subjects learned a list of word pairs either alone or in the presence of two other students. Some of the lists were designed to be easy and others to be quite difficult. The easy lists pairs were composed of words that have the same meaning or tend to be associated with each other, for example, adept–skillful and barren–fruitless. The other list's pairs were items that had no meaning in common and accordingly had weak associations, for example, arid–grouchy and dessert–leading.

Of course, the difficult list would be harder to learn under any circumstances, but we are primarily interested in the effect of the social situation on learning. The results show that the easy list was learned somewhat better when there was an audience than when the subject worked alone, whereas the difficult list was learned much slower when an audience was present. The presence of other people improved performance on the simple task where the correct responses were dominant, and inhibited performance on the difficult task where the correct responses were not strong to begin with.

Another study (Zajonc et al., 1969) tested this interpretation using cockroaches as subjects. High drive is expected to improve performance when the correct behavior is the dominant response, but interfere with performance when correct behavior is not dominant. In this study, cockroaches either alone or in pairs had to escape from a light by running down a straight alley or by learning a simple maze. In the alley, the dominant response would help the animals escape, but in the maze it would interfere. As shown in Table 6–1, the roaches did worse in the maze when they were in pairs, but did better in the runway—apparently being with another animal did increase drive and therefore strengthen the dominant response. A second study by the same authors demonstrated this effect even when the roach was by himself in the runway or maze but was being observed by other roaches nearby.

Hunt and Hillery conducted a study similar to Zajonc's but used humans as subjects. Once again the task was to learn a maze which was easy or difficult either alone or in company. The results of the experiment are presented in Table 6–1. They are almost identical to previous results obtained from experiments with rats. People learn the easy maze faster when other people are present but the difficult maze is learned faster alone.

Table 6–1

THE EFFECT OF AN AUDIENCE AND TASK DIFFICULTY ON PERFORMANCE OF COCKROACHES AND HUMANS

|  | EASY TASK | | HARD TASK | |
| --- | --- | --- | --- | --- |
|  | *Alone* | *Audience* | *Alone* | *Audience* |
| Cockroaches[a] | 40.48 | 32.96 | 110.45 | 129.46 |
| Humans[b] | 44.67 | 36.19 | 184.91 | 220.33 |

[a]Data on cockroaches adapted from Zajonc et al. (1969).
[b]Data on humans adapted from Hunt and Hillery (1972).

The research thus offers strong support for Zajonc's hypothesis that the presence of others arouses drive. There is some question, however, as to exactly what kind of drive it is and the specific conditions that are necessary to produce the effect. It seems likely that at least for humans the presence of other people tends to arouse feelings of competition and also concerns about being evaluated. People tend to interpret virtually every social situation as competitive. As we shall see below, they compete with each other in a simple game even though they know they would win more by cooperating. When two people are in a room, each may feel competitive with the other even when there is no explicit reason to feel so. They may think that there is an implied competition, that someone is comparing their performances, or that the other person is competing with them. Even ruling out these possibilities, the individual may compare his performance with the other person and want to do better, thus providing some sort of internal competition which does not depend on what the other person does.

Another perhaps more important motive that tends to be aroused by the presence of others is concern about being evaluated. When someone else is in the room, there is always the possibility that he is judging you. He may be looking at your appearance, your behavior, or your performance on a particular task. The other person may actually be totally unconcerned with you, but there is a tendency to assume that he is to some extent evaluating you. This concern about evaluation raises the drive level of the individual and produces the kinds of effects we have reported.

A number of studies have provided support for the notion that apprehension about evaluation is a crucial element in the situation. In one study (Cottrell et al., 1968), subjects performed either alone, with others, or with others who were wearing blindfolds. When the other subjects constituted an audience, dominant responses were increased over the alone condition. But when the other subjects wore blindfolds the performance did not differ from the alone condition. Although this is a somewhat strange situation, it does make it clear that the mere presence of others is not sufficient to produce the effect—the others must in some way be able to see or interact with the individual.

Two other studies provided more direct support for this idea. Henschy and Glass (1968) compared situations in which subjects thought they were being evaluated with others in which nothing was said about evaluation. Whenever subjects expected to be evaluated, the typical facilitation of dominant responses was observed. When no evaluation was expected, there was a much smaller difference between an alone condition and one in which nonevaluating spectators were present.

Paulus and Murdoch (1971) conducted a similar study and found the facilitation effect only when evaluation was expected, with no difference between the alone and the spectator conditions.

At the moment it seems safe to say that the presence of others under most circumstances increases drive which produces facilitation on simple tasks and interference on certain complex tasks. It seems likely that concern about evaluation is the dominant drive aroused, but there is also good reason to think that feelings of competition are also aroused under certain conditions.

Although the arousal of drive is probably the most important mechanism activated by the presence of other people, another aspect of the minimal situation is that other people are usually somewhat distracting. When an individual works alone in a room, it is quiet (or perhaps some music is playing) and there is little to attend to except his work. Another person working in the same room may shift around in his chair, chew on a pencil, breathe heavily, and so on. Suddenly, there is much more going on in the room and more to attend to; it becomes difficult to devote full attention to the work. A good example of this is a college library. At certain times, it is an almost ideal place to study. There are empty tables to work on and little noise or activity. But just before an exam period, it is very crowded. The other people talk, move around, sit close together, bump against chairs, etc. Under these circumstances, the presence of others is so distracting that performance is less efficient than if one were alone.

Evidence indicates that distractions caused by others are most annoying when one is trying to learn something new. Learning new material requires concentration on external stimuli (e.g., contents of a book), and extraneous external stimuli interfere with that concentration. When taking an exam instead of studying for one, external distractions are less bothersome—the material is already known and the ability to recall it is relatively unaffected.

Thus distraction should produce the same kinds of effects we would expect from the arousal of competitive or evaluation concerns. There is some research that indicates that distraction is a considerably less important factor in the situation, but under some circumstances it probably does contribute to the effects that are produced by the presence of other people. The effect depends largely on the task. If the task is familiar and reasonably simple, the increased motivation is generally more important than the distraction, so performance improves. If the task is unfamiliar and difficult, both motivation and distraction have adverse effects, so performance decreases. And if the task entails learning something new, the distraction is particularly harmful to performance.

COMPETI-
TION
VERSUS
COOPERA-
TION

In our discussion of social facilitation in a minimal social situation we have been assuming that the people involved are not interacting directly but are merely in the same place at the same time. When they are not members of the same group but do interact, people often have the choice of cooperating or competing. In most card and board games, one person's gain is another's loss. If you win a pot in poker, the other players lose. In Monopoly, if you land on Boardwalk with a hotel, you lose $2000 and someone else is that much richer. These are called zero-sum games because all the wins and losses add to zero, but in many real life situations, one side's gains need not be offset by the other's losses. They can both win or both lose. Whenever this is true, it is referred to as a non-zero-sum game (the total of gains and losses do not add to zero). In such a game, whether it involves interpersonal relationships, a business deal, or conflicts between nations, the players can cooperate to maximize their total gains or can compete. What determines their actions?

It might be thought that people would behave in all cases so as to maximize their rewards. If getting the most out of a situation meant cooperating, they would cooperate; if it meant competing, they would compete. As we shall see, this is not the case. Regardless of the complications in any situation, deal, or game, it is generally possible to specify the strategy that would produce the most profit. Mathematicians have developed what is called *game theory*—a mathematical analysis of games —which can be applied to complicated as well as simple games and which, in many cases, can tell an individual what he should do at each step in order to maximize his winnings. Game theory is an interesting and, in some contexts, useful exercise, but it is not applicable to our problem because people do not always follow ideal strategies. Even when it is obvious that cooperation is the best strategy, many, if not most, people compete rather than cooperate. The question, then, is not what is the best strategy, but what factors increase or decrease the tendency to compete.

Deutsch and Krauss (1960) conducted a classic experiment on this problem, in which pairs of subjects engaged in a simple game. Each subject was asked to imagine that she was running a trucking company (either the Acme or the Bold Company) and had to get a truck from one point to another as quickly as possible. The two trucks were not in competition; they had different starting points and different destinations. There was, however, one hitch—the fastest route for both converged at one point to a one-lane road, and they had to go in opposite directions. This is diagramed in Figure 6–1. The only way both could use the road would be for one of them to wait until the other had passed through. If either truck entered the road, the other could not use it; and if they both

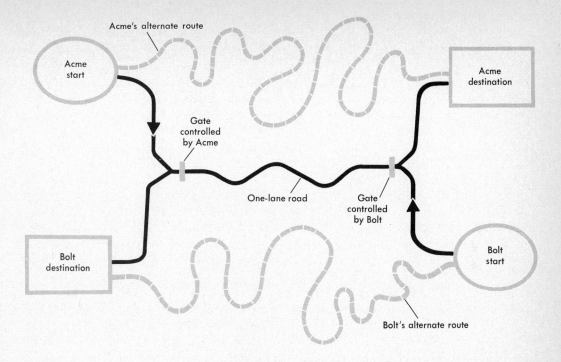

**Figure 6–1**

Road map of the trucking game. The players must get their truck to its destination as quickly as possible. Although they can do this efficiently only by cooperating and sharing the one-lane road, they often compete, particularly when gates are provided. (Deutsch, M., and Krauss, R. M., "The effect of threat on interpersonal bargaining," *Journal of Abnormal and Social Psychology*, 1960, *61*, p. 183. Copyright 1960 by the American Psychological Association, and reproduced by permission.)

entered the road, neither of them could move at all until one had backed up. In addition, each player had a gate across the direct route that he could raise by pressing a button. The gate prevented the road from being used. Each truck was provided with an alternate route that did not conflict with the other's, but the alernate was much longer; in fact, the game was set up so that taking the alternate route was guaranteed to lose points, whereas taking the direct route would gain points for both sides, even if they alternated at the one-lane section of the road. The players were told that their goal was to earn as many points as possible for themselves; nothing was said about earning more points than the other player.

The results of this experiment are quite striking. It was clear to the participants that the optimal strategy was to cooperate by alternating in

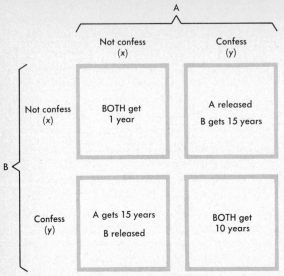

A

|  | Not confess (x) | Confess (y) |
|---|---|---|
| Not confess (x) | BOTH get 1 year | A released B gets 15 years |
| Confess (y) | A gets 15 years B released | BOTH get 10 years |

B

Figure 6–2

Prototype of Prisoner's Dilemma game. Two prisoners have the choice of confessing or not confessing. If they trust and support each other by not confessing, each receives a light sentence; if they both confess, they receive relatively heavy sentences; and if one confesses and the other does not, the former is released while the latter gets a very heavy sentence. The dilemma is that if either one has complete trust in the other, he would do best by being untrustworthy himself and confessing.

using the one-lane road. In this way, they could both use the direct route and one would be delayed only a few seconds while the other was getting through: Despite this, there was little cooperation between the players. Instead of allowing each other to use the one-lane road, they fought for its use, raised their gates, and both of them ended up losing points. In a typical trial, both sides would try to use the road and would meet in the middle head on. They would stubbornly stay there for a while, each refusing to retreat. The players might laugh nervously or make nasty comments. Finally, one of them would back up, erect the barrier, and use the alternate route. On the next trial, they would do the same thing. And so it went. An occasional cooperative trial might be interspersed, but most of them were competitive.

The tendency to compete is not due to the particular characteristics of the trucking game. It also occurs in other non-zero-sum games, such as one that is known as the Prisoner's Dilemma because it is based on a problem faced by two suspects at a police station. The district attorney thinks they have both committed a crime but does not have proof against either one. The prisoners are put into separate rooms and told that they have two alternatives—to confess or not to confess. If neither of them confesses, they could not be convicted of the major crime, but the district attorney tells them he could get them convicted of minor crimes and that they would both receive minor punishments. If they both confess, they will be convicted of the major crime, but the district attorney says he would ask for leniency for them. But if one of them confesses and the other does not, the confessor would be freed because he has helped the state, whereas the other suspect would get the maximum penalty. The situation is diagramed in Figure 6–2.

Obviously there is a conflict. If one suspect thinks his partner is going to confess, it is essential for him to confess also; on the other hand, the best outcome for both of them is for neither to confess and then for both to take the minor sentences. Thus, if the suspects trust each other, they should not confess and would do quite well. However, if one suspect trusts his partner and is convinced he will not confess, the first would do even better to confess and in that way be freed.

We do not know what real prisoners would do under these circumstances. In research on the problem, much of the drama is removed but the game is basically similar. Instead of playing for their freedom, subjects play for points or money. They play in pairs but usually are not allowed to talk to each other. Each player has a choice of two strategies, and each player's payoff depends both on what he does and on what his partner does. The exact pattern of payoffs varies—a typical one is shown in Figure 6–3. If both A and B choose *X*, they each get 10 points; if A chooses *X* and B chooses *Y*, the former loses 15 and the latter wins 15; and if both choose *Y*, they both lose 5. In other words, they can cooperate (choose *X*) and both win, or they can compete (one or both choosing *Y*) and try to win a lot but risk losing.

The players are told that they are supposed to score as many points as they can. It is clear to virtually all of them that the way to have the highest score is for both to select *X* (the cooperative choice) on every trial. But just as with the trucking game, there is a strong tendency for them to compete. In a typical game, only about a third of the choices are

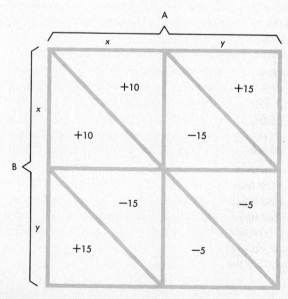

Figure 6–3

Typical Prisoner's Dilemma game matrix. The top figure in each square cell indicates A's payoff; the bottom indicates B's payoff. *X* is a cooperative choice, because it allows both members to win. The choice of *Y* is competitive, because only the one who chooses it has a chance. of winning and both may lose. With this matrix there is a great deal of competition.

cooperative. Moreover, as the game progresses (and the players are winning fairly few points), the number of cooperative choices actually goes down. The players choose the competitive strategy more and more, despite the fact that they know they can win more by cooperating.

It could be argued that in most of the Prisoner's Dilemma games, Y is the more rational choice, because the best single play is the competitive one. Let us analyze the game shown in Figure 6–3. If subject A selects the cooperative strategy, his payoff depends on what B does. If B chooses the cooperative strategy, A wins 10 points; if B chooses competitively, A loses 15 points. If A chooses the competitive strategy, once again his payoff depends on B. If B chooses the cooperative strategy, A wins 15 points; if B chooses competitively, A loses 5. Thus, in either case, A would do better by choosing the competitive strategy than he would by choosing the cooperative one. If B picks cooperatively, A wins 15 instead of 10; if B chooses competitively, A loses 5 instead of 15.

The dilemma is that over a long series of trials, A would be much better off if both he and B agreed to choose the cooperative strategy. They would both win on all trials rather than winning on some and losing on others. It is true that on any one trial, A would do better to pick the competitive strategy, regardless of what B picks. But over a long series of trials, the goal for both of them should be to choose cooperatively since doing so would maximize their gains. Nevertheless, particularly in a one-trial game, but even in longer games, there is strong pressure toward choosing the competitive strategy because it is the better one on any given trial.

This is not, however, an adequate explanation of why people choose competitively. Most of the players are bright enough to realize they would be better off if they and their partner could agree on picking cooperatively. The fact that they continue to pick competitively seems to indicate that they are, in fact, competing. This was forcefully demonstrated in a study (Minas et al., 1960), involving a game with the matrix shown in Figure 6–4.

This matrix is different from the others we have discussed, because there is no rational reason for picking the competitive strategy—it is always better to pick the cooperative strategy, because it would always result in a higher score. If player A chooses $X$, he would score more points than if he had chosen $Y$, regardless of what player B does. If B chooses $X$ also, player A wins 4; if B chooses $Y$, player A wins 1. Thus, depending on B's choice, player A wins either 4 or 1. In contrast, if A chooses $Y$, he would win either 3 or 0. From any point of view, both players should choose the cooperative strategy, because they would score more points that way.

The striking finding is that even with this kind of setup subjects

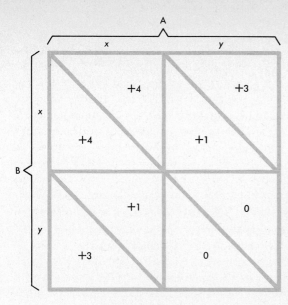

Figure 6–4

Matrix heavily favoring cooperative choices. Other than a desire to score more than the other person, there is no reason to choose Y. A player who chooses X scores more points than he would if he chose Y, regardless of what the other player selects. Nevertheless, players using this matrix make many competitive choices. (From Minas et al., 1960.)

tend to compete a great deal, rather than pick the cooperative strategy and quietly gain 4 points on each trial. The only advantage of the competitive choice is that one player can score more than the other, even though he always scores less than he would have if both had picked the cooperative choice. When subjects in these studies were questioned about their reasons for behaving as they did, many of them reported that they wanted to "beat" the other player. This occurred despite the fact that the experimenter had told them that the aim of the game was to score as high as possible. Apparently, subjects are relatively unimpressed by a game in which the only incentive is to score points; they prefer to compete even if it means they do less well from the experimenter's point of view.

### Factors Affecting Competition

**Incentive.** The competitive tendency changes somewhat when the incentive for doing well is increased. In most of the studies, subjects were playing simply for points, for imaginary money, or perhaps for small stakes. They earned no more by doing well than by doing poorly. In an occasional study, they could earn a few extra cents by scoring a lot of points, but the subjects, not only those who were fairly affluent college students but even the not so affluent high school students and working girls, were not impressed by the chance to earn an extra 15 or 20 cents. Therefore, their natural tendency to compete was predominant over their desire to earn the money. When the stakes are raised, however, and the subjects can earn as much as a few dollars, the desire to earn the money is relatively more important. Under these circumstances, there is a conflict between the competitive urge and the desire to maximize winnings. Yet the effect of incentive on competition is far from clear.

An experiment by Gallo (1966) demonstrated one effect of the size of rewards. Subjects played the trucking game, but for half the pairs, the payoffs were in real money, whereas the other pairs played just for points. With real money there was considerably more cooperation. Gallo and Sheposh (1971) obtained similar results when subjects who were given ten dollars to play with were compared to others who had only points. Once again those with real money earned more. And a study involving negotiation (Kelly et al., 1970) compared money with points in several different countries. They found that there were more agreements and they were reached more quickly when money was involved.

Other studies, however, have produced conflicting evidence on the role of monetary incentive. Gumpert, Deutsch, and Epstein (1969) found even more competition with real than with imaginary money in a prisoner's dilemma game. Oskamp and Kleinke (1970) conducted two experiments on this problem. In the first, each trial involved a range of payoffs from $.30 to $3.00 but the total earnings were based on a selection of trials and ranged only from $1.50 to $3.00. The second study had trials that were either no money (just points), pennies, or dimes with maximum earnings ranging from zero to $9.00. Although the effects of incentive were not strong, there was a consistent tendency for cooperation to be *greater* with lower payoff. Increasing the incentive actually decreased the amount of cooperative choices.

This research indicates that incentive does not have a simple effect on the amount of cooperation in these games. Sometimes it seems to increase cooperation, sometimes it decreases it, and sometimes it has little effect. A possible resolution of this seeming inconsistency is that people care more about winning when the stakes are greater, but that does not necessarily make them cooperate more. The temptation to pick a competitive choice and possibly win a big bonus exists both when points are involved and when there is a chance of winning money. Increasing the incentive may simply cause some subjects to concentrate on winning at least some money, but cause other subjects to maximize their winnings by competing. Knox and Douglas (1971) produced results that support this explanation. They compared subjects who were playing for pennies to those playing for dollars. The amount of cooperation was virtually identical for the two conditions, but there was three times as much variance when dollars were involved. This suggests that the higher incentive caused some subjects to play more competitively and others more cooperatively. Presumably when you care more about winning you will choose a more consistent and more extreme strategy, but there is no evidence that you will necessarily be more cooperative.

It is important to note that even when stakes are quite high and subjects can make a lot of money, they tend to make a large number of competitive responses. Apparently, the competitive urges are strong enough to cause people to compete despite the fact that it is to their disadvantage in terms of their total winnings. As we noted in our discussion of social facilitation, the presence of another person seems to arouse competitive feelings even when the situation includes no realistic reason for assuming that any competition is involved. Our present findings reinforce this. Taken together they seem to suggest that, at least in our society, one of the powerful, dominating factors in most interpersonal situations is the arousal of competitive feelings. This does not mean that people always compete nor that they feel competitive in all situations. But it does suggest that competition is a strong component in many interpersonal relationships even when the situation is structured to favor cooperation.

**Threats.**   In variations of the trucking game, one, both, or neither players were provided with threats in the form of barriers that could be placed across the one-lane road. When only one player had a barrier to use, the condition was called unilateral threat; when both players had them, the condition was called bilateral threat. Note that the barriers in no way prevented cooperation. The players did not have to use them; they could take turns using the road and forget about the barriers.

The existence of the barriers made a sizable difference in the amount of cooperation between the players. When neither one had a barrier to use, there was the most cooperation. When one of them had a barrier, there was less cooperation and the one who had the threat tended to do better than the other. On a typical trial, the two trucks met in the middle of the road and the question was which would back up first. If the one with the barrier backed up, she could erect the barrier and prevent the other one from benefiting from the direct route. They both lost but the one without the threat probably lost more. On the other hand, if the other backed up, there was no barrier to be erected and the first truck could roll through and gain a lot of points. Thus, the few cooperative choices that there were tended to favor the one with the threat, and she therefore got a better score. Finally, when both sides had a threat, there was the least amount of cooperation. The typical result was for both sides to erect their barriers and immediately take the long route. This was guaranteed to lose money but avoided the greater loss due to a stalemate at the narrow road.

Although threats can sometimes interfere with maximal performance, a person who has a threat does seem to have a distinct advantage over someone who doesn't. In the trucking game, when only one person has a gate, he does earn more points (or lose fewer) than the person who does not have a gate. In prisoner's dilemma and other bargaining games a player who has a threat of any kind is in a strong position. This is particularly true if he seems likely to carry out the threat (Guyer and Rapoport, 1970). Under these circumstances he will usually get the better of the bargaining—win more points or money or whatever is involved. On the other hand, someone who has power and does not use it may be considered weak and be taken advantage of. Swingle (1970) showed that subjects who have a threat and fail to use it are exploited more than subjects who do not have the threat in the first place. Apparently power is useful only when the other person is convinced that it may be used, and otherwise it may actually reduce the strength of a person's position by making him seem weak and ineffectual.

**Motivation.**   The evidence indicates that most people view the prisoner's dilemma game, at least in part, as a competitive situation. As we have seen, there is a strong tendency for players to compete rather than to try to maximize their own score independent of the other person. However, this competitive feeling can be influenced to some extent by what the subjects are told about the purpose of the game. In a study by Deutsch (1960), subjects were given one of three different instructions Cooperative instructions stressed concern for the other player's welfare; competitive instructions urged each player to win as much money as he could for himself and, in particular, to win more than the other player; and individualistic instructions stated that the only purpose was to win as much as possible and that the other player's outcome should be ignored.

The different instructions had a major impact on the amount of cooperation. The results are shown in the right-hand column of Table 6–2. Those subjects who were told to cooperate did so on over 90 percent of their choices. In contrast, the individualistic instructions resulted in

Table 6–2

*COMMUNICATION AND EFFECTS OF MOTIVATION ON COOPERATION*

| | PERCENTAGE OF COOPERATIVE CHOICES | | |
|---|---|---|---|
| *Motivation Instructions* | *No Communication* | *Communication* | *Average* |
| Cooperative | 89.1 | 96.9 | 93.0 |
| Individualistic | 35.0 | 70.6 | 52.8 |
| Competitive | 12.5 | 29.2 | 20.9 |

Source: Adapted from Deutsch (1960).

about 50 percent cooperation, and the competitive instructions produced only about 20 percent cooperation. Clearly, the tendency to view the game as competitive can be altered to a large extent by appropriate instructions.

It should be noted that instructing subjects to compete or to cooperate affects their behavior in situations other than the kinds of games we have been discussing. In several studies, groups that were working on problems were told either to maximize their individual efforts or to maximize the performance of the group as a whole. When they were urged to compete, there was less communication among the members of the group, they had less influence on one another and accepted one another less, and there was less division of labor and poorer productivity. When they were supposed to cooperate, there was more trust in one another, and the productivity of the group as a whole went up. Thus, in many, if not all, kinds of social interactions, having a cooperative goal produces more cooperation than seeing the situation as competitive.

**Communication.** Throughout our discussion of groups we have repeatedly stressed the importance of communication. The ability to talk to one's partner also plays a major role in determining the amount of cooperation between the two. In the study by Deutsch, described above, some subjects with each kind of motivation were allowed to communicate with their partner before playing. The effect of this communication was that cooperation increased markedly, regardless of the kind of motivation that had been aroused (see Table 6–2). However, the effect of communication was most dramatic in the individualistic condition. When subjects were trying to maximize their own winnings and were supposed to ignore those of the other player, being able to communicate increased their percentage of cooperative choices from 35 to over 70.

The Deutsch and Krauss trucking study included three different types of communication conditions. Some subjects were not allowed to communicate; others were given the opportunity to talk if they wanted to; and a third group was required to communicate. The effect was similar to that in the prisoner's dilemma game—there was more cooperation when communication was allowed than when it was not allowed and still more when it was forced. The effect was particularly strong in the unilateral threat conditions. When one player was provided with a barrier and not allowed to communicate, there was little cooperation, but when the players were forced to talk, the amount of cooperation increased dramatically.

This effect of communication was demonstrated even more convincingly by Wichman (1970). In a prisoner's dilemma game, some subjects were isolated from their partners; others could see their partners but could not talk to them; others could talk to their partners but could not see them; and still others could both see and hear each other. The amount of cooperation increased in that order. When there was no communication or only nonverbal communication, about 40 percent of the responses were cooperative. When verbal communication or both verbal and visual communication were allowed, cooperation occurred on more than 70 percent of the trials.

Assuming there is any tendency to cooperate, knowledge of the other person and particularly of what he is planning to do should facilitate it. Since the optimal strategy in these games depends almost entirely on the degree of trust in the other person, the ability to communicate is especially helpful. There may, however, be other games in which trust is less important or in which the tendency to cooperate is weaker, in which case being able to communicate might have relatively little effect.

One of the obvious reasons that communication should increase the amount of cooperation is that the players in these games often misperceive the others' intentions. Kelly and Stahelski (1970) showed that it was difficult for individuals in a prisoner's dilemma game to know what the other person was planning to do. More important, someone who was intending to make a cooperative choice was misjudged more often than someone who was planning to be competitive. Apparently there was a general tendency to assume that the other person would make a competitive choice. One of the reasons for this misperception was that the player who was planning to make a cooperative choice was often unable to follow through on this intention. If his opponent consistently made competitive choices, the player who wanted to play cooperatively was eventually forced to protect himself by making the competitive choice also. Thus the misperception of the cooperative player's intentions turned out often to be consistent with what the player actually did. This is another case of the self-fulfilling prophecy in which one player assumes that the other player will be competitive; accordingly he chooses a competitive response, eventually forcing the other person to be competitive also. The net result of this is that his initial perception that the other person is competitive will turn out to be correct only because he has in fact forced the other person to behave that way. As usual once you assume that the other person is a dangerous character and start treating him as an enemy, he will start acting like one.

The possibility of misjudging the other player is greatly decreased when communication is possible. Accordingly, allowing or forcing players to communicate makes it considerably easier for them to cooperate. They can discuss their plans, urge each other to cooperate, make promises, convince each other they are trustworthy, learn something about each other, and so on. Assuming there is any tendency to cooperate, knowledge of the other person should facilitate it.

### Applicability of the Research Findings

Many psychologists have attempted to relate the findings of the studies on these nonzero-sum games to the world situation and relationships between countries. Countries, too, cooperate or compete. In many cases, they could maximize their gains if they would cooperate, and yet there seems to be a tendency for them to compete. It was hoped that the research on games would reveal some of the basic factors determining relationships between countries.

The most significant finding of the work seems to be that people are motivated to maximize their profits from several points of view. As we would expect, in any bargaining or game situation, one of the strong considerations, and perhaps the dominant one, is to get as much as one can for as little as he can. But participants also want to maximize their gains in relation to other people. They want to "win" the exchange. Thus they might be willing to accept a slightly less advantageous deal if they felt it meant they were surpassing the other person. Some people refuse to accept a profitable arrangement merely because it means they would not win the exchange. Although they would be getting good value for their payment, the other person would receive equal value. Both the accumulation of goods and competition are motives that are probably present in almost all bargaining situations.

One implication of this is well known to salespeople. Customers want to feel that they are getting a good deal, that they are somehow winning the exchange. A used car salesman tries to make us feel that he has been talked into a deal that he never wanted to agree to, that we are very good bargainers. In that way, we feel we have won the exchange, he feels (probably rightly) that he has won, and everyone is happy. In countries such as Mexico where bargaining is a common mode of selling, this can be seen more clearly. If a vendor offers a rug for 200 pesos, the customer is not supposed to accept that price. It is deliberately high and the salesman would be surprised if it were accepted. Part of the selling is the bargaining itself, and both parties enter into it determined to win the deal. Most of the time they settle on roughly the price the vendor had in mind to begin with, but by this bargaining process, both people enjoy the sale more; they feel they have not only gotten good value but have also managed to beat the other person.

If the work on games is extended to relationships between countries, perhaps this is the important message. Countries also have competitive motives—they want to look good and to win an exchange. The ideal treaty or agreement between two countries is one that leaves each

188

side thinking it has won the conference. Perhaps the hope that countries will cooperate is unrealistic; it seems more likely that they will always compete, as people do. The hope, then, should be for them to compete in selling cars, playing ping-pong, or in building more impressive dams rather than in armaments. In that sense, the race to the moon and other space exploration has been constructive competition between the Soviet Union and the United States. Perhaps it is even better for the two countries to compete in this area than to cooperate; if they cooperated, they might seek other ways of competing in order to express their natural tendencies in that direction.

**PROBLEM SOLVING BY GROUPS**

Another question that has been given a great deal of attention concerns how groups compare with individuals in solving problems. We have seen that having another person present stimulates performance under some conditions but interferes with it under others. Stimulation and distraction also occur when a group is working on a problem together; and in this more complex situation, additional factors operate. We described above a common practice in business and government—the so-called brainstorming session, an unstructured, free type of group problem solving in which people get together and say anything that they think might be helpful. The idea is that they will stimulate one another into producing better ideas than each would produce alone. People also work together in more restricted types of groups. They can build a spaceship, design an experiment, solve a math problem, even write a novel in groups. In contrast, Thomas Edison invented the phonograph in virtual isolation; Albert Einstein devised the theory of relativity without discussing it with anyone; most novelists and artists work alone. How do groups compare with individuals in problem solving? Perhaps Edison would have been more effective in a work group at General Electric. Perhaps an advertising executive would think of a better slogan working alone than in a brainstorming group.

Although the question may seem to be straightforward and one that can be easily investigated, there is some difficulty in knowing just what to compare groups to. In some early studies, the same problem was given to groups of two, three, four, and five people and also to a number of individuals. The experimenters then compared the performance of the groups with the performance of each of the individuals. Examined in this way, the results are very clear. There is strength in numbers—by whatever criteria we choose, a group does better than a person working alone.

It quickly becomes apparent, however, that this is not the basic question. We really want to know whether four people working in a group would do better than the *same* four people working separately. To use the manpower we have most effectively, should we have them work in groups or alone?

In a classic study on brainstorming, (Taylor, Berry, and Block, 1958), subjects were assigned at random to either five-man groups or the individual condition. (Those in the groups had met together several times before.) The people in both conditions were then given five problems and twelve minutes to work on each one. One problem, for example, was stated as follows: "Each year a great many American tourists go to visit Europe, but now suppose that our country wished to get many more European tourists to come to visit America during their vacations. What steps can you suggest that would get more European tourists to come to this country?" The subjects were told that their task was to consider the problems and to offer as many and as creative solutions as they could. There were obviously no "correct" solutions. The following rules, taken from Osborne (1957, p. 84), were outlined to the groups:

1. Criticism is ruled out. Adverse judgment of ideas must be withheld until later.
2. Freewheeling is welcomed. The wilder an idea, the better. It is easier to tame down than to perk up.
3. Quantity is wanted. The greater the number of ideas, the more likelihood of winners.
4. Combination and improvement are sought. In addition to contributing ideas of your own, you should suggest how ideas of others can be turned into better ideas or how two or more ideas can be joined into still another one.

Subjects in the alone condition were divided at random into five-man nominal groups. That is, although each of these subjects worked alone, for purposes of the analysis they were considered a group and their total production was compared to the production of the actual five-man groups. In this way, Taylor, in essence, compared five man-hours of work done by a five-man group with five man-hours done by five individuals working alone. This is the only meaningful way to compare the efficiency of the two procedures.

The results (presented in Table 6–3) can be considered in terms of the quantity of ideas that were produced and also in terms of their originality. Quantity consisted of the number of *different* ideas produced by the real and the nominal groups. If two members of a nominal group produced the same idea, it was counted as only one idea. As can be seen from the table, the nominal groups (individuals working alone) scored

Table 6–3

PERFORMANCE BY REAL AND NOMINAL GROUPS

| Condition | Different Ideas | Unique Ideas |
|---|---|---|
| Real groups | 37.5 | 10.8 |
| Nominal groups<br>(five individuals working alone) | 68.1 | 19.8 |

Note: Figures are number of ideas.

Source: Taylor et al. (1958).

higher than the actual groups—the individuals produced an average of 68.1 ideas whereas the groups produced only 37.5. Similarly, the nominal groups produced more unique, creative ideas (19.8 versus 10.8). In other words, five individuals working alone produced almost twice as many solutions and unique ideas as five comparable people did working together. Someone working alone can concentrate better than he can in a group and also does not have to worry about competing with other people in order to express his ideas. If the group did provide any mutual stimulation, it was apparently more than offset by the interfering and distracting effects of other people.

### Limitations of the Research

Although the results of the study by Taylor et al. showed that groups are inferior to individuals working alone, this study has several limitations. The most important is that the groups had worked together for a relatively short time. It may be that people have to get to know each other and learn to work together before a group can become an effective unit. At least one study (Cohen et al., 1960) suggested that brainstorming in groups is quite productive when the individuals involved were specially selected to be compatible and were trained to work together.

Another question concerns the effect of dissimilarity of the group members on the quality of the solutions they produce. It appears that relatively heterogeneous groups, in which the personalities of the various members differ considerably, produce better solutions to most problems than do homogeneous groups. In a study by Hoffman and Maier (1961), the two kinds of groups were given problems to work on that varied considerably in terms of whether or not there was an objective solution, the kinds of issues involved, and so on. For example, one problem required the group to think of a way for men to cross a heavily mined road, whereas another involved settling a simulated argument between two of the group's members. The results showed that on several problems, there was a large difference—favoring the heterogeneous groups—

190

in the quality of the solutions offered by the types of groups. With other problems, the difference was considerably smaller. Overall, the results indicated that heterogeneous groups are superior to homogeneous groups on a wide variety of problems.

Another variable in this study was sex—some groups were composed only of men, whereas others had both men and women. There was some indication that the groups containing both sexes produced higher-quality solutions than did the all-male groups. Thus, heterogeneity, in terms of both personality and sex, seems to improve the performance of groups.

A further limitation concerns the type of problem tackled. How to use foreign aid or what slogan to adopt for a new polka-dot toothpaste, questions that were discussed in the brainstorming research, cannot be resolved by a logical process—these questions have no "correct" or unique solution. It would seem that any stimulating effect that a group might have on its members would be most beneficial and any distracting effect would be least harmful when such problems are considered. On the other hand, with problems that can be solved logically and that have unique, correct solutions (solving a math problem, building a spaceship, inventing the electric light, or solving a brainteaser), the stimulating effect of the group might be less important and the distraction more harmful. Groups do provide two important advantages—members can check one another's work and, collectively, they provide a variety of abilities that one individual would be unlikely to possess. However, because these characteristics of groups are helpful only with certain types of problems, the relative effectiveness of groups and individuals depends on the characteristics of the problem.

Groups are quite effective in working on problems that involve a large number of separate operations, such as complex arithmetic problems. In such cases, the ability of members to catch one another's mistakes is particularly important. A group provides a system of checks that is lacking when an individual works alone. On the other hand, with these problems, the group is not really working together—the individual members are working separately and then checking one another's work. This is quite different from brainstorming, but it does indicate that under some circumstances, groups perform better than individuals working alone.

It is obvious that problems requiring a number of separate skills tend to favor groups. If, in order to solve a problem, it is essential to know calculus, cellular biology, and organic chemistry, only an individual possessing all this knowledge would be able to find the solution. But even among individuals on a college faculty, it is unlikely that any one person would have all these skills. If, however, we form such a faculty into five-man groups, it is considerably more likely that a group of five professors would have, among them, the three necessary abilities. Thus in this admittedly somewhat specialized situation, groups would be better than individuals. It should be noted that many problems that require a number of skills can be worked on in stages. For example, the first stage may require a knowledge only of cellular biology; the second stage, a knowledge only of calculus; and the third, only of organic chemistry. With this kind of problem, it is not clear that groups are superior to individuals so long as we allow the individuals to work on the problem in stages and to distribute their findings at the end of each stage. Thus, the experiments in which groups have tended to be less effective than individuals may be somewhat misleading. We may conclude that groups set up at random and working together for a relatively short time almost certainly will be less effective than would be the same individuals working alone. However, the possibility remains that properly constructed and well-trained groups may sometimes be more creative and efficient than individuals.

One final point should be made about group problem solving. Particular characteristics of any of the individuals may have an inhibiting or even a destructive effect on the rest of the group. One person may talk so much that no one else is able to say anything. Or someone may be so critical of everyone else's ideas that the rest of the group becomes reluctant to contribute. Another common phenomenon, discussed in detail in chapter 5, is that persons of higher status in the group tend to have more influence than those of lower status.

In a study by Torrance (1955), airplane crews consisting of a pilot, navigator, and gunner worked on a series of problems together. A careful recording was kept of the solutions suggested by each group member and of the final solution agreed on by the whole group. It was found that the group almost always unanimously approved the solutions suggested by the pilot, whereas it was rarely influenced by the contributions of the gunner (the lowest-status person). This is not surprising and by itself need not have had an adverse effect on the group's performance. The striking finding concerned the group's reaction when either the pilot or the gunner had the correct answer. Torrance found that when the pilot had the correct answer, the group went along with him 100 percent of the time. However, when the gunner had the correct answer, the group accepted it only about 40 percent of the time. This means that if the three men had been working separately, at least the gunner would have been correct the other 60 percent of the time that he knew the answer; but when they worked as a group, all three members were incorrect on those occasions when the pilot disagreed with the gunner. The same effect has been found (Riecken, 1958) when a clue is given to various members of a group. When it is given to someone who talks a lot and is a leader, the

Drawing by R. O. Blechman; © 1958 *Punch*, London.

group solves the problem; when the clue is given to a relatively silent member, the group often fails to use it. This research demonstrates that groups introduce all sorts of complex interactions, conflicts, and pressures that are not present when individuals work alone and that these characteristics of the group are often disruptive.

To sum up, it seems that under most circumstances, groups are less efficient than individuals working alone. Group members distract, inhibit, and generally tend to interfere with one another. Groups do provide a means of catching errors, and on certain types of problems, this might overcome their relative inefficiency. Also, when differing skills are needed for a solution, groups have a big advantage. Finally, as in minimal social situations, group members tend to motivate each other to work harder, and they probably do this to an even greater extent than in the minimal situations. If other incentives have not already produced a sufficiently high motivational level, this would be an advantage of working in groups.

## Cohesiveness

As we mentioned in our discussion of group versus individual problem solving, interactions and feelings among the group members play an important role in the group's performance. It seems obvious that groups in which there is a lot of internal fighting, disagreements, and lack of cooperation will do poorly on tasks, whereas groups in which people generally agree and cooperate should do very well. In addition, groups in which all the members like each other and are strongly attracted to the group itself should do well. A group of this kind would have high morale, strong motivation, and strong pressures against conflicts that could interfere with performance. This quality of the group is called its *cohesiveness*. The more the members are attracted to one another and to the group and the more they share the group's goals, the greater the group's cohesiveness.

These considerations suggest that highly cohesive groups are more effective than those with less cohesiveness, and research has generally shown this effect (Husband, 1940; Berkowitz, 1956). However, it is important to take into account a group's norms and goals. The more cohesive a group, the more its members follow its goals. Thus, if the group's goal is to work hard and accomplish as much as possible, a cohesive group will be more productive than a less cohesive group. On the other hand, if for some reason the group's goals are to limit the amount of work, a highly cohesive group will be less productive than a less cohesive group (Schachter et al., 1951; Berkowitz, 1954). In other words, whatever the group as a whole decides to do, a cohesive group will do better.

Although it might seem that most groups would want to maximize their productivity, many groups deliberately limit production. A typical example is a union that places restrictions, formal or informal, on the amount of work each man is supposed to accomplish in a given period of time. The workers are expected to do that much and no more, and anyone who does more is considered a deviant and treated accordingly. (We shall discuss in detail in Chapter 7 how this was done by a group in a Western Electric Company plant.) Of course, in this situation the goal is set by an outside agency (the company management), and the group does not benefit directly from increased output. However, restricting productivity also occurs in more informal groups such as college fraternities and other living units. The members think that a certain amount of studying, for example, is appropriate, but anything more than that amount is "bad form." Someone who wants to study more than the accepted amount may be subjected to kidding, abuse, deliberate distractions, or even rejection. Thus, cohesive groups maintain performance at a set level better than do less cohesive groups, but the level of performance is not necessarily higher with greater cohesiveness.

**GROUPS AS MOBS**

Thus far we have been talking about groups in which the members work together to solve a problem. We have focused on the end result of this activity—the quantity and quality of the work accomplished. But groups do many other things and have many effects on individual members other than making them better or worse at problem solving.

The restaurant fire described at the beginning of this chapter is one example of a group acting as a mob. All the individuals wanted to escape. If they had cooperated and taken turns, they might all have escaped—or at least many more than actually did. Instead, they were disorganized, ignored one another, acted singly, and died.

With clouds of smoke billowing behind the diners, perhaps it was not surprising that they became frantic and disorganized. But this kind of phenomenon is not limited to such extreme circumstances. In the mild, innocuous, relatively placid setting of an experimental laboratory, each of a group of subjects was given one end of a string, the other end of which was attached to a small wooden spool (Mintz, 1951). The spools were placed in a large bottle, the neck of which was wide enough for only one spool to pass through at a time. The bottle then began to fill with water, and everyone was told to get his spool out before the water reached it. (The analogy to the restaurant fire is obvious.) The water rose slowly enough so that everyone could have gotten his spool out safely as long as only one person at a time tried. The scene was in plain sight, there was no bonus for getting one's spool out early, and, presumably, there was little or no actual fear of the water. Yet traffic jams almost always developed. Two or more people tried to get their spools through the bottle's neck at once, the spools got caught, and all those that were not already free were covered with water.

Harold Kelley and his associates (1965) repeated this study in a more controlled situation and, as shown in Table 6–4, got the same results. In addition, however, Kelley showed that increasing the actual level of fear (e.g., by threatening the subjects with electric shocks if they did not escape) produced more disorganization and more traffic jams. The main point of this research for our present purpose is that under even mild stress, a group sometimes acts in a disorganized, self-destructive manner and that this tendency increases with higher stress.

### Deindividuation

One of the most impressive aspects of groups is that people sometimes do things when together that they would not do if they were alone. This is most striking—and frightening—when the action involves immoral or violent acts—lynchings in the South, the killing of referees at soccer matches in South America, racial strife, and so on. Interviews with some of the people involved in riots indicate that they would never have considered performing the acts of violence had they been alone and that, when the riots were over, they were actually shocked at what they had done.

The explanation usually given for this phenomenon is that to some extent individuals lose their personal sense of responsibility when they are in a group. Instead of feeling, as they usually do, that they personally are morally accountable for their actions, group members somehow share the responsibility with one another, and none of them feels it as strongly as he would if he were alone. This is sometimes called responsibility diffusion or deindividuation, because the people are responding and being responded to, not as separate individuals, but as

Table 6–4

EFFECT OF THREAT ON ESCAPE IN A SITUATION
REQUIRING COOPERATION

| Threat | Percentage Escaping |
| --- | --- |
| Low | 69 |
| Medium | 56 |
| High | 36 |

Source: Adapted from Kelley et al. (1965).

part of the group. It has been shown that groups differ considerably in the extent to which they produce deindividuation. In addition, there is some evidence that the greater the deindividuation of any group, the more free and uninhibited is the behavior of its members.

One implication of deindividuation is that anything that makes the members of a group less identifiable increases the effect. The more anonymous the group members are, the less identifiable they are as individuals, the less they feel they have an identity of their own, and the more irresponsibly they may behave. In a mob, most of the people do not stand out as individuals. They blend together, are faceless, and, in a sense, do not have an identity of their own. Conversely, to the extent that they are identifiable and feel that they are, they retain their feeling of individuality and are less likely to act irresponsibly.

In an experiment by Singer, Brush, and Lublin (1965) to test this notion, some subjects were made easily identifiable and others were made difficult to identify. In the former condition, everyone dressed in his normal clothes, which meant that each was dressed differently from the others. In addition, the subjects were called by name and everything was done to make each one stand out as an individual. In the latter condition, all the subjects put on identical, bulky lab coats. The experimenter avoided using their names and, in general, tried to give the impression that their individual identities did not matter much. The group then discussed a variety of topics, including one that required the use of obscene language.

Groups in the low-identifiable condition showed much more freedom in all the discussions and, in particular, in the one involving obscene words. There were fewer pauses in the conversation, more lively discussions, and, most strongly, a greater willingness to use the obscene language that was necessary for a good discussion of the topic. Subjects who were more easily identified were much more constrained and appeared quite reluctant to use the taboo words.

A more dramatic effect of identifiability was provided in an experiment by Zimbardo (1959). Groups of four girls were recruited to take part in a study supposedly involving empathic responses to strangers. In one condition, the girls were greeted by name, wore name tags, and were easily identifiable. In another condition, the girls wore oversized white lab coats and hoods over their heads, were never called by name, and were difficult if not impossible to identify. All the groups were given an opportunity to deliver electric shocks to a girl not in the group. The subjects who were not identifiable gave almost twice as many shocks as the others. Apparently being less identifiable produced a marked increase in aggression, supporting the idea that loss of individuality is one cause of the violent, antisocial behavior that is sometimes exhibited by groups.

### Other Factors

Although responsibility diffusion is one part of the explanation of mob behavior, it seems likely that other factors are also operating. In a group, one extremely dominant, persuasive person can convince others to do something they would not do if he were not present. Moreover, this effect can snowball, because when the dominant one has convinced a few, they will convince others, and so on until everybody is convinced. As we shall see in the next chapter, when a large part of a group has taken a position, it can exert great pressure on the rest of the group to go along.

Another consideration is the protection afforded by a group. A crowd provides a certain amount of anonymity and, perhaps more important, makes it difficult for legal sanctions to be applied. An individual rarely could perform the acts a group can; but even if he could and did, it is more likely that he would be punished if he were alone than if he did the same things in a group. If one or even five people started breaking the windows of department stores, they would almost certainly be arrested and prosecuted. However, if five thousand people broke windows, only a small percentage would be caught and punished. Thus, from a purely practical point of view, people must be aware that they are more likely to get away with something when they are in a crowd than when they are alone.

It should be pointed out that the phenomenon of a group acting differently from an individual is not limited to immoral, violent acts. Groups sometimes perform socially valued acts that individuals would not perform alone. There are many anecdotal examples of people who band together to help survivors of disasters, rebuild someone's house that had been destroyed by fire, collect money for a sick child, etc. These deeds cannot be explained in terms of loss of moral inhibitions or fear of getting caught, since these considerations are not relevant to such positive actions. It appears that at times individuals are swept up in a positive group goal that, in essence, forces them to be better than they would otherwise be. The important point is that, despite our tendency to focus on the negative effect of groups, they have both negative and positive effects on their members—causing them to behave better or worse than they would alone.

## RISK TAKING

One interesting effect that groups seem to have on individuals' behavior concerns risk taking. People are often faced with a choice between a course of action that has only a small chance of working but the possibility of a large payoff and one that is more likely to work but would result in a much smaller payoff. For example, in roulette, betting $1 on red results in winning half the time (actually, slightly less than half the time because of the zeros, which are neither red nor black, but for this example we shall ignore them), with a payoff of $1. Betting $1 on a number results in winning about once in thirty-six times, with a payoff of $35. Thus, over many trials, the results would be equal. If either bet were made many times, the losses would be equivalent. The bets are, however, quite different in terms of expected gains and losses on any one trial. The first bet might be called conservative, because half the time, the player wins a small amount. The second bet is risky, because the player loses over 95 percent of the time, but when he does win, he wins a lot. A more practical example, perhaps, would be the case of a college senior considering graduate work. He might have to choose between entering a university that has such rigorous standards that only a fraction of the degree candidates actually receive degrees and entering one that has less of a reputation but where almost everyone admitted receives degrees. Here again, there is a risky strategy (entering the more difficult university). The question is whether individuals and groups favor different strategies.

In a series of studies (Dion et al., 1970; Marquis, 1962; Stouer, 1961; Wallach and Kogan, 1965; Zajonc et al., 1972) a number of complex situations were described to the subjects. In each situation, a variety of choices, ranging from very high risk to very low risk, was available. The subjects were asked to consider the situations carefully and decide what recommendations they would make or which alternative they would prefer. One situation was described as follows:

Mr. E. is president of a metals corporation in the United States. The corporation is quite prosperous and Mr. E. has considered the possibility of expansion by building an additional plant in a new location. His choice is between building another plant in the United States, where there would be a moderate return on the initial investment, or building a plant in a foreign counry, where lower labor costs and easy access to raw materials would mean a much higher return on the initial investment. However, there is a history of political instability and revolution in the foreign country under consideration. In fact, the leader of a small minority party is committed to nationalizing, that is, taking over all foreign investments.

Imagine that you are advising Mr. E. Listed below are several probabilities of continued political stability in the foreign country under consideration. Please check the *lowest* probability that you would consider acceptable in order for Mr. E.'s corporation to build in that country.

The chances are 1 in 10 that the foreign country will remain politically stable.

The chances are 3 in 10 that the foreign country will remain politically stable.

The chances are 5 in 10 that the foreign country will remain politically stable.

The chances are 7 in 10 that the foreign country will remain politically stable.

The chances are 9 in 10 that the foreign country will remain politically stable.

Place a check here if you think Mr. E.'s corporation should not build a plant in the foreign country, no matter what the probabilities [Kogan and Wallach, 1967, pp. 234–35].

After listening to this problem, the subjects made individual decisions. They did not discuss the issue; they did not know that they were going to discuss it later. When they had made their decisions, they were brought into a group and asked to discuss the problem to reach a unanimous decision. Under these circumstances, there was a strong tendency for the group decision to involve higher risk than the average of the decisions made by the individuals. For example, in one group, two individuals were for 9 in 10, two for 7 in 10, and two for 5 in 10 when they made their decisions individually. After the group discussion, the unanimous decision was to endorse 5 in 10—a clear shift toward a risky strategy. Moreover, the strong overall tendency to favor riskier choices in groups held for both males and females.

The results are striking. In virtually every study concerning this problem, groups favored more risky strategies than did individuals—even when the same individuals made a decision alone and then changed their decisions in groups. It is apparent that discussing a decision with a group makes people choose more risky alternatives.

This phenomenon has been referred to as the risky-shift. It has been demonstrated with a wide variety of decisions involving quite different kinds of materials and with many different subject populations. The risky-shift occurs with real life situations such as those just described. It also occurs when subjects have a selection of problems to work on that vary in difficulty and in the number of points they will get for solving them. This is the kind of choice a champion diver makes when he selects either very difficult dives which, if he does them well, will earn him many points, or somewhat simpler dives which are easier to do but will earn him fewer points even if he does them perfectly. And risky-shifts also occur (although somewhat less consistently) in gambling situations where there is a choice between low probability, high payoff alternatives, and higher probability but lower payoff possibilities. Most of the research has involved subjects (usually students) in the United States and Canada, but the risky-shift has also been demonstrated in England (Bateson, 1966), France (Kogan and Doise, 1969), Israel (Rim, 1963) and Germany (Lamm and Cogan, 1970). It is a stable, consistent finding which has attracted a great deal of research in recent years.

A number of explanations of this phenomenon have been offered. The testing and changing of these various explanations is an interesting case history of research on a specified problem in social psychology. Therefore let us consider some of the most plausible explanations in detail.

**Riskier People are More Persuasive.** One type of explanation is based on presumed differences between people who ordinarily favor risky choices and those who favor more conservative choices. If riskier people tend to be leaders of groups, participate more, play larger roles in group decisions, or be more persuasive for any reason, it would explain the risky-shift. Obviously if the group is more influenced by riskier people, the group as a whole will end up favoring riskier decisions after a discussion.

Although this is a plausible explanation, the evidence collected so far does not provide much support for it. There is some indication (Rim, 1964) that high risk people value leadership more and are generally *perceived* as more persuasive by the other members of the group (Flanders and Thistlewaite, 1967; Wallach et al., 1962; Wallach, Kogan, and Burt, 1965). On the other hand, two studies (Nordhoy, 1962; Rabow et al., 1966) have shown that in situations where conservative shifts occur, high risk people are seen as less persuasive. This indicates that the perception of how persuasive they are is probably not due to any inherent ability on their part, but rather to what happens in the group discussion. If the group is persuaded to be more risky, obviously those who initially favored high risk are seen as causing that shift; if the group ends up less risky, the conservative members of the group are seen as having caused the shift. Since there is no direct evidence that high risk people are more persuasive, we are forced to conclude that the risky-shift is not caused by any inherent differences in ability or persuasiveness among members of the group. This conclusion is reinforced by the fact that several studies (Blank, 1968; Teger and Pruitt, 1967) have shown that the risky-shift occurs without an actual discussion, but with only an exchange of each others' preferences. When no discussion occurs, differences in persuasiveness cannot account for the results. The available evidence thus does not support this explanation of the risky-shift, but the possibility remains that differences in persuasiveness may be a contributing factor in some situations even though not essential reason for the effect.

**Diffusion of Responsibility.** Individuals in a group may sometimes feel less personal responsibility for their own acts than they would if they were alone. To some extent the decision is made by the whole group and the burden of responsibility is accordingly shared. Even if the person makes the decision on his own following a group discussion, he may feel that he is less responsible for it because he is in a group. A second assumption is that most people would like to make risky decisions, but avoid them for fear of failure or other negative consequences. Being in a group reduces his feeling of responsibility, reduces his fear of negative consequences, and therefore allows him to pick riskier choices.

This is an interesting explanation of the risky-shift because it conceives of it as a true group phenomenon. Being in the group would be a necessary condition for the effect because group feelings and the accompanying diffusion of responsibility are the crucial elements producing the risky-shift.

The test of this explanation depends on whether group membership is, in fact, a necessary condition for a risky-shift. If the shift occurs without a discussion or even without the individual feeling that he is a member of a group, obviously it cannot be due to diffusion of responsibility. On the other hand, if giving the individual all the necessary information without actually having a group meeting does not produce a shift, it would suggest that diffusion of responsibility or some similar group phenomenon was the explanation. Unfortunately the evidence on this point is somewhat inconsistent. One study (Bem et al., 1965) demonstrated that having a discussion produced the effect while merely anticipating a discussion but not having it did not. Similarly Wallach and Kogan (1965) produced a risky-shift when the group had a discussion with a group consensus, when there was a discussion without a group consensus, but not when there was consensus without an actual discussion. On the other hand, watching others discuss the issue seems to be able to produce the effect (Kogan and Wallach, 1967), and, more damaging, some experimenters (Blank, 1968; Teger and Pruitt, 1967) have found the effect when the group knew each other's preferences but did not have a discussion. And making the group more cohesive, which might be expected to increase diffusion of responsibility, actually decreased the size of the risky-shift (Dion et al., 1970).

None of these studies entirely rules out the diffusion of responsibility explanation. The crucial question—whether the effect occurs when the individual does not feel that he is a member of a group—has never been fully tested. Even those studies that produced the effect without a group discussion did have groups, and perhaps simply being in a group is sufficient to reduce one's feeling of responsibility. Although we cannot confidently reject the explanation, the evidence in favor of it is somewhat questionable. No one has yet produced a study which directly demonstrates the feeling of reduced responsibility nor even that fear of failure is a basic reason for making conservative choices. Thus, although we cannot entirely rule out this explanation, at the moment the evidence in favor of it is not very convincing.

**Cultural Value.** The explanation that currently seems most plausible and most consistent with the evidence is based on the assumption that under most circumstances risky decisions are valued more highly than conservative ones. In many situations and many cultures, people admire, respect, and value the tendency to take chances. Discussing a decision with other people or even knowing other people's choices, makes this cultural norm more salient and therefore causes the individual to select a riskier decision than he would if he were alone. In other situations, the culture may value caution and when this is so, the opposite effect should occur—following a group discussion the choices should be more conservative than before. This explanation says in effect that the risky-shift is not truly a group phenomenon, but rather that being in a group is one way in which these culture values can be made salient. There would be other ways also and they too would produce the risky-shift. Thus group discussion or even group membership is not absolutely crucial, but is merely one effective procedure for producing the phenomenon.

Most of the evidence bearing on this explanation is indirect. To begin with, it is clear that the research on the necessity of group discussion is consistent with this explanation. As we have said, some studies (e.g., Wallach and Kogan, 1965) demonstrated that discussion was necessary in order to produce the effect; others (e.g., Teger and Pruitt, 1967) found risky-shift without discussion. In terms of the value hypothesis we would expect that a discussion would be more likely to produce the effect and would produce a stronger effect, because it would make the cultural norms particularly salient. On the other hand, if the information given to subjects about other's preferences is detailed enough and is presented in such a way as to make these preferences important, the effect should occur even without a discussion. Unfortunately there are several studies in which information about other's preferences was given to subjects in apparently considerable detail and yet no risky-shift was found (e.g., Kogan and Carlson, 1969; Zajonc et al., 1970). If the effect is due entirely to the salience of cultural norms, this kind of information should produce a risky-shift, and these studies in which it did not are somewhat damaging.

On the other hand, there is a considerable amount of supporting evidence from individual's stated preferences. People tend to say that they admire high risk choices in situations that have in fact produced the risky-shift effect (Levenger and Schneider, 1969; Pilkonis and Zanna,

1969) and to rate fictitious risk takers higher than more cautious people (Madaras and Bem, 1968). While in other situations which have produced shifts toward caution, people say that they admire cautious responses (Levenger and Schneider, 1969; Pruitt and Teger, 1967). In addition people perceive themselves as riskier than their peers in situations that produce risky-shifts (Baron et al., 1970) but see themselves as more cautious on items that produce a conservative shift (Levenger and Schneider, 1969; etc.). Thus, just as would be expected from the value explanation, when people value risk, the risky-shift occurs and when they value caution, a conservative shift occurs. This is strong evidence that the effect is produced by evaluation of the situation rather than by differences in individual persuasiveness or the diffusion of responsibility.

We have not presented all the possible explanations of the risky-shift nor all of the evidence for and against each of the three explanations discussed. There are other interpretations, some of them considerably more complex than these. Although none of the current explanations has been fully supported by the evidence, we do feel that the best at the moment is in terms of cultural values. It is, however, entirely possible that other mechanisms, while not sufficient to produce the effect alone, do play some role in increasing its strength. And, of course, still other explanations may appear to supersede the present ones.

## CHAPTER REVIEW

1. The presence of other people as facilitating or inhibiting performance.
2. Competition in non-zero-sum games.
3. The tendency to compete as affected by motivation and the ability to communicate.
4. Group versus individual problem solving.
5. Type of problems and membership of the group as affecting group problem solving.
6. People in groups engage in acts they would not perform alone.
7. Groups produce feelings of deindividuation and irresponsibility.
8. Individuals take more risks in groups than when they are alone.

## APPLICATIONS AND SPECULATIONS

1. How would you apply the findings from the trucking, Prisoner's Dilemma, and other non-zero-sum games to problems in the international situation such as the missile race or disarmament?

2. Nationalism and chauvinism within small groups are persistent but quite variable phenomena in the world today. The strength of these feelings differs greatly from one country to another and from one group to another. What might be some of the bases for and consequences of these feelings?

3. We have seen that individuals choose more risky alternatives in groups than they would alone. What are the implications of this for decisions made in open group meetings, for a judicial system with most decisions made by juries rather than judges, and for other decision-making processes in society?

SUGGESTIONS FOR ADDITIONAL READING

*Articles*

Bem, D. J., Wallach, M. A., and Kogan, N. Group decision making under risk of aversive consequences. *Journal of Personality and Social Psychology*, 1965, *1*, 453–60.

Cottrell, N. B., Rittle, R. H., and Wack, D. L. The presence of an audience and list type (competitional or noncompetitional) as joint determinants of performance in paired-associates learning. *Journal of Personality*, 1967, *35*, 425–34.

Dunnette, M. D., Campbell, J., and Jaastad, K. The effects of group participation on brainstorming effectiveness for two industrial samples. *Journal of Applied Psychology*, 1963, *47*, 30–37.

Gallo, P. S. Effects of increased incentives upon the use of threat in bargaining. *Journal of Personality and Social Psychology*, 1966, *4*, 14–20.

Oskamp, S., and Kleinke, C. Amount of reward as a variable in the prisoner's dilemma game. *Journal of Personality and Social Psychology*, 1970, *16*, 133–40.

Zajonc, R. B. Social facilitation. *Science*, 1955, *149*, 269–74.

*Books and Longer Discussions*

Cartwright, D., and Zander, A. *Group dynamics* (3rd ed.). New York: Harper & Row, 1968.

Dion, K. L., Baron, R. S., and Miller, N. Why do groups make riskier decisions than individuals? In L. Berkowitz (Ed.), *Advances in Experimental Social Psychology*, Vol. 5. New York: Academic Press, 1970. Pp. 305–77.

LeBon, G. *The crowd*. London: Benn, 1896.

# seven

# conformity

Human beings are remarkably diverse. Their behavior, attitudes, thoughts, feelings, and values have almost unlimited variations. They speak in hundreds of different languages. They believe in hundreds of gods, a Trinity, one God, or no god at all. In some cultures, men take many wives; in some, they take one; and in a few, women take many husbands. The "normal" position for sexual intercourse in one culture is considered indecent in another, and vice versa. In some cultures, pork is forbidden; in others, it is a delicacy. Some people like various forms of fried insects and others are nauseated by them. Almost every aspect of behavior—business, courtship, marriage, friendship, bargaining, communication—varies from culture to culture. Moreover, the diversity is so great that members of one culture find it difficult to exist in another unless they have studied it carefully. They cannot eat the food and do not know whether they are supposed to use their fingers or utensils. Their sexual practices are considered unnatural, their manners rude, their every act foreign and wrong. They continually offend people and in turn are offended themselves.

In contrast to this great diversity, however, people the world over have much in common. They are, after all, members of the same species; they have similar physical characteristics, needs, and abilities. Although they speak different languages, they all do have language and use it quite similarly; although they have different sexual habits, they all have family structures and prohibitions against incest; although they have different religions and moral codes, they almost all have some religion and share ethical values such as the condemnation of murder and stealing within the group. The exact forms of people's behavior may differ, but they do perform many of the same acts, play many of the same games, and have many of the same cares and problems. Thus, the huge differences among people must be seen against the background of basic innate, genetic similarities.

Moreover, within any subculture, the similarities tend to predominate. Just as there is fantastic diversity among cultures, great similarity exists within any given culture. Almost everyone speaks the same language and has the same values, the same behavior, and the same interests. In the United States, practically everyone likes hamburgers; in Japan, practically everyone likes sushi. The similarity of behavior and values is even greater in subcultures. The smaller the unit of society, the greater the similarity among its members. In the white, middle-class subculture in the mid-Western United States, almost everyone has similar attitudes toward marriage and courtship, behaves the same in business, and so on. Any outsider entering a different culture is immediately struck by the fact that everyone seems to be behaving similarly. From the outsider's point of view, it looks as though the people are all very conformist.

Drawing by Dunagin; courtesy Publishers-Hall Syndicate.

*"No wonder you people have identity problems. You all look alike."*

It is true, of course, that people in a culture do behave similarly. But it is important to note that, by and large, this kind of conformity is an adaptive and necessary phenomenon. Members of the society must be able to assume, to some extent, that others will behave in certain ways, will have certain values, will interpret behavior in particular ways, and so on. It makes life much simpler and allows society to operate; people can interact smoothly, interpret correctly what others are doing, and communicate easily. Perhaps the most dramatic instance of this is provided by language. If everyone spoke different languages or had different meanings for the same words, social interaction would be almost impossible. In the United States, we know that when we ask somebody a question and he answers "yes," it means that he agrees with us or that we are correct. We speak the same language; we use the same words and give them similar connotations. If we disagreed on the meaning of *yes*, we could not interpret the reply. In Japan, for example, people are reluctant to answer negatively. They reply to questions either positively or noncommittally. Therefore, in order to get an accurate answer, one must word his question so that the individual can give the information requested without having to say "no."

Language is only one form of behavior that is shared by members of a society. They have an almost unlimited number of conventions and behaviors in common. Accepted forms of ritualistic behavior, such as ways of addressing people and rules of courtesy, make social interaction easier. A friendly form of address quickly communicates a feeling different from that communicated by a stilted form. Signing a letter *love* or *best regards* gives a different impression from signing it *cordially yours* or *respectfully yours*.

Accepted conventions are even more important when the behavior involved is more significant than social greetings. For example, sexual relations tend to be highly ritualized and specific to a culture. How does one express affection for someone of the opposite sex without being improperly forward? How does one communicate that he wants to be friends but not lovers? How do two people of the same sex express friendship without implying a homosexual attraction? These questions are difficult to answer in any society, but the answers that do exist depend largely on the rituals and customs of that society. An arm around a waist, a light kiss, and holding hands are acceptable approaches in some societies but are improper in others. In some societies, they would show friendship; in others, they would be proposals of marriage. Two men kiss when they meet on the street. In many places, this is quite typical and demonstrates normal affection; in the United States, it is unusual and might be interpreted as a sign of a homosexual relationship. And so on. Not knowing these customs, or not following them, makes it difficult to make one's feelings and intentions known. By conforming to the norms of society, however, one can communicate his feelings unambiguously and avoid disastrous or embarrassing misunderstandings.

Similarity among the members of a culture is also due to similar backgrounds, experience, and learning. Children learn to do things in a particular way, to accept certain beliefs, and to develop certain motivations. To a great extent, all children in a society learn the same things. Then when they are adults, they behave in similar ways—not because they choose to, not because they even think about it, but because this is the way they learned to behave.

Conformity should therefore be considered within this context. Much of the similarity of behavior and beliefs that we see in society and that we call conformity is due to necessity and learning. Thus, although conformity usually has a negative connotation, there are often good reasons for people to be similar. In many circumstances, behaving differently from others would be maladaptive and destructive.

## TRUE CONFORMITY

There are times, however, when people behave similarly in the absence of common learning or necessity. Often a person who is free to behave in two different ways and who has no personal preference for either will do what he sees other people doing. If, when driving behind a number of other cars, one sees all the others turn left at a particular intersection, he would probably be strongly tempted to turn left, unless he had additional information about his correct route. When somebody on the street looks up, other people tend to look up also. If someone says that a Campbell's soup can twenty times its normal size is great art, someone else agrees and pays thousands of dollars for the privilege of having it in his living room.

Sherif (1935) provided a forceful demonstration of this kind of conformity. He took advantage of the perceptual effect known as the *autokinetic phenomenon*—a single point of light seen in the dark appears to move even though it is completely stationary. During World War II, pilots who were supposed to follow the lights of the plane ahead of them were bothered by this effect, because the lights seemed to move around in weird, erratic, and confusing ways. The pilots sometimes became disoriented and flew off course. Eventually, the problem was eliminated by using lights that blinked, which prevented the autokinetic effect. Two important characteristics of this effect for Sherif's purposes are that it appears to virtually everyone and that it is extremely difficult for the person watching the light to estimate how far it moves. Typically, it seems to move erratically, at varying speeds and in different directions.

In Sherif's experiment, each subject was taken into a totally dark

Crowded conditions in our cities and suburbs and the economy of building similar units produce startling uniformity in housing. The people in these identical houses may not have chosen to conform to a standard taste, but other conditions have forced them to.

room and shown a single point of light. The subjects were told that the light was moving (since they were unfamiliar with the autokinetic effect, they believed it) and that their task was to estimate how far the light moved. The estimates varied enormously. Several subjects thought the light moved only 1 or 2 inches, whereas one thought it moved as much as 80 feet. (Apparently, this subject thought he was in a gymnasium, although actually he was in a small room.) In other words, the distance the light moved was quite ambiguous. Although the subjects had some idea how far it moved, they were far from certain because they had no guidelines, no backgrounds on which to base their estimates.

Into this ambiguous situation, Sherif introduced another subject who was supposedly also judging how far the light moved. This other subject was, in fact, a confederate who had been told to make his estimates consistently lower or higher than those of the subject. The procedure worked as follows: There was a trial during which the light presumably moved, the subject gave his estimate, and the confederate then gave his estimate. The same procedure was repeated for a number of trials. Under these circumstances, the subject soon began to make estimates that were more and more similar to those of the confederate than the ones he had made at the beginning. For example, if the subject began by estimating that the light moved between 10 and 15 feet and the confederate said it moved only 2 feet, on the second trial, the subject would tend to lower his estimate, and on the third trial, he would lower it more. By the end of the series, the subject's estimates were very similar to those of the confederate.

This was a situation in which the subject was not sure of his position. He had some information but it was ambiguous. He encountered somebody else who seemed quite sure of himself, even though they both seemingly had the same information. (Note that the confederate gave consistent estimates over the course of the trials and, therefore, probably seemed much more sure of himself than the subject felt.) Thus, it was not simply a matter of the subject's conforming because he thought the other had more information. Rather, the subject was influenced because someone said something different from him, because this other person kept saying it, and probably because this other person seemed sure of himself. This happened even though the subject was told by the experimenter that the important thing was to give his own opinions because he was interested in the subject's perception of the situation.

This is quite a srong demonstration of agreement in the absence of a realistic reason, but it could be argued that it does not really show blind conformity. After all, the stimulus that the subject was trying to judge was extremely ambiguous. The subject had no idea how far the light moved, and he was essentially guessing when he gave his estimate. In contrast, the confederate seemed to have definite ideas about how far the light moved. It is true that there are large differences in the perceptual ability of individuals, and the subject might have thought that the other person was better than he at judging how far a light moved in a dark room. Under these circumstances, it would be reasonable for the subject to go along with the other person or at least to use the estimates of the other person as a frame of reference within which to make his own judgments. In other words, although it appeared to be blind conformity, it may have been that the subject had reason to conform.

This is the way Asch reasoned. He thought that once the effect of this frame of reference was removed, there would be little or no conformity. He felt that people are rational enough so that they would trust their own perceptions and beliefs when reality supported them and that they would accordingly remain independent even in the face of a group that unanimously disagreed with them. He constructed an experiment (1951) to test this expectation.

The procedure was quite simple. A group of subjects was assembled to take part in a psychological study of visual judgment. They sat around a table and were told that they would be judging the lengths of lines. Then they were shown one white card on which had been drawn three black lines of various lengths and another white card containing only one black line. The subjects' task was to choose the line on the first card that was most similar in length to the line on the second card. As shown in Figure 7–1, it was an easy task. One of the lines was exactly the same length as the standard, whereas the other two were quite different from it.

When the lines were shown, the subjects answered aloud in the order in which they were seated. The first subject gave his choice and each of the others responded in turn. Since the judgment was so easy, there were no disagreements. When all had responded, a second set of lines was shown, responses were given, and a third set was produced.

At this point, the experiment seems dull and pointless. On the third trial, however, the first subject looked carefully at the lines as before and then gave what was obviously the wrong answer. In the example in Figure 7–1, he might have said A rather than B. The next subject gave the same wrong answer, as did the third and fourth subjects. When it was time for the fifth subject to respond, he was quite disturbed. It was clear to him that the others were giving wrong answers. He knew that B was the line most similar to X. Yet everyone else said it was A.

This, then, is the perfect conformity situation. The first four "subjects" were confederates who had been instructed to give incorrect answers on certain trials. The one real subject did not know this and was faced with a terrible choice: he had either to disagree with a unanimous majority of seemingly normal, healthy, intelligent people or to give an answer he knew was incorrect by the evidence of his own, usually trustworthy senses.

Note that in this situation the other people supplied relatively little information about the physical world. The stimuli to be judged were right in front of the subject, they were shown clearly, and there was little

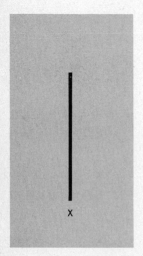
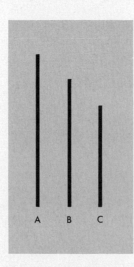

Figure 7–1

A representative stimulus in the Asch study. Subjects were shown the four lines simultaneously and asked which line was most similar in length to line X. When a number of confederates unanimously gave the incorrect answer (e.g., C), subjects conformed about 35 percent of the time.

question in his mind as to the correct answer. The others' responses did carry some information, of course—they told him what other people believed, what the normal, popular, usual response was in this situation.

The results did not support Asch's expectations. Even in this restricted situation, there was a great deal of conformity. Over many experiments and many trials within each experiment, subjects conformed on about 35 percent of the trials. That is, about 35 percent of the time they went against their own senses and gave the answer favored by the rest of the group. Some subjects never conformed; some conformed on all trials; but overall, the incorrect, conforming response was given about one time in three.

Conformity occurs even when individuals do not have to face one another. In the Asch study, the subjects were seated around a table, face-to-face. However, Gerard and Crutchfield devised a method of studying conformity when the subjects could not see the others who were making judgments. In this procedure, each subject is placed in a separate booth equipped with a panel of lights and three buttons. A stimulus is shown, and each subject is told to respond in turn by pressing one of the three buttons provided. As they respond, their answers are indicated by the lights on the panels. Thus, if subject 1 chooses A, all the subjects' boards would indicate this choice; then subject 2 would respond, and everyone would see his response; and so on. In this way, everyone sees the others' responses without actually being face-to-face with the group.

Actually, all subjects are told they are subject 4, and the experimenter controls all the lights himself. When subject 1 is supposed to respond, the experimenter merely causes the appropriate bulb to light in each booth; and the same for subjects 2 and 3. Then, when it is subject 4's turn, all the subjects respond and the experimenter records their responses from an indicator panel in front of him.

This procedure has several advantages over the standard Asch technique. It eliminates the facial expressions of the confederates that produce uncontrolled variations in the face-to-face situation; it enables the experimenter to test four subjects at a time; and it provides a comparison of face-to-face with anonymous conformity situations. The results of studies using this method confirmed Asch's findings. People did conform, and they did so even when they could not see the others in the group.

Conformity occurs when subjects are judging physical stimuli, opinion statements, statements of fact, logical syllogisms, and a variety of other materials. The answers with which they agree can be so obviously wrong that they are ridiculous. Asked to pick the line closest in length to an 8-inch line, subjects agreed with a majority that it was a $6\frac{1}{4}$-inch line, rather than another 8-inch line. Subjects have agreed that there is no population problem in the United States, because there is a distance of 6,000 miles between San Francisco and New York; that men are 8 to 9 inches taller than women on the average; and that male babies have a life expectancy of only twenty-five years. In other words, regardless of the type of stimulus and of how clear and unambiguous the correct choice is, when individuals are faced with a unanimous group opinion that differs from the correct one, the pressure exerted by the majority of the members is strong enough to produce an appreciable amount of conformity.

It is important to keep the unambiguousness of the situations in mind if one is to understand the phenomenon. There is a tendency to think that the conforming subjects are uncertain of the correct choice and therefore are swayed by the majority. This is not always the case. In many instances, the subjects are quite certain of the correct choice and, in the absence of group pressure, would choose correctly 100 percent of the time. When they conform, they are conforming despite the fact that they know the correct answer.

These results are very clear. People do conform to other people—even when to do so means they are going against their own perceptions of the world in an unambiguous situation. They do not really accept what the others are saying; in most cases, they believe themselves to be correct. Nevertheless, when asked to respond, they give the same response the others give. This is what we mean by conformity. People have an opinion and all the information necessary to support it, and yet they express an opinion that conforms to the opinion expressed by others.

## WHY DO PEOPLE CONFORM?

An individual in a conformity situation is under pressure from several sources. Most of the factors that affect conformity can be grouped into classes in terms of the kind of pressure they apply. There are those that determine the amount of trust an individual has in the group and in himself. These affect how much information the individual thinks the group's responses convey. Other factors in the situation affect the degree to which an individual wants to be similar to the group or, stated differently, how much he is concerned about being deviant. In addition, various characteristics of the individual himself determine his tendency to conform. Throughout our discussion of the variables that affect conformity, it will be helpful to keep these classes in mind. The operation of the specific variables can be most clearly understood in terms of these more general categories.

### Information and Trust

Other people are an important source of information. They often know something we do not, so by doing what they do, we may gain the benefit

Just
Say
No

Don't
do it
Kids

No.
Schachter

of their knowledge. A thirsty traveler at an oasis in the Sahara Desert who sees Arabs drinking from one well and avoiding another would do well to drink from the well they are using. Similarly, someone waiting for his turn at a Coca-Cola machine who sees someone lose a dime but then have success by using two nickels would do well to try the nickels before the dime. And a student who does not know an answer on a test and copies from the person sitting next to him is also indulging in an adaptive bit of conformity. All these people are doing what someone else is doing, because the other has or seems to have information they do not.

In a conformity situation, the individual initially holds one view and discovers that the group holds an opposing one. The individual wants to give the correct response. Therefore, the more he trusts the group or thinks it is a good source of information, the more likely he is to conform. At the extreme, if he thinks that the group is infallible, he will always go along with it, even though he might be quite certain of his own opinion. Similarly, if the group has vital information he does not have, conformity would be high. In either case, the individual would decide that he is mistaken and the group correct. In less extreme circumstances, the same mechanism operates. The more confidence one has in the group, the more shaken his own belief will be and the more he will conform. This does not necessarily mean that he is convinced by the group. It means his confidence in his own position is shaken enough so that he does not want to disagree. Therefore, the more the individual trusts the other members' opinions and distrusts his own and the more information he thinks their opinions convey, the more he will conform.

### Deviancy

An individual faced with a group that disagrees with him is reluctant to be deviant. He wants the group to like him, to treat him well, and to accept him. He is afraid that if he disagrees with them, they might dislike him, mistreat him, and consider him an outcast. He tends to conform in order to avoid these consequences.

This fear of being deviant is justified by the group's response to deviancy. In almost any group, there are strong pressures toward uniformity, and someone who does not conform risks grave consequences. When someone disagrees with the rest of the group, various efforts are made to get him to conform. The most straightforward is trying to convince him that he is wrong and the group right. This was shown in the study by Schachter (1951) that was described in Chapter 5. In that experiment, three confederates were included in a group—one of them consistently took a position deviant from that of the group, one started deviant and changed, and one took the same position as the group. Under these circumstances, the rest of the group spent a great deal of time trying to change the position of the two confederates who held deviant positions. They argued with the deviates, presented reasons to support their own position, cajoled, and did whatever they could to change the deviates' stand to agree with the group's.

Being the object of such an intensive campaign is not pleasant. The deviate feels great pressure to change in order to please everyone and to stop the attacks. If he does change, he is accepted and treated much like any other member of the group. If he maintains his deviant position, eventually the communication to him stops. The group decides that it cannot influence him and begins to ignore him. In the study, the group liked him less than someone who agreed with the group and tended to ostracize and reject him. When the time came to assign jobs, the deviate was never elected to top positions, was never the leader. Instead he was given the worst jobs.

Similar negative consequences of being deviant were found in the study by Freedman and Doob that was discussed in Chapter 4. A group of people who had never met before were brought together and given some information about each other. One of them was described as being different from the others, but just how he was different was not made clear. All the group knew was that his personality was in some way different from theirs. The group was then asked to choose one of their members to take part in a learning study. Whoever was chosen would have the job of responding, and whenever he made an incorrect response, he would receive an electric shock. It was clearly an unpleasant position to be in. The group chose the deviate overwhelmingly for the job of receiving the shocks. In another situation, the group had to choose someone to receive a reward of several dollars for taking part in a simple learning study. For this favorable position, the group avoided choosing the deviate and instead picked an average member. In other words, deviates are selected for painful, bad jobs and not for rewarding, good ones.

Drawing by Chas. Addams; © 1971 The New Yorker Magazine, Inc.

A group can also apply sanctions directly to a deviate. In a study at the Hawthorne plant of the Western Electric Company, observations were made of the behavior of a number of workers whose wages depended on their productivity. By working harder and accomplishing more, each worker could receive higher pay. However, the employees had developed their own standards as to the right amount of work to do in a day. Every day, after they had accomplished this amount of work, they slacked off. By working just this much, they earned a reasonable sum of money and did not have to work hard. Anyone who did work hard would make the others look bad and might cause management to increase its expectation of output. Thus, the group wanted to maintain its productivity at a fairly low average level.

In order to do this, the group exerted intense pressure on its members to be sure they did not surpass the established level. To begin with, the group set up a code of behavior. A person should not work too much or else he was a "rate buster." Nor should a person work too little— that would make him a "chiseler." In addition, the group devised a unique method of enforcing this code. Anyone who worked too fast or too slow could be "binged." Binging consisted of giving the deviate a sharp blow on the upper arm. Not only did this hurt but it was a symbolic punishment for going against the group's accepted behavior. Any group member could deliver the punishment, and the person who was binged could not fight back. He had to accept the punishment and the disapproval it indicated.

Binging is merely a dramatic example of the kinds of pressure present in all groups that cause members to conform to the accepted opinins, values, and behaviors. By persuasion, threats of ostracism, direct punishment, and offers of rewards, groups put pressure on individuals to conform. If they conform, they are accepted and treated well; if they remain deviant, they must face the consequences.

The strength of the desire not to be deviant varies considerably from person to person and from situation to situation. Some people probably do not feel it at all. In some circumstances, most people would probably like to be deviant. And there are some people who prefer to be deviant. These anticonformists deliberately take unpopular and different positions (Stricker et al., 1970). But for most people in most situations, there is a tendency to avoid being different and this fear of being deviant constitutes one of the important pressures that produces conformity.

The phenomenon of conformity is closely related to imitation and modeling. As we have discussed at various points throughout this book, particularly in the chapter on aggression, one of the major ways a behavior is learned or altered is through observing someone else performing that behavior. There is a strong tendency in humans and in most other animals to imitate what someone else does. Bandura (1965, etc.)

Drawing by Alex Graham; © 1963 *Punch*, London.

*"I fear we must have misread the invitation."*

demonstrated that children who watch someone behave aggressively are more likely to behave aggressively themselves. In fact if they watch someone who is aggressive, someone who is not aggressive, and someone who is moderately aggressive, they will behave aggressively, unaggressively, or moderately aggressively depending on whom they watch.

This phenomenon obviously has many similarities to conformity. In both cases the individual is doing what someone else does. And the underlying reasons for this kind of behavior are probably the same. Imitation occurs because the individual learns something from what the other person does, and also because he does not want to appear different from the other person. In the aggression situation he may learn that it is "correct" to be aggressive or that being aggressive will be rewarded, and these are very good reasons for behaving more aggressively. He may also behave more aggressively because he does not want to seem different from the other person—this is more like a conformity effect. In other words just as in the conformity situation, imitation is based partly on informational cues and partly on normative cues. (In most imitation situations, however, the emphasis is on informational cues rather than on normative cues as it tends to be in a conformity situation.)

### Characteristics of the Group

**Group Unanimity.**  An extremely important factor is the unanimity of the group opinion. When an individual is faced with a unanimous group decision that he disagrees with, he is under great pressure to conform. Under these circumstances, at least in the Asch situation, there is approximately 35 percent conformity with a majority of three. If, however, a group is not unanimous, there is a striking decrease in the amount of conformity. When there is even one person who does not go along with the rest of the group, conformity drops precipitously to about one-fourth the usual level. This is true when the size of the group is small, and it also appears to hold when the group is quite large, up to fifteen people. One of the most impressive aspects of this phenomenon is that it does not appear to matter who the other nonconforming person is. Regardless of whether he is a high-prestige, expert figure or has low prestige and is not at all expert, if he does not agree with the group, conformity tends to drop about three-fourths.

In one study (Malof and Lott, 1962), white Southern students were put into the standard Asch situation and faced with unanimous majorities who gave incorrect responses. Then, a black student in the group broke the unanimity by disagreeing with the majority. The amount of conformity—for both prejudiced and nonprejudiced subjects—greatly decreased. In fact, the black student disagreeing with the group caused conformity to decrease as much as did a white student disagreeing. Apparently, the presence of someone else who disagrees with the majority always makes it easier for an individual to express his own opinion, regardless of his feelings about the other person.

Moreover, this effect is found even when the other disagreer gives

Drawing by Handelsman; © 1972 The New Yorker Magazine, Inc.

*"Well heck! If all you smart cookies agree, who am I to dissent?"*

the wrong answer. If the majority says A, another person says C, and the correct answer is B, the subject is less likely to conform than if everyone agreed on one incorrect answer. Simply having some disagreement within the rest of the group makes it easier for one person to remain independent despite the fact that no one agrees with him.

In a study by Allen and Levine (1971) subjects were presented with either a unanimous majority, a three-man majority and a fourth person who gave the correct answer, or a three-man majority and a fourth person who gave a different answer but one that was even more incorrect than that of the majority. The subjects made three kinds of judgments—perceptual evaluations such as those used by Asch, information such as whether Hawaii was a state, and opinion items for which there was no actual correct answer but there were popular ones. The results are shown in Table 7–1. For all three items, the unanimous majority produced more conformity than either of the nonunanimous conditions. The effect was strongest for the perceptual items and weakest for the opinion items. The fascinating finding was that for both perceptual and information items, there was practically no difference in amount of conformity when the fourth subject gave the correct answer from when the fourth subject gave an even more incorrect answer than the majority. Even when the dissenter gave an answer further away from the subject's own impression than that given by the majority, conformity was cut approximately in half. The results were somewhat less clear for opinion items. On these, when the dissenter agreed with the subject's opinion, there was a little less conformity than when he gave an even more discrepant answer; but even then there was somewhat less conformity than when the majority was unanimous.

This effect appears to be due to several factors. First, the amount of

Table 7–1

CONFORMITY PRODUCED BY UNANIMOUS MAJORITIES, AND BY MAJORITIES WITH ONE DISSENTER WHO GIVES EITHER THE CORRECT OR AN EVEN MORE INCORRECT CHOICE

|  | TYPE OF JUDGMENT | | |
|  | Perception | Information | Opinion |
| --- | --- | --- | --- |
| Unanimous | .97 | .78 | .89 |
| One correct | .40 | .43 | .59 |
| One more incorrect than majority | .47 | .42 | .72 |

Source: Adapted from Allen and Levine (1969).

trust in the majority decreases whenever there is disagreement, even when the person who disagrees is less expert or less reliable than those who make up the majority. Of course, this is in a situation in which the person himself is also disagreeing with the majority. That is, he initially holds an opinion different from theirs, and he discovers that someone else does also. The mere fact that someone else also disagrees with the group indicates that there is room for doubt, that the issue is not perfectly clear, and, thus, that the majority might be wrong. This reduces the individual's reliance on the majority opinion as a source of information and accordingly reduces conformity. Second, if another person takes the same position that the individual favors, it serves to strengthen his confidence in his own judgment. As we shall discuss in more detail below, greater confidence reduces conformity. A third consideration involves the individual's reluctance to appear deviant. When he disagrees with everyone else, he stands out and is deviant in both his own and the others' eyes. When someone else also disagrees, neither of them is as deviant as he would be if he were alone. Thus, there is less tendency to conform in order to avoid being deviant and, consequently, less conformity.

This last result should probably be taken as encouragement to speak one's mind even when he disagrees with almost everybody. In the story "The Emperor's New Clothes," for example, the whole crowd watched the naked emperor in his supposedly beautiful new clothes. However, when only one person had the strength to say that the emperor was naked, everyone else found strength to defy the pressures of the majority; after a while the majority had become the minority and perhaps even disappeared. Certainly, this is a strong argument for freedom of speech, because it suggests that even one deviant voice can have a sizeable, important effect as long as there are other people who inwardly disagree with the majority but are afraid to speak up. It may also explain why in totalitarian states and some orthodox religions no dissent is allowed. Even one small voice disagreeing with the ruling powers could encourage others to do likewise. Then, after a while, the regime would be in danger of toppling. Perhaps it is dangerous to make too much of this one finding, but it does stand out as one of the most striking aspects of the conformity process.

### Characteristics of the Group

The strength of an individual's tendency to look to groups as sources of information and the strength of his desire to avoid being deviant are affected by many variables. The composition of the groups is very important.

**Group Size.**   Suppose there were two people in a room and one of them said that it was very warm. If the room was, in fact, quite cold, the second person would be unlikely to agree with the first. He would feel cold himself and would assume that the other was mistaken or feverish. If forced to make a public statement on the temperature of the room, he would probably say he thought it was rather cold.

If the room contained five people and four of them said it was warm, the situation would change markedly. Even if one person felt cold, he would be likely to doubt his own perceptions. After all, it is somewhat unlikely that all four of the others were feverish or mistaken. If he were asked how he felt, he might be uncertain enough to agree with the rest. He might say that the room was warm and then wonder what was wrong with him. When one person disagrees with you, he is feverish; when four others do, you must be sick yourself. Four people tend to be more trustworthy than one, in terms of both honesty and the reliability of their opinions; it is harder to mistrust a group than one person. Four people saying something offer better information than just one.

A series of experiments has demonstrated that conformity does increase as the size of the unanimous majority increases, at least up to a point. In some of his early experiments, Asch (1951) varied the size of the majority from two to sixteen. As shown in Table 7–2, he found that two people produced more pressure than one, three a lot more than two, and four about the same as three. Somewhat surprisingly, he found that increasing the size of the group past four did not increase the amount of conformity, at least up to sixteen. Thus, he concluded that to produce

Table 7–2

*GROUP SIZE AND CONFORMITY*

| *Size of Unanimous Majority* | *Asch Study (Males)* | *Gerard Study (Males)* | *Gerard Study (Females)* |
|---|---|---|---|
| 1 | 2.8 | 12.6 | |
| 2 | 12.8 | | 21.0 |
| 3 | 33.3 | 25.9 | |
| 4 | 35.0 | | 33.6 |
| 5 | | 24.1 | |
| 6 | | | 34.6 |
| 7 | | 30.1 | |
| 8 | 32.0 | | |
| 16 | 31.3 | | |

Source: Adapted from Asch (1951) and Gerard, Wilhelmy, and Connolley (1968).

the most conformity the optimal group size was three or four and that an additional increase did not have any effect.

Gerard, Wilhelmy, and Connolley produced somewhat different results in a more recent study (1968). They tested male subjects with unanimous majorities of one, three, five, and seven and female subjects with majorities of two, four, and six. The amount of conformity with each size group is shown in the table. It can be seen that there was a large increase when the group size was increased from one to three for men and from two to four for women. This is essentially what Asch found—the major effect of group size occurs when the group is increased beyond size two. Unlike Asch's results, however, these new data suggest that additional conformity is produced by still larger groups. Although there is a slight dip for men in groups with a majority of five, both males and females conform most when faced with the largest groups.

Using quite a different procedure and different measures, Milgram et al. (1969) produced similar results. The situation was very simple. On a very crowded street in New York City, a number of people played the old game of looking up in the sky to see whether anyone else would look up also. This time it was done as a deliberate experiment and careful observations were made of the passers-by. The confederates stood and looked up at the sixth floor window of an office building across the street. Either one, two, three, five, ten, or fifteen confederates stood around looking up at the window. The chief measure is what percentage of those who passed by actually stopped and looked up at the window also. When one person was looking up, only 4 percent of the passers-by conformed to his behavior; with five it went up to 16 percent; with ten it was 22 percent and with fifteen it was 40 percent.

Given these results, it is probably safe to say that within limits increasing the size of the group does put more pressure on the individual to conform. In some situations a group of three or four produces a great deal of pressure to conform and increasing the size of the group does not produce a comparable increase in the amount of conformity. In other situations a group of that size produces relatively little pressure and therefore the amount of conformity will increase substantially as the size of the group increases. In either case it may be that a much larger group, say five hundred, would produce a great deal more conformity. Although there is no evidence to support this, it seems plausible that it is harder to resist five hundred people who are, for example, all saluting than it is to resist only five or ten. For the moment, however, this is untested in an experimental situation and we are left with the general statement that a larger group produces more conformity up to some point and the increase in conformity then levels off.

**Expertise of the Group.** Another characteristic of groups that is relevant to conformity is the expertise of the group members. How much do they know about the topic under discussion? How qualified are they to give information?

The more expert a group is in relation to an individual, the more he should trust them and consider their opinion valuable information. If, in our example concerning room temperature, the other people in the room were ill with the flu or were Eskimos just off the plane from Alaska, the individual would probably be inclined to discount their opinions and trust his own. He would be less likely to conform than if the others were neighbors who were in good health. On the other hand, suppose the scene was shifted to the wilds of northern Alaska, and the problem was to discover the right way back to camp. If the individual had a strong feeling that the correct route was to the left but the rest of the group disagreed with him, he obviously would be more likely to trust four Eskimos than four neighbors from home. He would conform more to the Eskimos than to his neighbors. Although the evidence on this is somewhat meager, it appears that the more expert a group is relative to an individual, with expertise defined in terms of the specific judgments or opinions being stated, the more the individual will conform.

**Status.** The higher the status of the majority members, the more conformity occurs. In the Torrance study mentioned in chapter 6, the Air Force groups that were working on problems varied in status from pilot to gunner. In almost all cases, the group came to a unanimous decision on the simple problems. The striking finding was that when the gunner happened to arrive independently at the correct answer, if the pilot disagreed with him, the group often ended up with the wrong answer. On the other hand, when the pilot arrived at the correct answer, the group almost always arrived at the correct answer. In other words, the gunner, who was the lowest-status person, was not always able to convince the group that he was correct, even when he had the right answer. Instead, the group often convinced him that he was wrong. However, the pilot, even when he had the wrong answer, was often able to convince the group that he was right.

Just as high-status individuals have more influence than those with low status, so high-status groups produce more conformity than low-status groups. This effect may be understood most clearly in terms of the desire to be similar to the group and to avoid being deviant. An individual wants to be like the group so that the group will accept him; in addition, being similar imbues the individual with the qualities of the group. When the group has high status, he has more to gain by conforming. He acquires more status than from a low-status group, and it is more desirable to be accepted by the former than the latter. Thus, the higher a group's status, the stronger is one's desire to be similar to it and the more conformity occurs.

**History of Group Agreement.** The typical experimental conformity situation begins with a series of trials on which the subject and the rest of the group agree. The correct answer is given by the whole group, and when the subject's turn comes, he naturally responds correctly. This initial series of trials is designed primarily to make the situation believable, but it also increases the subject's confidence in his own and the group's ability to perform the task. The "conformity" trials follow—those in which the rest of the group give incorrect responses before it is the subject's turn to answer. When the first disagreement occurs, the subject is startled because the group has been agreeing with him all along. He is under considerable pressure to conform, because he feels the group is competent at making these judgments.

On the other hand, if disagreements occur during the initial series of judgments, the situation is quite different. If the whole group did not consistently agree with the subject, he has less confidence in his own ability and much less confidence in the group's ability. Perhaps most important, he realizes that disagreements are possible. When the first conformity trial occurs, he is, accordingly, less surprised and under less pressure to agree because the group appears less expert.

Several studies have investigated the effect on conformity of prior agreement. In a typical experiment on this problem (Julian et al., 1967), there were two series of twenty trials each. During the first series, the subject responded first and then was led to believe that varying numbers of the other subjects agreed with him. There were five conditions: (1) all four other members agreed with the subject (100 percent); (2) three agreed with him, with the one disagreeing changing from trial to trial (75 percent); (3) two agreed (50 percent); (4) one agreed (25 percent); and (5) none agreed (0 percent). The second series was run in the usual manner, with the subject responding last and the rest of the group giving the same incorrect response.

The results indicated, first, that the greater the agreement during the first series, the more confident the subject was of his performance, and, second, that the greatest amount of conformity occurred following 100 percent agreement, with all the other conditions producing considerably less conformity. There was conformity on 34 percent of the trials in the 100 percent agreement condition and only 19 percent on the average in the other conditions. Beyond that, the data were less clear.

The relationship between amount of prior agreement and conformity seems quite complicated. This particular study suggested that 0 and 75 percent prior agreement produced the least conformity, with the 50 and 25 percent conditions being higher and about equal. Exactly why this should be so is not apparent, although at least two studies have shown this pattern. At the moment, the one consistent result is that 100 percent agreement causes the greatest subsequent conformity, despite the fact that subjects in this condition were most confident of their own performance. In other words, although they were more confident, they were also more susceptible to group pressure. Their confidence in themselves was less important than their greater confidence in the group in the 100 percent condition and the greater acceptabiliy of disagreeing in the other conditions.

**Group Cohesiveness.** Another important dimension affecting conformity concerns the individual's relationship to the group. Do the members feel close to the group or not? How much do they want to be members of the group? The term *cohesiveness* has been used to include all these considerations. It refers to the total sum of the forces causing people to feel drawn to a group and that makes them want to remain members of it. The more the members like one another, expect to gain from group membership, feel loyalty, and so on, the more cohesive the group is.

Greater cohesiveness leads to greater conformity. When working for a valuable prize, a group produces more conformity than when there is no prize or a smaller one. A group that considers its task important or values itself highly produces more conformity among its members than one that puts less value on its task or itself. Moreover, group members conform more in a group with a lot of group spirit.

This increased conformity is due to the individuals' reluctance to be deviant. As we saw earlier, being deviant involves the risk of rejection. Someone who is deviant too often or on too important an issue may be mistreated and, in the extreme case, may be ejected from the group. The more one cares about the group, the more serious his fear of rejection is and the less likely he is to disagree. The less he cares about the group, the less serious his fear is and the more he would disagree. If someone is a member of a small group of friends, he has a tendency to avoid being a minority of one on any issue. Fear of rejection or expulsion is at least one reason for this. If, however, he no longer likes the group or feels that it is restricting his social life, this pressure to conform decreases. The worst that could happen if he deviates is that he would be thrown out of the group. When this ceases to be a serious threat, there is less reason for conforming and he feels freer to be deviant.

**Sense of Security.**   If we assume that an individual values a group and wants to remain a member, the strength of his position in the group should be an important determinant of his conformity to it. If he is sure of his acceptance by the group, he should be relatively unconcerned about being rejected, simply because he deviated on a particular issue. If, on the other hand, he is uncertain of his position and is not confident of his acceptance by the group, he should be more concerned about being rejected for deviating. Greater security should therefore produce less conformity.

A study by Dittes and Kelley (1956) provides some support for this analysis. Within limits, subjects who felt more accepted by a group conformed less than those who felt less accepted. Subjects who were low or very low on acceptance conformed less than those who were moderately well accepted. This was presumably due to these subjects' rejecting the group before it could reject them. Once the individual devalues the group, he no longer has to fear rejection and he therefore can conform less. Thus, a member of a group who is accepted enough so that he thinks he will be able to remain but not so much that he is overly confident would be most concerned about being rejected and would conform most.

### Characteristics of the Situation

**Anonymity.**   One interesting variable affecting conformity is whether or not the subject is actually facing the other members of the group. The method of using pseudogroups, described previously, provides a convenient way of comparing face-to-face with anonymous groups. In the typical situation, the individual sits at a table with several other people. A problem is presented, the others give their responses one by one, and then the subject must respond. All the others make the same response, and as each one answers, everyone looks at him. When it is the subject's turn, the others look toward him and wait for him to answer. This is contrasted with a situation in which the subject is alone in a booth. He cannot see the others nor they him. He hears their answers over earphones or sees them indicated by lights on a board. When his turn comes, he responds by speaking into a microphone or pressing a button. Experiments have shown that the face-to-face group produces more conformity. For example, in one study (Deutsch and Gerard, 1955), there were 30 percent conforming responses in the face-to-face situation and only 25 percent in the private booths. In another experiment (Mouton, Blake, and Olmstead, 1956), all the subjects were in separate booths, but the experimenters varied whether or not their responses were anonymous. In the public condition, the subjects announced their names before responding, whereas in the private condition, they did not give their names. There was more conformity in the public condition. And in a study by Raven (1959), some subjects thought their responses would be public while others thought they would be private. There was 30 percent conformity in the public condition and only 26 percent conformity in the private condition.

The effect of anonymity must be due primarily to an individual's perception of the consequences of being a deviant. When a subject's responses are entirely confidential and the rest of the group can never find out that he deviated, the risk of being rejected or mistreated is completely eliminated. Even when his responses are public knowledge but he is not actually facing the rest of the group, the risk is reduced somewhat. The group cannot sneer at him, ridicule him, or do anything else unpleasant to his face. He is hidden away in the relative safety of his booth. The group may mistreat him later, but he avoids the immediate unpleasantness. Thus, concern about possible rejection and mistreatment should be eliminated in anonymous and lowered in non-face-to-face situations, and these situations should accordingly produce less conformity.

Another factor is that in the face-to-face situation the responses of the majority members carry more weight. A person's voice heard through earphones may be trusted less than when it comes directly from the person. A response indicated only by a light on a board may not be imbued with the power, forcefulness, and credibility of the same response uttered in person. The sincerity on the faces of the group members may be an important component of the information they convey. Certainly politicians who travel in order to shake thousands of hands and utter a few remarks feel contact is important.

**Confidence in One's Own Judgment.** We have discussed the importance of trust in the group's opinion. Their response conveys information, and the more an individual accepts it, the more likely he is to conform. The motivation behind this is presumably a desire to be correct. The individual wants to give the right response, and, to some extent, he uses the group's response as an indication of what that is.

The desire to be correct also involves the characteristics of the problem itself and the individual's relationship to it. Another source of information in any situation is one's own perception of the physical stimulus or understanding of the cognitive problem and one's belief as to the correct answer. As we have seen, the more someone trusts the group, the more he conforms. Conversely, the more he trusts himself (and his perceptions), the less he conforms. If he trusts his own opinion, he will not be swayed by that of the group. Thus, any variables that increase an individual's self-reliance result in less conformity.

One factor that has a powerful effect on confidence and, consequently, on the amount of conformity is the difficulty of the judgment to be made. The more difficult the judgment, the less confidence the individual tends to have and the more likely he is to conform to others' judgments.

If someone asks us to name the capital of our home state, we know the answer and are sure we know it. Even if four other people gave a different answer, we probably would trust ourselves more than them. We are unlikely to conform, at least not because of lack of confidence in ourselves—we may still conform for the other reasons cited. However, if we are asked to name the capital of Sierra Leone, the question is more difficult. Even if we have some idea of the correct answer, we are probably less certain. Then, if four people disagree with us, we are more likely to trust them and conform. The same is true with any problem. As difficulty increases, our confidence decreases and we conform more.

Coleman, Blake, and Mouton (1958) presented subjects in a conformity situation with a series of factual questions that varied in difficulty. The correlation between difficulty and conformity was .58 for men and .89 for women. That is, the more difficult the item, the more likely the subject was to conform to an incorrect response.

Additional evidence supports the idea that this effect of difficulty was due to confidence. In a similar situation (Krech and Crutchfield, 1962, p. 510), subjects were asked to indicate how certain they were of their judgments on several items. On those items that the subjects were quite certain of, there was only 15 percent conformity; items that the subjects were fairly certain of produced 24 percent conformity; and when the subjects were somewhat uncertain, there was 36 percent conformity. It seems quite clear that as the subjects' judgments became less ambiguous, as the problems became easier, there was less conformity. Conversely, as the problems became more difficult and the subjects found it harder to make certain judgments, there was more conformity.

A related variable is how competent a person feels to make the responses. Obviously the question about Sierra Leone's capital would be easier for an expert on Africa than for a social psychologist. If one considers himself a math expert, he would be more confident of his answers to math problems than if he were not an expert; moreover, this holds even if the problems are quite difficult for him. Someone with good eyes would be more confident in making visual discriminations than someone with bad eyes.

This effect has been demonstrated in several studies (Mausner, 1954; Snyder, Mischel, and Lott, 1960), in which the subjects were made to feel more confident of their own ability relative to that of the rest of the group. The more expert they felt, the less they conformed. Regardless of the difficulty of a problem, someone who feels competent is more confident and conforms less.

With perceptual problems, one's confidence is affected by whether or not the stimuli are actually present. If someone is asked to judge which of three lines is longest, the greater the difference in length of the lines, of course, the easier it is to answer correctly. Regardless of the difficulty, however, most subjects are more certain of their choice if the lines remain in view. When the other people pick a different answer, the individual can look back at the stimuli to reinforce his own opinion. When the stimuli are removed before the responses are made, the individual has only his memory to rely on. Under these circumstances, the group's response differs not so much from the individual's perception and judgment as from his memory. Direct perception is something we all learn to trust almost completely. Our senses rarely deceive us in familiar situations, or at least we believe they do not. But our memories are much less reliable. We know that we often forget things, remember incorrectly, and so on.

Deutsch and Gerard (1955) compared the amount of conformity that occurred when the stimuli were present and when they were absent. In one situation, stimuli were shown and all subjects responded while they were still visible. In another situation, the stimuli were removed and three seconds later, the first confederate made his judgment. This meant that the subject did not respond until ten to fifteen seconds after he had seen the stimuli. There was an average of 34 percent conforming responses in the memory series but only 25 percent in the visual series.

Although confidence in one's own judgment is an important determinant of amount of conformity, it is important to remember that there was still some conformity when the situations were extremely unambiguous. For example, in the study on the effect of confidence levels described above, even on the items for which the subjects were certain, there was 15 percent conformity. In other studies, mentioned previously, it was found that subjects agreed with group opinions that were clearly and obviously incorrect. Greater confidence in his own judgment does increase a subject's ability to resist the pressure to conform, but this does not mean that conformity occurs only because the subject is uncertain of the correct choice. It merely implies that any degree of uncertainty (e.g., being 99 rather than 100 percent certain) makes it harder to resist the group and increases conformity.

**Commitment.** A different kind of factor that influences conformity is the degree of an individual's commitment to his initial judgment or opinion. We can define *commitment* as the total force that makes it difficult to give up a position, that binds the person to his position. Typically, we think of commitment in terms of an individual's feelings of being bound. Does he feel free to change his opinion or does he feel, for some reason, that he cannot or should not change it?

There are many ways of producing commitment to an initial judgment. The subject can write it down, say it aloud in the presence of others, or take any action that establishes his opinion in his own or others' eyes. In the standard Asch situation, the subject feels little commitment to his initial judgment. He has looked at the stimuli and presumably made a judgment. But he has not communicated this judgment to anybody. He has not said it aloud, written it down, or in any way made it a concrete decision. He would not embarrass himself by changing; he would not be admitting that he was wrong or that he was a weak person. There is no reason for him to stick to his initial judgment except a belief that it is correct. Under these circumstances, maximum conformity occurs.

Once the subject expresses his opinion, he becomes more committed to it. If others know his initial opinion, they would know that he has changed. The rest of the group accordingly might feel that he is allowing himself to be influenced by group pressure, that he does not have the courage of his convictions, and so on. The individual himself would feel this way. On the other hand, if he has never made his feelings concrete in any way, he can tell himself that his initial judgment was only a first impression, that he was never sure of it, that he changed because he thought it over more carefully. Thus, once one commits himself to a position, he is more reluctant to give in to group pressure and conforms less.

The degree of the subject's commitment to his first judgment was varied in a study conducted by Deutsch and Gerard (1955). Some subjects (no-commitment condition) saw the stimuli but did not make a public or private statement of their opinion until they had heard the judgments of the rest of the group. Others gave a minimal private commitment by writing their answers down on a magic pad before hearing any other responses. A magic pad is a familiar child's toy which has a piece of cellophane over a layer of graphite. When one writes on the cellophane, it presses into the graphite and the words appear. Lifting the cellophane causes the words to disappear. In this condition (self-commitment, magic pad), the subjects wrote their responses on the magic pad, heard the others' responses, gave their own response, and then erased the pad. In a third condition (strong self-commitment), the subjects wrote their answers on a sheet of paper that they knew was not going to be collected and that they did not sign. Finally there was a public-commitment condition, in which the subjects wrote their response on a piece of paper, signed the paper, and knew that it was going to be collected at the end of the study. Thus, the four levels of commitment were none; private, magic pad; private, written; and public.

The results are shown in Table 7–3. Clearly commitment reduces conformity. Even the magic-pad condition, in which the subjects knew that no one would ever see what they had written, produced less conformity than the non-commitment condition. The stronger commitments reduced conformity even further. Interestingly, there was no difference between public and strong private commitment, perhaps because the latter produced such strong commitment that conformity was already at a very low level.

A somewhat different type of commitment involves the behavior of conforming itself. Someone who, for one reason or another, does not conform on the first few trials tends to become committed to this non-conforming behavior. Similarly, someone who does conform at the beginning tends to get committed to that behavior. An individual can be induced to conform from the start by giving him difficult discriminations. When he is subsequently given easier problems, he tends to continue to conform. If, on the other hand, he is given easy problems at the beginning and does not conform to the obviously wrong answers of the other people, he will continue to be independent even when he is later given difficult problems.

This is particularly true when responses are public. When others know a subject's responses, they know whether or not he is conforming. This increases his commitment to a conformist or independent line. Thus, in a face-to-face situation, someone who conforms on early trials continues to conform, and someone who does not conform is generally independent throughout. In a non-face-to-face situation, this effect is less

Table 7–3

COMMITMENT AND CONFORMITY

| Commitment | Percentage of Conforming Responses |
|---|---|
| None | 24.7 |
| Private, magic pad | 16.3 |
| Private, written | 5.7 |
| Public | 5.7 |

Source: Adapted from Deutsch and Gerard (1955).

strong, and, in fact, there is a general tendency for most subjects to conform more on later trials. Commitment, therefore, can be to either a particular response (e.g., A is the right answer) or a type of behavior (e.g., conforming).

### Trust in the Situation

We should note that in studying conformity it is absolutely essential that the subject be unaware of any deception that is involved. If he knows that the other subjects are confederates or that their responses are faked, there will be little pressure toward conformity. When subjects are told of the deception (Horowitz and Rothschild, 1970) and asked to pretend that the responses are real, conformity is greatly reduced. As we shall discuss in chapter 14, role playing of this sort is generally not a useful technique of research. This is particularly true in the case of conformity where the pressure on the subject comes entirely from the apparent unanimity of the other peoples' responses. As soon as the subject knows that the others do not really believe what they are saying or even that they are not unanimous, the reason for conforming is removed. The subject's decision is whether to give the answer he favors and appear deviant and possibly wrong, or to give the other answer but go against his own senses. Obviously this dilemma exists only if he thinks that the other subjects believe in what they are saying.

The necessity of deceiving the subject is a problem in laboratory research on conformity. In the real world, however, people often find themselves confronted by a group that disagrees with them. This happens more on attitudinal or value issues than on perceptual judgments, but it is a fairly common occurrence. Thus the laboratory research on conformity does apply to actual situations. The difference is that in the laboratory one is usually forced to rely on some sort of deception to produce a conformity situation, and in these cases it is essential to make certain that the deception is effective.

### Characteristics of the Individual

Thus far, we have been talking about factors that vary with the group or the situation. These tend to operate in much the same way for all individuals. In addition there are variables that each person brings with him to a situation. There are enormous individual differences in how much people conform, even in the same situation. Some people conform on 100 percent of the trials; others conform on no trials. How do the conformers and nonconformers differ?

To begin with, although there are few controlled experiments on this variable, there appear to be differences in the amount of conformity shown by people of different nationalities. For example, a direct comparison of Norwegians and Frenchmen (Milgram, 1961) found that in a variety of situations and with a variety of different types of subject, the Norwegians conformed more than the French. Exactly why this occurred is not clear, but it seems to be consistent with the traditional emphasis on individuality in French life and the strong sense of social responsibility and group identification found in Norwegian society.

In another study (Frager, 1970) Japanese students were found to engage in anticonformity more than American students, i.e., they deliberately took a minority position, even when it was wrong. Anticonformity was also related to alienation—to rejection of contemporary Japanese society, and nostalgia for the old days of Japan. Schneider (1970) found that both black and white children conformed more when the majority was white than when the majority was black. However in this study, as in others on the matter, there was no general tendency for black children to be more conforming than white children, despite the common hypothesis that racial prejudice forces blacks to be more submissive than whites. It seems likely that there are considerable differences among other ethnic groups and subgroups, with some tending to conform a lot and others tending to conform relatively little.

There are also great differences in the amount of conformity shown by different individuals within a society. A number of studies have been conducted on this problem, but, unfortunately, the results tend to be somewhat weak and inconsistent. Nevertheless, we can make some generalizations in which we have a fair amount of confidence.

**Sex.** In past research, the strongest and most consistent factor that has differentiated people in the amount they conform is their sex. Women have been found to conform more than men. Julian et al. (1966) found that women conformed 35 percent of the time in a wide variety of experimental conditions, whereas men conformed only 22 percent of the time. In a later study (Julian et al., 1967), the comparable figures were 28 percent for women and 15 percent for men. These figures are representative of a wide variety of studies conducted during the 1950s and early 1960s which almost invariably found women to be more conforming than men. This finding was widely interpreted as evidence that cultural prescriptions for docility and submissiveness in the female overrode other personality variables that might differentiate among people.

For years this difference between males and females in amount of conformity was widely accepted as more or less a fact of life. However, the recent Women's Liberation Movement has brought about a heightened awareness of possible forms of subtle discrimination and unfair treatment of women. This in turn has caused experimenters to look more closely at the conformity situation in order to discover whether women are inherently more likely to conform or whether their greater conformity is brought about by other factors.

In particular, some investigators have begun to question whether the earlier findings reflected greater docility among women, or whether they were due to the use of male-oriented materials in experiments conducted by men, about which women would naturally not be especially expert or confident in their own judgment.

This suspicion has led to studies in which the sex relatedness of the materials has been varied, to test the hypothesis that women would be more conformist on male-oriented materials, and men would be more conformist on female-oriented materials. Perhaps women are quite conformist about sports and cars and politics, while men are more conformist about high fashion, cooking, perfume, child care, and other matters conventionally associated with the female sex role. Sistrunk and McDavid (1971) tested this hypothesis with considerable care. They began with a pool of 100 statements about a variety of everyday opinions and matters of fact; then had 53 subjects judge them for sex relatedness. Those items that at least 80 percent of these subjects judged as of greater interest and sophistication for men than women were used as "masculine" items, and a similar cut-off point was used to select "feminine" items. All these items (along with some neutral filler items) were then given to 270 new subjects from high schools and colleges in Florida, in four separate experiments. A faked "majority response" was indicated on each item, and the subject's conformity was measured by the extent to which he agreed with this "majority response."

The results are shown in Table 7–4. In all four experiments, there was no significant effect of sex by itself. Women were not appreciably

Table 7–4

AMOUNT OF CONFORMITY BY MALES AND FEMALES FOR ITEMS CONSIDERED MASCULINE, FEMININE, AND NEUTRAL.

|  | TYPE OF ITEM | | | |
| --- | --- | --- | --- | --- |
|  | Masculine | Feminine | Neutral | Total |
| Males | 34.15 | 43.05 | 39.65 | 38.95 |
| Females | 42.75 | 34.55 | 39.10 | 38.80 |

Source: Adapted from Sistrunk and McDavid (1971).

more conforming than men. On neutral items the two sexes conformed almost exactly the same amount. However, males conformed more on feminine items, and females conformed more on masculine items. Thus what has generally been accepted as a basic difference between men and women in terms of conformity may turn out to be simply a function of the particular experimental situation. The male experimenters who have done most of the research on conformity probably did not choose the items in order to discriminate against women by showing that they were more conformist. Yet because men were doing the research, they tended to choose items with which they were more familiar and thus unintentionally did produce a biased situation. As of now there has not been enough research using unbiased items to eliminate entirely the possibility that overall sex differences do exist, but this recent research casts considerable doubt on the previous findings to this effect.

**Intelligence.**  Another dependable finding seems to be that the amount of conformity varies inversely with intelligence. More intelligent people tend to conform less than those with low intelligence. It seems likely to us that the explanation lies simply in the individual's confidence in his own opinion. The more intelligent one is, the more likely it is that during his lifetime he has been correct in most of his judgments and that he therefore has built up a fair amount of self-confidence. When he finds himself in a situation in which his judgment is discrepant from that of the majority, because he has more self-confidence, he tends to be able to resist the pressure of the majority. A person of low intelligence, on the other hand, has often found himself to be incorrect in making judgments, and he therefore has little confidence in his own opinions. When he is faced with a majority that disagrees with him, he tends to give in more readily.

**Self-Esteem.**  The explanation of the effect of intelligence on conformity fits in nicely with the finding that people who conform a lot tend to have low self-esteem. They tend to have feelings of inferiority and inadequacy and to lack self-confidence. Conversely, people who conform little tend to have relatively high self-esteem, to be self-confident, and not to have feelings of inferiority and inadequacy. Once again, we find that the more confidence a person has in himself and his judgments, the less he tends to conform to the opinions of others when those opinions disagree with his (Consturzo, 1970).

In addition to these findings, which are fairly well documented, a number of other deductions about the personality of conformers and nonconformers are suggested by the data, but they are not yet supported by enough evidence for us to be certain of them. There are suggestions, for example, that conformers are more anxious, less able to cope with stress, less spontaneous, more repressed, more passive, and more distrustful of other people. The conformers also seem to have a lower tolerance for ambiguity and to be more rigid, more dogmatic, and more authoritarian. In general, the picture of the conformist that emerges from these suggestive findings, is one of a relatively weak, somewhat disturbed, somewhat narrow, and conservative person. However, it must be stressed that, at the moment, these findings are only suggestive and further research is necessary before we can be confident of them.

In closing the discussion of conformity, it is important to recall the distinction between adaptive and what we called blind conformity. Most of the chapter focused on the latter and described it in generally negative terms. It is clear, however, that in order for society to exist at all, its members must share, to some extent, certain conventions, attitudes, values, and behavior. The individual must conform to some of the ways of his culture—someone who never conforms cannot survive. This sort of conformity is adaptive and, within limits, highly desirable. In contrast, blind conformity, out of fear or rejection or lack of self-confidence, is generally not adaptive and ordinarily not desirable.

## CHAPTER REVIEW

1. People in a subculture as similar to one another; people in different cultures as often quite dissimilar.
2. Conformity as often highly adaptive.
3. People conform even when it means responding incorrectly.
4. The need for information and the fear of being deviant as two major factors affecting conformity.
5. A non-unanimous group produces less conformity than one that is unanimous.
6. Group size and confidence as affecting the amount of conformity.
7. Group cohesiveness as an important determinant of conformity.
8. An individual who commits himself to one position is less likely to conform to a new position.
9. Individual differences in amount of conformity.
10. Sex differences—a new look.

## APPLICATIONS AND SPECULATIONS

1. In our society and subcultures of our society, some classes of behavior are subject to more pressures toward conformity than others. Clothing, for example, is an area of fads and great conformity, but also of

innovation. Which behaviors in society seem to require the most conformity and why?

2. A related observation is that some people are permitted to be more nonconformist than others. Who and why?

3. Racial integration of housing, schools, jobs, and so on means that nonwhite minority members would be living, learning, and working in the midst of the white majority. This integration can occur in many different ways. In particular, the size and mix of the groups can differ considerably. The minority can be spread evenly throughout the society so that in any given situation they will be in a definite minority. Or relatively large groups of minority members can be placed in some groups of the society so that they will be in less of a minority in those groups but will have no representation in other groups. What would be the different effects of the two possibilities just described?

4. The Bill of Rights of the United States Constitution, liberal philosophers and politicians, and, currently, the American Civil Liberties Union argue that people should be allowed to express their opinions regardless of how unpopular they may be. In terms of the principles discussed in this chapter, what is the implication of allowing this form of dissent? Why do you think so many people get so upset by dissent?

*SUGGESTIONS FOR ADDITIONAL READING*

### Articles

Allen, V. L., and Levine, J. M. Social support and conformity: the role of independent assessment of reality. *Journal of Experimental Social Psychology*, 1971, 7, 48–58.

Deutsch, M., and Gerard, H. B. A study of normative and informational social influences upon individual judgment. *Journal of Abnormal and Social Psychology*, 1955, 51, 629–36.

Dittes, J. E., and Kelley, H. H. Effects of different conditions of acceptance on conformity to group norms. *Journal of Abnormal and Social Psychology*, 1956, 53, 100–107.

Malof, M., and Lott, A. J. Ethnocentrism and the acceptance of negro support in a group pressure situation. *Journal of Abnormal and Social Psychology*, 1965, 65, 254–58.

*Books and Longer Discussions*

Freedman, J. L., and Doob, A. N. *Deviancy.* New York: Academic, Press, 1968.

Riesman, D. *The lonely crowd.* New Haven, Conn.: Yale University Press, 1950.

# eight

# attitudes:
# theoretical background

W hat makes someone a Republican or a Democrat, a conservative or a liberal, a Protestant or an atheist? Why are some people anti-Semitic, others anti-black, and still others not prejudiced at all? Why do people decide that one toothpaste is best or that drugs are horrible? What determines whether or not someone will change his mind about toothpastes or drugs? If someone is a Republican, how can we convince him to vote for a Democrat? Conversely, how can we prepare someone to meet an attack on his opinions so he will be able to resist the attack? These are the kinds of questions that form the basis for the extensive work on attitude formation and change, which in a sense has been the central core of social psychology in the United States for many years.

In 1937, in the first textbook mainly devoted to experimental studies in social psychology, Murphy, Murphy, and Newcomb wrote, "Perhaps no single concept within the whole realm of social psychology occupies a more nearly central position than that of attitudes [p. 889]." Concentration on this problem has continued to increase, and it is safe to say that in the past twenty years or so, social psychologists have devoted more time to the study of attitude formation and change than to any other topic. This is due, in part, to the great interest in interpersonal influence, with attitude change being one of the forms this influence takes. It is also due to an increasing emphasis on cognitive development and cognition in general. The work on attitudes, therefore, reflects both these major concerns of social psychologists. By concentrating on how attitudes are developed and changed, we can gain insight into the process of social influence and cognitive structure and how these two phenomena affect behavior.

**DEFINITION**    Attitudes have been defined in a number of different ways. Each of the traditional definitions contains a slightly different conception of what an attitude is or emphasizes a somewhat different aspect of it. G. W. Allport (1935) proposed that "an attitude is a mental and neural state of readi-

244

ness, organized through experience, exerting a directive or dynamic influence upon the individual's response to all objects and situations with which it is related [p. 810]." He saw an attitude primarily as a set to respond in a particular way. His emphasis clearly was on its behavioral implications.

In contrast, Doob (1947) defined an attitude as "an implicit, drive-producing response considered socially significant in the individual's society [p. 138]." He emphasized what an attitude is rather than its implications—his statement did not include overt behavior, although it contained a clear assumption that an attitude would affect how an individual acts. This definition was derived from a learning or stimulus-response tradition, and it conceptualized an attitude as simply another response, albeit an implicit rather than explicit one.

Today a third definition is most commonly held, to some extent incorporating the other two. An attitude toward any given object, idea, or person is an enduring system with a cognitive component, a feeling component, and an action tendency. The cognitive component consists of beliefs about the attitude object; the feeling component is equivalent to Doob's affective component, which is to say that there is some emotional feeling connected with the beliefs; and the action tendency is what Allport referred to as the readiness to respond in a particular way. For example, a student's attitude toward Mick Jagger might include the *knowledge* that he is a man, a leader of the Rolling Stones, a musician, and an actor; *feelings* of attraction and liking; and the *behavioral* tendencies to buy all his records, see his movies, and go to his concerts. This is the definition that most social psychologists today seem moderately content with and the one we shall use throughout our discussion.

Before considering the definition of attitudes in more detail, it is important to distinguish between attitudes and facts. Although it is difficult to draw a sharp dividing line between the two, the main distinguishing characteristic of attitudes is that they involve an evaluative or emotional component. A scientist believes that it is 250,000 miles to the moon or that human beings have forty-six chromosomes. He also has a complex collection of other facts about the moon and chromosomes. But under most circumstances, he does not have any emotional feelings toward either—he does not think that the moon is good or bad, he does not like or dislike chromosomes. In contrast, he also has a collection of facts about Mick Jagger or poison gas, but he does have emotional feelings about these. We can distinguish between facts and attitudes, to some extent, in terms of either the presence or absence of an evaluative component.

This distinction is important because facts and attitudes function somewhat differently. The crucial difference between them is that attitudes, once established, tend to be much more resistant to change. The scientist who believes that humans have forty-six chromosomes in most cases has no strong commitment to that belief or strong feelings about it one way or the other. Not so many years ago, scientists were convinced that humans had twenty-four chromosomes. Then somebody discovered that there were forty-eight. Those who originally believed we had twenty-four chromosomes probably changed their opinion quite readily when they saw the evidence. Certainly high school and college biology students, who were in no way involved in the controversy, changed their "knowledge" almost instantaneously. Originally they had the "fact" that there were twenty-four chromosomes; they changed that to forty-eight chromosomes. When, several years later, it turned out that the "correct" answer is forty-six chromosomes, that change was also accomplished readily. Unless someone was involved with the research, he had no reason not to change his mind when the new research results appeared.

This is different from the way people react when their attitudes are

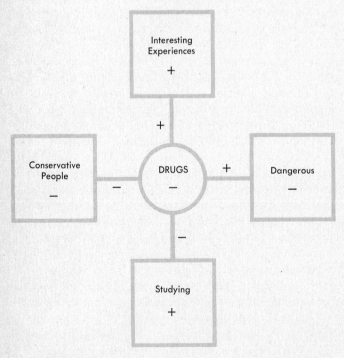

Figure 8–1

Schematic representation of an attitude toward hard drugs. The core object is surrounded by a cluster of cognitions, which are all related to it. The individual's overall evaluation of drugs is determined in part by his relationship to the separate items in the cluster.

concerned. As we shall see, attitudes tend to be highly resistant to change, they do not generally respond to a few new facts, they are more complicated in this respect than facts. People do not change their attitudes without putting up a fight and being exposed to a considerable amount of pressure. The presence of the evaluative component seems to change the dynamics considerably; it makes the attitude-change process much more difficult.

Thus we conceive of an attitude as a collection of thoughts, beliefs, and knowledge (cognitive component), and as including positive and negative evaluations of feelings (affective component), all relating to and describing a central theme or object—the subject of the attitude. This knowledge and feeling cluster tends to produce certain behavior. Figure 8–1, which is a schematic representation of a hypothetical person's attitude toward hard drugs, is one example.

Around the central object are clustered the *cognitions* that are related to it in the person's mind. These cognitions describe the object and its relations to other objects. The relations can be many and varied. The surrounding cognitions may be simply descriptions or characteristics of the core object—in our example, drugs are expensive, dangerous, exciting, fun. They may be causally linked—drugs produce interesting experiences, cause psychosis, expand the mind. They may be evaluative— freaks like drugs, my roommate likes them. We have indicated all the positive relations (i.e., the characteristics of drugs, the results of taking them, and the favorable evaluations) with a plus sign on the connecting lines. There are also negative relations: drugs are illegal, they prevent one from working effectively, conservative people dislike them. These are indicated by minus signs.

For simplicity we have shown only a few of the multitude of cognitions that an individual could have regarding drugs, but these should be sufficient to give a picture of the attitude. Drugs are seen as causing interesting experiences, as being dangerous, as preventing one from doing well in school, and as being condemned by the conservatives in society. Remember, however, that the real cluster would contain all the person's thoughts in connection with drugs.

Next, there is the affective or evaluative component. Many of the separate cognitive elements themselves have positive or negative feelings connected to them, and the central object does too. Positive and negative evaluations of the elements and central object are indicated by plus and minus signs, respectively. The individual in our example has a strong negative evaluation of drugs. He dislikes and is afraid of them. This is shown in the diagram by the minus sign in the central circle.

There are also a number of other factors to be considered, which we have not included in the structure. For example, each of the cognitions can vary in its importance (e.g., the fact that drugs are expensive is probably less important than the fact that they are illegal) and in the strength of its valence (e.g., it may be good or very good to be exciting). As you can see, the picture can get quite complex, potentially including a great many cognitions that vary in the nature of their relationship to the core and in their evaluative component. So this picture is an oversimplification, in some cases, of the way attitudes are in real life. For example, just think of the Pandora's Box opened up by the fact that the related cognitions are often related to one another and to many other cognitions, rather than existing in a vacuum. The thought that conservative people hate drugs is meaningful only when an attitude toward conservatives is considered. And then attitudes toward conservative people can bring in attitudes toward parents, teachers, politicians, and so on.

Nevertheless, for most purposes our diagram is, if anything, overly complex. Most people have rather simple attitudes about most things. When the average citizen is asked about a hot debate going on in Congress, let us say about a foreign economic aid bill, he will say, "Unnnhhh, I don't know, . . . I suppose we have to help out some, but . . . unnnhhh, . . . how much do they want to give again?" The interviewer usually finds that further probing is useless. Even in thinking about Mick Jagger, most people most of the time do not consider all the things they know about him—they do not remember many details of his music, his movies, or his personal life; rather, they simply have a positive attitude, consisting mainly of feeling attracted to him. Or in thinking about hard core drugs, most police do not think of the scientific facts they once were told, or the preaching against drugs in their childhoods. Rather, the drugs are illegal, and the people they see on drugs are pathetic and abhorrent, so they simply hate drugs. The multitude of cognitions exists in their minds and may have some influence on them, but by and large, their attitude, particularly the evaluative component, is less complex.

There have been many demonstrations of this simplicity of most attitudes. One is provided by the work on the semantic differential, described in Chapter 2. Osgood showed that much of the variance in our conceptions of objects, people, and so on, is accounted for by a simple evaluative factor. Whatever is being considered, a large part of an individual's conception of it or reaction to it consists of liking or disliking.

Second, survey research has repeatedly shown that most people have rather little information about political matters and that their political attitudes tend not to be tightly interrelated. Regarding most political matters, most people have relatively few cognitions, and even these are not tightly interwoven (Sears, 1969). In one survey taken of a representative sample of the American public at the height of the Vietnam War, it was found that attitudes toward escalation were only minimally related (inversely, of course) to attitudes toward deescalation (Verba et al., 1967). That is, a voter who was in favor of *escalation* (e.g., sending troops into North Vietnam) was almost as likely as someone opposed to it also to be in favor of *deescalation* (e.g., bringing all the boys home). This suggests that the basis for attitudes is not ordinarily a complex series of arguments, that cognitive content does not determine affective feelings to any large extent. Finally, Anderson has shown that attitude change can persist even after the content that produced it is forgotten, emphasizing that the affective component is more durable and central than the cognitive component. Thus, although the total structure of an attitude is complex, one important part of it, the part consisting of affects or feelings, is often very simple.

The contrast between the cognitive complexity of the attitude and the apparent evaluative simplicity is extremely important. For example, both policemen and drug users know a great deal about drugs, have all sorts of complicated pieces of information, understand a variety of inter-relationships between drugs and other aspects of the world. And each of these pieces of information to some extent influences their general feelings toward drugs and has a substantial effect on their behavior. Knowing what drugs look like, how much they cost, where they can be obtained, the difference among various kinds, and so on, affects the activities of both the users and the narcotics squad. Nevertheless, the relatively simple evaluative component of the attitude is the major determinant of behavior. Although the details of users' and policemen's behavior toward drugs is influenced by the knowledge they have, the general direction of their behavior is influenced primarily by their overall evaluation—whether they consider drugs as positive or negative.

There are thus two facets of attitudes that must be kept in mind. First is the contrast between the cognitive complexity and the evaluative simplicity. Second is that all elements of the attitude, such as they are, can be interrelated, and that each can therefore have some effect on the total attitude and on the other separate elements.

**THEORETICAL FRAMEWORKS FOR STUDYING ATTITUDES**

Now that we have a general view of an attitude, we can consider the theoretical frameworks within which attitudes have been studied. The major approaches to attitude formation and change have been (1) conditioning and reinforcement, (2) incentives and conflict, (3) functionalism, and (4) cognitive consistency. The conditioning approach sees attitudes as habits, similar to anything else that is learned; principles that apply to other forms of learning also determine the formation of attitudes. The incentive theory is that a person adopts the attitude that maximizes his gains. There are reasons for accepting each side of an issue, and the side for which the reasons are better, from the individual's sometimes selfish point of view, will be adopted. This approach implies a maximization of gains. A variant of this approach considers attitudes in terms of what function or use they serve for the individual. Finally, the cognitive consistency theory asserts that people tend to seek harmonious relations among their cognitions and behavior. It emphasizes acceptance of ideas that are consistent with previous attitudes. Individuals tend to accept attitudes that fit into their overall cognitive structure. The four approaches are not contradictory or inconsistent. They represent different theoretical orientations and differ primarily in the factors they emphasize when explaining attitude formation and change.

## Conditioning and Reinforcement

The conditioning and reinforcement model is most closely associated with Carl Hovland and others at Yale University. The basic assumption behind this approach is that attitudes are learned in much the same way as other habits. Just as people acquire information and facts, they also learn the feelings and values associated with these facts. A child learns that a certain animal is a dog, that dogs are friends, that they are good; finally, he learns to like dogs. And he learns this attitude through the same processes and mechanisms that control other kinds of learning.

This means that the basic processes by which learning occurs should be directly applicable to the formation of attitudes. In developing an attitude, the individual acquires information and feelings by the processes of *association, reinforcement,* and *imitation.* Associations are formed when stimuli appear at the same time and in the same place. If a police chief, a parent, or a television reporter shows us a dirty, broken-down, evil-looking man and says the word *drug,* an association is formed between the image and the word. When the newspapers, television, and magazines talk about drugs being dangerous, when ministers and parents say drugs are evil, when we see people who have taken drugs looking miserable, these images become associated with drugs. Similarly, we may be exposed to positive things that can become associated with drugs: a friend says they are good; we see a movie in which someone on drugs seems to be having a pleasurable time; we take a drug and have a good experience.

Learning the characteristics of an object, a person, or an idea is obviously an important aspect of developing an attitude toward it. Although the studies described in the chapters on person perception and liking were conducted in a somewhat different context, many of them illustrate this effect. For example, Norman Anderson conducted experiments in which he listed a number of attributes of a person and then asked subjects to state their impression of that person. The subjects formed their attitudes on the basis of the listed characteristics (warm, friendly, intelligent, ambitious, courageous, and so on). Having learned the characteristics, the subjects, in a sense, also learned an attitude.

Similarly, Donn Byrne told subjects that someone either agreed or disagreed with them on a variety of issues and values. Presumably, each time the other person agreed with them, it was a positive attribute and each time he disagreed with them, it was a negative attribute. The subjects learned that these were the characteristics of the other person and on the basis of these characteristics, they formed an attitude toward the other person, including a feeling about how much they would like him.

This process works as well for things as for people. Individuals learn the characteristics of a house, a country, an idea, a bill pending before Congress, or anything else. An attitude consists of that knowledge plus some evaluative component based in part on that knowledge and in part on other factors (which we shall discuss later). The simplest factor in the formation of attitudes is thus the development of associations between the object and other words or qualities.

Learning also occurs through reinforcement. If one takes a drug and has a pleasant experience, the act of taking the drug is reinforced— he would be more likely to take the drug in the future. Similarly, if one says "Drugs are great" and someone else applauds, making the statement is reinforced. Then both these acts (taking drugs and saying they are good) become part of the cluster that forms his attitude. One element is the knowledge that he takes them and another that he tells people they are good.

Finally, attitudes can be learned through imitation. As we mentioned before (Chapter 4), people imitate the behavior of others, particularly if the others are strong, important people. Children tend to imitate their parents, and this imitation extends to both behavior and attitudes. In this way, a child learns and accepts the values and attitudes of his parents even when they are not overtly rewarding the child.

Imitation is not limited to the parent-child relationship. Teachers, friends, public figures, baseball players, actors, and so on, are imitated. Individuals learn many different attitudes by imitating different people; as we shall discuss below, they often find they have learned contradictory values from different people and are under great stress to resolve the conflicts. This is typical of college students who suddenly find themselves confronted with ideas and values different from those they had previously learned from their parents.

Association, reinforcement, and imitation are the major mechanisms by which learning occurs. Other principles of learning have been applied to the study of attitudes, but for the moment these are the important ones to keep in mind. The learning approach to attitudes is relatively simple—it views the individual as primarily passive; he is exposed to stimuli, he learns through one of the learning processes, and this learning determines his attitude. The final attitude contains all the associations, values, and other bits of information the individual has accumulated. His ultimate evaluation of, say, drugs depends on the number and strength of the positive and negative elements he has learned.

### Incentives and Conflict

The theory based on incentives and conflict is particularly relevant to attitude change. It views the attitude situation in terms of an approach-avoidance conflict. The individual has certain reasons for accepting one position and other reasons for rejecting it and accepting the opposite position. He thinks drugs are dangerous; he knows they are illegal; and he wants to finish college and get into law school. These considerations produce a negative attitude. However, he believes drugs are exciting, and he knows many of his friends take them. These considerations tend to give him a positive atitude. According to the incentive theory, the relative strength of these incentives determine his attitude. If his initial attitude were negative, it would become more positive only if there were greater incentive for taking this new position than for maintaining the original one.

This view is similar to the learning approach in that the attitude is determined more or less by a sum of the positive and negative elements. The difference is that the incentive theory emphasizes what the individual has to gain or lose by taking a particular position. Whether or not his friends would like him, how enjoyable the experience is, etc., are the critical considerations. When there are conflicting goals, the individual adopts the position that maximizes his gains. Unlike the regular learning approach, cognitive elements that do not involve gains or losses are relatively unimportant.

The formulations in terms of learning principles and incentives have pervaded much of the work on attitude change. They have led to the specific model described in detail on page 266, to the acknowledgement of the importance of alternative modes of reducing pressures in the situation, and to an emphasis on motivational factors as determinants of attitude change. These are only a few of the consequences of these approaches. We shall see in this and succeeding chapters that they have been an important influence in virtually every problem in the attitude-change area.

### Functionalism

Another, more specific, version of this same approach is the functionalist approach. Here the individual selects his initial attitude, or changes to a new attitude, in terms of what psychological function or use it serves for him. In the most detailed forms of this approach—those of Katz (1960) and Smith, Bruner, and White (1956)—a limited set of functions has been identified as most crucial.

An attitude may be adopted because it is *instrumental* to some goal the individual has. It may serve his economic self-interest, as in the case of a businessman voting for a conservative Republican who promises to cut corporate income taxes, or it may serve a social adjustment purpose, as in the case of a bride accommodating herself to the dogmatic political beliefs of her new mate.

Attitudes may also serve an *ego-defensive* function. For example, some historians and psychoanalysts have hypothesized that white Southern men are so violently anti-Negro and so punitive of even the slightest trace of sexuality between black men and white women (whether rape or gentle seduction), because this attitude serves them as an ego-defense mechanism. In olden times, Southern Womanhood is said to have been on a pedestal, unapproachable, pure and chaste, and white Southern men are said therefore to have been inhibited in their sexual approaches to them. However, this inhibited sexuality was then projected onto black men, and was violently condemned and suppressed. The white man could thus control his own sexuality by suppressing the black man's sexuality. Other attitudes have similarly been analyzed as serving an ego-defensive function; e.g., pacifism for those with intrapsychic conflicts about the expression of aggression, cynicism for those with conflicts about the expression of love and tenderness, and so on.

The other major category of commonly identified functions is *knowledge* or *object appraisal*. Some attitudes simply help the individual understand his world, and develop readiness to behave with respect to attitude objects he might encounter. Presumably people respond to much of what they see on television or read in the newspaper in this fashion. They adopt attitudes about a great many things that will never have any instrumental value to them, and are of no great help in resolving unconscious conflicts, simply to understand and place things.

The functionalist approach to attitude formation and change has not stimulated much research. A few studies have attempted to measure the individual's needs, or have tried to vary his needs experimentally, and then have tried to determine whether or not he would be especially responsive to need-satisfying attitude positions. However, this line of research has not provided much supporting evidence. More often, the functionalist approach has been used by historians, political scientists, and sociologists as a way of explaining *after the fact* why certain individuals or groups of people have held the attitudes they have.

### Cognitive Consistency Theory

The other major framework within which attitudes have been studied is cognitive consistency theory. Actually, there are a number of somewhat similar theories associated with Lewin, Heider, Abelson, Festinger,

Osgood, and others. The theories differ in some important respects, but the basic notion behind all of them is the same. They begin with the assumption that there is a tendency for people to seek consistency among their cognitions and that this is a major determinant of attitude formation. An individual who has several beliefs or values that are inconsistent with one another strives, according to these theories, to make them more consistent. Similarly, if his cognitions are consistent and he is faced with a new cognition that would produce inconsistency, he strives to minimize the inconsistency. Since this theoretical approach has been developed primarily with reference to attitudes, rather than to other psychological phenomena, we shall consider it in some detail.

**Balance Theory.** In Chapter 3 we described a simple cognitive system to which consistency theory may be applied. Such a system consists of two objects (one of which is often another person), the relationship between them, and an individual's evaluations of them. In the system, there are three evaluations—the individual's evaluation of each of the objects and of the relationship of the objects to each other. Assuming that each evaluation is positive or negative, with no differences in strength, the four possible situations are shown in Figure 8–2: all evaluations can be positive, two can be positive and one negative, one can be positive and two negative, or all can be negative. The first and third situations are considered balanced or cognitively consistent. This approach to cognitive consistency, proposed by Fritz Heider (1958) and others, has been called the *balance model*. The major point of the model is that a system in a state of imbalance will move toward a state of balance.

This approach need not be limited to the simple situation just de-

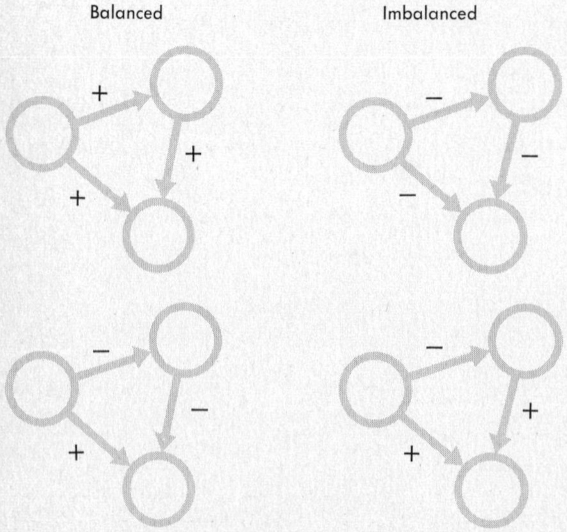

Balanced                    Imbalanced

Figure 8–2

Balanced and imbalanced cognitive structures. Plus and minus signs indicate positive and negative relationships, respectively; arrows indicate the direction of the relationships. The theory states that imbalanced structures tend to change and become balanced.

scribed. Theoretically, it could apply to any number of pairs of objects, although most of the research has used situations involving two persons, an object, and the relationships among them. This is convenient for the study of attitude formation and change, because it can deal with the basic situation of one person receiving information from a second person about some object. However, research has also been conducted on situations in which there are interpersonal relations among three people and the cognitive structure of one person thinking about two objects.

The main value of this research is that it describes the notion of cognitive consistency in extremely simple terms and provides a convenient way of thinking about and conceptualizing attitudes. The balance model makes it clear that in a given situation there are many ways to resolve an inconsistency. It focuses our attention on one of the most important aspects of attitude change—the factors that determine which of the various modes of resolution are adopted. We shall return to this in the next chapter.

**Congruity Theory.**   Congruity theory, proposed by Osgood and Tannenbaum (1955), is another useful model of cognitive consistency. Dealing with simpler situations than does the balance model, congruity theory is concerned entirely with the effect of one person taking a positive or negative position toward another object or person—perhaps the simplest attitude-change situation. When person P says something good or bad about object $X$, what effect does it have on our attitude toward both P and $X$?

To begin with, the theory measures our evaluation of any person or object on a scale from $-3$ to $+3$. A rating of $+3$ means that we have a maximum positive evaluation of the object; a rating of $-3$ means we have a maximum negative evaluation of it; and a rating of 0 means we have a neutral attitude toward it. An example of this type of scale, with a variety of items, is pictured in Figure 8–3.

The theory makes several predictions about how another person's evaluation of the object affects our evaluation of both of them. First, to achieve congruity, our evaluation of the two must change an amount equal to the discrepancy between them, so our final evaluation depends on the discrepancy between our initial evaluations of them. If someone we like moderately ($+2$) says something positive about something we also like moderately, there is no discrepancy. If we rate one of them $+2$ and the other only $+1$, there is some discrepancy, but they are almost equal. If someone who is rated $-2$ praises something at $+2$, there is quite a bit of discrepancy (4 points). The same principle holds for negative evaluations, except in reverse. The farther apart the two are, the more natural it is for the person to dislike the object and the less discrepancy exists; the closer they are, the more inconsistent dislike is and the greater the discrepancy. If someone at $+2$ attacks a $-2$ object, there

| | |
|---|---|
| +3 • | Student leader |
| +2 • | College president |
| +1 • | Liberal congressman |
| 0 • | Unknown politician |
| −1 • | Conservative senator |
| −2 • | Reactionary alumnus |
| −3 • | John Birch member |

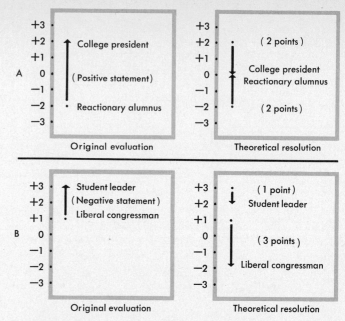

Figure 8–3

A representation of one person's feelings, perhaps a liberal student's, in terms of the congruity model. Every person is evaluated between maximum positive (+3) and maximum negative (−3). According to the model, those who are evaluated similarly should like (make positive statements about) each other; those evaluated differently should dislike each other. If there is any discrepancy, congruity is reestablished by changes in evaluation. (A) Congruity prediction for a positive statement. When the alumnus (−2) praises the president (+2), the amount of discrepancy is 4 (subtract −2 from +2). Congruity is reestablished by each one moving 2 points toward the other, producing equilibrium at 0. (B) Congruity prediction for a negative statement. When the congressman at +1 criticizes the student leader at +3, discrepancy is 4 (add the two), because we do not expect a positive person to criticize another positive person. Equilibrium is at +2 and −2, with the congressman, who is less extreme, moving three times as far as the student leader.

is no discrepancy. If they are at +2 and −1, there is 1 point of discrepancy; and if both are at +2, there are 4 points. The amount of discrepancy is ascertained by subtracting the rating of one from that of the other if there is a positive statement or by adding the two ratings if there is a negative statement.

Second, a positive association between the two induces attitude changes toward consistency, which would be identical evaluations of the person and the object. Conversely, a negative association between the two induces change toward opposite evaluations of them. In all cases, the ratings of the two would be equally extreme, but they would be on the same side of neutral (e.g., both +2 or both −2) after a positive association (P says he likes $X$), and on opposite sides (e.g., one −2 and the other +2) after a negative association (P says he dislikes $X$).

Third, the *amount* that each evaluation changes depends on its initial extremity. Since extreme opinions tend to be held more firmly than moderate ones, the more extreme an evaluation, the less it will change. Specifically, the two evaluations would change by an amount inversely proportional to their initial extremity. Thus, someone starting at 3 (+ or −) would change one-third as much as someone starting at 1 (+ or −).

Consider some examples. Suppose a reactionary alumnus whom we evaluate −2 praises the college president whom we evaluate +2. This is quite discrepant, because someone we dislike appears to like someone we like. The amount of discrepancy is 4 (subtracting one from the other). Since the statement is positive, the two men should end up being evaluated identically. And finally, because initially they are at equally extreme positions, they should change the same amount. To eliminate 4 points of discrepancy, each person must change 2 points—and they must change toward each other. Accordingly, the president and the alumnus both end up at neutral (0). The president is hurt in our eyes, because if a reactionary person likes him, he must not be as good as we thought; and the alumnus gains, because if he likes the popular president, the alumnus must not be as bad as we thought.

Or consider a situation in which a local congressman whom we like moderately (+1) criticizes a much-liked student leader (+3). Someone we like should not criticize someone we like even more, so there is considerable discrepancy (4 points—the two positions are added because the evaluation is negative). The two men should end up at opposite sides of neutral, because they dislike each other. And the student should change one-third as much as the congressman, because the former's initial rating is three times as extreme. Thus, the congressman changes 3 points and the student leader 1 point; they end up at +2 and −2, respectively. The student goes down in our evaluation, because he was attacked by someone we liked, but the congressman goes down even more because he attacked someone we liked a great deal. Note that if the student had attacked the congressman, the result would have been the same—in this model, the direction of attack or praise does not affect the outcome.

The main application of congruity theory is in the prediction of a communicator's effectiveness in producing attitude change. Yet one must not forget that changes in our evaluation of the communicator occur, and the theory is also applicable to this situation. In political life one can observe many instances of politicians attempting to build their reputations by attaching themselves to popular and attacking unpopular causes. An unknown conservative running for governor may try to become popular by attacking campus radicals, whom the general public tends to oppose. A neutral source (0) attacking unpopular people (−3) yields +3 for the politician and −3 for the radicals. (Note that the neutral source does all the moving.) This is known as the "I'm against sin" ploy. The opposite tactic finds an unknown politician taking a stand in favor of safe streets and a strong America. A neutral source (0) supports a popular cause (+3), resulting in a popular figure (+3). This is the "I'm in favor of motherhood" gambit. Both tactics are effective, and thus most politicians try to find unpopular causes to attack and popular ones to support—not to affect the popularity of the causes but to increase their own popularity.

The numerical predictions of the congruity theory have been supported in part by several experiments. However, they must be considered only rough approximations of what occurs in real-life situations. Clearly, a positively evaluated college president does not go all the way to neutral merely because some right-winger praised him; nor does a congressman who is liked become strongly disliked because of one criticism of a popular student leader. If these were the only considerations, if we knew nothing else about the president or the congressman, the predictions of the theory might be precisely correct. But the fact that we know a great deal more means that the resulting changes may be much less dramatic. However, the theory does indicate the direction and relative magnitude of the effect these situations tend to produce. The president is hurt by the praise, the congressman is hurt by his attack, and the congressman is hurt more than the president. There is some pressure to change in the direction indicated by the theory, and the more change predicted, the more pressure there is. If a large number of such relations existed, enough pressure would build up to change our evaluation. For example, if many negative people praised the president, he might become considerably less positive in our eyes.

One contribution of this analysis is that it emphasizes the existence of varying degrees of positive or negative evaluations. The balance model considers objects as either positive or negative, but congruity theory takes into account the fact that the strength of evaluations is an important factor in attitude-change situations.

Congruity theory also highlights the fact that there are alternative modes of resolving inconsistencies. In the examples above, both attitude change (toward $X$) and change in evaluations of the communicator (toward P) occur. Other modes are also possible. For example, if a racist hears that George Wallace has said something good about the Black Panthers, this is clearly an incongruous or imbalanced situation. We have seen that there should be a strong tendency to resolve the inconsistency.

By the straightforward congruity model, Wallace at $+3$ and the Panthers at $-3$ would both end up neutral. They are equally extreme and therefore move the same amount. This is one possible solution to the inconsistency.

It is, however, not the only one. Congruity theory has built into it what is called a *correction for incredulity*. There are times when the information we have is so unlikely that rather than change our attitudes to resolve the inconsistency we decide that the information is not believable. In the example, the racist could decide that Wallace could not have said something good about the Black Panthers and he would simply not change his attitude at all. This is the point of maximum incredulity, which occurs when someone at $+3$ says something good about someone at $-3$, or vice versa. There can also be some incredulity at intermediate levels, which would reduce the amount of change rather than eliminating it entirely. The point is that we have two options—we can change our attitudes to reduce the inconsistency or, if we are incredulous, we can reject the information.

**Interrelations within Cognitive Structure.**   One of the interesting and important aspects of the entire cognitive consistency approach is the emphasis on interrelations and mutual interdependency of the various elements in the cognitive system. Rather than picturing a cognitive structure with a lot of elements—ideas and notions—that have relatively little interconnection, consistency theories depict one in which there are bonds among many of the elements and in which these bonds have some tendency to be consistent.

This is most apparent within the system composing a particular attitude. An individual's evaluation of drugs is greatly influenced by his evaluations of the other elements related to drugs in his attitude structure. Looking back at Figure 8–1 on page 246, we see that the types of relationships between the surrounding elements and the core object are similar to those in the simple balance model. A positive element—excitement—can be positively linked to drugs—drugs produce it. According to cognitive consistency, this system would be balanced only if drugs were also positive. It would then consist of a positive object causing something positive $(+ + +)$. Thus, having the cognition that drugs cause excitement should tend to make someone like drugs. Similarly, a negative relationship to a negative object—for example, conservative people dislike drugs—should also lead to a positive evaluation, producing a balanced system $(+ - -)$. Conversely, a positive relationship between drugs and something bad—drugs are dangerous—should make him dislike drugs $(- + -)$, as should a negative relationship between drugs and something good $(- - +)$—drugs prevent one from working effectively.

Each of the first two relationships tends to increase the positive evaluation of drugs; each of the latter two increases the negative evaluation. The more there are of the former, the more positive the attitude is; the more there are of the latter, the more negative it is. Naturally, the strength of the relations and the individual's evaluations of the elements vary. It is probably more important to most college students that drugs are dangerous than that they are disliked by ministers and farmers. The more important the element and the stronger the negative or positive evaluation, the greater impact this element has on the total attitude.

Of course, it is true, as we said earlier, that most people do not have very elaborate cognitive structures regarding most things in the news. So they mostly learn to like or dislike things on the basis of rather skimpy knowledge. And they ordinarily do not self-consciously and deliberately add up positive and negative elements in order to determine their overall evaluation of an object. Often they are not even aware of the adjustments they make as they move toward consistency. Nevertheless, cognitive consistency indicates that the relations between the various elements and the core object are important in determining the total evaluation. Much of the work on attitude change supports this view in one form or another.

The interrelatedness of the evaluations of the core object and the surrounding elements means that a major change in any of the items tends to produce corresponding changes elsewhere in the structure. Most dramatically, in the example on page 246, changing the core object (drugs) from negative to positive would produce a large amount of stress in the system. Practically everything was in a nice state of balance or consistency or congruity when the core object was negative; if, for some reason, the object suddenly became positive, practically every relationship pictured would be imbalanced and there would be pressures toward resolving the imbalance.

Rosenberg (1960) provided a striking demonstration of the ramifying changes created by a change in the core object. He obtained from subjects a comprehensive description of their attitudes toward blacks, integration, and the whole question of relations between blacks and whites. He then hypnotized the subjects and told them that their attitude toward blacks moving into their community was the opposite of what it had previously been. If the subject had previously been strongly against integrated housing, he was told that he now was in favor of it, and vice versa. The subjects were then awakened from their hypnotic trance and questioned about their current attitudes about blacks and integration.

Rosenberg found that the change he had produced under hypnosis in one cognitive element was followed by many dramatic reversals in the subjects' other attitudes—in the direction that would be consistent with the hypnotically produced change. Thus, the other changes tended to reduce the imbalance that had resulted from the induced change. As the theories of cognitive consistency would predict, there were pressures toward reducing inconsistency, which resulted in a variety of cognitive changes.

**Dissonance theory.**   The last, and perhaps most important, of the cognitive consistency theories is cognitive dissonance theory, first proposed by Leon Festinger in 1957. The most distinctive focus of dissonance theory has been upon inconsistencies between beliefs and overt behavior. As originally proposed, dissonance theory focused upon two principal sources of belief-behavior inconsistency: the effects of making decisions, and the effects of engaging in counterattitudinal behavior. Such inconsistencies produce cognitive dissonance, which may be reduced in a number of different ways. We will discuss this theory only briefly here, because Chapter 11 is largely devoted to spelling out its numerous interesting predictions and the ingenious research it has led to.

Festinger proposed that each alternative involved in a decision could be thought of as having positive and negative attributes. When a person makes a decision between two alternatives, the positive attributes of the chosen alternative, and the negative attributes of the rejected alternative, are consistent (or consonant, in the terms of dissonance theory) with the decision. That is, these attitudes about the choice alternatives are consistent with the overt behavior of deciding. However, dissonance arises because these are not the whole story with either alternative: usually the chosen object has some bad attributes, and the rejected object has some good ones. Both represent cognitions that are dissonant with the decision. And most decisions carry with them some dissonance, no matter how deliberate or rational they are. If we decide to buy a Jaguar instead of a Volkswagen, the Jaguar's comfort, speed, and stylishness, and the Volkswagen's crampedness and homeliness, are consonant with the decision. But the Jaguar's price, and its penchant for expensive repairs, and the inexpensiveness and ease of upkeep of the VW, are dissonant with the decision.

There are also cases in which people engage in behavior which is counter to their attitudes. Sometimes they are forced into it, because they have been drafted into the army, or because a hated regime has taken over their country. Sometimes they are simply seduced into it, or charmed into it; sometimes guilt makes them do it. In Chapter 12 we will discuss a number of the reasons why people do things they do not believe in. The point here is that engaging in behavior discrepant from attitudes leads to cognitive dissonance.

Dissonance theory spells out a number of the conditions affecting the magnitude of dissonance, and the mechanism of dissonance reduction most likely to occur. In cases involving attitude-behavior discrepancies, clearly the two major modes of dissonance reduction are revoking the behavior in some way (or claiming it really didn't matter very much), or changing one's attitudes.

We have not described the balance model, the congruity model, or dissonance theory in great detail. Only the main points of the theories have been presented, because they have been influential per se and they give some idea of the basic notions behind the theories of cognitive consistency. They differ mainly in the phenomena they address, rather than in the predictions they make. Balance theory has been used most widely to deal with attraction in interpersonal relationships, and especially with similar attitudes as a basis for attraction between people. It has also been widely applied to consistency among various subparts of an attitude structure. Congruity theory has been applied principally to inconsistencies arising in mass communication situations when a communicator takes a position disagreeing with his listener's opinion. And dissonance theory has been mostly concerned with how an individual resolves inconsistencies between his attitudes and his overt behavior. Nevertheless, all these models agree on two major points: when there is inconsistency, there is a tendency for a system to move toward a more consistent structure; this move can be accomplished in a variety of ways, with the individual generally choosing the easiest mode of resolution.

The formulations that we have called the conditioning-reinforcement, incentive-conflict, and cognitive consistency approaches are the bases for virtually all the work in the area of attitudes. They provide the framework within which most of the research has been conducted and serve as basic principles with which to explain the findings. It should be noted that at times there have been conflicts between the approaches, particularly between consistency and incentive. Researchers have tended to work within one of these two frameworks and have tended to be suspicious of derivations from and results of experiments conducted within the other one. Despite this occasional friction, it seems clear to us that the approaches are not mutually exclusive but, on the contrary, are complementary. In the succeeding three chapters, we shall see that in some areas one approach is more useful, in some the other, and in some the experimental results can be explained only by recourse to a combination of theoretical approaches. Throughout the discussion, we shall refer to one or more of the theoretical positions in an attempt to fit together and explain what is known about attitude formation and change.

## CHAPTER REVIEW

1. Attitudes defined in terms of cognitions, affect, and behavior.
2. Attitudes as distinguished from knowledge.

3. Attitudes as highly complex and, in some respects, very simple.

4. Reinforcement, incentive, functionalism, and cognitive consistency theories as major approaches to the study of attitude formation and change.

5. Balance, congruity, and dissonance theories as examples of the cognitive-consistency approach.

## APPLICATIONS AND SPECULATIONS

1. I like my dog, my dog likes dog food. In terms of a balance model, I should like dog food. How would you resolve this?

2. The theories of cognitive consistency assume that people seek consistency among their cognitions and beliefs. Why should people like consistency? You might think about this primarily in terms of decision making and the consequences of decisions.

3. We described two techniques that we called "I'm against sin" and "I'm in favor of motherhood." What politicians that you like and dislike use these methods, and does one method seem more effective than the other?

## SUGGESTIONS FOR ADDITIONAL READING

### Articles

Katz, D. The functional approach to the study of attitudes. *Public Opinion Quarterly*, 1960, *24*, 163–204.

Osgood, C. E., and Tannenbaum, P. H. The principle of congruity in the prediction of attitude change. *Psychological Review*, 1955, *62*, 42–55.

### Books and Longer Discussions

Insko, C. A. *Theories of attitude change.* New York: Appleton-Century-Crofts, 1967.

Kiesler, C. A., Collins, B. E., and Miller, N. *Attitude change: a critical analysis of theoretical approaches.* New York: John Wiley, 1969.

McGuire, W. J. The nature of attitudes and attitude change. In G. Lindzey and E. Aronson (Eds.), *Handbook of social psychology*, Vol. III. Reading, Mass.: Addison-Wesley, 1969. Pp. 136–314.

Sears, D. O. Political behavior. In G. Lindzey and E. Aronson (Eds.), *Handbook of social psychology*, Vol. V. Reading, Mass.: Addison-Wesley, 1969.

# nine

# changing attitudes

In 1959, Carl Hovland and Irving Janis suggested a useful model of attitude change. Figure 9–1 illustrates a model based largely on theirs but simplified and changed to bring it more in line with recent work in this area. It begins with what Hovland called the observable persuasion stimuli. There must be a *communicator* who holds a particular position on some issue and is trying to convince others to hold this position. To do so, he produces a *communication* designed to persuade people that his position is correct and to induce them to change their own positions in the direction of his. This communication is presented in a given *situation*. These, then, constitute the attack—the source, the communication, and the surroundings.

In the typical attitude-change situation, an individual is confronted

Figure 9–1

Model of the attitude-change situation, showing examples of important factors at each stage. The amount of attitude change that occurs is determined by variables at each point in the process.

with a communication that espouses a position discrepant from the one he holds. He may have a negative attitude toward marijuana and someone tells him that it is really very good; he may be a Democrat listening to a Republican campaign speech; he may be a smoker reading the Surgeon General's report that claims that cigarette smoking causes cancer. Under these circumstances, stress is produced by the discrepancy between the individual's attitude and the attitude expressed in the communication. This stress has been called conflict, incongruity, imbalance, or just inconsistency. Whichever model we choose, there is general agreement that there is pressure on the individual to resolve the discrepancy.

The focus of most of the research has been on ways of increasing attitude change. If the individual changes his attitude in the direction advocated by the communication, the discrepancy between these two positions is reduced. Since this discrepancy is the source of the stress, reducing the discrepancy reduces the stress. This is, however, only one alternative. Throughout our discussion of the factors affecting the amount of attitude change in such a situation, it is important to keep in mind that the subject has open to him a variety of ways of resolving the stress. The emphasis on so-called alternative modes of resolution is one of the important contributions of Carl Hovland's model of attitude change and of the cognitive consistency models.

One of the assumptions generally made about the various modes of resolution is that they tend to be additive in their effect. To the extent that one of them is used in a given situation, the others need not be used. There is a certain amount of stress to be reduced or resolved in the attitude-change situation; any mode of resolution, if used successfully, would reduce some of that stress. For example, if there are five units of stress, they may be reduced by any one or any combination of the modes of resolution. But only those five units need to be reduced. The individual who rejects the communicator is less likely to change his opinion or distort the communication; the individual who changes his opinion is less likely to reject the communicator; and so on. This assumption is made most explicitly in congruity theory.

From the point of view of the communicator, this means that one of his major problems is to maximize the likelihood that the target will choose attitude change as his mode of resolution and to minimize or eliminate the use of alternative modes of resolution. Therefore, one of the most critical factors in any attitude-change situation is whether or not alternative modes of resolution are present and, if they are, the extent to which they are used. Before discussing attitude change in detail, we shall describe briefly the most important alternative mechanisms the individual can use rather than change his attitude.

**Refuting the Arguments.** An individual can attempt to refute the arguments contained in the discrepant communication. He can engage in a debate with the content of the communication and attempt to demonstrate to himself that his own position has more merit than the other one. This debate can be implicit or explicit, verbal or nonverbal, perhaps even conscious or unconscious. He can argue against the discrepant communication, produce evidence to support his own position, show how the other side is illogical or inconsistent, and in general do anything he can to weaken the impact of the communication. To the extent that he is able to refute these arguments, the stress should be reduced.

The problem with this mode of resolution is twofold: usually a rather lazy recipient is up against a more expert communicator. Most people, most of the time, are not very motivated to analyze in close detail the pros and cons of complex arguments. Moreover, persuasive messages are usually designed so that it is difficult to reject them on purely logical grounds. The authors of the communication naturally present as strong a case as they can, and the communicator is generally better informed on the topic than the recipient of the communication. Therefore, although arguing against the discrepant communication and attempting to reject it is a rational mode of resolution, it is often difficult to employ.

**Rejecting the Arguments.** This is probably the most common mode of resolution. Rather than trying to refute the arguments on logical grounds or weakening them by attacking their source, individuals seem to be able simply to reject arguments for no apparent reason. A typical response by a smoker to a well-reasoned, logical attack on cigarette smoking is to say that the arguments are not good enough to make him stop. He does not answer them; he just does not accept them. When someone who believes in capital punishment is shown overwhelming evidence that it does not serve as a deterrent to homicide, he tends to be unconvinced. He essentially shrugs off the evidence, says he does not believe it, and continues to maintain his position. It often takes more than a good argument to convince people of something. Much of the time they respond in an illogical, nonrational manner to discrepant communications. They merely say "No, that's not right." We do not understand this mechanism very well because it has not been directly studied, but it seems to be an alternative that is often employed in attitude-change situations.

**Derogating the Source.** Someone who is faced with a discrepant communication can reduce the stress by deciding that the source of the communication is unreliable or negative in some other way. Referring to the balance or congruity models, we can see that there is nothing inconsistent about disagreeing with a negative source. In fact, people expect to disagree with a negative source. Thus, by deciding that the source is negative or the information unreliable, one can balance the system and remove all stress.

Such an *ad hominum* attack on the source of a communication is common in politics, informal debating, courtroom trials, and practically every kind of adversary proceeding. The defense attorney in a trial tries to discredit the damaging witness when he cannot rebut his evidence. The politician calls his opponent a Communist or a Fascist or some other negative term when he finds it difficult to argue on the issues themselves.

This device is extremely effective because it not only eliminates the threat from the current argument but also makes all future arguments from the opponent much less powerful. When an opponent has been discredited, anything he says carries less weight. Thus, attacking the source of the communication is an effective way of reducing the stress produced by a discrepant communication.

**Distorting the Message.**   Another type of resolution people sometimes employ is distorting or misperceiving the communication so as to reduce the discrepancy between it and their own position. The Surgeon General says it is extremely dangerous to smoke because smoking has been shown to be a significant cause of lung cancer. The confirmed smoker reads this message and decides that the Surgeon General is recommending a decrease in smoking but that the evidence on lung cancer is not yet conclusive. The smoker may do this by a gross misperception of the article when he reads it, by distorting the article in his memory, or perhaps by reading only part of the article and reconstructing the rest of it in his own mind. However he accomplishes it, the result is the same—the message becomes considerably less discrepant.

Alternatively he may exaggerate the extremity of the communication so as to make it ridiculous. Many student activist groups have argued that students should have a greater voice in running their schools. The administrators and faculty who disagree with this are antagonistic to these groups. One fairly common distortion of the students' position is that they want to take over the school and make all the decisions themselves. Actually this is a much more extreme position than the one taken by even the most extreme groups. The distorted position is so unreasonable to the administrators and faculty that they need not take it seriously —they can simply reject it.

Hovland has suggested that the distortion of the message follows certain rules. When a discrepant position is quite close to that of an individual, he perceives it as closer than it actually is. When it is quite far away, he perceives it as farther away than it is. These two processes are called *assimilation* and *contrast*, respectively.

In order to test this notion. Hovland, Harvey, and Sherif (1957) asked subjects to rate communications that were designed to be either similar to their views, moderately different, or extremely different. The issue chosen was one that the subjects felt strongly about—the issue was prohibition, and they were living in a "dry" state. Shortly before the study began, the state had voted, by a narrow margin, to retain the existing prohibition laws. The "dry" subjects consisted of members of the Women's Christian Temperance Union, a group of Salvation Army workers, and students in the ministry or in strict denominational colleges. Moderate positions were represented by college students in classes in journalism, speech, education, and chemistry, etc. A group of "wet" subjects was secured on the basis of personal knowledge of their views.

All the subjects listened to a tape-recorded speech described as having been made by a proponent of the stand advocated. A "wet" (repeal) communication was presented to the extreme "dry" and moderate subjects. The "dry" (prohibition) communication was presented to the extreme "wet" and moderate subjects. And the moderate communication was presented to everyone. After listening to each communication, the subjects indicated where they thought it fell on a scale ranging from extreme dry to extreme wet.

The results supported the expectation that assimilation and contrast would occur. Subjects who held a strong wet position rated the moderate communication as much dryer than did the moderate subjects; subjects who held an extreme dry position rated it much wetter than did the moderates. In fact, the extreme dry subjects judged the moderate communication to be a wet communication, despite the fact that it was, by any objective criterion, quite moderate.

Both kinds of misperceptions should reduce the stress in an attitude-change situation. Assimilating the discrepant position makes it seem closer than it actually is. This reduces the amount of discrepancy and, accordingly, the amount of stress. The opposite tendency, exaggerating the discrepancy of an already distant communication, makes the communication so extreme that it loses its credibility. As we have seen, specifically in the congruity model, when a communication or its source becomes unbelievable, there is no pressure on the individual to change his position in response to it. Thus, both assimilation and contrast are effective means of reducing pressure caused by a discrepant communication.

**Rationalization and Other Defensive Procedures.** An interesting article by Abelson (1959) has described a number of ingenious, complicated modes of resolution, similar, in some ways, to the defense mechanisms for emotional conflicts described by Anna Freud. The individual intellectualizes, encapsulates, denies, displaces, and, in general, does whatever he can to minimize the stress in a situation. Abelson described how a person can decide there is no discrepancy because he and the other person are talking about different things. A man who thinks he is for civil rights and freedom for everyone but is also against laws that prohibit discrimination in housing would seem to be a prime subject for attitude change. We may say to him that denying blacks fair housing is denying them freedom. But he avoids the issue, and the stress, by saying that we and he mean different things by *freedom*. He wants people to be free to do as they please, and forcing people to rent their houses to blacks abridges freedom. He says he wants blacks to be free to rent any house that both they and the owner agree on, but that we should not force anyone to do anything. As far as he is concerned, after this distortion by separating the argument into two issues, there is no discrepancy.

There are many such ways of distorting, shifting, explaining away discrepancies. They probably produce other stresses in an individual's cognitive system, but they often are successful in reducing stress due to discrepant communications. The challenge for the communicator is to block their use and create attitude change instead.

**FACTORS AFFECTING ATTITUDE CHANGE**

Although there are many variables that affect attitude change, they can all be described in terms of two general factors—trust in the persuasive message and the strength of the message itself. If the target does not trust the message or its source, he will not accept the communication nor change his attitude. Similarly, if the message is not strong enough to convince him or discrepant enough to attack his own position, there will be no pressure on him to change. Thus, in order to effect an attitude change, a message must be both trusted and powerful.

Since a persuasive communication presents a position that is discrepant from the one held by the target, there is always some tendency for him to disbelieve or mistrust it. This lack of trust usually centers around the source of the communication—he is dishonest, stupid, misinformed, etc.—but can be produced by the communication itself—it is so extreme or biased that it loses credibility. To the extent that mistrust is aroused, the individual is unlikely to be influenced. As we have said, rejection of the source and of the message are two alternatives to attitude change, and the less trust he feels, the more likely the target is to use these alternatives. Conversely, the more trustworthy the source and the message, the more likely the target is to accept what the communication says and to change his attitude.

Largely independent of the trust factor is the power of the communication itself. How much pressure does it put on the individual to change his attitude? A perfectly trusted, clearly heard, and clearly understood communication would still produce little change if its arguments were weak and presented in a faltering, unimpressive manner. The same message presented twice—or fifty times, as in television advertising—has more power than if shown only once. The discrepancy between the position of the individual and that of the message is also a determinant of power—the larger the discrepancy, the more stress the message produces. The power of the persuasive communication is especially related to the target's ability to refute, distort, or ignore its arguments. The weaker the message, the more likely he is to use these alternatives rather than changing his attitude. Thus, assuming a communication is heard and is perfectly trusted, the amount of attitude change it can produce still varies, and this variance is due largely to what may be called its power or force.

It is not always possible to say that a particular variable involves only trust or only power, but most factors do seem to affect one more than the other. In any case, keeping these two dimensions in mind will help in understanding how each factor determines the effectiveness of a persuasive attempt.

With this background, we can turn to a consideration of the specific factors that increase or decrease the amount of attitude change produced by a persuasive communication after it has reached its target. Following the model on page 266, these factors are divided into several classes: factors involving the communicator, factors concerning the communication itself, factors in the surrounding environment that are extraneous to the communication and the participants, and factors that involve characteristics of the individual who is the target of the persuasive attempt.

### The Source of the Communication

**Prestige of the Communicator.** One of the most straightforward and reliable findings is that the greater the prestige of the communicator, the more attitude change is produced. By *prestige* we refer primarily to how expert the communicator is perceived to be in the area of concern and how much he is respected by the individual receiving the communication. For example, when evaluations of a new medicine are attributed to a noted doctor, they are more persuasive than when they are attributed to a housewife. If T. S. Eliot says that a certain poem is good, he should have more influence that a barber saying it is good. This effect of prestige was demonstrated in a study by Hovland and Weiss (1952).

Subjects heard communications concerned with four issues: the advisability of selling antihistamines without a prescription, whether the steel industry was to blame for the then-current steel shortage, the future of the movie industry in the context of the growing popularity of television, and the practicality of building an atomic-powered submarine. Each communication came from either a high- or low-prestige source.

For example, the communication on atomic submarines was supposedly either by J. Robert Oppenheimer, a noted, high-prestige physicist, or from Pravda. The results indicated that communications attributed to high-prestige sources produced more change than those from low-prestige sources.

In another study (Aronson, Turner, and Carlsmith, 1963), subjects were told they were in an experiment on aesthetics and were asked to evaluate nine stanzas from obscure modern poems. They then read someone else's evaluation of one of the stanzas they had not liked very much. The communication argued that the poem was better than the subject had indicated. It was described as being either somewhat better, much better, or very much better than the subject had thought. The crucial variable was that the communication was supposedly from either T. S. Eliot or Agnes Stearns, who was described as a student at Mississippi State Teachers College. After reading the communication, the subjects reevaluated the poems. Regardless of the level of discrepancy between

Drawing by Alan Dunn; © 1965 The New Yorker Magazine, Inc.

*"Before I begin, I'd like to make a brief statement on American foreign policy."*

the communication and the subject's initial position, there was more change with the high-prestige communicator than there was with the low-prestige one.

An interesting question, not yet answered, is whether an expert in one field can transfer the influence of his expertise to another field. If T. S. Eliot, who is highly respected in the field of poetry, took a stand on politics or education, would his opinion carry more weight and produce more attitude change than someone less well known? Although there is little evidence on this question, it seems likely that an expert may be able to transfer some of his influence to *related* fields. For example, T. S. Eliot would probably be quite influential if he discussed the teaching of English or even of music. However, as the area of concern became more different from his own area, the fact that he was an expert would matter less and he would be less able to transfer his power of persuasion. His comments on the teaching of English would probably be quite persuasive even though teaching is not his major field; his comments on the teaching of music or on contemporary theater would also be quite persuasive; his comments on politics or ethics would be less persuasive; and his comments on space technology or submarine warfare would probably be no more persuasive than anybody else's. However, for the moment this is just speculation. The question of the transferability of prestige is an open question, which should be more fully investigated in the future.

Politicians often try to transfer their own popularity and prestige to another politician. An outgoing President tries to campaign for his party's candidate. A popular senator may campaign for local candidates in his home state. Although the popular figures do attract large crowds, there is little evidence that their popularity is transferred to the other person. In the 1972 elections, Senator Kennedy drew crowds but won few votes for McGovern, while Nixon scored a huge victory yet was little help to Republican congressional candidates. Although this is not exactly the same thing as transferring prestige from one area of concern to another, it does suggest the difficulty of any such transfer.

It might be noted that many advertisements involve famous athletes or movie stars endorsing a product. Obviously the advertising companies believe that this helps sales. Whether or not it does is not known for certain, but if it does, it might be due to a somewhat different phenomenon than the one we have been discussing. The football star who shaves with a particular razor blade may help sales of that blade by associating his popularity with it. He is not convincing anyone that he knows much about blades or that they are better blades but is lending the glamor of his name to the blade and thereby making it seem more attractive. He is not the source of the message in the usual sense but is part of it.

**Intentions.** Regardless of the expertise of the communicator, it is extremely important for the listener to trust his intentions. Even though someone may be the world's greatest expert on poetry, we would not be influenced by his writing reviews of his own poetry or of poetry written by a friend of his. We would not be concerned about his inherent ability to write accurately; we would be concerned about his objectivity and, therefore, his trustworthiness. As we saw in our discussions of ingratiation (Chapter 3) and attribution in general (Chapter 2), to the extent that a communicator is not a disinterested observer, his trustworthiness may be in doubt and what he says will have less effect. If he is perceived as having something to gain from the position he is advocating or if he is taking that position for any other personal reasons, he would be less persuasive than someone perceived as advocating the position for entirely objective reasons.

A major problem for a communicator is how to convince an audience that he is a disinterested observer. One way is for him to argue for a position that appears to be counter to his self-interest. A district attorney, whose main role is supposed to be procuring convictions, would be expected to argue in favor of greater power for law-enforcement agencies. But if he does so, his credibility would be lessened, because he clearly has something to gain from this position. On the other hand, if he argues for greater protection of the rights of individuals and against strengthening law-enforcement agencies—that is, if he argues against his self-interest—his credibility should be enhanced. We would expect that a district attorney would be more persuasive and produce more attitude change when he takes the latter rather than the former position. A study by Walster, Aronson, and Abrahams (1966) concerned the effect of a communication from a convicted criminal. When the criminal argued in favor of more individual freedom and against greater powers for the police, he produced virtually no attitude change. When he argued in favor of a stronger police force, he produced a great deal of attitude change. Thus, even a low-prestige and highly doubtful communicator appears to have a considerable amount of influence when he argues in favor of a position that would hurt rather than benefit him.

A similar effect is produced when the target thinks the communicator does not intend for him to hear the communication. People tend to be more influenced when they "accidentally" overhear a persuasive communication than when it is directed at them (Walster and Festinger, 1962; Brock and Becker, 1965). This effect also seems to be due to the perceived credibility of the communicator. If he knows people are listening, he may try to convince them and may not be entirely honest. If he does not know anyone is within earshot, it is less likely that he is being dishonest. People are more likely to believe the message in the latter case and are therefore more likely to be convinced.

Given these findings, it might be thought that perception of intent to influence would have a major impact on attitude change. If the target thinks the communicator is trying to change his opinion, presumably the target should be more suspicious and change his attitude less. The research on this variable, however, has produced mixed results. The target's perception of the source's intent to persuade sometimes decreases the effect of the communication but sometimes increases it.

When the communicator has extremely high prestige or is well liked, perceived intent to persuade produces more positive attitude change. Under these circumstances, the individual generally does whatever he can to please the communicator. When he knows exactly what the communicator would like him to do, he is more likely to do it than when the communicator's intent is disguised. For example, Mills and Aronson (1965) showed that men were more influenced by a girl they liked when they knew she was trying to influence them than when her attempt to influence was less obvious. This enhancement of the effect should generally occur whenever the source of the communication is a liked figure whom the target wants to please and has no particular reason to distrust. Thus, although at first glance it seems that intent to persuade would always decrease the effect of the communication, there are times when it has the opposite effect.

In general, any characteristic of the communicator that implies that he either knows what he is talking about (is an expert) or is being honest (has no ulterior motive) increases the effectiveness of the communication. Since derogation of the source of the communication is one of the major ways of avoiding attitude change, these variables relating to the communicator are extremely important. Any lack of trust in the competence or credibility of the communicator makes it relatively easy to reject the message by attacking him; in this way, the target frees himself from the pressure of worrying about the complex details of the message itself. Therefore, preventing this particular mode of resolution by emphasizing the honesty and expertise of the source of the communication is a major concern in the attempt to influence. In most cases, it is clear that the communicator is trying to change one's attitude, and he is therefore already somewhat suspect. It is usually quite difficult to convince an audience that he is a disinterested commentator, and thus, at least in politics and advertising, there is great emphasis on the sincerity of the speaker and on his basic integrity and honesty.

**Liking.** A communicator who is trusted is more difficult to reject, and his message should produce more attitude change. A somewhat different process underlies the effect of liking for the source of the communication. As we discussed in detail in the chapter on liking, there is a strong tendency for people to like others who have views similar to theirs. This follows from any of the cognitive-consistency models and is clearly supported by the available evidence. The consistency models also predict that there is a tendency for people to agree with others whom they like. If one thinks that marijuana is terrible but his friend says it is great, the system is imbalanced. One way of reducing the imbalance is to change his attitude toward marijuana and agree with his friend. In contrast, if someone he dislikes has an attitude different from his, there is no imbalance and no pressure to change his attitude. Thus, the more that people like the source of a discrepant communication, the more likely they would be to change their attitude.

The psychological process by which liking produces attitude change is, however, somewhat different from that by which expertness works. According to a theory proposed by Kelman (1961), liking produces attitude change because people try to identify with a liked communicator, and thus tend to adopt whatever attitudes, tastes, modes of behavior, modes of dress, etc., he does. His reasons or arguments for his attitudes are not very important. On the other hand, expertness produces attitude change because people pay more attention to an expert's arguments, and consider them more seriously, than they do a nonexpert's arguments. Mills and Harvey (1972) tested this theory by varying the timing of information about the communicator: some subjects were told of the communicator's attractiveness (or expertness) before reading his message, and others learned about the communicator only after reading his message. Mills and Harvey reasoned that the attractive source would produce attitude change in either case, because all the subject needed to know was the communicator's opinion in order to identify with him and accept his position. On the other hand, learning after the message that the communicator was an expert would do no good, because the opportunity to scrutinize and consider his arguments more carefully would have been lost by that time. As shown in Table 9–1, that was how their data came out. The attractive communicator was equally effective in producing attitude change whether he was described before or after the message, but the expert communicator produced attitude change only when he was described before the subjects read the message.

**Similarity.** People tend to be influenced more by people who are similar to them than by people who are different. This is partly because of the tendency to like people who are similar and, as just noted, to be more influenced by people we like. But similarity also increases influence for another reason. Suppose someone is similar to us in terms of national, economic, racial, and religious background, and we also share many ideological values. If he then says that he thinks drugs are bad, we

Table 9-1

AMOUNT OF AGREEMENT WITH ATTRACTIVE AND EXPERT COMMUNICATORS WHEN INFORMATION ABOUT THEM WAS RECEIVED BEFORE OR AFTER THE COMMUNICATION

| | INFORMATION ABOUT COMMUNICATOR GIVEN | |
| --- | --- | --- |
| | *Before Communication* | *After Communication* |
| Attractive Communicator | 8.2 | 9.3 |
| Expert Communicator | 9.5 | 1.9 |

Source: Adapted from Mills and Harvey (1972).

would probably assume that he made this judgment on the same bases that we would. He is not using irrelevant or incorrect (in our eyes) criteria. Accordingly, his judgment tends to carry considerable weight. If he were different from us in terms of background and values, his attitude toward drugs would be less meaningful, because we could assume it was based on criteria different from those we would apply. Thus, in terms of both increased liking and shared perspectives, the greater the similarity between the source and recipient of a discrepant communication, the more attitude change is produced.

The balance model would suggest the same effect of similarity. If someone is similar to us on many dimensions and agrees with us on most things but disagrees with us on one issue, some imbalance is produced by the disagreement. We can resolve this imbalance by changing either all the things on which we already agree, thereby making us disagree on everything, or our stand on the one source of disagreement. Obviously it is easier to change our attitude on the one issue, and that is what would be expected.

**Reference Groups.**  One of the strongest sources of persuasive pressure is a group to which an individual belongs. The group could be as large and inclusive as all American citizens or the middle-class or a labor union or college students or all liberals or all blacks. It can also be a much smaller, more specialized group, such as a college fraternity, social psychologists, the Young Republicans, or the Elks Club. And it can be extremely small, such as a group of friends, a bridge club, a discussion group or just five people who happen to be in a room together.

As we saw in the chapter on conformity, there is a strong tendency for individuals to go along with the group, particularly when everyone else in the group holds the same opinion or makes the same response. In these cases, however, there is little actual change in the individual's opinions—he conforms to the group overtly but does not change his internal attitude. Nevertheless, the opinion of the group can also be an

Drawing by Kraus; © 1964 The New Yorker Magazine, Inc.

*"And I thoroughly understand the problems of the cave-man, because I'm a caveman myself."*

extremely persuasive force and can cause the individual to change his internal attitude on an issue. If the Young Republicans endorse a particular candidate, there is a tendency for all the members of the club to feel he is a good candidate. If a group of friends tells us they are in favor of student activism or like a particular movie, we probably are convinced by them. If most of the members of a fraternity think initiations are a good idea, the rest of the members may agree with them.

There are two important reasons why reference groups are so effective at producing attitude change and creating attitudes. If people value a group, it is a high-prestige, highly credible, highly esteemed source of communication. When the group says something, each member tends to trust it and believe the message. In addition, because they consider themselves members of the group, they tend to evaluate themselves in comparison with it. In essence, the group serves as the standard for their own behavior and attitudes. They evaluate the group highly and want to be similar to the other members. When the other members express a particular opinion, each member thinks his own opinion wrong if it is different. Only when their opinion is the same as the group's would it be correct or "normal." Therefore they tend to change their opinion so as to make it agree.

Attachment to the group can also serve to prevent somebody from being influenced by a communication from an outside source. If the group agrees with the individual's opinion, they provide him with strong support. Consider a fraternity member whose fraternity believes strongly in initiations. He may occasionally be exposed to an attack on initiations from someone outside the fraternity. Whenever he is so exposed, knowledge that his group agrees with him provides strong support and makes it easier for him to resist persuasion.

This dual effect of groups—changing a member's opinion to make it coincide with the rest of the group and supporting a member's opinion so he can resist persuasion from without—depends to some extent on how strong the individual's ties are to the group. The more he wants to be a member of it and the more highly he evaluates it, the more he would be influenced by the group's beliefs. Kelley and Volkart (1952) demonstrated the effect of attachment to the group on members' resistance to outside influence. A communicator attempted to change some Boy Scouts' opinions on various issues that were closely related to their troop's norms. The more the Scouts valued their membership in the troop, the less effect the communicator had on their opinions.

Another way of demonstrating the potent effect of group norms is to show how changes in the group's position can pull people away from their old positions. Kelley and Woodruff (1956) played subjects a tape recording of a speech arguing against their group's norm—they were education students, and the speech argued against "progressive education." The speech was interrupted periodically by applause which the experimenters attributed to faculty members and recent graduates of the college in one experimental condition ("members' applause"), or to an audience of college-trained people in a neighboring city, interested in community problems related to education ("outsiders' applause"). Attitude change toward the speech, away from old group norms, was much greater in the "members' applause" condition. This gives additional evidence of the potency of groups in producing or blocking attitude change; in this case, subjects confronted with an apparent change in their group's norm were likely to change their own attitudes to line up with the group's new position. This study was repeated recently with some variations (Landy, 1972) and produced essentially the same results: fellow group members (in this case, fellow students) applauding a communication discrepant from the subject's initial attitude created major attitude change compared to the applause of a less attractive group.

**The Sleeper Effect.**   An interesting and important phenomenon connected with the source variables we have been discussing is the so-called sleeper effect. It appears that the effect of the source of a communication is strongest immediately after exposure to the communication and is much less important some time later.

Kelman and Hovland (1953) conducted an experiment in which high school students heard a communication that argued for lenient treatment of juvenile delinquents. The communicator was made to appear either competent, fair, and generally positive, or biased, uninformed, and generally negative. Immediately after hearing the communication, the students indicated their attitudes on the issue. Three weeks later, the subjects again gave their attitudes on the same issue, but just before doing so, half the subjects were reminded of the source of the communication, that is, whether it was positive or negative.

The results are shown in Figure 9–2. It can be seen that the immediate effect of the positive communicator is greater than that of the negative communicator. After three weeks, however, when the subjects are not reminded of the source of the communications, the effect of the positive communicator has declined while that of the negative communicator has increased. This is called the sleeper effect because the influence of the negative communicator is greater than it appears at first.

The explanation usually given for this effect is that individuals forget the source of a communication quicker than the content. Although they remember the message, they do not spontaneously connect it with the person from whom it came. The effect of the communicator disappears or declines with time, whereas the effect of the message remains

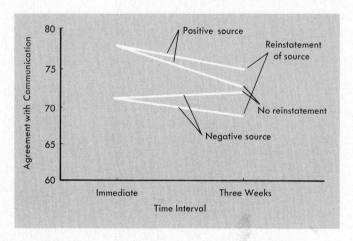

Figure 9–2

The effects of the prestige of the communicator, time, and reinstatement of the source on attitude change. The high-prestige communicator produces more immediate change but loses strength over time; the low-prestige source is less effective immediately but gains strength. Reinstatement of the source minimizes the effect of time, thus indicating that the effect of time is primarily due to forgetting the source.

relatively constant. Originally, the subjects' attitudes were changed more by the communication from the positive source than by the one from the negative source. The former increased the effectiveness of the message by lending it his prestige and trustworthiness; the latter decreased the message's effectiveness by associating it with his own low prestige and untrustworthiness. When the source was forgotten or was no longer spontaneously associated with the message, both effects declined. The positive communicator no longer helped the message; the negative communicator no longer hurt it. Thus, forgetting the source should decrease the effect of a message from a positive source and increase the effect of one from a negative source.

The results of the reinstatement condition in the Kelman and Hovland experiment supported this interpretation. When the students were reminded of the sources of the communications, the sleeper effect disappeared. Those who had heard the positive communicator and were reminded of this showed more change even after three weeks than did those who were reminded that they had heard the message from a negative communicator.

These results highlight the difference between getting a message through and getting people to accept it. Presumably, people hear a message and learn its content regardless of how they feel about the communicator. Although they accept the message less if they hear a negative communicator, they still retain it. Then, when they forget the source of the communication, the message begins to have more effect, because it is no longer damaged by being connected with a negative source.

### The Communication

Social psychologists tend to concentrate on factors that increase the effectiveness of a persuasive message rather than on the content of the message itself. This is because we are looking for general laws that determine the effectiveness of all messages. We do not mean to give the impression that the content of the message is unimportant. Naturally it is easier to sell something good than something less good. Crest toothpaste was successful in part because it offered protection against cavities; the automobile became popular because it was a great product; and some political candidates are more qualified than others. A good campaign does better than a poor one, but a really terrible product would be difficult to sell even with great advertising. Given a particular product or opinion to sell, however, a number of variables in the communication itself have important effects on the amount of attitude change that is produced.

**Discrepancy.** As mentioned earlier, the major source of stress in any influence situation comes from the discrepancy between the target's initial position and the position advocated by the communication. The greater the discrepancy, the greater the stress. If a smoker is told that smoking may cause his teeth to turn yellow (a mildly negative statement), there is less stress than if he is told that smoking causes cancer (an extremely negative statement). If someone who thinks John Kennedy was a great president hears a communication arguing that he was only moderately successful, the individual's attitude is under pressure; if the communication argues that Kennedy was a terrible president, there is much more pressure. If on a scale there are 2 points of discrepancy, 2 points of attitude change would eliminate it. If there are 5 points of discrepancy, 5 points of change are necessary. An individual who changes his attitude under the pressure of a discrepant message must, accordingly, change it more with greater discrepancy. Therefore, within a wide range, there is more attitude change with greater discrepancy (Fisher and Lubin, 1958; Hovland and Pritzker, 1957).

However, the relationship between discrepancy and amount of change is not always this simple. There is more stress with greater discrepancy, but this does not always produce more change. The complicating factors are that as discrepancy becomes quite large, the individual finds it more difficult to change his attitude enough to eliminate the discrepancy and that extremely discrepant statements tend to make the individual doubt the credibility of their source. Suppose someone thinks Kennedy was a very great president and is faced with a discrepant opinion from a teacher of political science. What happens as the discrepancy between his and the teacher's opinions increases? This is diagrammed in Figure 9–3.

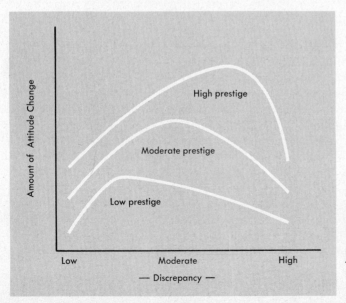

Figure 9–3

Discrepancy, prestige of the communicator, and attitude change. Maximum change is always produced by intermediate levels of discrepancy, but the point at which it occurs is determined by prestige. The higher the prestige, the greater the discrepancy that produces the maximum change.

We shall consider this situation in terms of two modes of resolution —attitude change and rejection of the communicator—and, for the moment, shall ignore other modes. If one can reject the communicator, he need not change his opinion; if he cannot reject the communicator, he must change his opinion. At low discrepancy, when the teacher says he thinks Kennedy was not a great president but still a pretty good one, the individual is likely to be somewhat influenced. There would be some pressure on him to change his opinion in the direction of the teacher's, and if the teacher presented a fairly persuasive argument, the individual would probably do so. In this situation, it is difficult to reject the moderately prestigeful communicator but is easy to change one's opinion the little bit required to reduce the discrepancy. It is fairly easy to decide that Kennedy was not a great president but only a good one; it is considerably more difficult to decide that a teacher in political science is not a valid source of information about politics. Since attitude change is easier than rejection of the communicator, the individual would tend to resolve the situation by changing his attitude. He would, however, change his attitude only slightly, because that is all that is necessary to reduce the discrepancy.

With somewhat greater degrees of discrepancy (e.g., the teacher thinks Kennedy was a mediocre president), it becomes harder to reduce the discrepancy by changing one's attitude. It is one thing to change from thinking Kennedy was great to thinking he was only good; it is more difficult to change from great to mediocre. Nevertheless, it may still be easier to change his opinion than to reject the communicator, and the research indicates that this is what happens. With moderate discrepancy, subjects still resolve the situation primarily by changing their attitudes rather than by rejecting the communicator. Note that moderate discrepancy results in more attitude change than small discrepancy because greater change is necessary in order to reduce the discrepancy. Thus, as discrepancy increases from slight to moderate, the amount of attitude change also increases.

As the discrepancy becomes extreme, however, it becomes still harder for the individual to reduce the stress by changing his opinion. A greater change in his opinion is necessary in order to reduce the discrepancy, and the greater the change that is necessary, the more difficult it is for the person to make it. It is extremely difficult for someone who thought Kennedy was great to decide that he was terrible.

As discrepancy increases, something else important happens. Congruity theory points out that a communicator who makes an extremely discrepant statement tends to lose credibility. If one thinks Kennedy was great and someone says he thinks Kennedy was terrible, there is a tendency to decide that this communicator does not know much about government or men. The extremity of his statement compared to the individual's initial belief tends to cast doubt on his credibility. Thus, as discrepancy becomes quite large, it becomes relatively easy to reject the source of the communication. One decides he is dumb, ignorant, or biased.

There are thus two factors operating as discrepancy increases— attitude change gets more difficult and rejection of the communicator gets easier. At some point, rejection becomes easier than attitude change as a means of removing the stress. Perhaps it is when the teacher says he thinks Kennedy was a poor president; perhaps it is when he says he thinks Kennedy was a very bad president. When this degree of discrepancy is passed, people begin to reject the communicator rather than change their attitudes and the amount of attitude change decreases. Thus, as discrepancy increases, the amount of attitude change produced increases up to a point and decreases beyond that point. Conversely, rejection of the communicator is relatively slight until the maximum point of discrepancy is reached, and then rejection becomes the primary mode of resolution. This relationship between discrepancy and attitude change has now been well documented (Freedman, 1964; Bochner and Insko, 1966; Rhine and Severance, 1970; Eagly and Telaak, 1972).

The effect is heightened by the tendency to assimilate or contrast the position advocated in the discrepant communication. As mentioned earlier, discrepant positions that are close to the individual's are often seen as closer than they actually are, whereas those that are far away are seen as farther away than they are. Exaggerating the closeness of a discrepant position makes it easy to change enough to reduce the small discrepancy, or it may eliminate change by making the two positions essentially identical. Exaggerating the remoteness of a position makes it easier to attack the credibility of the person advocating it, by making his position even more extreme and less reasonable.

Thus far we have been considering situations in which the communication comes from a person of moderate prestige. Higher prestige makes it more difficult to reject the source. If one's most respected teacher says that Kennedy was a poor president, it is harder to decide that he does not know what he is talking about. Only extreme statements from him could make the individual come to this conclusion. Therefore, the greater the prestige of the communicator, the higher the level of discrepancy at which rejection, rather than attitude change, starts and at which the maximum of change occurs. Similarly, a lower-prestige source makes rejection relatively easy and the maximum point occurs at lower levels of discrepancy. The study by Aronson, Turner, and Carlsmith (1963) described earlier demonstrated this effect. Subjects read opinions about poetry that were slightly, moderately, or greatly discrepant from their own. When the discrepant opinion was attributed to T. S. Eliot, maximum attitude change occurred with the highest discrepancy. When another student was the source, maximum change was produced by the moderately discrepant message. Presumably, even T. S. Eliot's prestige has some limits, and if discrepancy became great enough, attitude change would begin to decline.

This relationship is nicely illustrated in Figure 9–4 which shows the effect of discrepancy and prestige on opinion change. Bochner and Insko (1966) found more change at moderate than high levels of discrepancy with messages from both a Nobel prize winner and a YMCA instructor. In addition, as expected, the optimal level of discrepancy was greater for the high prestige source.

Thus, the level of prestige does not change the basic relationship between discrepancy and attitude change, but it does change the point at

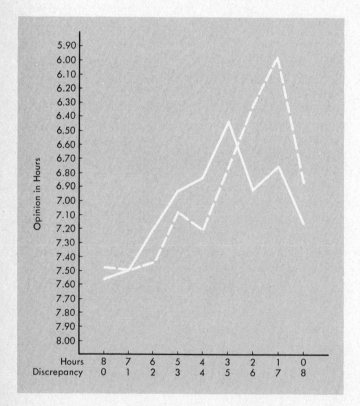

Figure 9–4

Opinion change produced by high- and low-prestige communicators at low, moderate, and high discrepancy. (Bochner and Insko, 1966.)

which maximum change occurs. A similar effect is produced by any other factor that affects the difficulty of rejection or the difficulty of changing. The more difficult it is to reject the communicator, the greater the discrepancy at which maximum change occurs; the more difficult it is to change one's attitude, the lower the discrepancy producing maximum change. This example illustrates how an interplay of forces determines which mode of resolution is adopted in a given situation and how the use of one mode implies that there is less use of another.

**One-sided versus Two-sided Communications.** To produce the maximum effect, should a communication argue entirely on one side of the issue or should it contain some arguments on the other side? Should a man trying to sell a Chevrolet tell a customer that a Ford is a good car and rides smoothly before launching into his arguments in favor of the Chevrolet? Or should he never say anything nice about competitive cars and concentrate entirely on the virtues of the Chevrolet? These approaches can be seen in political campaigning. Some candidates make a point of occasionally saying nice things about their opponent. Others are extremely careful not to say favorable things about their opponent and sometimes not even to mention their opponent's name in public. What is the effect of these two tactics?

It appears that under most circumstances, the two-sided communication is more effective. This approach produces more attitude change when the listener initially disagrees with the position advocated by the communication and when the listener is relatively well informed and intelligent. One likely, though as yet unproven, explanation is that including some arguments on the other side tends to make the speaker seem less biased, better informed, and, in general, more credible. A speaker who is willing to concede some point to the opposition probably seems more objective than one who denies that there are arguments other than those favoring his position. By demonstrating that he is familiar with these other arguments, he suggests that he has arrived at his own position after considering both sides of the issue. This would make him seem not only well informed but also careful and thoughtful.

The two-sided communication has another advantage. As mentioned above, when someone thinks a speaker is trying to make him change his mind, he tends to be influenced less. It seems likely that the intent to persuade is somewhat more disguised when the communication contains both sides of an issue. Other things being equal, it sounds less like a propaganda message and more like a dispassionate talk. Thus, the two-sided communication makes the speaker appear more dispassionate, better informed, more objective, and less obviously attempting to persuade the listener. All these factors increase the credibility of the communication and tend to produce greater attitude change.

However, there appear to be times when a one-sided communication is preferable. Although the evidence on this point is somewhat weak, there is reason to believe that a one-sided communication is more effective when it is directed mainly at poorly informed, relatively unintelligent individuals who already generally agree with the position advocated in the communication. Under these circumstances, presenting arguments on both sides of an issue seems merely to confuse the listeners, to give them counter-arguments they had not thought of before, and to result in a weakened effect. Moreover, because the listeners generally agree with the communication already, it does not arouse suspicion and its main effect is to strengthen their existing attitudes.

Factors that increase the credibility of the communicator or communication increase its effectiveness only when the audience has some reason to doubt the credibility of the message. When there is no such doubt, the relatively subtle factors, such as using two-sided communications, disguising the fact that the speech is intended to persuade, and pretending that the speech is not directed at the individual, may have the effect of diverting the audience from the main content of the speech and therefore lessening its power. Thus, a teacher who is trying to instruct his class on how to solve a problem in algebra or on the chronology of the Kings of England should be as direct as possible. Since the class has no reason to doubt his credibility, he should simply present his arguments as clearly and forcibly as possible, and he should make it explicit that he is trying to convince the class of the correctness of his position. On the other hand, if an instructor in English is trying to change the political attitudes of his class, the situation is different. Politics is not his area of expertise, and the class might well doubt his credibility on the issue. In order to have maximum effect, he should use all the techniques described to increase his credibility and to disguise the fact that he is trying to change their opinions.

In Chapter 2 we mentioned the effect of one's first impression on his ultimate judgments of others. The question of whether first impressions tend to be dominant has also been of considerable interest to psychologists studying attitude formation. There are plausible reasons why either the first or the last impression would be dominant. A primacy effect, that is, the first impression dominant, could be caused by the person's becoming committed to his first position and thus, as cognitive consistency would lead us to expect, rejecting subsequent, discrepant information. On the other hand, a recency effect, that is, last dominant, might be caused by the last piece of information being more vivid and salient. The results of research on this problem have been inconsistent, however. Whether primacy or recency occurs seems to depend on the particular situation.

**Stating a Conclusion.** When presenting arguments to support a particular position, the communication can either state the conclusion explicitly or leave it unstated. Stating the conclusion has the advantage of making the speaker's position clear and thus avoids the possibility that anyone in the audience could misinterpret it. On the other hand, leaving it unstated has two advantages: the speaker may appear less intent on convincing the audience of a particular position and therefore may seem more credible; and the audience is encouraged to reach the conclusion without aid, which may increase its effectiveness. In much the same way we discussed above, it is a question of whether enough is gained from the greater clarity to make up for the trust that may be lost by the low credibility of the explicitly stated conclusion.

The data indicate that the relative effectiveness of the two procedures depends on the conditions of the situation. Although the findings are somewhat inconsistent, it appears that the effect of stating the conclusion is similar to that of using a one-sided communication. It is more effective when the audience is composed primarily of less intelligent people or when the communication contains complex arguments with which the audience is unfamiliar and that concern an issue that is not highly involving. In one study (Hovland and Mandell, 1952), a talk concerning current economic theory, the financial status of the United States, and the possibility of devaluating American currency was presented under two conditions. In one case, the conclusion that the currency should be devalued was clearly stated; in the other, it was not. Although the same conclusion could logically be drawn from the arguments that were presented, a large percentage of the andience that did not hear it stated explicitly was probably unable to deduce it themselves, and more attitude change occurred when the conclusion was stated.

With a relatively intelligent, well-informed audience and familiar arguments and issues, the effect appears to be different. Under these conditions, stating the conclusion does not produce an increase in attitude change and, in fact, may actually produce less change than leaving it unstated. Once again, the clarity that is gained by the explicit statement may be balanced or perhaps outweighed by the loss of credibility. In addition, if the listener is able to draw the conclusion himself, he may be influenced more because of the effort he has exerted. Linder and Worchel (1970) showed that the more difficult it was to draw a conclusion, the greater effect it had on those who initially disagreed with it. Thus, whether or not to state the conclusion depends on many factors. What does seem to be clear is that the intelligence, sophistication, and involvement of the audience, plus the complexity of the issues, appear to be important determinants of the relative effectiveness of the two methods.

Throughout this discussion, we have been assuming that the stronger the communication in terms of the quality and quantity of its arguments, the more effective it is. The more arguments there are, the more logical they are, the more evidence presented to support them, the more important the implications of the arguments are, and so on, the more influence they should have. There is little solid evidence to support this, because, in a sense, we define the quality of the arguments by how effective they are. But from any theoretical and even practical consideration, it must be assumed that, other things being equal, four pieces of evidence to support an argument make the argument more convincing than only two pieces of evidence supporting it. In other words, the stronger the arguments on purely logical grounds, the more attitude change should be produced.

Much of our discussion has been dealing with ways in which to make the arguments more trustworthy. There are probably also a number of factors that directly affect how strong the arguments appear to be. The clarity of the presentation, the forcefulness with which the arguments are pressed, and other such rhetorical considerations have a great effect on the strength of the arguments themselves. A clear presentation may, however, reveal the weakness of arguments that are not very strong to begin with. Thus someone who is on weak ground may want to present his arguments unclearly so the audience cannot realize how poor they are. If a handsome, attractive, liked, and trusted speaker says nothing, he has more impact than if he utters clear but weak statements. This does not contradict the idea that a better presentation in rhetorical terms strengthens the arguments that do exist. But it does mean that sometimes speakers want to rely not on the arguments but on the effect of the communication.

A few studies deal with specific characteristics of the communication itself. For example Zilman (1972) showed that in some circumstances rhetorical questions were more persuasive than simple declarative statements. Subjects listened to the defense summation in a trial. One form of the summation used sentences such as, "But he never used a knife before." Another form of the summation was identical in every respect except that a number of key sentences were put into the form of rhetorical question such as, "But did he ever use a knife before?" The use of rhetorical questions caused more subjects to agree with the defense lawyer's position. Other studies have shown that repeating a message can increase its effectiveness, and still others (Haas and Linder, 1972) demonstrate that the structure of the message in terms of when and how counter arguments are presented can increase or decrease the amount of persuasion it produces.

There has been relatively little work on these kinds of factors and probably for good reason. It seems likely that the effect of repetition or rhetorical statements or any other structural aspect of the message depends on specific variables in the situation. For a given message, communication, issue, and audience one kind of structure may be more effective; but changing any aspect of the situation might reverse the effect. At the moment we know very little about the detailed interactions between message structure and these other factors. Further research along these lines must take into account that any finding may be severely limited in terms of its generality. Nevertheless the important point from this research is that minor changes in the structure of the message can produce substantial differences in its persuasive impact. Perhaps social psychologists would do well to devote more attention to these internal factors that affect the strength of a persuasive communication.

**Novelty of the Information.** One factor that probably always affects the strength of the arguments is the novelty of the information being presented. A communication that contains new information on an issue should be more effective than one that simply contains information with which the audience is already familiar. Presumably, the audience has not taken into account the new information when they took the position they presently hold, and therefore, when they receive new information, they should be more willing to change than when they receive old. Thus, in presenting an argument, the more new information included, the more attitude change should be produced.

One implication of this effect is that regardless of the actual novelty of the information, it is desirable to make it seem new. Even if the information is quite familiar, the speaker may be able to convince the audience he is presenting something new and may therefore increase the effectiveness of his argument. In a study of this problem (Sears and Freedman, 1965), all subjects were presented with an identical persuasive communication, but some were told that it contained novel arguments and information whereas the others were told that all the information was material with which they were already familiar. Those who were expecting novel information were significantly more influenced by the communication than those who were expecting familiar information. Simply being told that the information was new made it more effective.

**Fear Arousal.** Arousing fear is one of the most natural ways of trying to convince someone of something. A mother tells her young son that he will be run over if he crosses the street without her. Religious leaders frighten their followers with threats of eternal damnation and suffering. Political philosophers and candidates warn that if their opponents are elected, the country will be ruined, people will starve, and civilization will collapse. And opponents of fluoridation tell us that fluorides cause cancer, heart disease, hardening of the arteries, calcification of the brain, etc., while supporters of fluoridation warn that without it, children's teeth will decay. Given a particular argument in favor of a position, how does the amount of fear aroused affect the success of the argument?

The original study in this area was conducted by Janis and Feshbach in 1953. They showed high school students a film that emphasized the importance of brushing one's teeth three times a day, after every meal. The film described the dangers of not doing this and explained the advantages of good dental care. High fear was aroused by showing pictures of badly decayed teeth and gums, close-ups of diseased teeth, mouths in which the gums had pulled away from the teeth, etc. They were extremely vivid and dramatic. In the mild-fear condition, subjects saw less dramatic and less frightening pictures. And in the no-fear, or control, condition, the subjects saw no pictures of diseased teeth. The subjects in the high-fear condition reported being more impressed by the presentation and agreeing with it more. However, a week later it was found that the subjects in the no-fear condition had changed their behavior more than had subjects in either of the fear conditions. The authors concluded that the maximum effect was produced by the persuasive arguments without the fear-arousing slides.

This result has generally failed to replicate in later experiments. Much of the work done in recent years has produced the opposite result. For example, a series of experiments conducted by Howard Leventhal at Yale University (Leventhal, Jones, and Trembly, 1966; Leventhal and Singer, 1966) have shown that the arousal of fear tends to facilitate both attitude and behavioral change. In one study (Dabbs and Leventhal, 1966), college students were urged to get inoculations for tetanus. The disease was described in detail—it was pointed out how serious it was, that it was often fatal, and that it was easy to catch. In addition, the students were told that the inoculation was extremely effective and that it gave almost complete protection against the disease.

The message was delivered under several different conditions of fear arousal. In the high-fear condition, the descriptions of the disease were extremely vivid, the symptoms were made very explicit, and everything was done to make the situation as frightening as possible. In the second condition, a moderate amount of fear was aroused; and in the third, very little. Students were then asked how important they thought it was to get the inoculation and whether or not they intended to get one. The university health service, which was nearby, recorded how many of the students went for inoculations during the next month.

The findings (Table 9–2) are straightforward and impressive. The greater the fear aroused, the more strongly the subjects intended to get shots. Perhaps more important, higher fear induced more subjects actually to go to the health service and receive inoculations. Thus, fear arousal not only produced more attitude change but also had a greater effect on the relevant behavior.

Various other studies have used a wide range of issues, including automotive safety, atom bomb testing, fallout shelters, and dental hygiene, to study the effects of fear. Higbee (1969) has made quite a careful review of these many studies. He concludes that there is an overwhelming weight of evidence favoring the positive effect of fear. There were only five studies that clearly showed low fear having more effect (e.g., Janis and Feshbach, 1953; Janis and Terwilliger, 1962), whereas over twenty experiments conducted by a number of different experimenters have shown fear facilitating attitude change (e.g., Berkowitz and Cottingham, 1960; Haefner, 1964; Insko, Arkoff, and Insko, 1965; Rogers and Thistlewaite, 1970; and the work by Leventhal). Harris and Jellison (1971) even showed that simply making subjects *think* they were more afraid increased persuasion. They used the false physiological feedback technique discussed in Chapter 2, telling some subjects they were very upset and others that they were less upset by a communication. The former actually changed their opinions more, even though everyone received the same message. Some studies, such as Dabbs and Leventhal (1966) and Evans et al. (1970), also indicated that high fear had a greater effect on relevant action, although the evidence for this is somewhat less consistent. From all of this research, it seems clear that under most circumstances fear arousal increases the effectiveness of a persuasive communication.

Table 9–2

EFFECTS OF FEAR AROUSAL ON ATTITUDES AND BEHAVIOR

| Condition | Intention to Take Shots[a] | Percentage Taking Shots |
|---|---|---|
| High fear | 5.17 | 22 |
| Low fear | 4.73 | 13 |
| Control | 4.12 | 6 |

[a]The figures are ratings on a scale from 1 (lowest) to 7 (highest).

Source: Adapted from Dabbs and Leventhal (1966).

**Mark Waters was a chain smoker. Wonder who'll get his office?**

Too bad about Mark. Kept hearing the same thing everyone does about lung cancer. But, like so many people, he kept right on smoking cigarettes. Must have thought, "been smoking all my life... what good'll it do to stop now?" Fact is, once you've stopped smoking, no matter how long you've smoked, the body begins to reverse the damage done by cigarettes, provided cancer or emphysema have not developed.

Next time you reach for a cigarette, think of Mark. Then think of your office—and your home.

**American Cancer Society**

Campaigns to stop smoking are based on the knowledge that smoking is harmful. But the advertisements can be designed to differ enormously in how much fear they arouse. These excellent ads range from quite frightening (with a specific reference to dying and being replaced) to almost amusing (with only a veiled reference to health).

There may be some situations, however, in which fear does reduce the effectiveness of a communication. Janis has suggested that the relationship between fear and attitude change depends on the level of fear involved. He argued that at low levels, greater fear produces more attitude change but that at some point, the fear becomes too intense, arouses defensive mechanisms, and thereby produces less change. This would explain the seemingly contradictory results that have been found, because the studies have involved different amounts of fear. Janis has reanalyzed a number of experiments in these terms, and although not all the data fit this model, most of the results appear to be consistent with it.

To sum up, the evidence strongly indicates that under most circumstances arousing fear increases the effectiveness of persuasive communications. But arousing too much fear may be disruptive. Causing a person to be too frightened can make him either so paralyzed that he is unable to act or so threatened that he tends to deny the danger and reject the persuasive communication. Aside from such extreme cases, however, it appears that fear-arousing arguments are more effective in producing attitude change than are arguments that arouse little or no fear.

### Characteristics of the Target

Even after a message from a particular source has reached the target, the problems of attitude change are not over. Various characteristics of the individual's personality and factors in his immediate and past experience are important determinants of his reaction to the message. These factors affect primarily his tendency to trust the message or its source, his ability to argue against the message, his motivation not to change his opinion, and his confidence in his own position.

**Commitment.** One of the important aspects of the attitude-change situation is the power or force of the persuasive communication. The corresponding factor in the target is the strength of his commitment to his own attitude, that is, the extent to which he feels reluctant to give up his initial position. If one has just bought a house, he is more committed to the belief that it is a fine house than if he had not yet bought it. Changing his opinion of the house has broader implications for him if he owns it than if he is only thinking about buying it. Someone who has just stated on television that he thinks smoking is bad for health and is an evil, dirty habit is more committed to this attitude than if he had made these statements only to his wife or had kept them to himself. Changing his attitude is harder if he expressed it on television, because then the change would involve publicly admitting he was wrong. Anything that means that changing an attitude would cause the individual to give up more, suffer more, or change more of his other attitudes or behaviors increases his commitment to his initial attitude and makes it more difficult for him to change it.

Two factors that affect the strength of commitment are action taken on the basis of the attitude and public statement of the attitude. In addition, it appears that freely choosing a position produces a greater feeling of commitment than being forced. In a study on this problem (Freedman and Steinbruner, 1964), subjects were given information about a candidate for graduate school and asked to rate him, under circumstances of either high or low choice. The subjects were made to feel either that they had made up their own minds and freely selected the particular rating or that they had virtually nothing to do with the decision and had been forced to select the rating. The subjects were then exposed to information that strongly contradicted their initial rating and were allowed to change their rating if they desired. Those who had made the first rating with a feeling of free choice changed less than did those in the low-choice condition.

A fourth factor affecting commitment is the extent to which the attitude is imbedded in other behaviors and attitudes. Someone in favor of fluoridation of drinking water may feel very strongly about it, but this attitude probably stands by itself to a large extent. Most people have taken no action related to fluoridation and have few attitudes related directly to it. Changing their attitude toward it from favorable to unfavorable would involve relatively few other changes in their cognitive systems. This is not so for a dentist who has been fighting tooth decay for years, who has been coating teeth with fluorides, who has donated money to fluoridation campaigns, and who has read extensive literature supporting fluoridation. Changing his opinion about it would involve many contradictions, inconsistencies, and, eventually, changes in his cognitive and behavioral system. Thus, he is more committed to his attitude and would find it harder to change.

The effect of commitment of this kind is to reduce the amount of attitude change produced by a persuasive communication. Greater commitment makes it harder for the individual to change his attitude and means that he is more likely to use other modes of resolution instead. Thus, the greater the commitment to the initial position, the less attitude change occurs.

The relationship between commitment, discrepancy, and attitude change is similar to that of prestige. As described previously (page 286), the prestige of the source does not change the relationship between discrepancy and attitude change but does affect the point at which maximum change occurs—the higher the prestige, the greater the discrepancy at which there is maximum attitude change. Commitment to one's initial position also shifts the maximum point, but in the opposite direction. The harder it is to change his position, the lower the discrepancy at which rejection of the source is easier than change. Therefore, the greater the commitment, the lower the discrepancy at which maximum attitude change occurs (Rhine and Severance, 1970).

**Inoculation and Support.**   Another source of resistance to change in the target comes from his past experience with the issue. William McGuire and his associates conducted a series of experiments on the effects of giving people experiences designed to increase their ability to resist persuasion. McGuire has used a medical analogy to describe the influence situation. He pictured the individual faced with a discrepant communication as being similar to somebody being attacked by a virus or a disease. The stronger the persuasive message (virus), the more damage it would do; and, of course, the stronger the person's defenses, the better able he is to resist persuasion (disease). There are two different ways of strengthening someone's defense against a disease. We can strengthen his body generally, by giving him vitamins, exercise, and so on; and we can strengthen his defenses against that particular disease by building up antibodies. McGuire argued that these two approaches are also applicable to the influence situation.

To begin with, he identified a number of *cultural truisms*—opinions that are so universally held in our society that they are almost never subjected to any kind of attack. One example is the belief that it is good to brush one's teeth three times a day. Probably almost everybody in the United States believes that this is basically a good idea in terms of dental health. And, also, most people have never heard anything to the contrary. Thus, someone holding this opinion is analogous to an individual who has never been exposed to the smallpox germ. He has never been forced to defend himself from attack so has never built up any defenses against attack.

One procedure that strengthens resistance is to build up the person's opinion directly, by giving the individual additional arguments supporting his original position. If he believes that it is good to brush his teeth three times a day, he is shown a study by the United States Public Health Service that shows that people who do so have fewer cavities than those who brush their teeth less often or not at all. Giving individuals this kind of support for their position does, in fact, increase their resistance to a subsequent persuasive communication. Thus, one way of increasing somebody's resistance to persuasion is simply to give him more reasons for believing what he already does. This gives him more ammunition to use in the coming argument, and he therefore changes his opinion less.

A different approach is to strengthen the individual's defenses against persuasion rather than to strengthen his opinion. McGuire has argued that, as with diseases, the most effective way of increasing resistance is to build up defenses. If a person is given a mild case of smallpox that he is able to fight off, his body produces antibodies, which in the future provide an effective and strong defense against more powerful attacks of smallpox. Similarly, if a particular opinion has never been attacked, it is extremely vulnerable because no defenses have been built up around it. When such an opinion is suddenly and surprisingly subjected to persuasive pressure, the individual does not have a set of defenses immediately available, and the opinion tends to be relatively easy to change. However, if the opinion has been attacked and the individual has successfully defended himself, he should be better able to resist subsequent attacks because he has built up a relatively strong defensive system around that opinion. In other words, McGuire argued that it is possible to inoculate individuals against persuasive attacks just as we can inoculate them against diseases.

This is accomplished by weakly attacking the individual's attitude. The attack must be weak or it would change his attitude and the battle to maintain his attitude would be lost. To be certain that this does not occur, the target is helped to defend himself against the mild attack. He is given an argument directed specifically at the attack or is told that the attack is not very good and he should be able to refute it.

One study by McGuire and Papageorgis (1961) used both the supportive and inoculation methods to build up defenses. There were three groups of subjects: one group received support for their position; one group had their position attacked weakly and the attack refuted (the inoculation condition); and the third group received neither of these procedures. Afterward, all groups were subjected to a strong attack on their initial position. Table 9–3 shows how much each group changed as a result of the attack. It is clear that the supportive method helped subjects resist persuasion—the group receiving support changed less than the group that had no preparation. But the inoculation method helped even more—subjects receiving this preparation changed least of all.

Later research has shown that support tends to be particularly effective when the subsequent attack contains arguments similar to the content of the supporting arguments, but it is relatively ineffective when new arguments are used. In contrast, inoculation is effective even when the attack includes new arguments.

The specific mechanism by which inoculation operates is not yet

Table 9–3

*SUPPORT, INOCULATION, AND RESISTANCE TO PERSUASION*

| Condition | Amount of Attitude Change |
|-----------|---------------------------|
| Support | 5.87 |
| Inoculation | 2.94 |
| Neither | 6.62 |

Source: Adapted from McGuire and Papageorgis (1961).

clear. It may be that in refuting the mild attack, the individual uses and therefore exercises all his defenses—by preparing arguments supporting his own position, constructing counterarguments against the opposing position, derogating the possible sources of opposing views, etc. This would make each of these defensive mechanisms stronger and would provide the individual with a generally more effective defensive position.

Another explanation is that giving the target a counterargument or telling him that the original argument is not good strikes at the reliability and credibility of the source of the discrepant communication. Showing an individual an argument against his position and then telling him that this argument is all wrong is the standard technique of setting up a straw man and then knocking it down. This probably serves to make anyone who takes the other side seem somewhat foolish, misguided, and ignorant. The person is told, in effect, that these are the stupid kinds of arguments that some people have put forth against a commonly held idea. Then, when he comes across another argument against the position, even if he is not capable of refuting it himself, he may assume that it is just as stupid as the first argument and therefore may not be influenced by it. Thus, the refutation serves as an attack on the source of any discrepant message and is effective even when subsequent messages have different content. The opposition has been made to look unreliable; anything they say is suspect and unpersuasive.

**Personality Factors**

Some people are generally more persuasible than others, regardless of the issue involved or the type of influence being attempted. Experiments have been conducted (Hovland and Janis, 1959) in which subjects were exposed to persuasive communications on a variety of issues with different types of appeals and arguments and in different attitude-change situations. They indicated that the subjects who were highly persuasible under one set of conditions tended to be highly persuasible under others.

The effect is not very strong; it explains only a small percentage of the total variance. But considering the diversity of the situations and issues studied, the consistency found offers convincing support for the existence of the trait of general persuasibility. However, relatively little is known about the specific sources of this trait. Quite a number of personality characteristics have been suggested as affecting persuasibility, but only a few of these suggestions have been supported by the data.

**Self-esteem.** One fairly consistent finding has been that subjects with low self-esteem tend to be more persuasible than those with high self-esteem. The variable has been defined in various ways by different experimenters. Low self-esteem has been considered to entail feelings of inadequacy, social inhibitions, social anxiety, and test anxiety. Self-esteem has also been defined as the discrepancy between the ideal and the actual self, with greater discrepancies indicating lower self-esteem. Although the actual measures have varied somewhat, the basic notion has been similar. Self-esteem is defined implicitly or explicitly as the worth the person places on himself or how much the person esteems himself.

Cohen (1959) gave subjects a chance to influence one another and found that high-self-esteem subjects tended to make more attempts to influence others than did low-self-esteem subjects and that low-self-esteem subjects were more easily persuaded than were high-self-esteem subjects. Another study (Janis and Field, 1959) found low but significant correlations between feelings of inadequacy and persuasibility for men but not for women. Sears (1967) found that making subjects socially anxious by threatening them with criticism for their views increased their susceptibility to persuasion. Other work has generally confirmed the relationship between self-esteem and persuasibility, although the correlations tend to be rather small.

Cohen explains the effect of self-esteem in terms of the kinds and effectiveness of the defenses used by high- and low-self-esteem people. He proposed that high-self-esteem people tend to be better able to deny or forget information that attacks them or their ideas. Low-self-esteem people, on the other hand, tend to be relatively sensitive to negative information and are therefore more affected by it.

The more traditional explanation of the relationship between self-esteem and persuasibility is that low self-esteem people place a low value on their opinions just as they do on everything else about themselves. Since they do not value their own opinions, they are less reluctant to give them up and are more likely to change them when they are attacked.

McGuire (1969) has added one complexity to this theory. While he grants that low self-esteem should be related to acceptance of a message, he hypothesizes that it will at the same time be negatively related to comprehension of the message. Thus a low-self-esteem person may be quite gullible, accept almost anything someone tells him, and thus be likely to show a great deal of attitude change. However, he may at the same time have trouble understanding complex communications, frequently miss the point of their arguments, and, as a result, show reduced attitude change.

This hypothesis has been tested most directly by Zellner (1970). She reasoned that low self-esteem should be strongly related to influence in very simple situations where the subject would have no trouble understanding the point advocated, while it would be negatively related to influence in complex situations, where the low-self-esteem subject's gullibility would be of little help, since he would have trouble understanding the communication. She tested the effects of self-esteem on influence in three situations ranging from simple to complex. In the simple ("suggestion") situation, the subject was required to write out the message, in a sentence, repeatedly; in the moderate ("conformity") situation, the message consisted of four "facts" in a list of fifteen "facts" the subject was supposed to learn; while in the complex ("persuasion") situation, the messages were complex essays. As expected, the data showed that low self-esteem was positively related to influence in the simple situation, while the reverse held in the complex situation. This provided support for the hypothesis that self-esteem affects persuasibility both by affecting the tendency to accept influence, and by affecting comprehension of the communication.

**Intelligence.** One factor that has often been said to affect persuasibility is intelligence. It has seemed likely to many people that individuals with high intelligence would be less persuasible than those with lower intelligence. Research has not, however, supported this assumption; there is no evidence that level of intelligence is consistently related to degree of persuasibility. On the average, people of high intelligence are persuaded just as much as people of low intelligence.

Although intelligence has no overall effect on persuasibility, there is reason to believe that it does have some effect on the kinds of persuasive appeals that are most effective. People of high intelligence are influenced less by inconsistent and illogical arguments than are people of lower intelligence, and the latter may be influenced less by complex, difficult arguments. Some evidence for this was provided in the work, described above, on the relative effectiveness of stating or not stating a conclusion. The research suggested that stating the conclusion was more effective for relatively uninformed and less intelligent audiences and not stating the conclusion was more effective for relatively informed and intelligent audiences. It is important to note that the lack of an overall correlation between intelligence and persuasibility does not necessarily mean that intelligence is entirely unrelated to the influence process. Rather, it indicates that the relationship is complex and that level of intelligence affects how much the individual is influenced in any given situation.

**Sex Differences.** There is a considerable amount of evidence that women are generally more persuasible than men. Women change their attitudes more (Janis and Field, 1959) and, as we mentioned in Chapter 7, also conform more to others' opinions. The usual explanation is that, at least in our society, men are supposed to be independent and dominant, whereas women are allowed or perhaps encouraged to be submissive and dependent. Most men are taught that they should make up their own minds and should not be influenced by other people. This may not necessarily make them able to do so, but it should certainly make them more determined to resist influence and more resistant to admitting they have been influenced. An additional piece of evidence that fits the role explanation is that the difference between the sexes is present in high school students but not in first-grade students (Abelson and Lesser, 1959). Presumably, six-year-old children have not yet learned their sex roles clearly enough for the difference to appear.

However, these findings of sex differences should be considered with great caution. As recent work on conformity demonstrated (see pp. 236 ff.), the effects may be due to the specific materials used in the research. If the materials are issues and objects that are generally of more interest to men than to women, the women may be more persuaded because they are less committed to their initial position or feel less expert in the area, not because they are generally more persuasible.

**Defensive Styles.** One of the explanations offered for the effect of self-esteem on persuasibility was in terms of the types of defenses used by different people, specifically, that people of high self-esteem tend to deny or forget unpleasant information, whereas people of lower self-esteem do this to a lesser extent. Whether or not this is a sufficient explanation of the effect of self-esteem, the kind of defensive process an individual uses to protect himself from negative information does determine to some extent how much he is influenced by a particular persuasive attempt.

Defenses can be divided broadly into two types—those that are relatively cognitive and logical and those that are relatively non-cognitive and illogical. The former have been discussed at length. They include refuting the arguments; producing counterarguments; attacking the credibility of the source; and, in general, responding directly to the content, meaning, and reliability of the persuasive message. The illogical defenses correspond more or less to what Freud called the *defense mechanisms*. These include denial of the conflict between the persuasive message and the original position; distortion of the message; repression of or forgetting the message; reaction formation, which is moving in the direction opposite from that advocated by the message; and projection, which in this case would be attributing to the source of the message some of one's own characteristics or beliefs. These defenses do not attempt to attack or weaken the content of the communication but, rather, to protect the individual's opinion in less logical but nevertheless often extremely effective ways.

People differ considerably in the extent to which they rely on cognitive and noncognitive defenses. Katz, Sarnoff, and McClintock (1956) investigated the effect of the two types of defenses on reactions to persuasive communications. They divided the subjects into those who relied heavily and those who relied less heavily on defense mechanisms (high- and low-defense users). They then presented two kinds of persuasive communications dealing with prejudice against Negroes. One message, which they called an information appeal, contained a variety of facts about Negroes and whites, all of which were designed to show that prejudice was not based on sound reasoning. The other message, which they called the insight appeal, described the psychodynamic relationship between defense mechanisms and prejudice.

The results showed that the high- and low-defense users responded quite differently to the two appeals. The highly defensive subjects were hardly affected by the insight appeal and were more influenced by the information appeal; those who used defense mechanisms relatively little were more influenced by the insight appeal. The authors explained these results by saying that the high-defense subjects strongly resisted the attack on their defensive mechanisms, whereas the low-defense subjects were relatively open to this kind of attack.

Other experiments, principally by Sarnoff, have shown that the specific defense mechanism a person tends to use may determine to some extent how much he is influenced by a given appeal. In order to be maximally effective, an appeal should attack a weak defense and should be designed not to arouse the defenses that are favored and strong. If someone tends to deny or ignore negative information, the appeal should attempt to introduce the information in a subtle way so that the target is exposed to it before he can put the mechanism of denial into operation.

On the other hand, if he does not use denial but tends to argue against persuasive messages, it is important to concentrate on the strength of the attack and not to worry too much about how it is presented. Knowledge of the kinds of defensive mechanisms a person tends to use should enable the communicator to concentrate on avoiding the target's strongest defenses and attacking his weakest.

In summary, relatively little is known about the effect of personality on persuasibility. We know that some people are generally more persuasible than others, and we are fairly sure of a number of personality traits that affect this trait. Other than the evidence for the few factors that have been mentioned, however, there is little to support hypotheses about how other aspects of personality affect persuasibility. There have been many suggestions (e.g., authoritarianism, richness of fantasy), but the evidence for any of these is rather weak at the moment. We are therefore left with few solid findings except consistent evidence that personality does affect persuasibility. A detailed specification of which dimensions of personality are most important is not yet possible.

### Situational Factors

The factors described thus far are concerned solely with the communicator and his message, and in that sense deal only with factors that are in his control. Yet mass communications usually are delivered within a broader context in which other things are happening, and these also often prove to have decisive effects upon the success of persuasion attempts. Let us now consider some of the most important situational variables in an attitude change setting, above and beyond the communicator himself.

**Forewarned Is Forearmed.** If someone is told ahead of time that he is going to be exposed to a persuasive communication, he is better able to resist persuasion by that message. In a study by Freedman and Sears (1965), teen-agers were told ten minutes beforehand that they were going to hear a talk titled "Why Teenagers Should Not Be Allowed to Drive." Other teen-agers were not told about the talk until just before the speaker began. Thus, one group had a ten-minute warning and the other group had no warning at all. Under these circumstances, those who had the warning were less influenced by the talk than were the others. In some way, the warning enabled the teen-agers to resist better. Dean, Austin, and Watts (1971) found a similar though somewhat weaker effect.

This is certainly a plausible finding, and it seems to be believed by many people in the business of persuasion. For example, we often find an advertisement on radio or television introduced with no warning that this is going to be an advertisement. Instead, the station sneaks in the ad before we are fully aware of what it is. Thus, a hit tune ends and immediately another "hit tune" begins—but it turns out to be an ad for Coca Cola. A similar, although more altruistic, example is the dentist who warns us that something is going to hurt. He seems to feel that we will be better able to withstand the pain if we are warned. In fact, there is some experimental evidence that subjects who are warned ahead of time that they are going to receive an electric shock report that it hurts less than subjects who are not warned. All this sounds plausible and reasonable, but why does it occur? Why does a ten-minute warning help people resist persuasion more than a two-second warning?

It is important to keep in mind that all the subjects know as soon as the talk or the discrepant message begins that it is, in fact, discrepant. In these studies, there is no attempt to fool the subjects. Thus, the explanation cannot be in terms of greater acceptance of the message simply because the subjects do not know that the speaker is against them. Everybody knows that the speaker disagrees with them—the only difference is that some people know it ten minutes ahead of time and others know it only just before the speech. The greater resistance shown by those with the longer warning is due to some process, some mechanism that goes on during those ten minutes between the warning and the speech.

Drawing by Stevenson;
© 1958 The New Yorker Magazine, Inc.

It seems likely that this process resembles that which is produced by the inoculation procedure. In some way, the individual's defenses are exercised or strengthened. In the inoculation situation they are strengthened by the person actually using them to refute an argument; in the forewarning situation they are strengthened by the person preparing to refute an argument. The net result, however, is quite similar.

Although there is little evidence that directly demonstrates the kinds of processes that go on during this period, we can cite those that the individual *probably* indulges in. He tries to marshal and strengthen his defenses, and in doing this, he employs all the defensive maneuvers and tactics we discussed previously. He constructs arguments supporting his own position and attempts to refute the arguments that will possibly come from the opponent. In the inoculation situation, he is provided with some of the opponent's arguments and works at refuting them. At the same time, he thinks about other arguments that might be presented and tries to refute them. In the warning experiment, the teen-agers probably say to themselves, "The message is going to present arguments against teen-age driving. It will probably say that teen-agers don't drive as well as adults. Well, that's not true. I know teen-agers drive better, so that's a bad argument." The teen-agers would also think about arguments in favor of teen-age driving, such as "Old enough to fight, old enough to vote and drive." They would also employ derogation of the discrepant source. As discussed above, the person who has been through the inoculation procedure has ample opportunity to derogate the opponent. Similarly, the forewarned person has ten minutes to convince himself that the communicator is unreliable, prejudiced, and misinformed. In other words, the individual who is warned or who has just experienced a mild attack is like a fighter who has prepared for a match. He has been through training, so when the fight comes, he is in better shape and better able to meet his opponent. He also spends time convincing himself that his opponent is not very good and that he, himself, is great. This makes him more confident and better able to fight his best.

In some cases, though, forewarning has the opposite effect—it actually helps to precipitate attitude change. In most such cases, the person is unlikely from the start to cling very tightly to his original attitude, and the forewarning seems to operate as a cue to propel him along the road he was destined for sooner or later anyhow. For example, Apsler and Sears (1968) hypothesized that forewarning would facilitate attitude change among subjects who were not personally involved in the topic, while it would help block it among highly involved subjects. They gave subjects a persuasive communication advocating replacement of professors by teaching assistants in many upper division courses, a change opposed by almost all subjects. Some subjects were told the change would come quickly, in time to affect their own education (high involvement), while others were told it was several years off and would not affect them (low involvement). Forewarning helped block change among the highly involved subjects, just as it had among the teenagers who were highly involved in the issue of teenage driving in the Freedman and Sears experiment. However, it facilitated change in the low-involvement condition.

The effects of forewarning frequently can be detected even before the subject receives the communication. The person seems to begin to change or to resist before he is even exposed to the forthcoming communication. In one experiment, subjects highly committed to their initial position became more extreme (and presumably more resistant to change) when forewarned of a forthcoming debate, while weakly committed subjects became more moderate (and presumably more receptive to change) while anticipating the debate (Sears, Freedman, and O'Connor, 1964). This anticipatory effect is similar to what happens *after* a debate. Almost everyone who heard the Nixon-Kennedy debates in 1960 thought his man had won. And Berkowitz (1970) found that prowar spectators at anti-Vietnam parades became more prowar while antiwar viewers became more antiwar. Cooper and Jones (1970) have shown that these anticipatory changes are due to the subjects' expectations of exposure to the communications and their likely effects, rather than just to the knowledge of their existence. Weakly committed subjects changed anticipatorily when forewarned of forthcoming exposure to the communication, but not when merely told that such a communication existed without any implication of forthcoming exposure.

The most popular explanations for these effects of forewarning are twofold. In cases where forewarning increases resistance to change, most researchers assume that the subject begins generating counterarguments, or rejecting the forthcoming position, prior to actual exposure. Some of these cases of anticipatory attitude change seem to be accounted for by the assumption that weakly committed subjects have little resistance to change, and if they anticipate powerful arguments, nothing restrains them from granting the point from the start. In other cases it appears that subjects are more motivated to resist change, but are worried about their ability to stand up to counterarguments. They therefore tend to change in advance so they will not have to go through the embarrassment and loss of self-esteem of knuckling under later on. Anticipatory change allows them to maintain a positive self-concept.

We do not mean to give the impression that all these maneuvers are done deliberately. Especially in the forewarned situation, most people probably do not decide to strengthen their defenses. There is no evidence that they worry about the coming attack, feverishly preparing themselves either to defend their positions to the death, or give them up quietly and gracefully. Rather, they tend to think about the issue a little, go over some of the points in their minds, and in this way prepare for exposure. As far as we know, the process is all quite casual and almost accidental. But the effects are clear.

**Distraction.** In parts of our discussion, we have described the individual as actively fighting the persuasive message. Although he may sometimes be quite passive, the person whose opinions are attacked usually tries to resist changing. He counterargues, derogates the communicator, and generally marshals all his forces to defend his own position. One important implication of this is that the ability to resist persuasion is weakened by anything that makes it harder for the individual to fight the discrepant communication. In particular, distracting his attention from the battle may enable the persuasive message to get through without being fought.

A study by Festinger and Maccoby (1964) demonstrated this effect of distraction. Subjects listened to a speech against fraternities while watching a film. For some of the subjects, the film showed the person making the speech. For others, the film was "The Day of the Painter," a funny, somewhat zany satire on modern art. Presumably, those watching the irrelevant film were more distracted from the antifraternity speech than were those watching the person speak. Subjects who initially disagreed with the speech (who were in favor of fraternities) were more influenced in the distraction than the nondistraction condition. Taking the subjects' minds off the speech increased its effectiveness.

There is some debate about how reliable this finding is, and about the mechanism that is responsible for it, if it is reliable. As indicated in a review of several subsequent studies, the results have been quite mixed, with as many failing to find distraction advancing attitude change as those finding it doing so (Osterhouse and Brock, 1970). It seems to occur primarily when the subjects are initially strongly opposed to the position being advocated, when they are quite familiar with the topic, when they attend to the distraction rather than to the message (Zimbardo, Snyder, and Gurwitz, 1970), and when they have the opportunity to develop counterarguments in the absence of the distraction. Consequently, Osterhouse and Brock (1970) have argued that when distraction works, it does so by blocking a subvocal process of developing counterarguments. So far the evidence on this point is mainly inferential, since no one has yet devised a technique for directly measuring subvocal arguing.

In any case, the effect logically must depend on the right amount of distraction. As usual, there is a conflict between getting the message through and getting it accepted. Obviously, too much distraction prevents the persuasive message from being heard at all and reduces its effectiveness to zero. Advertisers may want to distract television viewers from the main point of commercials by having irrelevant pictures and action going on during the speech. They do not, however, want to have the irrelevancies so fascinating or interfering that the message is lost. Having a beautiful girl in the background during a soap commercial may help sell soap; having her in the foreground may even help; but having her in the foreground singing so loud that the commercial can barely be heard would certainly reduce the effectiveness of the ad. Thus, the effect of distraction may work under limited conditions, but it is important that the distraction be not too great or the effect will be reversed.

**The Arousal of Aggression.** One interesting explanation of the effect of motivational arousal on attitude change concerns the appropriateness of the motive aroused. In most of the studies on fear arousal, the persuasive communication contains information about a real danger such as cancer, tetanus, or reckless driving. When fear of cancer is aroused by vivid pictures, the fear is appropriate, because it is realistic to be afraid of cancer, with or without pictures. Perhaps more important, the messages are urging the subjects to take steps that would reduce the danger and the fear. If one takes a tetanus inoculation, one is, in fact, less liable to get tetanus and should no longer fear the disease. In situations such as these, the arousal of fear is appropriate to the attitude-change situation, and therefore the arousal should increase susceptibility to the message.

A study by Weiss and Fine (1956) on the arousal of aggression is relevant to this explanation of the effect of motivation. Some subjects were put through an annoying, frustrating experience designed to make them feel aggressive. Other subjects had the opposite experience—they went through a pleasant, satisfying experience. Then, both groups of subjects were exposed to a persuasive communication that took either a lenient or a punitive attitude toward juvenile delinquency. Thus, the experiment exposed aggressive and nonaggressive subjects to lenient or punitive persuasive communications.

The experimenters hypothesized that the subjects who had been made to feel aggressive would be more likely to accept the punitive communication than the lenient one and that the nonaggressive subjects would be more likely to accept the lenient communication. The rationale was that the punitive message would satisfy the motivational needs of the aggressive subjects by providing them with a way of displacing their aggression and that the lenient message would be more likely to satisfy the relatively nonaggressive needs of the other subjects. The results were in line with these expectations—the aggressive subjects were more influenced by the punitive communication, and the nonaggressive subjects were more influenced by the lenient one.

Another demonstration of this effect came in a study by Cohen (1957), in which the order of the arousal and the message was varied. In one condition, subjects were made nervous about their grades and were then given a communication describing how the new system of grading on a curve would solve some of their problems. In another condition, the communication about grading on a curve was given first, and then the subjects' concerns about their grades were aroused. The study found that when the need was aroused before the communication was presented, there was significantly more attitude change than when the communication was presented before the need was aroused. Thus this work indicated that arousing strong motivations increases the effect of a communication that is directly relevant to that motivation but may actually decrease the effect of nonrelevant communications.

**The Effect of Reinforcement—"Things Go Better with Coke."**   Much of our discussion has been influenced by the reinforcement or incentive approach to attitude change. One of the basic ideas of this approach is that an attitude-change situation consists of an interplay of forces—some pushing the individual to change his attitude and some pulling him back to his initial position. All the arguments in the persuasive communication are, in a sense, a motivation for changing his opinion or approaching the new position. On the other hand, all the reasons he initially had for maintaining his own position are reasons for continuing to maintain it and for avoiding the new position. Under these circumstances, anything that associates additional incentive with either position should affect the outcome.

This argument suggests that associating the persuasive message with some reinforcing stimulus increases the effectiveness of the message. A simpler line of reasoning is that the more positive the persuasive message is seen to be, the more effect it has, and reinforcement simply makes the message more positive. Whatever the rationale for the prediction, conceptualizing the situation in terms of approach-avoidance and positive and negative reinforcements does suggest this effect.

The advertising industry and political campaigners have been acting on this assumption for some time. Television commercials are one example. They have recently been referred to as "one-minute movies," because they are so elaborate and so much care goes into making them as attractive and even enjoyable as possible. We are not simply shown a sleek car and told how powerful, quiet, and comfortable it is. Rather, while the message is being delivered, we are shown beautiful women, handsome men, and lovely children, with perhaps a couple of graceful horses or cute dogs cavorting around. And, as mentioned earlier, the car may be endorsed by a famous athlete or movie star. Presumably, all this beauty, fame, and popularity are reinforcing; and the reinforcement becomes associated with the message, which is asking us to buy the car, and with the car itself. The hope is that the reinforcement will increase our positive feelings toward the car and thus increase the likelihood that we will buy it.

Research has provided some support for this widespread idea. Subjects were presented with a persuasive communication in the usual manner, but some subjects were given an extraneous reward whereas others were not given the reward. For example, while reading a persuasive communication on foreign aid, some subjects were given a Pepsi Cola to drink and others were not given anything (Janis et al., 1965). In this study, the reward, or positive stimulus, had nothing to do with the content of the persuasive message or the issue itself. Nevertheless, the subjects receiving a reward tended to be influenced more than those who did not receive a reward.

One possible alternative interpretation of this finding is that the reward acted primarily to make the subjects feel more positive toward the experimenter and the experimental situation as a whole. Or, it may simply have put them in a better mood, which would probably have had the effect of making the subjects feel positive toward everything and therefore less likely to disagree with the persuasive communication— particularly when that communication came directly or indirectly from the experimenter. In other words, it may have been simply a halo effect. This explanation is considerably less interesting than that involving the reinforcement theory, which implies that the subject is actually more influenced, but at the moment it is difficult to choose between the two. We do know that giving a reward increases the amount of agreement with the persuasive communication, but the specific mechanism behind this effect is as yet somewhat unclear.

Thus many factors affect attitude change primarily by increasing the trust in the communication, by strengthening the persuasive message, and, in general, by determining how much the individual believes what is being said. An attempt to influence someone's opinion need not, however, be done in an entirely logical, unemotional, cognitive situation. The situation may, and often does, involve strong motivations, appeals to deep-seated needs, and a great many factors that are extraneous to the logical arguments contained in the message itself. An entirely rational, cognitive man would be influenced only to the extent that the arguments presented were logically sound. But since there are few, if any, entirely rational beings, motivational and emotional factors are also important in determining the effectiveness of a persuasive communication.

*CHAPTER REVIEW*

1. Different mechanisms for resisting persuasion.
2. Prestige of the communicator.
3. Intentions, liking, and similarity of the communicator.
4. The sleeper effect.
5. Communication discrepancy.
6. How many sides? Present the conclusion? Novel information?
7. Fear arousal.
8. Prior commitment.
9. Inoculation.
10. Personality and persuasibility.
11. Forewarning.
12. Reinforcement.

*APPLICATIONS AND SPECULATIONS*

1. Innovation of new ideas and values is a crucially important ingredient in society. Since people tend to be quite resistant to anything new, only people of high prestige and credibility are generally able to introduce new ideas. However, such a person risks losing his credibility if he tries to be innovative. What are the implications of this conflict between the need to have high prestige in order to be innovative and the danger of losing that prestige by being innovative?
2. Intentionally or otherwise, the advertising industry uses many of the principles we have discussed. Reinforcement, prestige sources, familiarity, distractions, warnings, and so on all appear in television commercials and other forms of advertising. Think of specific examples of their use and try to estimate their effects.

3. Arguments have been made for and against allowing speakers to present unpopular views on college campuses. What do you think the effects are of allowing such speeches to be made? Can you think of arguments for and against allowing them?

4. The intensive antismoking campaign has tried to arouse people's fear of lung cancer, tuberculosis, and other diseases. Do you think this is an effective tactic, and how might you improve it?

5. What do you think is the effect of humor in persuasive communications? Some of the factors that might be relevant are exposure level, memory, distraction, and reinforcement.

6. We have concentrated on the positive effects of persuasive attempts. That is, we have talked about how much attitude change was produced in the direction of the communication. It is also possible that an attempt to persuade would have a reverse effect, would cause the target to move in the opposite direction. This is usually referred to as a "boomerang" effect. Do you think it ever occurs? (Note that this is a tricky, complicated issue, which has not been fully resolved.)

*SUGGESTIONS FOR ADDITIONAL READING*

*Articles*

Abelson, R. P. Modes of resolution of belief dilemmas. *Conflict Resolution*, 1959, *34*, 3–352.

Aronson, E., Turner, J., and Carlsmith, J. M. Communicator credibility and communication discrepancy. *Journal of Abnormal and Social Psychology*, 1963, *67*, 31–36.

Dabbs, J. M., Jr., and Leventhal, H. Effects of varying the recommendations in a fear-arousing communication. *Journal of Personality and Social Psychology*, 1966, *4* (5), 525–31.

Janis, I. L., Kaye, D., and Kirschner, P. Facilitating effects of "eating-while-reading" on responsiveness to persuasive communications. *Journal of Personality and Social Psychology*, 1965, *1*, 181–86.

Janis, I. L., and Mann, L. Effectiveness of emotional role-playing in modifying smoking habits and attitudes. *Journal of Experimental Research in Personality*, 1965, *1*, 84–90.

McGuire, W. J., and Papageorgis, D. The relative efficacy of various types of prior belief-defense in producing immunity against persuasion. *Journal of Abnormal and Social Psychology*, 1961, *62*, 327–37.

*Books and Longer Discussions*

Hovland, C. I., Janis, I. L., and Kelley, H. H. *Communication and persuasion.* New Haven, Conn.: Yale University Press, 1953.

Lane, R. E., and Sears, D. O. *Public opinion.* Englewood Cliffs, N.J.: Prentice-Hall, 1964.

McGuire, W. J. The nature of attitudes and attitude change. In G. Lindzey and E. Aronson (Eds.), *Handbook of Social Psychology,* 2nd ed., Vol. 3. Reading, Mass.: Addison-Wesley, 1968.

# attitude formation and change in real life

Hovland pointed out (1959) that the success of persuasion depends in part on whether it is attempted in an experimental laboratory or in the real world. In the controlled environment of a psychologist's laboratory, it is often easy to change practically any attitude one wishes. Even a simple written essay can produce changes in attitudes toward foreign aid, atomic submarines, tuition rates in college, brushing teeth, cancer and cigarettes, the quality of a poem, and so on. A subject reads or hears a communication, is asked to state his own belief, and tends to agree with the communication more after he reads or hears it than he did before (or than does a control group that did not read or hear it). In contrast, attempts to change people's attitudes in the world outside the laboratory tend to be quite unsuccessful. Advertisers, politicians, and other propagandists know, or at least should know, this. In general, campaigns conducted through the mass media are not successful in producing mass changes in attitudes.

There are some exceptions. A high-powered, clever advertising campaign built around a grammatical error (*"like* a cigarette should") catapulted Winston cigarettes from a small seller to the most popular cigarette in the United States. Similarly, Crest toothpaste (which did have something substantial to offer in the way of protection from decay) became one of the largest sellers after its introduction. Occasionally, a person who is virtually unknown at the beginning of a political campaign can win the election by virtue of intensive advertising and face-to-face contacts.

In spite of these exceptions, it is usually extremely difficult in a short period of time to produce any sizable change in people's opinions on any issue they really care about and are involved in. Most Americans know after the nominating conventions how they are going to vote in the presidential election in November, and the tens of millions of dollars spent during the intervening months does not produce much change. The results of surveys of American elections are shown in Table 10–1.

Table 10-1

CHANGES IN PARTY PREFERENCES DURING ELECTION CAMPAIGN

| Year of Survey | First Poll | Last Poll | Percentage of change |
|---|---|---|---|
| 1940 | May | November | 8[a] |
| 1948 | June | August | 8[b] |
| | August | October | 3[b] |
| 1960 | August | November | 7[c] |
| 1964 | August | November | 10[c] |

Sources:
[a]Lazarsfeld, Berelson, and Gaudet (1948, pp. 65–66).
[b]Berelson, Lazarsfeld, and McPhee (1954, p. 23).
[c]Benham (1965).

The data show that the way a person says, early in the campaign, that he is going to vote in November is a good predictor of how he actually will vote.

Only 7 to 10 percent of those surveyed changed parties during the campaigns. True, those who have not decided in May may be influenced by a campaign, but these people did not yet have an opinion. The campaign, therefore, did not change an opinion—it *produced* one, which is quite a different matter. Of course, because the undecided votes often decide an election, the campaign can be extremely important. The 8 percent who do change their opinion can be decisive if more of them change in one direction than in the other. Nevertheless, the data indicate how difficult it is to change the opinion of those who have already made a decision.

Other attempts at persuasion have had similarly meager effects. The campaigns to induce people to stop smoking are a case in point, at least in this country. There has been a slight decrease in the amount of smoking immediately following each intensive antismoking campaign by the Public Health Service, but the changes evaporated quickly. As far as we can tell, there has been little or no lasting effect of these scientific campaigns. Again, the National Safety Council's admonitions against unsafe driving and the warning that "The life you save may be your own" does not seem to have made people drive any more safely. And the campaigns by all the doctors, dentists, health officials, and teachers in a town to introduce fluorides into water in order to improve children's teeth are often unsuccessful because of preexisting emotional prejudice against adding things to water, particularly when this prejudice is stirred up by even a slight antifluoridation campaign conducted by conservative groups.

A final example of failure to influence opinions is provided by the so-called brainwashing that occurred during the Korean War. American prisoners were subjected to an intensive long-term campaign to make them give up their belief in American democracy and adopt the principles of Chinese communism. In this situation, the campaign did not have to fight counterpropaganda and the Chinese could do just about anything they wanted, since the soldiers were held captive. The situation was ideal for changing attitudes.

A great deal has been made of the fact that some Americans were influenced by this campaign and that a small number actually defected to Communist China. But in fact, the campaign was remarkably unsuccessful. A great many prisoners were subjected to this intensive campaign under ideal circumstances, but only a handful were influenced appreciably. Practically all the American soldiers—even the uneducated, unsophisticated, tired, weak, lonely, and perhaps not strongly pro-American ones—were able to resist the Communist attempt to change their opinions.

From our discussion in the previous chapter, it should be obvious that a critical factor in attitude change is the subject's commitment to his initial attitude. Indeed, in the examples here we are dealing with important, deeply held attitudes that generally have been built up over many years, are related to a great many other attitudes and beliefs, are supported by strong emotional feelings, and, accordingly, are highly resistant to change, even though they can sometimes be influenced by long-term, powerful persuasion. In contrast, many attitudes are quite susceptible to influence. People change their attitudes toward politicians, products, ideas, and behavior all the time.

To understand why some attitudes are almost impossible to change while others are easy to change, we need to understand the individual's history: why is he more or less committed to his position? This question must take us first to his childhood.

**THE DEVELOPMENT OF ATTITUDES**

As mentioned earlier, the cognitive components of attitudes are assumed to be learned in the same way as are any facts, knowledge, or beliefs. The basic processes of association, reinforcement, and imitation determine this acquisition. A child is exposed to certain things about the world. He is also reinforced for expressing some cognitions or attitudes or, perhaps, for actually acting on the basis of them; thus he learns them. In addition, imitation or identification is important in the learning process. A child spends a great deal of time with his parents and after a while begins to believe as they do simply by copying them—even when they do not deliberately try to influence him. The same process works with figures other than parents, such as peer groups, teachers, or any important figures in a child's life.

For example, how has the American child traditionally built his attitude toward his country? Very early in life he was told that he was an American. He learned the name of his country and heard people say positive things about it. The words *great, good, strong, beautiful, free, bountiful, rich*, etc., became associated with *America*. When the child made positive statements about America, everyone smiled and rewarded him; when he said negative things, people frowned and punished him. He soon realized that his parents, teachers, and friends thought America was a great country; by a process of imitation, he tended to accept this view. Thus, by the mechanisms of association, reinforcement, and imitation he learned that his country is great.

One of the significant aspects of this process is that the child was exposed primarily to one view of his country. Everyone, or almost everyone, he knew had a similar belief. Of course, this varies somewhat for different children and different issues. Not all adults have a purely positive evaluation of their country. Some may even make an occasional negative statement about it in front of their children. And on other issues, there is even more conflict. A child tends to be exposed to both sides of the issue of smoking, particularly if one parent smokes and the other does not. But, as we discussed in the chapter on liking, by and large a child in any culture grows up in an extremely homogeneous environment in terms of attitudes and values. His parents and their friends tend to belong to one nation, come from the same ethnic and class origins, prefer the same political party (typically, 90 percent of marriage partners vote for the same party), have similar views on religion and morality, have similar prejudices and tastes, and so on. Thus, the child is exposed to a very biased sample of the available information, even on those issues that, outside family, are highly controversial. The child's own friends are similarly determined to an important degree by his parents' environment. The daughter of a rich white Republican businessman, living in the suburbs, is very unlikely to be close friends with a poor black girl from the central city, or an Arab guerilla's daughter, or an auto mechanic's daughter. This has been called *de facto* selective exposure because the child is exposed to only a selective, rather than a representative, subsample of the attitudes other people have, and because the selectivity arises merely out of the fact of the child's life circumstances, rather than from any special motivation in the child, or by law, or any other deliberate choice (Sears and Freedman, 1967).

The effect of this selective exposure is that children tend to adopt the same attitudes as their parents. For example, as shown in Table 10–2,

Table 10-2

RELATIONSHIP BETWEEN PARTY PREFERENCES OF PARENTS AND CHILDREN

| PARENT (AS INDEPENDENTLY REPORTED) | HIGH SCHOOL SENIORS (N = 1852) | | | |
| --- | --- | --- | --- | --- |
| | Democratic | Independent | Republican | Total |
| Democratic | 32.6% | 13.2% | 3.6% | 49.4% |
| Independent | 7.0 | 12.8 | 4.1 | 23.9 |
| Republican | 3.4 | 9.7 | 13.6 | 26.7 |
| Total | 43.0 | 35.7 | 21.3 | 100.0 |

| PARENTS (AS RECALLED BY RESPONDENT) | ADULT RESPONDENTS (N = 1281) | | | |
| --- | --- | --- | --- | --- |
| | Democratic | Independent | Republican | Total |
| Both Democrats | 36.9% | 8.2% | 6.2% | 51.3% |
| Split, one uncertain, both shifted | 7.1 | 6.1 | 5.6 | 18.8 |
| Both Republicans | 4.8 | 6.0 | 19.0 | 29.8 |
| Total | 48.8 | 20.3 | 30.8 | 99.9 |

Source: Adapted from Sears (1969).

a high percentage of high school seniors favored a given political party when both parents agreed on that party, with only about 10 percent having the opposite preference. Thus, the fact that on many issues the child is exposed to only one position results in his attitudes reflecting this selective exposure.

Even after a child develops an attitude, he continues to be exposed primarily to information that supports it. At this stage, various socio-economic factors determine what he hears. His neighborhood, news-paper, school, church, friends, etc., tend to be more homogeneous than the rest of the world. If he is wealthy, he would live in an expensive house and be realtively conservative politically. His neighbors would also have money and tend to be conservative. If he attended a public school, his classmates would come from his neighborhood and have attitudes similar to his. If he attended a private school, the similarity in financial and religious backgrounds (in parochial schools) would be even greater. His parents would read the *Wall Street Journal* to keep up with the financial news, and accordingly he would be exposed to its conserva-tive views. And so on. All these factors would continue to present him with biased information that would be consistent with the attitudes he had already developed.

### Strong Commitments

Early socialization of this kind instills strong attitudes in most American children on a certain number of social and political issues. The most common are racial attitudes, attitudes toward nation and toward the prevailing system of political authority, identification with a political party and sometimes with a social class, certain democratic slogans (e.g., freedom of speech, the right to vote, etc.), occasionally very well-known public figures (e.g., Hitler, FDR, the Kennedys, the president), and numerous general social values (e.g., the value of hard work, obedience of constituted authority, physical aggression is mostly bad, etc.). On these matters, most Americans arrive in adulthood with strong attitudes already in place (Sears and Whitney, 1973). Thus it is easy to see why some of the propaganda campaigns we mentioned above failed to be very effective—the Chinese Communists or presidential candidates were attacking these strongly held attitudes.

However, it is equally obvious that a great many matters of opinion are not included in this list, and presumably attitude change is much easier to accomplish in those cases. Moreover, it is easy to overrate the parents' importance in this early attitude formation. The best evidence at hand suggests that adolescents do have a pretty clear idea of their parents' political and social attitudes on some of the topics named above, and generally tend to agree with their parents. This is particularly true for political party identification, presidential candidate preferences, and to a lesser extent for racial attitudes. In the nationwide study of high school seniors cited earlier, 92 percent could correctly identify which presidential candidate their parents had favored in the campaign that had just concluded, and 71 percent could correctly identify their parents' party preference (Jennings and Niemi, 1968). However, aside from the most visible issues, most adolescents do not even know how their parents feel, so it is not surprising that they do not simply fall into line behind them. For example, in this same study, both parents and high school students were asked how they felt about allowing a Communist who had won an election to take office. Agreement between parents and offspring was only slightly above the level of purely random association. In these cases, children must pick up their attitudes from their social environment more broadly, rather than simply from their parents.

**OBSTACLES TO ATTITUDE CHANGE**

Given that most people come into adulthood with rather fixed attitudes on at least the most important and controversial issues in our society, what happens when someone makes an attempt to change their attitudes? To understand this, we can go back to the model of the attitude change situation that we introduced in the last chapter (Figure 9–1, p.

266). There, it will be remembered, we said that four conditions were necessary for attitude change to take place: (1) a powerful communication must reach the target from (2) a credible communicator, (3) the target must not be too resistant to change, and (4) situational variables must be propitious. What normally happens in real life?

### Communication Interferences

Although our model of the attitude-change situation begins with a communicator, we shall first discuss the factors that intervene between the source and the target. To paraphrase a familiar expression, "what you don't hear can't change your attitude." If a message does not reach its target, for all intents and purposes there is no attitude-change situation. Thus, these intervening variables are the first hurdle that must be cleared in order to influence someone.

**Low Levels of Exposure.**   People in the business of trying to affect attitudes are generally aware that their most critical and difficult problem is reaching the people they want to influence. Advertisers, politicians, propagandists, and teachers must devote a considerable amount of their efforts to making sure that their messages reach the targets to which they are directed. Teachers have the least trouble in this respect, because they can require attendance in class. This does not guarantee that the students are listening, but at least the vibrations caused by the teachers' speech are striking the students' ears. This is a major advantage. An advertising man has to spend millions of dollars and use great ingenuity to accomplish the same thing. He must select some medium, say, television, find a program that people watch, and then try to keep them from leaving their seats or turning down the sound or switching channels during the ads. And even when all this is achieved, he reaches only a small percentage of his prospective audience—perhaps 30 percent of those owning sets if he selects the most popular program on the air.

The propagandist and political campaigner have even more difficult tasks. Almost no one watches discussions of public affairs on television. The Nixon-Kennedy debates during the 1960 presidential campaign were a remarkable and almost unique exception. Eighty million people watched at least one of these debates, but other political programs are lucky to get eight million viewers. If a typical presidential hopeful buys prime television time at perhaps $50,000 for thirty minutes, he cannot expect more than a few million people to tune in. Many would not be watching television at all, and most of those who were would be watching other shows. Most viewers consider a football game, a western, or a good movie more interesting than a political speech.

Some indication of the low level of exposure to political information can be obtained from surveys in which people in the United States are asked various questions relating to politics. The range of knowledge (and ignorance) is indicated in Table 10–3. (The data are from a number of studies conducted over the fifteen-year period from 1947 to 1962.) It is perhaps reassuring that practically everyone knew who the president was. Unfortunately, when we move beyond this level, ignorance was rampant. Only 57 percent could name even one of their senators, 35 percent could name both, and 38 percent were capable of reporting the name of their congressman. The same held for issues. An encouraging 96 percent were familiar with the United Nations and 71 percent were familiar with the Peace Corps, but only 22 percent knew what the Common Market was and only 26 percent had even heard the term "bipartisan foreign policy."

This lack of knowledge is not surprising, however, when we look at the extent to which people are exposed to this kind of information. In the 1958 congressional campaign, which was more hotly contested than most, only 24 percent of the people had heard something about both candidates in their district and only 54 percent had heard something about either of them. This means that 46 percent of the people had been exposed to *no* information about any candidate. No wonder they could not name their congressman—they had never heard of him.

Thus, getting through to people is exceedingly difficult and chancy. Particularly in the area of politics and public affairs, people tend to be

Table 10–3

*PUBLIC'S INFORMATION ABOUT POLITICS*

| Item | Percent Correctly Identifying Person or Issue |
|------|-----------------------------------------------|
| **Person:** | |
| President | 98 |
| Vice President | 69 |
| Secretary of State | 66 |
| One senator | 57 |
| Both senators | 35 |
| Congressman | 38 |
| **Issue:** | |
| United Nations | 96 |
| Peace Corps | 71 |
| Bipartisan foreign policy | 26 |
| Common Market | 22 |

Source: Adapted from Sears (1969).

exposed very little to persuasive messages. And regardless of the topic, the percentage of the potential audience that is reached by any message tends to be quite small.

**Two-Step Flow of Information.**    There is evidence that some of the material does reach its intended audience through the mass media, but only indirectly. As we have said, most people do not watch public affairs programs or read editorials. But some people do, and they tend to be the most influential members of their community or group. Called "opinion leaders" because of their considerable impact on the attitudes of their associates, these people are exposed to the persuasive information through the mass media and, to some extent, pass it on to their friends. By means of this two-step flow of communication, some of the persuasive material does eventually reach the people. Thus, reaching the opinion leaders is critical. If they hear a candidate's speech, many others will be exposed to the material it contained. Since generally the candidate cannot reach many people directly, this is one way of increasing exposure to his message. Overall level of exposure is still low, and the exposure that does exist tends to be through these relatively influential and informed members of society.

The major implication of the low level of exposure is that it is one explanation of the relatively slight effects of most mass campaigns. Obviously, if the messages do not even reach most of the people, there is going to be little general effect. The person who watches a favorite program on TV and misses the candidate's speech on another channel is not going to be influenced by what the candidate says. If it does reach him, it may still be ineffective, but it must reach him to have a chance.

**Selective Exposure.**    As difficult as the low level of exposure makes life for a propagandist, he has other problems. When a message does get through to someone, it is likely that the person it reaches already agrees with it. This is the phenomenon of *selective exposure* we mentioned earlier. Persuasive communications tend not to reach the very people they are designed to influence. People tend to be exposed relatively little to information that disagrees with them. Democrats hear talks mostly by other Democrats; Republicans hear talks mostly by other Republicans. Religious people hear talks in favor of religion; nonreligious people hear talks against religion; and members of any particular religion obviously hear ministers of that religion rather than ministers of some other religion. Similarly, businessmen tend to read articles in favor of businessmen, and farmers tend to read articles in favor of farmers; doctors read articles in favor of doctors; and lawyers, in favor of lawyers; and so on.

Almost every attempt to assess exposure to the mass media systematically has come up with the same kind of findings. For example, in the 1958 California gubernatorial campaign, Senator William Knowland was the Republican candidate running against Edmund Brown, the Democratic candidate. In a last effort to swing some votes, Knowland spent twenty-nine hours on television trying to convince the people to vote for him. A survey conducted just after the telethon showed that only 10 percent of the Democrats watched any part of it, whereas more than twice as many Republicans did. And among those who watched, the Republicans watched twice as long. Thus, Senator Knowland spent twenty-nine hours on television and failed to reach 90 percent of the Democrats he was trying to reach. It is clear he was not getting to most of the people whom he wanted to hear him. (He lost the governorship by over a million votes.) The same phenomenon seems to occur in every political campaign and in practically every area in which mass media campaigns are used. Thus, in addition to the low level of overall exposure, another explanation of why campaigns in the mass media are less than overwhelmingly effective is that they fail to reach the very people they are trying to reach. But why does this type of selective exposure occur?

It is obvious that there are many reasons for watching or not watching a particular television program other than, and more important than, the product being advertised. Few people decide to watch a particular program because it is advertising a particular product. They decide to watch it because they like the program or because it is at a convenient hour or for some other reason that is entirely irrelevant to the program's commercial message. Similarly, people choose a newspaper for a variety of reasons, most of which are more important to them than its political persuasion. Businessmen read the *Wall Street Journal* primarily because it is useful to them—it contains business news, stock-market reports, and so on. Psychologists tend to read the *American Psychologist*, because it contains a lot of information they are interested in. The fact that the *American Psychologist* is also biased in favor of psychology is more or less irrelevant for purposes of exposure. The Republican businessman's daughter plays with a stockbroker's daughter because she lives next door.

In all these cases, the individual is exposed primarily to information and ideas with which he already agrees. The businessman who reads the *Wall Street Journal* reads editorials that are favorable to businessmen. The psychologist who reads the *American Psychologist* reads propsychology editorials. The businessman's and stockbroker's daughter both reflect their parents' conservative Republicanism. In Senator Knowland's case, it is possible that the Republicans were more familiar with him and more interested in seeing him than were the Democrats. The Republicans, therefore, watched in greater numbers, not necessarily because they supported Knowland for governor but because they were interested in hearing him.

These examples could be multiplied almost indefinitely—people tend to be exposed disproportionately to opinions and information that agree with them. It is tempting to interpret these findings as being caused by a general preference for supportive information. Perhaps people typically expose themselves to information mainly on the basis of what they agree with. However, selective exposure may be caused by factors other than a preference for supportive information. Probably the most important factor producing selective exposure is the disproportionate availability of supportive information. Most people live in an environment that contains more information supporting than not supporting their attitudes. A Republican tends to live and work near other Republicans, to read a Republican newspaper because his town has only one newspaper and it is Republican, to be sent Republican literature through the mails, and so on. The same would be true of an advocate of black power, fluoridation, and practically every other attitude.

Other important factors are utility and believability. People tend to expose themselves to useful, believable, and interesting information more than to information that lacks these qualities. And apparently supportive information has these characteristics more than nonsupportive information. The *Wall Street Journal* illustrates how utility tends to go along with supportiveness. The editors and reporters are interested in and concerned about business and tend to be Republican. The newspaper therefore contains financial news and has Republican editorials. The news is useful to other businessmen, who tend to agree with the editorials. A liberal Democrat could publish the *Journal* or be a reporter on it, but he would be less likely to be interested in financial news and therefore less likely to be associated with that kind of newspaper. This is even more obvious with specialized journals such as the *American Psychologist*, which is actually edited by a psychologist.

We have seen that selective exposure is a good explanation of why people resist persuasion by the mass media or in society in general. However, unless we can be certain that selective exposure is produced in part by real preferences for supportive information, it would not be a good explanation of how people resist persuasion in relatively controlled situations in which they are given a choice between positive and negative information. That is, does an individual tend to listen more to a speaker who agrees with him than to one who disagrees with him? Do people deliberately avoid information that disagrees with them and deliberately seek out information that agrees with them?

There has been a great deal of research on selective exposure in controlled situations, but unfortunately, the evidence is somewhat inconsistent. In an early study (Ehrlich et al., 1957), individuals who owned new cars were asked to choose among envelopes that contained advertisements on a variety of cars, including their own. It was found that people preferred to read material about their own car. This seems to indicate that people, at least in this situation, want to expose themselves primarily to information supporting their own decision—information consistent with their own actions.

In another study, Mills, Aronson, and Robinson (1959) told students in a college class that they were going to be given an exam. The students were given the choice of taking a multiple-choice or an essay exam. After they chose, they were told that some articles about the two kinds of exams were available and they were shown their titles. Some of the articles were in favor of the type of exam they had chosen and others were in favor of the other type. The students preferred to read information favorable to their own decision. Those who had decided to take a multiple-choice exam preferred articles in favor of that type, and those who chose the essay exam chose to read articles favoring essays.

However, a follow-up study, conducted by Rosen (1961), indicated a strong preference for nonsupportive information. The procedure was the same as in the earlier study. Two of the articles were designed so that one would be supportive and one nonsupportive. The nonsupportive article was titled, "Why Students Who Prefer a Multiple-Choice Exam Should Have Chosen an Essay Exam." Any student who had chosen a multiple-choice exam would consider this article extremely nonsupportive, because it was telling him he had made the wrong choice. Nevertheless, there was a strong tendency to choose this article over a supportive article. Even when the students were told that the exam would count for 70 percent of their grade and was therefore extremely important, they preferred to read the article that indicated they had made the wrong choice.

People who smoke cigarettes are strongly committed to that behavior. Presumably they enjoy smoking, many have smoked for a long time, and most of them would find it exceedingly difficult to stop. An article that argued that cigarettes cause lung cancer would be a nonsupportive communication for these people. On the other hand, such an article would be supportive, or at least neutral, for people who do not smoke. When Feather (1963) gave smokers and nonsmokers a choice of reading either an article that indicated that smoking causes cancer or one that indicated that it does not cause cancer, there was no difference between smokers and nonsmokers in their preferences. There was no indication of selective exposure for either group.

During the great antiwar protests of the spring of 1968, many college men signed an antidraft petition—called the "We won't go" pledge, and many others gave a great deal of thought and deliberation to the possibility of it. It was an issue of great personal importance to young men who thought they might be drafted, and possibly killed, in a war they regarded as immoral. Janis and Rausch (1970) tested for selective exposure to propledge and antipledge communications among four different kinds of Yale students: those who immediately refused to sign the pledge, those who refused after some deliberation, those who favored the pledge and said they might sign, and those who had already signed it. Each student was given the titles of eight articles on the war, four of which supported the pledge and four opposed it. Each student then rated the articles for his interest in reading them. Selective exposure would have been reflected in a propledge student's greater interest in propledge than antipledge messages, with the reverse holding for antipledge students. In fact, however, Janis and Rausch found selective exposure in only one of the four groups (those who might sign but hadn't yet), while both groups opposed to the pledge were primarily interested in counterattitudinal information. So in this study, if anything, the general trend was for subjects to be interested in messages *opposing* their own position.

Other studies have also shown that people sometimes actually prefer information that *disagrees* with them to information that agrees with them. In a study by Freedman (1965), subjects listened to an interview and were then asked to rate the person who had been interviewed. After they had made their rating, they were given a choice of reading an evaluation of the individual that agreed or one that disagreed with their own rating. There was a strong tendency for the subjects to prefer the evaluation that disagreed with them. All but one subject chose the nonsupportive evaluation.

Overall, the findings of the various studies range from a strong preference for supportive information to a strong preference for nonsupportive information. Of the studies in this area, there are just about as many producing a preference for supportive information as there are producing a preference for nonsupportive information, and a large number show no difference at all (Sears, 1968).

The most likely conclusion from the research seems to be that whether or not selective exposure occurs depends, to a great extent, on the situation. Under some circumstances, as yet unspecified, people do avoid nonsupportive information and seek out supportive information. In other circumstances, the opposite is true. Therefore we cannot conclude that a preference for supportive information is a strong or prevalent phenomenon. When a person is given a clear choice between negative and positive information, selective exposure does not operate strongly, if it operates at all. In these relatively well-controlled situations, in which a person can expose himself easily to either supportive or nonsupportive information, the mechanism of selective exposure is not an important explanation of how people resist persuasion.

Much research has also been done on other avoidance mechanisms, especially selective learning and selective retention. Here the idea is that people avoid discrepant information by not learning it, or by forgetting it quickly. Yet a number of careful studies have been done in recent years which show that people do not learn supportive information more quickly than nonsupportive information, nor do they retain it longer or more completely (Smith and Jamieson, 1972). They do learn familiar information more quickly, but apparently not because it agrees with their position; they learn familiar discrepant arguments quite quickly also (Greenwald and Sakumura, 1967).

Thus the work on selective exposure indicates that the communicator does not have to worry too much about the target person *deliberately* avoiding nonsupporting information. If the communicator can get his message near the target and give him a clear choice as to whether or not to listen to it, the target will not avoid it simply because he disagrees with it. On the contrary, there is even some evidence that he prefers information that disagrees with him to information that supports his position. Thus, the difficulty of getting a message to someone who disagrees with it is due primarily to the sociology of people's life circumstances, as described above, rather than to the preference of the individual.

### Resistance to Persuasion

Assuming that the communicator has been successful in getting his message to the target, he is still a long way from changing the target's opinion, as could be expected from the research presented in the previous chapter. For example, both Democrats and Republicans watched the Kennedy-Nixon TV debates in 1960, but they differed enormously in their evaluation of them. The overwhelming journalistic consensus was that Kennedy had "won" the first debate. To the extent that impartial observers existed, they agreed with this evaluation. Yet, as you can see in Table 10–4, only 17 percent of pro-Nixon viewers thought Kennedy had won the debate. Consistency thus has a major impact. New information is interpreted in terms of existing attitudes as much as it is evaluated on its merits, and sometimes more so.

In general, attitudes that have been socialized early in life and to which the person is highly committed, do not change very much in adulthood. They are largely unaffected by mass communications (Klapper, 1960), or by such life changes as aging, geographical mobility, or social mobility, which would seem to put considerable pressure upon them

Table 10–4

WHO DID THE "BETTER JOB" IN THE FIRST NIXON-KENNEDY DEBATE IN 1960
AS RATED BY PRO-NIXON, PRO-KENNEDY, AND UNDECIDED VIEWERS

|  |  | Kennedy | No Choice | Nixon | Total Percent |
|---|---|---|---|---|---|
| Pre-debate Preference | Kennedy | 71 | 26 | 3 | 100 |
|  | Undecided | 26 | 62 | 12 | 100 |
|  | Nixon | 17 | 38 | 45 | 100 |

Source: Adapted from Sears and Whitney (1973).

(Sears, 1969). Nor do they change very much as the consequence of public events, such as hotly contested election campaigns, the presence of charismatic candidates on the opposite side, and so on (Campbell et al., 1960).

What happens instead to new communications if attitude change does not occur? Pressures toward cognitive consistency cause the beliefs and values that fit into the already existing structure to be more easily accepted than those that do not fit in. For example, if someone had developed a negative attitude toward drugs, he would be more likely to accept negative statements about marijuana than he would be to accept positive ones. Similarly, if both his parents were Democrats and he, therefore, considered himself a Democrat, he would be extremely selective in what he believed about Democrats and Republicans. He would be more likely to believe positive things about the former and negative things about the latter. He would also be more likely to favor ideas proposed by Democratic politicians than to favor those proposed by Republicans. His attitude toward a bill in Congress that he had never heard of before would be shaped, to a large extent, by these preexisting attitudes. Given entirely equal information about the two sides of an issue, an individual tends to accept the side that fits better into his already existing cognitive and attitudinal structure.

**Cognitive Consistency in Everyday Life**

How important is consistency in real life? Some survey studies have shown amazingly low levels of consistency between beliefs that are apparently related. On issues of domestic economic policy, Converse (1970) has estimated that as few as 20 percent of the public have genuine stable and consistent attitudes across policy areas. On matters of civil liberties, there have been repeated demonstrations that the widespread consensus on abstract slogans of support for libertarian principles (e.g., "I believe in free speech for all") is wholly contradicted in concrete situations, whether among adults (Prothro and Grigg, 1960; Stouffer, 1955) or children (Zellman and Sears, 1971). When we are concerned with the general public, then, it is a grave error to assume that consistency exists among apparently related attitudes.

However, consistency does exist at a very high level under the right circumstances, and we know enough now to specify some of them. First of all, consistency is extremely common with respect to the early socialized, high commitment attitudes we listed earlier. Party identification, which most people do not change during their lifetimes, is strongly related to how people vote—for president, and for all sorts of lesser offices (Wolfinger and Page, 1972). Racial attitudes, attitudes toward nation and authority, and the other core attitudes all affect voting, evaluations of public figures that take prominent stands on such matters, evaluations of public events, and so on (Sears, 1969). And as we have mentioned in connection with the Knowland telethon and the Kennedy-Nixon debates, people strongly tend to evaluate media presentations in terms of their core attitudes, when relevant (and on most important issues they are relevant).

Second, consistency is more common when people are highly involved in the issue in question. Congressmen tend to have much more consistent attitudes on matters of public policy than does the public at large (Converse, 1964); women using birth control techniques tend to have much more consistent attitudes on a wide variety of birth control issues than do women not using birth control (Insko et al., 1970); college students in Montreal have consistent attitudes about French-Canadian separatism (Rothbart, 1970), and blacks living in Watts had highly consistent attitudes about the Watts riot after it had happened (Sears and McConahay, 1973).

Finally, people with greater education generally have more consistent attitudes than the less educated, and their attitudes generally tend to revolve more around abstract ideological principles. This suggests a caution for college students and for professors as well. Since we circulate primarily among people with some college education (other students and professors), we are likely to overestimate the degree of consistency present in the general public's attitudes. Nevertheless, it is true that consistency is probably the single most important determinant of people's reactions to communications from other people, at least on the most hotly controversial issues involving strong commitment to attitudes deriving from early socialization.

### Changing High Commitment Attitudes

Even if change of high commitment attitudes is the exception, it must occur sometimes. What are the occasions on which it is most likely? To start with, there are, broadly speaking, two possible reasons for this lack of change. One is that the environments that people construct around themselves tend to expose them selectively to information supporting their pet beliefs, so their attitudes are only infrequently challenged. The other possibility is that people are so committed psychologically to their attitudes in these areas that even massive assaults on them are ineffective.

One way of choosing between these explanations is to look at cases in which the wall of selective exposure breaks down. Selectivity is of course never perfect, whether deliberate or accidental. Throughout his life and particularly as he grows older, an individual is exposed to information that disagrees with his attitudes. The extent to which negative, inconsistent information reaches him varies greatly and is more prevalent for some issues than for others. For example, most people develop attitudes in favor of honesty, peace, and motherhood, and they are rarely exposed to information inconsistent with these attitudes. Similarly, a belief that democracy is the best political system is not often attacked in the United States. In contrast, a devout Catholic or an atheist and a conservative Republican or a liberal Democrat would be exposed to information that disagrees with their attitudes on religion or politics. Although they would be exposed to more supporting than nonsupporting information, they would have to face occasional disagreement.

A sudden exposure to conflicting opinions is an almost universal characteristic of the first year of college. Students who have spent most of their years living in their parents' house and surrounded by childhood friends are introduced to an environment containing many different kinds of people with many different beliefs. This seems to be particularly true of students raised in a conservative political household and of students who have strong religious beliefs, but it is also true of students with liberal views on politics or little religious background. Most college students find themselves in a more heterogeneous environment, in terms of attitudes, than they were in previously. They are exposed to ideas, beliefs, facts, and attitudes that they may never have heard before. Not surprisingly, this exposure has a profound effect on many of them. They change many attitudes they had held since childhood; they reevaluate other attitudes in the light of the new information; and, in general, much of their belief system may undergo considerable reorganization.

We mentioned that most people adopt the political preference of their parents. This is the tendency in early childhood, but it decreases with age. Whereas almost 80 percent of grade school students agree with their fathers in party preference (Hess and Torney, 1965), only 50 to 60 percent of those in college do so (Goldsen et al., 1960).

Bennington College is a small, exclusive girls college in Vermont that was started, with a very liberal faculty, in the early 1930s. In a famous study (1943), Newcomb traced the changes in attitudes that some students experienced during their college years. Most of the students came from affluent and conservative homes, yet there were large and marked changes toward liberalism as the girls progressed through the school.

Perhaps the most interesting finding of the study concerned the students' attitudes after they left school. Did their new-found liberalism persist or did they regress to their parents' conservatism? Newcomb and his associates (1967) studied the girls twenty years later and found that their political views had remained remarkably stable. Those who left college as liberals were still liberals, and the conservatives were still conservatives. More precisely, the girls' senior-year attitudes were better predictors of their ultimate attitudes than were their freshman attitudes.

Newcomb attributed this stability to the social environments the girls moved into after college. He found almost perfect political agreement between the graduates and their husbands; these affluent-but-liberal girls had found affluent-but-liberal husbands. Moreover, the occasional attitudinal regressions could be attributed to the fact that some liberal girls had married conservative husbands or, at least, husbands in

Drawing by Saxon; © 1963 The New Yorker Magazine, Inc.

*"They sent her to Bennington to lose her Southern accent, and then she turned her back on **everything**."*

occupations, such as banking or corporation law, in which they could be expected to move in a conservative world.

This study emphasized, as an important determinant of an individual's opinions, the attitudinal environment in which he lives. His social acquaintances, family, spouse, and so on have a major impact on his political views. The study also emphasized the malleability of the young, *if* they are placed in a sufficiently monolithic environment. However, it is a rare college that embodies the political homogeneity of the small, exclusive, isolated, and highly liberal Bennington campus (Newcomb's follow-up revealed that today even Bennington does not embody the same degree of liberalism). And the college experience is in some sense unique as an opportunity to be exposed to new ideas, because it is specifically designed to be just that. Most of society is not designed for this purpose, and in the past many people were never exposed to views that contradicted some of those they learned in childhood. They continued to be surrounded by people who held views similar to their own and never had an opportunity even to hear the other side of issues. It seems likely that, to some extent, the growth of television changed this. Although people still may not hear both sides of unimportant issues or issues on which only a small minority disagrees, most people in our society probably are now exposed to both sides of any important, controversial issue.

Even college students seem to be immune to anything short of massive assaults on their pet attitudes. The literature on attempts to reduce anti-Negro prejudice reads like a dirge of smashed hopes. Ashmore (1970) has done the most careful job of summarizing the vast number of studies on prejudice reduction, and concludes that only under a very limited set of circumstances can much headway be made—extensive interracial contact under conditions of equal status, and shared coping to accomplish shared goals. Stuart Cook (1970) has done research attempting to validate this hypothesis. He tested the racial attitudes of a group of white Southern college girls, hidden amidst a long battery of tests on other subjects. He selected the most prejudiced of these students. Then, in a completely different setting (actually at another college) and with different personnel, he put each student through a one-month-long experiment, that involved about 40 hours of close contact with a black coworker. Most of this time was spent in coordination with the black woman as a coworker on a complicated and difficult task that required complete cooperation between them. The rest of the time was spent in casual contact—mostly lunch breaks. Then a few months later, all the subjects were retested for racial prejudice, again in surroundings completely removed from the experimental procedure.

Cook found that about 35 percent of the subjects became less negative toward blacks, as indicated on measures of attitude toward segregation and attitudes about interracial situations in general. This was considerably greater than the positive change shown by a control group that had not participated in the contact experience. Yet a substantial number of experimental subjects changed in a more negative direction, and a large number did not change at all. So even when a massive effort is made, under seemingly most propitious circumstances—all the correct social-psychological variables, with relatively young and open-minded college students—still rather little change took place. And this is a typical finding of even the most massive efforts to change racial attitudes, or other attitudes of high commitment—once people reach adulthood, the return is pretty small.

More generally, it appears that low commitment attitudes are fairly easy to change in adults once a communicator can break through the usual barriers of lack of interest, low levels of exposure, and de facto selectivity; while high commitment attitudes tend to be very difficult to change regardless of the circumstances. As indicated in the previous chapter, a high credibility communicator who makes a fairly low discrepancy appeal probably can achieve small amounts of attitude change, though nothing very dramatic. And as the Bennington example or Cook experiment illustrate, sometimes young adults can be exposed to strong influence, from a dominant social environment, and substantial changes will occur. And finally of course the early socialization of children can readily be influenced (though parents and school boards and other supporters of status quo do strongly resist tampering with children). In short, exposure seems to be the largest problem for children and adolescents, while the resistance born of commitment is most important for adults.

Thus attitude formation begins primarily as a learning process. An individual is exposed to information and experiences relating to a particular object and forms an attitude toward that object by processes of reinforcement and imitation. Once the attitude begins to be formed, however, the principle of cognitive consistency becomes increasingly important. The individual is no longer entirely passive; he begins to process new information in terms of what he has previously learned; in particular, he strives to form a consistent attitude. He tends to reject or distort inconsistent information and to accept more readily consistent information. Presumably this is a continuing process, with attitudes always subject to change, even after they have existed for a long time.

### Attitude Change vs. Behavior Change

We have emphasized the difficulty of changing attitudes in adults in real life. Antiprejudice campaigns, presidential election campaigns, and even the Chinese brainwashing attempts seem to have had only slight impact upon their targets' attitudes. As we will see in the next few chapters, however, it is not nearly as difficult to change people's overt behavior. There are tried and true techniques of social influence (or other forms of power) that can produce behavior that is wholly contradictory to the person's attitudes, or even his perceptions of reality. Subjects freely administer shock to inoffensive people, when they are told to, or express beliefs that wholly contradict their sense perceptions. In considering these dramatic cases it is well to contrast the ease of behavior change with the manifest difficulty of attitude change, at least of attitudes that matter.

## CHAPTER REVIEW

1. Minimal change in real-life propaganda campaigns.
2. Acquisition of attitudes in early life.
3. Low levels of exposure and information.
4. De facto versus motivated selective exposure.
5. Pressures toward consistency in information evaluation.
6. The Bennington study.
7. The difficulty of prejudice reduction.

## APPLICATIONS AND SPECULATIONS

1. Voluntary audiences to mass communications tend to be biased in advance in favor of the speaker's viewpoint. How could you explain this fact without invoking a general tendency for people to seek out supportive information (i.e., without invoking motivated selectivity)?

2. If people do not change their party identification very often, and if propaganda campaigns typically do not have a major effect, how would you account for the substantial swings from year to year in the outcomes of presidential, senatorial, and gubernatorial elections?

3. During the 1960s, student protests broke out repeatedly at universities across the country. The rhetoric of the protest expressed much disaffection with the American system. Yet these students had generally been socialized earlier to a trusting view of the system. What parallels can you see between this change and the Bennington study?

4. In the long run, political debate is intended to help people make polit-

ical decisions that maximize their interests. Do you think the operation of cognitive consistency in evaluating mass communications promotes or impedes such rational decision making? What might be said on each side of the issue?

## SUGGESTIONS FOR ADDITIONAL READING

### Articles

Hovland, C. I. Reconciling conflicting results derived from experimental and survey studies of attitude change. *American Psychologist*, 1959, *14*, 8–17.

Newcomb, T. M. Persistence and regression of changed attitudes: long-range studies. *Journal of Social Issues*, 1963, *19*, 3–14.

Schein, E. H. The Chinese indoctrination program for prisoners of war. *Psychiatry*, 1956, *19*, 149–72.

Sears, D. O. The paradox of de facto selective exposure without preferences for supportive information. In R. P. Abelson et al. (Eds.), *Theories of cognitive consistency*. Chicago: Rand McNally, 1968. Pp. 777–87.

### Books and Longer Discussions

Ashmore, R. D. Prejudice: causes and cures. In B. E. Collins (Ed.), *Social psychology*. Reading, Mass.: Addison-Wesley, 1970.

Cook, S. W. Motives in a conceptual analysis of attitude-related behavior. *Nebraska symposium on motivation*, 1970. Pp. 179–231.

King, B. T., and McGinnies, E. (Eds.). *Attitudes, conflict, and social change*. New York: Academic Press, 1972.

Sears, D. O. Political behavior. In G. Lindzey and E. Aronson (Eds.), *Handbook of social psychology*, 2nd ed., Vol. 5. Reading, Mass.: Addison-Wesley, 1969.

Sears, D. O. Political socialization. In F. I. Greenstein and N. W. Polsby (Eds.), *Handbook of political science*, Vol. 3. Reading, Mass.: Addison-Wesley, 1974.

# eleven

# dissonance and attitude-discrepant behavior

In the previous chapters, we discussed attitude change produced by persuasion—one person trying to change another's attitude by means of a persuasive communication. As we have seen, there is a tendency for people to change their opinions under pressure from a discrepant message. In this chapter, we shall discuss attitude change produced by inducing the individual to perform an act that is discrepant from an attitude he holds and a theory that accounts for this effect. Suppose a young man has strong pacifist feelings. He hates war and thinks all forms of violence are unnecessary and evil. However, he has not been able to get himself declared a conscientious objector and is drafted into the army. Sometimes later he finds himself in the midst of the fighting, firing his gun and wounding enemy soldiers. Or consider a doctor who believes that cigarettes cause lung cancer but cannot give up smoking. Or a liberal congressman from Texas who has to advocate protection for oil companies to please the powerful oil interests in his district.

All these people are saying or doing things that run counter to their beliefs. How does it affect them? Individuals' relevant attitudes tend to change in the direction of their behavior. The pacifist becomes less opposed to violence, the doctor may decide that the relationship between smoking and cancer is not as strong as he thought before, and the congressman may decide that the oil interests really need protection. Engaging in behavior that is discrepant from an attitude puts pressure on the attitude and causes it to change.

One way of conceptualizing this process is in terms of cognitive consistency. As we discussed in Chapter 8, there is a tendency for individuals to seek consistency among their cognitions. When inconsistency exists, the relevant cognitions tend to change in order to reduce it. One cognition is a person's knowledge of his own behavior; another would be his attitude on an issue. When his behavior is inconsistent with his attitude, either can change. If the behavior has already been performed, however, it cannot change and there is a strong tendency for the

task to the next subject as very enjoyable. There was also a control group, the members of which were not asked to tell the lie. Soon afterward, the experimenter had all the subjects indicate how much they had actually enjoyed the task. Deciding that the task was quite enjoyable would reduce any dissonance the subject might have felt. As expected, all the experimental subjects increased their ratings of how enjoyable the task was more than did the controls.

The interesting finding, however, was the comparison between the $1 and $20 conditions (Table 11–4). Those who were paid $1 rated the task more positively than those who were paid $20. This is what dissonance theory would predict. The larger amount of money served as an additional reason for performing the task; therefore it was a consonant element in the situation and reduced the overall amount of dissonance. The less dissonance, the less attitude change. Thus the more the subjects were paid for performing the discrepant behavior, the less attitude change they experienced.

One point regarding rewards, punishments, and any other kind of justification must be stressed. In order to effect attitude change, it is absolutely essential to produce the discrepant behavior. The justification must be large enough to produce the behavior. Only if the person engages in attitude-discrepant behavior would any dissonance be aroused and any attitude change produced. Once the behavior has been induced, then the less the reward or punishment used to induce it, the more attitude change is to be expected. This means that according to dissonance theory, the optimal amount of change is produced by using an amount of reward or punishment that is just large enough to produce the behavior. Any less and the individual would not perform the behavior so there would be no change at all; any greater reward or punishment would serve as additional consonant elements in the situation and would produce less attitude change.

A demonstration of this was provided by the study on eating grasshoppers that was described earlier. For the subjects who ate the grasshoppers (that is, performed the discrepant act), the more justification there was (pleasant experimenter), the less attitude change occurred. They liked the grasshoppers somewhat more with the unpleasant experimenter. This contrasted markedly with the reactions of those people who refused to eat the grasshoppers. For those who did not perform the discrepant act, the pleasantness of the experimenter had the opposite effect. They rated the grasshoppers more negatively when the experimenter was unpleasant than when he was pleasant. Presumably the unpleasantness of the experimenter made them dislike the grasshoppers even more than before, whereas the pleasant experimenter may have convinced them slightly that the grasshoppers were not so bad. The dissonance effect of greater change with less justification occurs only when the justification is great enough to induce the person to perform the discrepant behavior.

### Dissonance Theory Versus Learning Theory

Thus far, we have described the effect of discrepant behavior on attitudes entirely in terms of the theory of cognitive dissonance. An alternative conceptualization of the situation has been made in terms of learning or incentive. Someone who engages in attitude-discrepant behavior tends to be exposed to information and experiences he otherwise would not be. A child who is induced to taste spinach, which he thinks he hates, will discover what spinach tastes like; a pacifist who joins the Marines will discover a lot more about the Marines than he knew before; and a policeman who is somehow induced to argue in favor of legalizing marijuana may think of some arguments he would not otherwise have heard or listened to. Exposure to this information may, in itself, change the individual's attitude. He may discover that spinach tastes good or that the Marines are a great group. Moreover, someone who argues against his own position may convince himself. If he tries to come up with the best possible arguments, he will be exposed to very persuasive communications. Thus, rather than than dissonance reduction causing the attitude change, it may be due to the usual process of persuasion.

An impressive illustration of the learning effect of engaging in discrepant behavior was provided by Irving Janis. In his work on convincing people not to smoke (Janis and Mann, 1965), cigarette smokers playacted the role of someone who has lung cancer. The subjects became extremely involved in their roles—they looked at X-rays, pretended they were talking to the doctor, playacted their response to the news that they had cancer, imagined themselves waiting for the operation and finally undergoing it, and so on. It was an intense, emotionally arousing experience for them. Janis reported that subjects who went through this experience were more likely to be successful in giving up cigarette smoking than were people who did not participate in this kind of emotional role playing. In a follow-up survey six months later (Mann and Janis, 1968), a large percentage of the people in this condition were still not smoking cigarettes. The subjects who went through less involving experiences, who engaged in less intensive playacting, were considerably less successful in giving up smoking. Apparently, the intensive role playing was an unusually effective persuasive device.

Although the two explanations of the effect of attitude-discrepant behavior are quite different, they are not inconsistent. Both cognitive dissonance and learning play a role in the effect of discrepant behavior on attitude change and, under most circumstances, reinforce each other. Each explains a portion of the effect. Individuals do change their attitudes in order to make them consistent with the discrepant behavior; and people are to some extent influenced by their experiences while engaging in the discrepant behavior. Both processes usually work in the same direction. Operating together, they make the effect of discrepant behavior even stronger than it would be if one of them operated alone.

The one apparent contradiction involves the effect of incentives. Dissonance theory predicts that there is more change with less incentive. The learning explanation predicts that, under some circumstances, greater incentive for performing the discrepant act produces more attitude change than less incentive. This occurs when the added incentive in some way exposes the individual to more convincing information. For example, if someone is induced to make a speech defending a position opposite from his own, it might be expected that the more he is paid for doing so, the harder he would work and the better job he would do. Doing a better job means constructing better arguments and presenting them more forcefully, The better the arguments, the more convincing they are. This holds for the individual making the speech as well as for those listening to it. Therefore, if the larger sum of money caused the individual to make a better speech, he would convince himself more and we would expect more attitude change.

The same argument could hold for other kinds of discrepant tasks. Someone who is paid more or given better reasons for engaging in a particular act may perform the act better, become more involved in it, pay more attention to it, and, in general, perform the act more thoroughly and completely. His greater involvement would tend to expose him to more information, might cause him to appreciate the act more, and would tend to convince him of the worth of the act. Any time that greater incentive causes an individual to perform a discrepant act more fully, there should be some tendency for him to be more persuaded by the act itself and there would be more attitude change.

Another consideration in terms of learning theory is that, as discussed previously, reinforcement can increase the effectiveness of a persuasive communication. Extraneous reinforcement increases attitude change, and the learning approach predicts that related reinforcement would also. If giving someone a Pepsi while he is reading an essay makes him agree more with the essay, paying him $20 for writing an attitude-discrepant essay should make him agree more with the essay he writes. Moreover, this should hold even if the additional reward does not make him write a better essay—the reinforcement alone should increase persuasion.

Thus, there are several reasons, from the learning or incentive point of view, why greater rewards for performing a discrepant act should produce more (not less) attitude change. Since dissonance theory makes the opposite prediction, there is a clear conflict between the two approaches. As might be expected, there has been a considerable amount of research attempting to determine which prediction is correct, and an unequivocal assessment of the results is difficult. Greater rewards have been shown to increase change, to decrease change, and to have no effect on change. Although it is difficult to weigh this kind of inconsistent evidence, more and somewhat stronger studies have supported the prediction of dissonance theory than that of learning theory. In addition, all the work on other forms of justification, particularly threats, is in line with the dissonance predictions. Since learning theory treats threats in much the same way as it does rewards, data that show greater change with small threats provide strong support for the dissonance interpretation. Thus, it seems that, in general, the dissonance analysis of discrepant behavior has been shown to fit many situations, though not all of them.

This does not mean, however, that one should discard the learning analysis. As we stated earlier, both approaches are relevant, and together give a fuller understanding of the effect of discrepant behavior on attitudes. The apparent contradiction between the two explanations can be resolved by noting that the dissonance effect is dominant under some circumstances, whereas the learning effect is dominant under others. The critical factor is whether or not dissonance was aroused in the first place. If a considerable amount of dissonance has been aroused, most of the effect would be due to dissonance reduction and there would be more change with less incentive; if relatively little dissonance has been aroused, most of the effect would be due to learning and there would be more change with more incentive.

An experiment by Carlsmith, Collins, and Helmreich (1966) demonstrates both these effects and supports this way of resolving the conflict. Individuals were induced to take a stand discrepant from their own opinion by having them take part in a dull task and then say that it was really fun, interesting, and exciting. The assumption was that telling this lie would produce dissonance, primarily when it was told directly to another person. Under these circumstances, the subjects were clearly misleading the other person, making a statement they did not believe, and doing all this in public.

Some subjects, as in the Festinger-Carlsmith study described previously, told the lie in a face-to-face situation to someone who was supposedly another experimental subject. This condition was expected to arouse a considerable amount of dissonance. Other subjects were told to write an essay describing the task as enjoyable. However, these essays were to be anonymous, would never be shown to other subjects, and would be used only as sources of phrases and ideas for an essay the experimenter himself would eventually write. This condition was expected

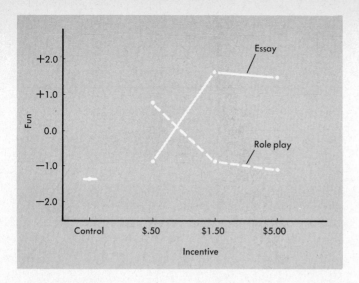

**Figure 11–3**

Forced compliance, incentive, and attitude change. When dissonance was aroused (the roleplay condition), greater incentive produced less attitude change; when dissonance was not aroused (essay condition), greater incentive produced more change. (Carlsmith, Collins, and Helmreich, "Studies in forced compliance," *Journal of Personality and Social Psychology*, 1966, *4*, p. 9. Copyright 1966 by the American Psychological Association, and reproduced by permission.)

to arouse little or no dissonance, because the subject was simply performing an exercise and was in no way committing himself publicly to the discrepant message. Some subjects in each condition were paid $5 for performing the task; some were paid $1.50; and some were paid $0.50. After performing the discrepant behavior, all the subjects were asked to rerate how enjoyable the original task had been.

The results are shown in Figure 11–3. It is apparent that they are consistent with the explanation above. When the task was designed to arouse dissonance, there was more attitude change with less incentive. The most change occurred in the $0.50 condition, the least in the $5 condition. When the task was designed not to arouse dissonance, the opposite was found—there was more change with $5 than with $1.50, which, in turn, produced more change than $0.50.

Two experiments by Linder, Cooper, and Jones (1967), in which the perception of choice was the crucial factor determining the arousal of dissonance, produced similar results. Subjects wrote an essay that disagreed with their opinion on an issue. Some subjects were made to feel that they had free choice about whether or not they wrote the essay, whereas others were given no choice. Half the subjects in each condition

Table 11–5

*REWARD, CHOICE, AND ATTITUDE CHANGE*

| Condition | No Choice | Free Choice |
|---|---|---|
| Experiment 1: | | |
| $0.50 reward | 1.66 | 2.96 |
| $2.50 reward | 2.34 | 1.64 |
| Experiment 2: | | |
| $0.50 reward | 2.68 | 3.64 |
| $2.50 reward | 3.46 | 2.72 |

Note: The figures are ratings on a scale from 1 to 7. The higher the figure, the greater the attitude change.

Source: Adapted from Linder, Cooper, and Jones (1967).

were paid $2.50, and half were paid $0.50. The amount of attitude change in the four conditions for the two experiments is shown in Table 11–5.

With free choice, the typical dissonance effect appeared—there was more change with less reward. With no choice, the learning effect was obtained—more change with greater reward. As we suggested earlier, perception of choice is necessary for the arousal of dissonance. When there is no choice, dissonance is not produced and the dissonance analysis does not apply.

A related finding was reported in the study by Freedman (1963; see p. 361), in which subjects were given either high or low justification for performing a dull task. Some subjects were given the high or low justification before they performed the task. When it was over, the standard dissonance effect was seen—those given the high justification said they enjoyed the task less. However, other subjects were given either high or low justification after they had performed the task. Under these circumstances, the typical incentive effect was found—those given the high justification said they enjoyed the task more.

The explanation of these opposite effects of justification is very much like that offered by Carlsmith, Collins, and Helmreich in their study. When given before the task, the justification served as a consonant element and reduced dissonance. It is less dissonant to perform a dull task when one has high justification.

Once the task was performed, however, the justification instructions should not affect the amount of dissonance produced. They have the same status as totally unexpected consequences which as we discussed before have no effect on dissonance. The subject has willingly performed a dull task presumably with some notion as to how useful it is. When he later hears that it is either more or less useful than he imagined, he need not feel responsible for this new information. There is no way that he could have known ahead of time what the experimenter just told him, and therefore the amount of dissonance aroused by performing the task should not be affected by the new information. Under these circumstances the justification served as either positive or negative reinforcement. When the subject heard that the task was more useful than he imagined, he was positively reinforced and liked the task more; when he heard that it was less useful, that acted as a negative reinforcement and he liked the task less.

Other studies have also demonstrated that the effect of rewards and other forms of justification depend to some extent on particular conditions. More detailed specification of these conditoins will be made possible by further research. For the moment, we can say that greater incentives for performing a discrepant act result in less attitude change if dissonance is aroused and more change if dissonance is not aroused.

Note that we are referring only to change produced by attitude-discrepant behavior. In these circumstances the dissonance effect is usually the dominant one. Most of the research discussed in Chapters 8, 9, and 10 did not refer to attitude change produced by attitude-discrepant behavior. When change is produced by a persuasive communication or information of any kind, the learning effect is dominant; then, the more incentive there is in the situation, the more attitude change we expect. Thus, the dissonance explanation is particularly relevant to the effect of discrepant behavior on attitudes, and the learning explanation is more relevant and powerful in the attitude-change paradigm involving discrepant communications from someone else.

### Dissonance Theory Versus Attribution Theory

Several alternative explanations of the dissonance phenomena have been offered in terms of one form or another of attribution theory which is discussed in detail in Chapter 2. The most interesting reinterpretation was offered by Daryl Bem (1967) who described the typical forced compliance situation in terms of what he called self-persuasion. He argued that all of our attitudes are based on our perceptions of our own behavior. If we eat oranges and somebody asks us how we feel about oranges, we say to ourselves, "I eat oranges; therefore I must like oranges." Accordingly we tell the person that we like oranges. Similarly if we vote for a Republican, we assume that we have Republican attitudes; if we go to church, we assume that we are religious; and so on.

It is easy to see how this might apply to the forced compliance situation. A subject is induced to tell someone that a particular task was very enjoyable. When the subject is subsequently asked how enjoyable he thought the task was, he says to himself, "I said that the task was enjoyable and I must think that it is." Therefore after he had said that the task was enjoyable, he will be more likely to rate it as enjoyable. But there is more to the situation than that. If he has been paid one dollar to say that the task was enjoyable, he says to himself, "I said that the task was enjoyable and I was paid only one dollar. One dollar is not enough to make me lie, so I must really think that the task is enjoyable." On the other hand if he is paid twenty dollars, that is a sufficient amount to tell a lie, and he is therefore less likely to believe that he thinks that the task is enjoyable. Thus this explanation makes the same predictions as dissonance theory—the more the subject is paid to make the discrepant statement the less he will believe it. Similar explanations can be offered for virtually all of the dissonance phenomena. The major difference is that instead of the subject reducing cognitive consistency by changing his attitudes (as in dissonance theory), the subject simply bases his response to an attitude questionnaire on his perception of the situation.

Personally we find this an extremely implausible view of the situation. We believe that subjects do have attitudes that endure from one moment to another and are not based entirely on current behavior. We do not believe that a subject decides whether or not he likes spinach on the basis of whether or not he has recently eaten spinach. We think he has real feelings toward spinach and it is these feelings that determine his responses. However, due to the nature of the two theories, it is quite difficult to design an experiment that tests between them. Various studies have purported to provide such a test, but with sufficient ingenuity, proponents of one theory or the other can always explain away negative results. Much of this research has been of the simulation or role playing variety which we believe has little value.

There is, however, one crucial difference between the theoretical positions. Dissonance theory contends that the existence of inconsistency is uncomfortable, that it acts as a drive much like hunger, and that the subject does what he can to reduce this discomfort. Bem's analysis is entirely cognitive and certainly would not expect these situations to arouse any kind of discomfort or drive. Fortunately this difference between theories is directly testable. Waterman (1969), Pallack (1970), and Pallack and Pittman (1972) provide such a test and seem to show clearly that a drive is aroused. In the latter study subjects first performed a dull task with high or low choice. According to dissonance theory, voluntarily performing such a task should be dissonance arousing and the subject should experience some increase in drive level. According to Bem, of course, there should be no change in the level of drive. Subjects then tried to perform a task that involved either high or low levels of competing responses. It has been demonstrated in the experimental literature that tasks with high competition (i.e., there are several competing responses rather than one obvious correct response) are more difficult under high drive than under low drive; while tasks with low competition are easier under high drive than under low drive. The results appear in Table 11–6.

Table 11-6

THE EFFECT OF CHOICE ON DRIVE AROUSAL AS MEASURED BY ERRORS ON HIGH AND LOW COMPETITION TASKS

| | TYPE OF TASK | |
| --- | --- | --- |
| | Low Competition | High Competition |
| High Choice (High dissonance) | −.39 | +1.61 |
| Low Choice (Low dissonance) | +.41 | +.62 |

Note: A positive score means an increase in errors.

Source: Adapted from Pallack and Pittman (1972).

As expected by dissonance theory, under high choice and therefore high dissonance or high drive, performance on the high competitive task was made worse while performance on low competitive lists was improved. In a second experiment, only the high competitive task was used and subjects performed a dull task under high or low choice and with high or low justification. According to dissonance theory only the high choice low justification condition is high dissonance and accordingly only this condition should have high drive. Sure enough this one condition did better on the high competitive task than any of the others. Thus, as dissonance theory predicted, a dissonant situation produced exactly the results that would be expected if drive were aroused.

Although it is difficult to dismiss an alternative explanation entirely on the basis of a few experiments, it seems to us that the dissonance interpretation is more plausible and more consistent with the current results than the self-persuasion explanation. Under some special circumstances subjects may indeed base their attitude purely on their current behavior and therefore act according to Bem's analysis in terms of self-persuasion. But by and large, in most of the situations to which it is relevant, dissonance theory is closer to the truth. People really are bothered and upset by inconsistencies in their cognitions and they do try to reduce these inconsistencies. One of the ways they do this is to change preexisting attitudes to make them consistent with current behavior. They do this not because their attitudes are "defined" by their current behavior, but because they want to reduce the dissonance that is aroused by the discrepancy between attitudes and behavior.

## ATTITUDES AND BEHAVIOR

The research we have examined in our discussion of attitudes has dealt almost exclusively with the question of how to influence attitudes. Underlying this research has been the implicit, and sometimes explicit, assumption that changes in attitudes produce corresponding changes in behavior. When a politician tries to persuade a voter to have a positive attitude toward him, he is not doing this just because he wants to be liked—he wants the vote. He assumes that the more the voter likes him, the more probable it is that he would vote for him. He assumes that changing the person's attitudes will also produce a change in his behavior Is this assumption correct?

Although virtually all of the interest in attitude change has been generated by the assumption that attitudes do affect behavior, there has recently been some questioning of this assumption. In reviewing some of the relevant literature, Wicker (1969) concluded that attitudes rarely have a strong relationship with the relevant behavior. Tittle and Hill (1967), Fishbein (1972), and others have agreed with this assumption. But it seems to us that this is incorrect. We feel that these authors have made a mistake partly because they have incorrectly analyzed the existing data, partly because they tend to overemphasize those studies that supported their position, and partly because they failed to distinguish between two quite different aspects of the question. We should not ask whether attitudes and behavior are always consistent—rather we must ask whether attitudes tend to affect behavior. It is unreasonable to expect someone always to behave in accord with his attitudes. There are so many other reasons for performing a particular behavior, so many conflicting attitudes and motives that no single attitude should ever be entirely consistent with any single behavior. As Leonard Berkowitz recently stated, "Considering all of the conditions that could intervene between attitude expression and behavior, it is surprising that attitude indicators predict action successfully as often as they do" (1972, p. 49).

It is important to state the question in two parts: do attitudes affect behavior and are attitudes and behavior always consistent? The answers to these questions are yes for the first and no for the second. The politician who tries to make people like him is generally operating on a sound principle. If he can make the voter like him, he is more likely to get his vote. Similarly, if he can persuade the person to consider himself a Democrat, that voter is likely to vote Democratic. If one believes in God, he is more likely to attend church than if he does not. And obviously, if he accepts Catholic dogma, he would attend a Catholic church, whereas if he accepts Protestant dogma, his church would be Protestant. If he thinks fluoridation is good for teeth and not harmful, he would vote in favor of it. If he thinks it is harmful, he would vote against it and almost certainly would avoid drinking fluoridated water. If he likes a Chevrolet more than a Ford, he would buy the former and not the latter. And so on. What people believe, the opinions they hold, the evaluations they make, their attitudes have enormous influence on their behavior.

This does not mean, however, that behavior is always perfectly consistent with attitudes nor even that a change in an attitude always produces a change in behavior. It is true that attitudes always produce *pressure* to behave consistently with them, but there are factors other than attitudes that determine behavior, and these other factors are sometimes dominant. Consider the examples above. A person who considers himself a Democrat and who holds other attitudes that define him as a Democrat tends to vote for the Democratic candidates. True. But he may sometimes vote for a Republican. Millions of Democrats voted for Nixon in 1972 because they mistrusted McGovern's policies even more than they disliked Nixon. If one believes in God, he is more likely to attend church than if he does not. True. But many people who believe in God do not attend church— and probably many who attend church do not believe in God. There are other reasons for and against church attendance. It is socially required in some communities, it is a place to meet friends, it takes time, it may be inconvenient, and it may not seem to serve any real purpose. This is a case where other attitudes (e.g., it serves no purpose) and other considerations (e.g., time) might conflict with the individual's positive attitude toward God and cause him to behave seemingly inconsistently with his attitude.

Another case of this kind of conflict is our example of the Chevrolet and the Ford. Someone who is in the market for a car may look at Chevrolets and Fords and may much prefer the Chevrolet. But he buys the Ford. Why? Maybe because the Ford is cheaper. Or because the Chevrolet dealer is out of cars and he would have to wait a week, whereas the Ford dealer has a car available. Or because he happens to work for a supplier of Ford parts and there is strong pressure to buy Fords. His attitude favors the Chevrolet, but he buys the Ford because there are other reasons for doing so.

Consider the person who thinks there is nothing wrong with stealing. He feels no moral compunction about it and, in fact, has a somewhat positive evaluation of the successful thief, perhaps based on movies in which the thief is the hero. If a good opportunity presented itself, if he needed the money, and if all other things were equal, this person would be more likely to steal than would someone who thought stealing was wrong. But all things are never equal. He may go through life and never steal anything, because he has everything he needs, because he is afraid of getting caught and understands the consequences, or just because he never has a good opportunity.

Another example, with practical implications, is the relationship between feelings of prejudice toward a specific group and actual behavior toward that group. Once again, all things being equal, someone who is prejudiced against blacks is more likely to treat them badly than someone who is not prejudiced. But again, all things are not equal. In a coal mine, for instance, blacks and whites work together. At least while they are in the mine, it is important for them to get along. For many whites, this necessity would override any prejudice they might feel and would cause them to treat the blacks as well as they treat other whites. More to the point, those whites who are in closest contact with blacks in the mine and most dependent on them as coworkers should show the least prejudice in their behavior, regardless of their actual attitudes. Thus, some whites who are very bigoted against blacks would treat them better than would other whites who are less prejudiced but who are under less external pressure to get along with them. Outside the mine, the pressures are reduced, and we would expect a closer correspondence between attitudes and behavior toward blacks.

In a classic study (LaPiere, 1934), a white psychologist and a well-dressed Chinese couple went to a large number of motels and asked for rooms for the night. Although at that time in the United States there was strong prejudice against Orientals, virtually all the motels agreed to give them a room. Some time later, a letter was sent to the same motels asking whether they would accept Orientals as guests. Almost all those responding said they would not. The inconsistency between their behavior and their response to the letter does not mean that they were lying or that they were not prejudiced. It means, first, that what one says he would do is not always what he actually does and, second, that the pressure in a situation can override inner feelings. Well-dressed, respectable-looking people asking for rooms are hard to refuse, despite personal feelings of prejudice against them. The external pressures are clearer when there is a law requiring rental to anyone. Under these circumstances, even the most prejudiced person must rent to Orientals, blacks, or anyone else unless he wants to close his motel.

We can now see why research on the relationship between attitudes and behavior has produced quite inconsistent results. As Wicker (1969) accurately pointed out, sometimes the relationship is strong, sometimes it is weak, and sometimes it is virtually nonexistent. Although Wicker summarizes the results by saying that there are few studies in which a strong relationship was found, that is not an accurate assessment. Even in Wicker's review, he mentions many studies that produced a very strong or moderately strong relationship. In a recent, more extensive survey of the literature (Freedman and Tyler, 1973), the authors listed every relevant study that they could find. Although it was clear that there was a range of findings, this extensive survey indicates that attitudes often (more often than not) do have moderate or strong relationships with relevant behaviors.

It is also important to realize that the failure to find a relationship is sometimes due to poor methodology. The measure of attitudes could be faulty or have low reliability. If the subjects do not give correct answers, if they are unable to answer the question intelligently, if they do not understand the question, or if the question is so vague that it is difficult to answer, the questionnaire is then not measuring the attitude it is supposed to be measuring, and a lack of relationship with a relevant behavior would be understandable. Similarly if the behavior chosen is not directly relevant to the attitude measured, one would not expect to find a strong relationship. For example, several studies have asked subjects whether they believe in God or consider themselves religious, and then noted whether the subjects attended church. Typically there was only a weak relationship between the answers to those two questions and church attendance. But attending church is not directly related to a belief in God nor even to being religious. Many people believe in God and even consider themselves religious and do not think that attending church is meaningful to them. Similarly, other people do not believe in God and may not even consider themselves religious, but attend church for a variety of reasons having nothing to do with these particular beliefs. Thus, it is not surprising that the answers to these two questions do not relate directly to church attendance. On the other hand, if the subjects were asked whether they thought attending church was a good idea, presumably the relationship to actual church attendance would be much stronger.

To summarize: we believe that there is a great deal of evidence supporting the idea that attitudes affect behavior. It seems correct to say that attitudes always produce pressure to behave consistent with them. However, external pressures and extraneous considerations can cause people to behave inconsistently with their attitudes. Any attitude or change in an attitude tends to produce behavior that corresponds with it, but this correspondence often does not appear because of these other factors that are involved in the situation.

CHAPTER REVIEW

1. Dissonance exists when the opposite of one cognition follows from another.
2. The magnitude of dissonance as dependent on number and importance of inconsistent cognitions.
3. Decisions, dissonance, and regret.
4. Disconfirmed expectancies as arousing dissonance.
5. Attitude-descrepant behavior as a source of dissonance.
6. Choice, justification, and incentives affect the magnitude of dissonance.
7. Dissonance and learning theories and some resolutions.
8. Dissonance and attribution or self-perception.
9. Do attitudes affect behavior and are they always consistent?

APPLICATIONS AND SPECULATIONS

1. One of the crucial aspects of raising children is the use of discipline to control aggression and to instill feelings of morality and ethics. In the chapter on aggression, we discussed the effect of harsh and permissive discipline on aggression within and outside the home. In terms of dissonance, what would be the effects of too harsh and too soft discipline on a child's aggressive behavior and the development of morality?

2. It has often been argued that you "cannot legislate morality." This has been used as an argument against laws requiring integration or prohibiting bias. It has also been used as an argument in favor of local control and against Federal control. What are the pros and cons of this issue?

3. The United States Army has a relatively low salary scale for enlisted men and used to rely heavily on the draft for recruiting men into the service. What might be the implications of this for the fighting ability of the Army, its loyalty, and its belief in what it is doing? What affect might the recent change to an all-volunteer army have?

SUGGESTIONS FOR ADDITIONAL READING

*Articles*

Bem, D. Self-perception: an alternative interpretation of cognitive dissonance phenomena. *Psychological Review*, 1967, 74, 183–200.

Carlsmith, J. M., Collins, B. E., and Helmreich, R. L. Studies in forced compliance: I. The effect of pressure for compliance on attitude change produced by face-to-face role-playing and anonymous essay writing. *Journal of Personality and Social Psychology*, 1966, 4, 1–13.

Freedman, J. L. Long-term behavioral effects of cognitive dissonance. *Journal of Experimental Social Psychology*, 1965, 1, 145–55.

Gerard, H. B., and Mathewson, G. C. The effects of severity of initiation on liking for a group: a replication. *Journal of Experimental Social Psychology*, 1966, 2, 278–87.

Pallack, M. S., and Pittman, T. S. General motivational effects of dissonance arousal. *Journal of Personality and Social Psychology*, 1972, 21, 349–58.

Walster, E. The temporal sequence of post-decision processes. In L. Festinger (Ed.), *Conflict, decision and dissonance*. Stanford, Calif.: Stanford University Press, 1964. Pp. 112–28.

*Books and Longer Discussions*

Brehm, J. W., and Cohen, A. R. *Explorations in cognitive dissonance.* New York: John Wiley, 1962.

Festinger, L. *A theory of cognitive dissonance.* Stanford, Calif.: Stanford University Press, 1957.

Festinger, L., Riecken, H. W., and Schachter, S. *When prophecy fails.* Minneapolis: University of Minnesota Press, 1956.

# twelve

# compliance, obedience, and altruism

In the last five chapters, we have discussed social influence of various kinds. We have seen that an individual can be made to conform to a group's unanimous opinion even though it is wrong, and we have described in detail many of the factors that determine the extent to which this conformity occurs. We have also considered how one person can change another's attitudes and how engaging in attitude-discrepant behavior causes an individual to change his own attitudes. However, except in the chapter on conformity, we have not dealt with factors that influence an individual's behavior directly. As noted earlier, interest in attitude change is based in part on the assumption that change in an attitude tends to produce a corresponding change in behavior. But this is an indirect approach. In this chapter, we turn to a consideration of social factors that can directly influence how a person behaves.

How can a person be induced to do something he would rather not do? How does one elicit compliance or obedience? Answers to this question are relevant to practically every phase of social life—from doing assigned homework to obeying laws against drugs, from serving in the Army to buying a particular brand of detergent, from supporting civil rights to supporting the United Fund. In all these instances, some people would rather not perform the action and others try to get them to do so.

Much of the work in this area has focused on eliciting altruistic behavior, rather than compliance in general. Many of the experimenters have concentrated on discovering factors that determine the extent to which an individual will give help. Therefore, in addition to the general question concerning compliance, this chapter deals with the more specific issue of factors that affect altruistic behavior.

**EXTERNAL PRESSURE**   One way to produce greater compliance is to increase external pressure on the individual to force him to perform the desired behavior. The use of rewards and punishments is a familiar means of eliciting compliance.

Drawing by George Dole;
reprinted by permission, *True Romance Magazine.*

*"It keeps him home nights."*

The mother who wants her twelve-year-old son not to smoke often uses threats or bribes. She threatens to revoke his allowance, give him a beating, or deprive him of his favorite TV program if he disobeys her. Or she may promise him a bigger allowance or extra TV if he obeys. A third alternative is the use of cajolery, reasoning, and argumentation. She can tell him the medical reasons why he should not smoke, or that it is unattractive, or anything else she thinks will convince him. All these methods work.

Under most circumstances, offering rewards, threatening punishment, or giving justification of some other kind tends to increase compliance. Note that we are concerned here with producing behavior by external pressure—not with the possible effect of such behavior on attitudes. A woman with acne who is offered $10,000 for giving a testimonial for a skin cream is more likely to agree to have her scarred face appear on television than is one who is offered only $1. Someone who is told that LSD may cause irreparable brain damage and psychosis is more likely to avoid taking the drug than is someone who is told that it will make him dizzy (assuming they both believe what they are told). A child threatened with severe penalties or offered large rewards will smoke less than if the penalties or rewards were smaller. Within limits, the more the reward, threat, or justification, the more the compliance.

Social pressure is also effective in producing compliance. As we saw previously, a group can often cause an individual to make a statement he does not believe in order to conform to the group's opinion. The larger the group (up to a point), the more conformity it produces. A group that is face-to-face with an individual is more effective than one that is not actually present. And a unanimous group produces more conformity than one in which there is even one disagreeing member. All these factors increase social pressure, and the stronger the pressure, the more likely the individual is to comply with the group's wishes.

Compliance can also be affected by modeling and imitation. As with many other behaviors, an individual will tend to do what he sees someone else do. In an aggression situation, if the other person behaves aggressively, he will tend to became more aggressive; if the other person is not aggressive, it will reduce his own aggression. The same kind of effects occur with compliant behavior. If the individual witnesses someone else being highly compliant, he will tend to be more compliant than he might otherwise have been. In contrast, if he witnesses somebody being noncompliant, he will tend to be less compliant than he might have been. This kind of effect has been amply demonstrated by Bryan and Test (1967), Grusec (1970), and others.

At least for compliance, however, the effects of modeling appear to be somewhat limited. White (1972) demonstrated that imitating someone who donated money produced a smaller increment in donations than when the subject actually went through the motions of donating the money himself. That is, if the subject could be induced to give a donation on one occasion, even if he did this under considerable pressure and supervision, he would be much more likely to continue donating than if he merely watched someone else giving money in the first place. And Grusec (1970) showed that to be effective the model must actually engage in the behavior and not just talk about it. The situation was one in which subjects could either share rewards or not share them. There were three conditions—no model, a model who said that she would share her rewards but did not actually do it, and finally, a model who did share her rewards. Those subjects who had witnessed a model sharing were more likely to share themselves than those for whom there was no model. But those who merely heard a model say that she would share did not themselves share any more than if there was no model present. In other words, as with many things in life, it appears to be not what the model says that has the effect,but what she actually does. A further note on this interesting study is that the personality of the model and her behavior toward the subject did not have much effect on the extent of imitation. A highly nurturent, warm, comforting model was copied no more than a model who was not at all nurturent.

As might be expected, direct instruction by telling the subject how to behave also had a considerable effect on his degree of compliance. For example, telling a subject that he should donate money and reminding him when he does not causes him to donate more even when he is later left alone (White, 1972). Similarly, telling a subject ahead of time that he must not enter a particular room inhibits him from subsequently going into that room to help someone who is in distress; whereas, specifically telling him that he can enter the room naturally increases the likelihood that he will (Staub, 1971). When the experimenter specifically tells someone how to behave, it is to be expected that under most circumstances the subject will be more likely to behave in that way than if he had not been told.

### Pressure from the Situation

The effect of direct instructions and social pressure varies considerably depending on the circumstances. One way to maximize compliance is to place the individual in a well-controlled situation in which everything is structured to make noncompliance difficult. The individual is asked to do something and is free to refuse. However, refusal is made difficult because everyone expects him to comply. The possibility of refusal is never mentioned, and he feels obligated to comply because of his role in the situation. A familiar example of this phenomenon can be seen in a doctor's office. Someone is sitting quietly, enjoying a magazine while he waits the usual forty minutes to see the doctor. Then the nurse asks him to come into the doctor's office. He knows the doctor is still busy with two other patients and will not be ready to see him for another fifteen minutes. He would be more comfortable staying where he is, and there are no obvious threats for refusing the nurse or rewards for complying. Nevertheless, he walks docilely into the office and waits uncomfortably, this time without his magazine and maybe without his clothes— all because the nurse asked him to do so and the situation is set up so that it is difficult for him not to comply.

The phenomenon is even more clear in psychology experiments. Subjects find it extremely difficult to deny the experimenter anything. They have agreed to take part in a study. By doing so, they have, in effect, put themselves in the experimenter's hands. Unless the experimenter deliberately frees them from this obligation, the subjects tend to agree to virtually any legitimate request. If a group of subjects are brought into a room and asked to eat dry soda crackers, they will do their best to eat as many as they can. After they have eaten several dozen and their mouths are parched and they are extremely uncomfortable, the experimenter can simply go around and say "Would you eat just a few more," and the subjects try to cram a few more soda crackers down their throats. They will do so even though they are given no justification, offered no direct rewards, and threatened with no punishments. Students have been reported to eat huge numbers of crackers in this situation. Through it all they are suffering but trying their best to comply with the experimenter's request.

A dramatic study by Milgram (1963) demonstrated the phenomenon even more strikingly. Subjects took part in what was described as a learning experiment and were told that their job was to deliver electric shocks to another "subject" (actually, a confederate) who was in a separate room. Each subject sat in front of a large, impressive "shock machine" containing a number of levers, each lever supposedly delivering a different level of shock. The levers were labeled in terms of the number of volts of current they would produce, starting low (15 volts) and going up to 450 volts. Above the numbers showing the voltages were labels describing the severity of the shock; they ranged from "Slight Shock" to "Extreme Intensity Shock" and finally to "Danger: Severe Shock."

The subject's job was to read a list of word pairs to the confederate and then to test him on them. The confederate was supposed to learn the second member of each pair. Whenever he made a mistake, the subject was to tell him that he was wrong and deliver a shock. For each mistake, he was to deliver a higher level of shock.

Drawing by Dave Huffine; reprinted by permission, *Parade Magazine*.

Before the testing began, the confederate told the subject that he had a slightly weak heart but that he had been assured by the experimenter that the shocks were not dangerous. Then, the experimenter gave the subject a "sample shock." It was actually fairly severe and hurt considerably, but the subject was told that it was a very mild shock. This made him think that the shocks he was delivering were extremely painful.

During the testing, the confederate made a number of deliberate errors. The subject told him he was wrong and delivered a shock. Whenever a shock was given, the confederate grunted to indicate that it had hurt. As the level of shock increased, the confederate's reactions became increasingly dramatic. He yelled, begged the subject to stop shocking him, pounded the table, and kicked the wall. Toward the end, he simply stopped answering and made no response at all. Through all this, the experimenter urged the subject to continue. "The experiment must go on. It is necessary for you to continue. You must continue." He also said that the responsibility was his, not the subject's.

Under these circumstances, a large number of subjects dutifully delivered supposedly severe electric shocks. More than half of them continued to the end of the scale and administered the shocks labeled 450 volts and marked XXX. They did this even though the person they were shocking screamed for mercy, had a heart condition, and was apparently experiencing great pain. The pressures of the situation, the urging of the experimenter, the lack of perceived choice (although, of course, they could have stopped at any time), and the acceptance of full responsibility by the experimenter made refusal difficult.

Any factors that make the individual feel more responsible for his own behavior or which emphasize the negative aspect of what he is doing will reduce the amount of obedience. In subsequent studies (1965) Milgram has shown that bringing the victim closer to the subject has a substantial effect. In the extreme case when the victim is placed not in another room but actually right next to the subject, compliance decreases dramatically. Tilker (1970) supported this finding and more importantly demonstrated that reminding the subject of his own total responsibility for his actions makes him much less likely to administer the shocks. These results demonstrate that under these circumstances the subject feels enormous pressure from the situation and from the demands of the experimenter. Opposed to his feelings are this pressure of responsibility and concern for the welfare of the victim. As long as he can shift the responsibility to the experimenter and minimize in his own mind the pain that the victim is enduring, he will be highly compliant. To the extent that he feels responsible and is aware of the victim's pain, he will tend to be less compliant.

Another demonstration of the extreme compliance that can be elicited by appropriate manipulations of the situation is provided in a study by Orne and Evans (1965), which involved some subjects who were hypnotized and several groups of nonhypnotized subjects. One group (simulators) was told that they were controls in a hypnosis study and that their task was to try to fool the experimenter by pretending to be deeply hypnotized. Another group was also told they were controls but were not asked to simulate hypnosis. A third group was not told that they were in an experiment, and nothing was said about hypnosis.

All the subjects were asked to perform a variety of dangerous actions. They were shown a rattlesnake in a cage and were asked to reach in and touch it. They were shown a beaker of nitric acid, into which a coin was dropped. After the coin began to dissolve, thus making it clear that the liquid was really acid, the subjects were told to reach in and pick up the coin. Finally, they were told to throw the acid in the experimenter's face. Naturally, all these tasks were arranged so that no one would be hurt, but the subjects did not know this. The actions appeared dangerous and frightening. Ordinarily, virtually no one would perform any of them.

The behavior of the subjects is summarized in Table 12–1. Hypnosis produced considerable compliance. Under deep hypnosis, many subjects performed all or most of the tasks. Even more striking, however, was the behavior of the control subjects. All the simulators performed all the tasks, and the other control group also complied to a great extent. In contrast, those who were not told they were in an experiment refused to perform any of the objectionable tasks. Apparently, subjects in an experiment will do practically anything they are asked.

We have described these studies in terms of the pressure exerted

Table 12–1

COMPLIANCE TO DANGEROUS REQUESTS BY HYPNOTIZED AND
CONTROL SUBJECTS

| Condition | Grasp Venomous Snake | Take Coin from Acid | Throw Acid at Experimenter |
|---|---|---|---|
| Hypnotized | 84 | 84 | 84 |
| Simulation control | 100 | 100 | 100 |
| Nonsimulation control | 50 | 84 | 84 |
| Nonexperimental | 0 | 0 | 0 |

Note: Entries are percentage of subjects performing task.

Source: Adapted from Orne and Evans (1965).

by the situation. The subjects agreed to take part in the study, found themselves asked to do things they would rather not do, and did not feel free to refuse. The person running the study gave no indication that it was possible to refuse and the subjects submitted.

Another aspect of these situations, and probably a crucial one, is that the subjects gave up all responsibility for what they did. In the shock study, they continually asked the experimenter if he assumed complete responsibility. He said he did, and then many of the subjects continued delivering the shocks. The same was true of the hypnosis study—both hypnotized and control subjects put themselves into the experimenter's hands. It was his responsibility, not theirs, so they could do whatever he asked. This is similar to the deindividuation that occurs in groups, which, as we discussed in Chapter 6, partially explains mob behavior. The individual surrenders to the group or to the high-status experimenter, does not feel personally responsible, and therefore performs acts he would not ordinarily perform.

### The Hawthorne Effect

One of the most effective ways of exerting pressure on an individual to persuade him to do something is to make him happy and to show him that we really care about him and want him to do this thing very much. This is probably implicit in most laboratory situations. The experimenter is sincere, presumably is dedicated to what he is doing, and talks individually to the subject to tell him what he wants him to do. The subject has put himself in the experimenter's hands, feels that the experimenter wants him to perform the acts, is having a lot of attention paid to him, and finds it hard to refuse any request that is even remotely reasonable. He feels obligated to the experimenter and therefore wants to help him.

In a classic study (Homans, 1965), the purpose of which was to investigate the effect of various working conditions on rate of output, six women from a large department at the Western Electric Company's Hawthorne plant were chosen as subjects. The experiment took place over a period of more than a year. The girls, whose job consisted of assembling telephone relays, worked in their regular department for the first two weeks (the first period) to provide a measure of their usual rate of output; they were average workers. After this initial period, they were removed from their department and put into a special test room, which was identical to the main assembly room, except that it was provided with a method of measuring how much work each woman did. For the next five weeks (the second period), no change was made in working conditions. During the third period, the method of paying the women was changed. Their salary had previously depended on the amount of work turned out by the entire department (100 workers); now it depended only on the amount of work turned out by the six women. During the fourth experimental period, five-minute rest pauses were introduced into the schedule —one in the morning and one in the afternoon. In the fifth period, the length of the rest pauses was increased to ten minutes. In the sixth period, six rest periods of five minutes each were established. In the seventh, the company provided a light lunch for the workers. During the three subsequent periods, work stopped a half hour earlier each day. In the eleventh period, a five-day workweek was established, and finally, in the twelfth experimental period all the original conditions of work were reinstituted, so that the circumstances were identical to those with which the girls had begun.

From the point of view of the experimenters, this seemed like a good, scientific way of testing the effect of various working conditions. Presumably the rate of work would be influenced by the conditions, so it could be determined which ones promoted work and which interfered with it. The results, however, were not what the company expected. Regardless of the conditions, whether there were more or fewer rest periods, longer or shorter work days, each experimental period produced a higher rate of work than the one before—the women worked harder and more efficiently.

Although this effect was probably due to several reasons, the most important was that the women felt that they were something special, that they were being treated particularly well, that they were in an interesting experiment, and that they were expected to perform exceptionally. They were happy, a lot of attention was paid to them, and they complied with what they thought the experimenter (their boss) wanted. They knew that the main measure of their work was the rate at which they produced, they knew that this was what was being watched, so it did not matter what changes were introduced, they always assumed that the changes were for the good, that they were supposed to increase their work— therefore they worked harder. Each change stimulated their efforts further.

Making someone feel special by manipulating his environment, by setting him apart, by watching his work particularly closely exerts a lot of pressure on him. If he knows what is expected of him, he will do everything he can to go along with it as long as there is no particular reason why he wants to resist. Just as in a typical psychological experiment in a laboratory, the women at the Hawthorne plant knew they were being studied and tried their best to produce the appropriate result, although what the women thought was appropriate was not what the experimenters actually expected. In a controlled situation, people are compliant and do whatever the experimenter wants or at least what they think the experimenter wants.

### Limits of External Pressure

We have described a number of ways of increasing compliance. The most straightforward is to exert pressure on the individual, which can be done with threats, rewards, justification, or social pressure. He can also be exposed to a model who is doing what the experimenter wants, and the individual will usually imitate him. A different approach is to place the person in a highly controlled situation designed to put subtle pressure on him and to make refusal difficult. It is important in this technique to give the impression that the subject is expected to comply, that the possibility of his not complying was never considered, that the experimenter is dependent on him, and that he, in essence, agreed to comply when he entered the situation. Another factor in this technique is the assumption of responsibility by someone other than the subject. The experimenter or someone else relieves the individual of personal responsibility, so he feels freer to do whatever is required. The consequences are not his concern, nor his fault.

These procedures tend to increase compliance. However, they are not foolproof. Someone trying to elicit compliance often does not have large rewards, threats, or justifications at his disposal; and it is rare that he has sufficient control over the situation to produce the conditions necessary to make refusal difficult. In less ideal circumstances, people find it fairly easy to refuse even simple requests.

There are also times when the amount of external pressure that it is possible or appropriate to use produces less compliance than desired. The heroic soldier refuses to divulge the secret information even when subjected to unbelievable tortures; the typical nonheroic smoker refuses to give up cigarettes despite the tremendous danger of cancer and heart disease; the letter writer refuses to use zip codes despite a variety of threats and cajolements from the Post Office. In these cases, increasing the amount of external pressure would increase compliance, but for one reason or another, it is impractical or undesirable to increase the pressure beyond a certain point.

**Reactance.**   In addition, increasing the amount of external pressure sometimes actually decreases the amount of compliance. Under certain circumstances, too much pressure causes the person to do the opposite of what he is asked to do. A series of studies conducted at Duke University by Jack Brehm (1966) explored this phenomenon, which Brehm calls *reactance*. The basic notion behind his work is that people attempt to maintain their freedom of action; when this freedom is threatened, they do whatever they can to reinstate it. Whenever increasing the pressure on an individual is perceived by him as a threat to his freedom of action, he protects it by refusing to comply or by doing the opposite of what is requested. We are all familiar with the child who, when told to do something, says "I won't," but when his parents then say, "All right, then, don't," the child goes ahead and does what was requested. This kind of "countercontrol" or reactance also occurs in adults.

The clearest demonstration of reactance is an experiment (Brehm and Cole, 1966) in which subjects had a choice of two problems to work on. The problems were essentially identical, but the subjects were told that some people were better at one and some at the other and, therefore, the experimenter was giving them their choice. Into this simple situation was introduced external pressure in the form of a note from another subject who was supposedly making the same choice in another room. In one condition, the note read, "I choose problem A." The other subject was expressing his preference, and this put some pressure on the subject to agree with the choice. In the other condition, the note read, "I think we should both do problem A." With this note, the other subject was not only expressing his preference but also directly trying to influence the subject's choice. Although the external pressure was greater in the second condition, it produced less not more compliance. In the low-pressure condition over 70 percent of the subjects complied, by choosing the problem suggested on the note. In the high-pressure condition only 40 percent of the subjects complied—60 percent of them chose the other problem. Thus, by increasing the pressure on the subjects in such a way that they felt their freedom of choice threatened, reactance was aroused and the amount of compliance actually decreased. This study demonstrated that even when it is possible to exert more external pressure on an individual, it may not always produce the optimal amount of influence. It may sometimes boomerang and result in less influence than would milder pressure.

This effect has been shown in a variety of situations. It seems to work with both behavior and attitudes. Thus, although increasing the amount of external pressure is usually an effective way of increasing compliance, there are many situations in which it is necessary to find other ways of doing so. When the possible amount of external pressure would produce less compliance than desired, when increasing the pressure would arouse reactance and therefore decrease compliance, or when it is important to produce the desired behavior with little or no obvious pressure in order to maximize its subsequent effect (attitude-discrepant behavior, discussed in Chapter 11)—in all these situations, it is important to look for factors other than external pressure that affect the amount of compliance. It is these other factors that we shall primarily be dealing with in this chapter.

**OTHER FACTORS**

In order to make an individual more likely to comply with a request, it is possible, rather than increasing external pressure on him, to expose him to some experience or situation that would have the same effect. Ordinarily such an experience would occur before the request was made (instead of at the same time), but it would increase subsequent compliance.

### The Foot-in-the-Door Technique

Sometimes one's goal is to get someone to agree to a large request that people ordinarily would not accept. One way of increasing compliance in such cases is to induce the person to agree first to a much smaller request. Once he has agreed to the small action, he is more likely to agree to the larger one.

This technique is employed explicitly or implicitly by many propaganda and advertising campaigns. Advertisers often concentrate on getting the consumer to do something, anything, connected with their product—even sending back a card saying they do not want it. The advertisers apparently think that any act connected with the product increases the likelihood that the consumer would buy it in the future.

A study by Freedman and Fraser (1966) demonstrated this effect. Experimenters went from door to door and told housewives they were working for the Committee for Safe Driving. They said they wished to enlist the women's support for this campaign and asked them to sign a petition, which was to be sent to the senators from California. The petition requested the senators to work for legislation to encourage safe driving. Almost all the women contacted agreed to sign. Several weeks later, different experimenters contacted these same women and also others who had not been approached before. At this time, all the women were asked to put in their front yards a large, unattractive sign, which said "Drive Carefully." The results were striking. Over 55 percent of the women who had previously agreed to sign the petition (a small request) also agreed to post the sign, whereas less than 17 percent of the other women agreed. Getting the women to agree to the initial small request more than tripled the amount of compliance to the large request. This effect was replicated in a recent study by Pliner, Hart, Kohl, and Saari (1974).

Why this technique has such a strong effect is not entirely clear.

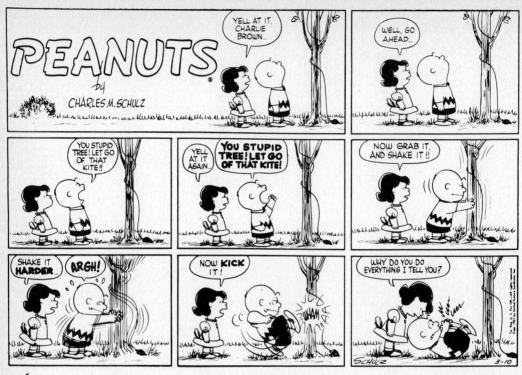

Drawing by Charles Schulz; © 1957 United Feature Syndicate, Inc.

The most likely explanation is that people who agree to a small request get involved and committed to either the issue itself, the behavior they perform, or perhaps simply the idea of taking some kind of action. Any of these involvements would probably make someone more likely to comply with future requests.

Another explanation might be that in some way the individual's self-image changes. In the safe-driving experiment, for example, a woman may have initially thought of herself as the kind of person who does not take social action, who does not sign petitions, who does not post signs, or, perhaps, who does not even agree to things that are asked her by someone at the door. Once she had agreed to the small request, which was actually difficult to refuse, she may have changed her perception of herself slightly. Since she agreed to sign a petition, perhaps, after all, she is the kind of person who does this sort of thing. Then, when the second request was made, she was more likely to comply than she would have been otherwise.

Thus, performing the first action changes an individual's attitude toward either himself or the action itself. In either case, this change makes him less resistant to performing a similar act in the future, even when the second request entails a much more extensive commitment than the first one. There is also some evidence that the effect spreads to requests that are not directly related to the first one, as long as they are similar in some way. For example, the issues involved in the two requests need not be identical. If the first request involved a program to keep America beautiful and the second one, safe driving, there would still be increased compliance to the second request when compared with the situation in which there had been no first request.

### Transgression and Guilt

The idea that a feeling of guilt tends to lead to expiation is probably as old as the concept of guilt itself. Guilt is aroused when someone does something he considers wrong. When one feels guilty, he generally tries to reduce his guilt. This can be accomplished in several ways: the individual can perform a good act to balance the bad one; he can subject himself to some kind of unpleasantness and thereby punish himself for his misbehavior; or he can attempt to minimize the negative aspects of the guilt-arousing action. The first two techniques would make the person more likely to comply with an appropriate request. If the request involved doing somebody a favor, performing a good act, or subjecting himself to unpleasantness or pain, compliance would tend to reduce the individual's guilt. Therefore, people who feel guilty should be more likely to comply with this kind of request than people who do not feel guilty. A number of experiments have demonstrated this.

Carlsmith and Gross (1969) conducted a study using a situation similar to the learning and shock study described previously. Each subject was told that he was taking part in a learning experiment. One person would be the learner and the other the teacher. In all cases, the subject was the teacher and a confederate played the part of the learner. The subject's job was to press a button whenever the learner made a mistake. For one group of subjects, pressing the button sounded a buzzer and supposedly delivered an electric shock to the learner; for the other group, the button only sounded a buzzer. Thus, half the subjects were doing something quite unpleasant—shocking another subject. The other half were doing something innocuous—simply signalling when the other person made a mistake.

After a series of trials, the experimenter indicated that the study was completed and asked both the subject and the confederate to fill out a short questionnaire. While they were doing this, the confederate turned to the subject and, in a casual way, made the critical request. He asked the subject whether he would be willing to make a series of calls in connection with a campaign to save the California redwood trees. (In all cases, the confederate did not know which condition the subject was in.)

The measure of compliance was whether or not the subject agreed to make any calls and, if he did, how many he agreed to make.

The results are shown in Table 12–2. Presumably, shocking the confederate made the subjects feel guilty, whereas delivering buzzes did not. If guilt increases compliance, subjects in the shock condition should have agreed to make more calls. This is what occurred. Those subjects who thought they had delivered electric shocks were more likely to comply than were those who delivered only buzzes.

Other studies involved other kinds of transgressions. In one study (Freedman, Wallington, and Bless, 1966), the experimenter told the subjects that it was extremely important that they not know anything about the test they were going to take, and the situation was set up so that virtually all the subjects said they knew nothing about it. Some of the subjects, however, had been told about the test by a confederate. Thus, these subjects were lying to the experimenter. Telling a lie and thereby perhaps ruining an experiment is expected to arouse guilt. It did. There was almost twice as much compliance among the "liars."

In another experiment by the same authors, the subjects sat at a table waiting for the experiment to begin. In some conditions, the table was specially prepared so that the slightest touch would tip it over and scatter index cards, which had been described as needed for somebody's thesis, all over the room. When the subjects tipped the table, they presumably felt responsible and guilty for mixing up the cards. In one control condition, the table was tipped by a confederate. In another, the table was stable and the cards were not scattered. Once again, there was more compliance in the guilt than in either control condition.

This effect of guilt on voluntary helping was demonstrated in two very nice studies (Konečni, 1972; Regan et al., 1972). In the former, the subject was a pedestrian strolling along a street in Toronto. As he walked along, one of the experimenters suddenly dropped some index cards in front of him and gave the subject an opportunity to help pick

Table 12–2

GUILT AND COMPLIANCE

| Condition | Compliance | Noncompliance |
|-----------|-----------|---------------|
| High guilt (delivered shocks) | 75 | 25 |
| Low guilt (delivered buzzes) | 25 | 75 |

Note: Entries are percentages.

Source: Adapted from Carlsmith and Gross (1969).

them up. The measure of compliance was simply how many cards were picked up. In some instances the experimenter brushed against the subject and made it appear that this encounter caused the cards to fall. This was called a "restitution" condition because the subject had caused the harm but was being given an immediate opportunity to make up for it. In another condition the innocent subject strolling along the street "ran into" one of the experimenters causing him to drop some books. The experimenter immediately picked up the books and walked off, obviously upset by the encounter. Subsequently a second experimenter dropped the index cards in front of the subject who then had an opportunity to help him. This was called a "generalized guilt" condition because the subject had caused harm to one person and was given the opportunity of helping another. In a "sympathy" condition the experimenter watched as someone else bumped into the experimenter knocking his cards down. The one who supposedly knocked the cards down kept walking, but the subject who had witnessed this sad event could help if he wished to. And finally there was a control condition in which nothing happened except that the cards were accidently dropped in front of the subject.

The results are shown in Table 12–3. As before it was found that subjects who had themselves caused the accident or who had caused an accident previously (the restitution and guilt conditions) helped considerably more than those in the control conditions. Unexpectedly, subjects in the sympathy condition who had merely watched someone else knock the cards down helped even more than those in the guilt conditions. Causing harm yourself does tend to increase compliance, but simply witnessing harm done by another sometimes also increases compliance.

The results of these and other experiments involving transgressions have been consistent. Regardless of the type of transgression— whether it consisted of lying, scattering valuable notes, delivering electric shocks, breaking an expensive machine, or taking something valuable

Table 12–3

THE EFFECT OF GUILT, SYMPATHY, AND RESTITUTION ON VOLUNTARY HELPING

| | Condition | | | |
|---|---|---|---|---|
| | Control | Sympathy | Restitution | Guilt |
| Percentage Helping | 16 | 64 | 39 | 42 |

Source: Adapted from Konecni (1972).

from a partner—subjects complied more when they had transgressed than when they had not. The obvious explanation is that the transgression aroused guilt, which, in turn, led to the increase in compliance.

It is important to note that in most cases the effect was not caused simply by sympathy or compassion for someone who had been hurt. In Carlsmith and Gross's study, for example, there was one condition in which subjects did not push the button themselves but watched the confederate receive shocks. There was no difference in compliance between this group and one that merely delivered buzzes. And in the card-mixing study, when the table was tipped by the confederate rather than the subject, there was no more compliance than when the table was not tipped by anyone. Simply watching someone suffer does not usually increase compliance.

The research also shows that the person making the request need not be the one about whom the subject feels guilty. In some of these studies, the request was made by someone other than the person whom the subject had hurt. Even then, guilty subjects complied more than nonguilty ones. In addition, it appears that the request need not even benefit the victim. Subjects in several of the experiments were asked to do something that had nothing to do with the person they had injured. Once again, guilty subjects complied more than did nonguilty ones. This seems to indicate that the effect of guilt is not entirely specific to the person injured. People can reduce their guilt by doing a good deed for someone else. Thus, someone who feels guilty for any reason is more likely to comply with a request even when that request is not directly related to the cause of his guilt.

Some of the evidence suggests that although the subject would like to help his victim, he also wants to avoid contact with him. Guilty subjects have a tendency to comply less when the request involves associating with the victim than when they need not actually meet the person they injured. A guilty person seems to have two different motivations. On the one hand, he wants to make up for his guilty act by helping the victim or by doing something good for someone; on the other hand, he wants to avoid confronting his victim, probably because he is afraid of discovery or embarrassment. This implies that the effect of guilt is maximized when the guilty person can comply without having to come into contact with the person about whom he feels guilty.

An interesting aspect of the relationship between guilt and compliance involves the effect of confession. One of the common assumptions about confession is that it is good for the soul, by which we presumably mean that it is a form of expiation. This, in turn, implies that confession should reduce feelings of guilt. If confession does reduce guilt, it should also reduce compliance. Studies by Carlsmith, Ellsworth,

Table 12–4

*GUILT, CONFESSION, AND COMPLIANCE*

| Condition | Number of Hours Volunteered |
|-----------|-----------------------------|
| Guilt | 4.33 |
| Confession | 2.67 |
| Control | 1.92 |

Source: Carlsmith et al. (1968).

and Whiteside (1968) and by J. Regan (1968) supported this prediction. In the first study, subjects believed they had ruined an experiment because they used information they were not supposed to have. Some of them were allowed to confess what they had done; others were not given this opportunity; and a third group, who did not think they had ruined the study, served as a control. All the subjects were asked to volunteer for further experiments.

The results are shown in Table 12–4. It is clear that guilt increased compliance—those who used the illicit information complied more than those who did not have the information. It is also clear that confessing, which reduced guilt, also reduced compliance—those in the guilt condition who confessed complied little more than those in the control group.

Regan's study, which used a different method for creating guilt, compared guilty subjects who were allowed to talk about what had happened, although not necessarily confess what they had done, with others who were not allowed to talk and with control subjects who had not transgressed. As usual, guilt increased compliance, this time in the form of contributing money to an experimental fund. And again, those guilty subjects who talked complied less—they gave less money than did the guilty subjects who were not allowed to talk and the same amount as the controls. Presumably, talking reduced their guilt and they had no more reason to comply than did the controls. This work demonstrated that someone who is made to feel guilty and then confesses his wrongdoing complies less than if he is not given a chance to confess.

A series of studies (Berscheid and Walster, 1967; Lerner and Matthews, 1967) showed that when guilt is aroused specifically by harming another person, its effect on compliance depends to some extent on other aspects of the situation. The guilty person wants to make reparations to his victim. If he has the opportunity to do so, he will. If he cannot pay him back fully or if the only available payment is much too great, he reacts in other ways. He tends to decide that the victim deserved the harm inflicted—that the victim is not nice or that he did something wrong himself. He devalues the victim, reduces his liking of him, and in other ways justifies hurting him. He may also minimize the amount of harm he did by deciding that it was not serious, that electric shocks do not hurt much, etc. Finally, he may seek justification in other ways, such as by deciding that he caused the harm for a good reason, for science, or because he was ordered to. Thus, one response to guilt is to expiate it by doing something good in return; another response is to minimize the guilt in any way available.

It is interesting to note that in describing the brainwashing attempts in Korea and China, Schein (1956) mentioned arousal of guilt and the foot-in-the-door technique as the two major techniques used by the Chinese Communists. To effect compliance by the later method, the Communists first asked the prisoners to do something inconsequential. For example, they might have asked them to lead a discussion group on the Communist system or to say that democracy was not a perfect system—things that were quite reasonable and difficult not to do. These small concessions were used to build up to larger concessions, until the individual was asked to comply with whatever the Communists wanted. The methods used to arouse guilt were considerably more dramatic. Individuals were encouraged to confess all their misdeeds, ranging from very small ones to extremely large ones. In a sense, the two compliance techniques were combined in this case, because the individual was first induced to confess something small and then led to larger and larger confessions. Apparently, toward the end of this confession procedure, which extended over a considerable period of time, some prisoners were pouring out their innermost secrets and were even confessing fantasies they had. This procedure aroused an enormous amount of guilt, so the person was essentially submerged in guilt for much of the time. Under these circumstances, it was relatively easy for the Communists to elicit compliance. In a few cases, the combination of the two techniques did succeed in producing basic changes in an individual's views of the world.

### Social Justice and Equity

One of the norms that appears to affect relationships between people has been called distributive or social justice (Homans, 1961) or equity (Adams, 1965). The idea is that each person should get what he deserves and that when he does not, others feel pressure to see that he does. In particular, when two people exert the same amount of effort, time, skill, or anything else on a job, their rewards should be equal. If one receives more than the other, inequity exists. The one receiving the larger share tends to reduce this inequity and restore social justice by giving something to the other.

This does not mean that everyone is always fair with everyone else, that greed does not exist in the world, or that people are not pleased when they get more than they deserve. The point is that, to some extent, people do feel pressure toward social justice, and they show some tendency to act so as to achieve it. One implication of this phenomenon concerns the effect on one's compliance when he has caused someone to lose something, or even observed somebody lose something, and when he, himself, has not suffered the same loss. If someone has lost, say, $5, someone else at the same time has gained $5, and neither of them had apparently done anything to deserve their particular fate, a state of inequity would exist between them. One gained while the other lost, when they both deserved to be treated equally. The feeling of inequity would probably be most strong if the person who gained $5 had caused the loss to the other person but should hold even if he was simply aware that the other had lost the money. The feeling should exist whenever the one who gained deserved no more than the one who lost. In some sense, it is unjust for one to gain while someone else loses when they both had exerted the same amount of effort; therefore, there is a feeling that injustice has been done. The important point is that there is a tendency to redress this imbalance and produce a state of equity.

A number of studies have demonstrated this. In several of them (Berscheid and Walster, 1967; Berscheid et al., 1969), subjects played a game in which one, through no fault of his own, won a lot of money or trading stamps while the other one lost. At the end of the game, the winner (the real subject) was given an opportunity of returning some of the money to the other subject. Under these circumstances, there was a strong tendency to give back some of the winnings, even though they had been won legitimately. In contrast, when the winnings are equal, there was little tendency for the subject to give any winnings to the other player.

Schmitt and Marwell (1972) also found evidence for equity. When one member of a team was given two, three, or five times as much as his partner, he tended to give some of his money to his partner in order to make their rewards more equal. In addition the overrewarded partner often chose to play a different game when he was assured that this would result in more equal partitioning of the rewards. In other words, not only did he give up some of his own money in order to produce a more equitable division, but he avoided the situation which produced the inequity in the first place.

Leventhal, Michael, and Sanford (1972) found that a subject who was asked to divide money among the members of a team gave higher rewards to better performers. But there was some evidence that apparently in order to prevent conflict in the group the worst performer was given somewhat more than he might have deserved and the best performer somewhat less. That is, the difference in rewards was somewhat smaller than their performance would have warranted.

Other results of this seeking of equity or social justice are less altruistic. Apparently the individual is also very concerned about receiving just treatment himself. If one member of a team is given all of the money to divide, under most circumstances it seems that he will divide it equally. But if the amount of money he is given is either less than he expected or considerably more, there is a tendency for the individual to give himself more than he gives his teammates (Lane and Messé, 1972). Presumably, the person doing the dividing wants to make sure that he gets at least what he deserves (in the case where there is less money than there should have been) or that he benefits particularly from the excess when there is more money than he expected. This is not exactly fair or equitable, but it does fit in some odd way with a sense of social justice (at least for himself). Similarly, if the person doing the dividing feels that he is better at the task than his teammate, he will tend to take more than half of the available money, while if he is worse than his teammate he will actually take somewhat less than half (Leventhal and Lane, 1970; Leventhal and Anderson, 1970). In other words, given the chance, the individual will try to give each person what he deserves in terms of his performance. But when there is either too much or too little money, selfishness seems to be predominant and the divider protects his own interests first.

**Receiving a Favor.** Another implication of the notion of equity concerns the effect of doing a favor for someone. If we are working in a hot, stuffy room and someone brings us a cold, refreshing drink, he has done us a favor. We are grateful; we feel pressure to repay him. If he subsequently asks us to do something for him, we are more likely to agree than if he had not done us the favor. Similarly, if we are working on a dull, tedious task and someone comes along and offers to help, we would be more likely to help him in return than if he had not helped us.

When someone does a favor, he has upset the precarious balance of equity. He has done something for us; we have not done anything for him. We owe him something. In order to restore equity, we must do a favor for him. We would be under considerable pressure to comply if he made a request. Even if he asked us to do something that involves more effort than he exerted in doing us the favor, we would find it hard to refuse.

Berkowitz investigated this phenomenon in a number of studies (Berkowitz, 1968; Berkowitz and Daniels, 1964; Goranson and Berkowitz, 1966). In his experiments, each subject worked on a task and a confederate offered to help him. Later, the subject had an opportunity to help the confederate on a similar task. A subject was more likely to offer help when he had previously been given help than when he had not been helped. In these experiments, the favor done for the subject was the same as the one he did for the favor-doer. A study by Regan (1968) demonstrated a similar effect when the favors were different. College students were tested in pairs, one of each pair actually being a confederate of the experimenter. The study was described as dealing with perceptual and aesthetic judgment. The subjects were put in separate rooms, shown a series of pictures, and asked to rate how much they liked each of them. After they had rated one series of pictures, there was a short break and the subjects were told they could do what they wanted as long as they did not talk about the experiment. At this point, the confederate got up, left the building, and returned several minutes later carrying two bottles of Coke. He handed one to the subject, saying, "I asked him [the experimenter] if I could get myself a Coke and he said it was okay, so I brought one for you, too." The subject took the Coke, and the experimenter then gave them a second series of pictures to rate. In another condition, the experimenter went out, returned with two Cokes, and handed one to the confederate and one to the subject, saying, "I brought you guys a Coke." In the third condition, no Coke was given to the subject.

After the second series of pictures was rated, there was another short break, during which the confederate asked the experimenter (loud enough for the subject to hear) whether he could send a note to the subject. The experimenter said that he could as long as it did not concern the experiment. The confederate then wrote the following note:

> Would you do me a favor? I'm selling raffle tickets for my high school back home to build a new gym. The tickets cost 25 cents each and the prize is a new Corvette. The thing is, if I sell the most tickets I get 50 bucks and I could use it. If you'd buy any, would you just write the number on this note and give it back to me right away so I can make out the tickets? Any would help, the more the better. Thanks [Regan, 1968, p. 19].

The measure of compliance was how many tickets the subject agreed to buy. The data are shown in Table 12–5. When the confederate gave the subject a Coke and then asked him to do a favor, there was considerably more compliance than when the experimenter gave the subject a Coke or no Coke was given. Compliance in the latter two conditions did not differ appreciably. According to this study, it appears that having a favor done for us and then receiving a request from someone

Table 12–5

*EFFECT OF DOING A FAVOR ON COMPLIANCE*

| Condition | Number of Tickets Bought |
|---|---|
| Confederate gave Coke | 1.73 |
| Experimenter gave Coke | 1.08 |
| No Coke | .92 |

Source: Adapted from Regan (1968).

other than the person who did the favor does not make use more likely to comply with the request. But the study does show that one way of increasing compliance is by doing somebody a favor. The recipient of the favor feels obligated to the favor-doer and is more likely to comply with a subsequent request by him than if no favor had been done.

The tendency to reciprocate a favor seems to be quite strong, but it is affected by various factors in the situation. For example Greenberg and Frisch (1972) found that a larger favor was reciprocated more often than a smaller favor. In addition when the initial favor was viewed as intentional, reciprocation was higher than when it was seen as somewhat accidental. Similarly, Goranson and Berkowitz (1966) showed that this effect depends in part on the individual's perception of why the other person helped him. In their study, the confederate either offered help voluntarily or was ordered to do so by a supervisor. When the help had been given voluntarily, subjects were more likely to reciprocate by helping the confederate than when the help was compulsory. Apparently, relatively little feeling of obligation is aroused when an offer to help is not made by choice. The study also suggested that the feeling of obligation is felt primarily toward the person who offered the help. Subjects who had been helped by someone tended to repay that person but showed considerably less tendency to offer help to someone else.

In addition to feelings of obligation, another possible explanation of the effect of doing a favor on compliance is in terms of liking. Doing a favor is usually perceived as a friendly act. The recipient will tend to like the favor-doer more than he would like someone who did not do him a favor, and this liking may lead to greater compliance. At the moment, however, there is little evidence that liking is an important factor affecting compliance, so this explanation must be considered as speculative. In any case, it seems likely that the effect of doing a favor is due primarily to feelings of pressure toward social justice and equity.

Although the effect of receiving a favor does not appear related to liking for the other person, there is some evidence that having something nice happen to you more or less accidently does increase the tendency to help others. Isen and Levin (1972) found that giving subjects a cookie or a dime made them more likely to offer help than if they had not received an unexpected gift. In one of the studies, subjects in a phone booth were pleased and surprised to find a dime sitting in the coin return. When they subsequently were in a position to help someone who had dropped some packages, they were much more likely to help than someone who had also been in a phone booth but had not gotten a dime. Now obviously the ten cents was not a large enough reward to make the big difference in the subjects' financial condition. It seems likely that the effect is due to the pleasure associated with this kind of unexpected gift from heaven (or in this case, the telephone company). Whatever the reason, this kind of unexpected, unasked for gift from an unknown source does increase the person's altruistic behavior far out of proportion to the size of the gift itself.

### Motive Arousal

People comply or are obedient for a variety of reasons. They are afraid of the consequences if they do not comply, they are seeking rewards if they do, they feel internal obligations that cause them to comply, and so on. In any situation, some of these reasons are stronger than others. Whether or not compliance occurs depends to some extent on whether the situation makes salient the particular concern that at that moment is important to the individual. If the person is primarily worried about being punished, for example, a situation that involves the threat of punishment should be more effective in evoking compliance than a situation involving only rewards. Conversely, someone who is unconcerned about punishment but desirous of rewards would comply most in a potentially rewarding situation. This is analogous to the operation of other drives. If someone is hungry, food is a good incentive; if he is thirsty, water is better than food; and so on.

In a study by Carlsmith, Lepper, and Landauer (1969), some children were asked by a threatening adult to pick up 150 tennis balls. Some children picked up all of them, some picked up 40 or 50, and some picked up only a few. Overall, there was a considerable amount of obedience. Other children were asked to perform the same task by a warm, rewarding adult. Again, some of them picked up a lot of the balls and some picked up a few, but the average number of tennis balls picked up was quite high. Both threats and promises are reasonably successful means of inducing obedience.

The situation changed dramatically when some of the children were frightened and some were not. In the former condition, children had just watched a frightening movie, while the others had watched a happy, lighthearted movie. The frightened group should have been par-

Table 12–6

*MOTIVE AROUSAL AND COMPLIANCE*

| Movie | Stern | Warm |
|-------|-------|------|
| Scary | 108.5 | 62.4 |
| Neutral | 69.9 | 99.8 |

Note: Entries are the number of tennis balls picked up.

Source: Adapted from Carlsmith, Lepper, and Landauer (1969).

ticularly concerned about being punished, about negative things happening to them. These concerns would be especially strong when the adult was someone whom they knew might punish them if they disobeyed him. If he asked them to pick up the tennis balls, they should obey him more (from fear of being punished) than they would someone whom they knew was a nice, rewarding person. In contrast, the children who had watched the happy movie should be relatively unconcerned about negative outcomes and more concerned about positive ones. The threatening adult should not impress them because they were not frightened. Instead, they would respond more to the nice adult because he would give them what they want—rewards. As may be seen in Table 12–6, this is what happened. The frightened children obeyed the stern, punishing adult more than the warm, rewarding adult, whereas the children who were not frightened obeyed the warm adult. This result was repeated by Pepper (1970) using a somewhat different situation. He found that subjects who were made anxious responded more strongly to negative than to positive reinforcements while less anxious subjects showed the opposite preference, responding more strongly to positive than to negative reinforcements. Any situation or person that makes salient the particular motive that is dominant at the moment produces maximum obedience.

**BYSTANDER INTERVENTION**

As we mentioned earlier, much of the work on what we have been calling compliance has focused on the conditions under which people spontaneously help other people. Interest in this question was stimulated by a series of incidents in which people who desperately needed help were not assisted by people who could easily have come to their aid. Latané and Darley, who have done much of the work on this problem, cite the four incidents described below.

Eleanor Bradley was walking on crowded Fifth Avenue in New York City when she suddenly tripped and broke her leg. She lay on the sidewalk crying for help while hundreds of people passed by, but for forty minutes no one stopped.

Seventeen-year-old Andrew Mormille was stabbed in the stomach in a New York subway. His assailants fled, leaving him bleeding badly. None of the eleven other passengers in the subway car helped him, and he bled to death.

At 3 A.M. a young woman named Kitty Genovese was attacked and killed on a public street in Kew Gardens, New York. Her screams of terror and cries for help awakened at least thirty-eight neighbors, who came to their windows and tried to see what was happening. Despite her continued cries and the fact that she was not killed until a half-hour after her first scream, no one came to her aid or even called the police.

An eighteen-year-old switchboard operator was raped and beaten in her office in the Bronx. She eluded her assailant and rushed out into the street, naked and bleeding. It was during the day and a crowd of forty people gathered. No one, however, helped her when the rapist attempted to drag her back into the building.

The work on this problem is closely related to that on compliance but has a somewhat more specific focus. Whereas those who studied compliance have concentrated primarily on factors that increase the tendency to comply, those investigating helping have tried to answer the question why people do not help, even under extreme circumstances.

One of the striking findings is that the presence of other people seems to inhibit the likelihood of intervention. In one experiment (Latané and Darley, 1968), subjects were put in a room either alone or with other subjects. Smoke began to pour into the room through a small vent in the wall. The critical measure was whether or not and how soon the subjects reported the presence of the smoke to the experimenter. When a subject was alone in the room, there was a very strong tendency to report the smoke soon after noticing it. Of the subjects in this condition, 75 percent reported the smoke within six minutes of the time they first noticed it and 50 percent reported the smoke within two minutes. In contrast, when other subjects were present, there was a strong tendency not to report the smoke at all. In various other conditions, the number of people reporting the smoke ranged from 38 percent to as low as 10 percent. Simply having other people present reduced the likelihood that the subjects would report the presence of smoke pouring into the room.

In another experiment (Latané and Rodin, 1969), subjects also waited either alone or with others, but they were given the opportunity to help a lady in distress. When the subjects arrived, they met an attractive young woman who gave them a questionnaire to fill out and said that she would be working for a while in the adjoining room. She went into the room, shuffled papers, opened drawers, and made other noises

Drawing by Whitney Darrow, Jr., © 1972 The New Yorker Magazine, Inc.

*"Hang in there, old man. There's bound to be a Good Samaritan along any time now."*

for a few minutes; then she went into a carefully rehearsed act designed to make it appear that she had fallen off a chair and hurt herself. The subjects heard a chair fall loudly, the woman scream and then yell "Oh, my God, my foot . . . I . . . I . . . can't move. . . . it. Oh . . . my ankle. I . . . can't get this . . . thing . . . off me." The whole thing lasted just over two minutes, and the main dependent variable was whether or not the subjects did anything to help the victim. Of the subjects who were waiting alone, 70 percent offered to help the victim in some way. When two strangers were present, only 40 percent of the groups went to the aid of the victim. When a passive confederate was present, only 7 percent of the subjects intervened. Once again, the presence of other people generally inhibited the tendency to intervene in this emergency.

Subsequent research has tried to pin down the specific reason for this effect. One plausible explanation is that when others are present the subject feels that they can help and that therefore he doesn't have to. Schwartz and Clausen (1970) had subjects waiting in groups of two, six, or six including a medical student. They then heard a person in distress who obviously needed medical care. The females in the experiment were more likely to help in groups of two than in groups of six and were least likely to help when the group of six included the medical student. For some reason, however, the effect was confined to females—the males were unaffected by the composition of the group. Bickman (1971) and Ross (1971) lend more convincing support to this notion. In Ross's study, for example, individuals waited alone, with two children, or with two adults and the tendency to help decreased in that order.

Although the ability of others to help may play some role in this phenomenon, it seems likely that, as Latané and Rodin suggested, the effect was due in large part to the individual's interpretation of the situation being affected by how others reacted. When there are other people present and they sit calmly, minding their own business, the individual may decide that the situation is less serious than he might otherwise have imagined. When three people in a room ignore cries of distress, perhaps (so the subject may think) there is no emergency. As we have seen time and time again, we interpret the world to some extent in terms of what other people are doing. If other pople are upset we get upset; if other people are calm, we remain calm. And in the present context, if other people seem to have decided that a cry for help need not be answered, there is a tendency to draw the same conclusions.

Recent studies that have not obtained the typical results seem to support this interpretation. When the situation is so unambiguous that the subject must recognize the existence of an emergency, the presence or absence of other individuals has little effect. This has been found by Clark and Word (1971) and by Piliavin, Rodin, and Piliavin (1969). The latter study involved victims who collapsed on a New York subway train. The confederate who posed as the victim either appeared sober and carried a black cane, or pretended to be drunk. In the cane condition the victim received spontaneous help 62 out of 65 trials. The number of people in the subway car and their proximity to him had no effect at all. When someone seems ill and is obviously in distress, people appear to offer help whether or not there are others who could also give assistance. The "drunk" victim received help only 19 of 38 trials (the lower rate presumably due to less concern for a drunk and some fear of getting involved) but even here the amount of help given was unrelated to the number of people present.

A study by Smith, Smythe, and Lien (1972) also lends support to the notion that a subject's interpretation of the situation is determined in part by how the other people behave. These authors report the typical finding that there was less helping when the subject was alone than when others were present. In addition, they found that the similarity of the other people to the subject was a critical factor. When the others were dissimilar there was more helping than when the others were similar. This is what would be expected from an explanation in terms of normative behavior. The subject's interpretation should be more influenced by people who are similar than by those who are not. When similar others sit and do nothing it should reduce the subjects tendency to help even more than when dissimilar others do not help.

Thus there are a variety of explanations of this effect. Other people are available to give help and it is therefore less necessary for the subject to help. Others are not helping and therefore the situation is interpreted as less serious. In addition, there may be some diffusion of responsibility—each person waits for the other to offer help and feels less personally responsible. Finally, the individual may face a higher likelihood of being embarrassed by intervening when other people are present than when he is alone. If it turns out that it was inappropriate for him to offer help or he finds himself in some other embarrassing situation, he would probably prefer to be alone. Whenever others are present, it increases the possibility of embarrassment and accordingly reduces the likelihood that the individual will take the chance of acting in this ambiguous situation.

APPLICATIONS AND SPECULATIONS

1. Milgram has related his findings on obedience to the situation in Nazi Germany, where seemingly normal, ordinary people allowed and even participated in brutal aggressive acts against the Jews and others. What do you think is the significance of his research for the Nazi situation?
2. American involvement in Vietnam led, by a complex route, to a situation in which the country found itself entangled in an extremely unpopular war. How would you explain our involvement in terms of the principles discussed in this and the preceding chapter?
3. Some of the phenomena described in this chapter should be relevant to techniques of salesmanship. Can you think of salesmen who use these techniques? How could the techniques be applied?
4. It has been suggested that many white Americans feel guilty for the way blacks have been treated in our country. Do you think this is true, and if so, what are its possible implications?

SUGGESTIONS FOR ADDITIONAL READING

*Articles*

Carlsmith, J. M., and Gross, A. E. Some effects of guilt on compliance. *Journal of Personality and Social Psychology*, 1969, *11*, 232–39.
Freedman, J. L., and Fraser, S. C. Compliance without pressure:

the foot-in-the-door technique. *Journal of Personality and Social Psychology*, 1966, 4, 195–202.

Milgram, S. Behavioral study of obedience. *Journal of Abnormal and Social Psychology*, 1963, 67, 371–78.

Regan, D. T. Effects of a favor and liking on compliance. *Journal of Experimental and Social Psychology*, 1971, 7, 627–39.

*Books and Longer Discussions*

Brehm, J. W. *A theory of psychological reactance.* New York: Academic Press, 1966.

Latané, B., and Darley, J. M. *The unresponsive bystander—why doesn't he help?* New York: Appleton-Century-Crofts, 1970.

Macaulay, J. R., and Berkowitz, L. (Eds.), *Altruism and helping behavior.* New York: Academic Press, 1970.

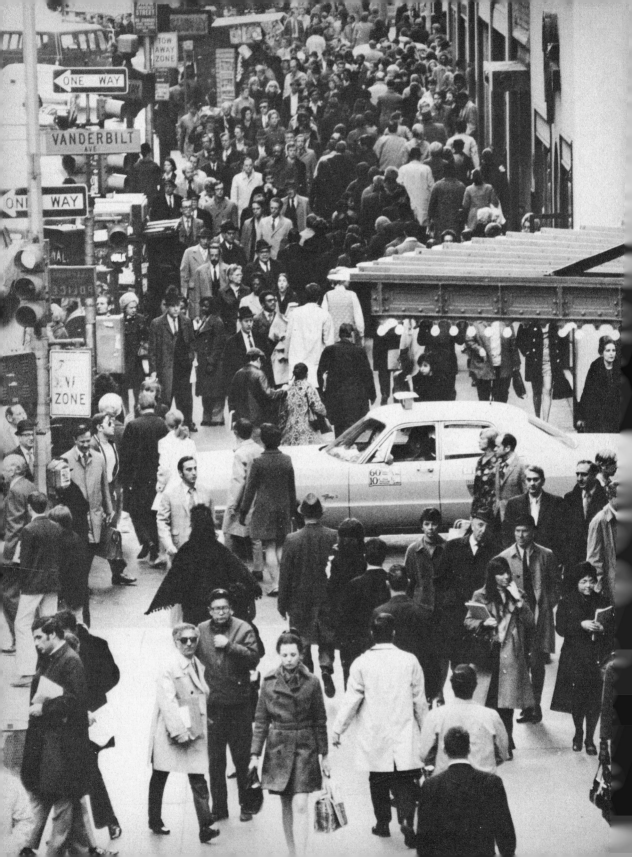

# thirteen

# environmental and urban psychology

We live in a world populated with vast numbers of people, and our interactions with these people and behavior toward them has been the major concern of this textbook. Social psychologists naturally deal primarily with how people respond to other people. Until recently social psychologists generally ignored the fact that we live in a world that is largely shaped and defined by machines, structures, institutions, and whole environments that are created by man. We respond not only to other people, but also to what other people have created. Thus it is both fitting and important that social psychologists turn their attention more and more to the effects of the social environment on peoples' attitudes, emotions, and behavior.

This is a new field in social psychology. Although more and more work is being done in it, thus far there is relatively little research and it is concentrated in a few specific areas. Much of the work grows out of the acknowledgment that most people in the United States, and other highly industrialized countries, live either in or near a city, and that the urban environment confronts the individual with stimuli, stresses, and social situations different from those that exist elsewhere. Social psychologists have accordingly investigated certain of these stimuli in order to understand how they affect the people who are exposed to them.

**AN URBAN WORLD**    The United States is now primarily an urban society. In 1800 most of the people in the country lived on farms or in small rural communities. This pattern of distribution changed slowly during the nineteenth century and at an ever increasing rate in the early part of the twentieth century. In 1970, over 70 percent of the population lived in or near urban areas, and 200 metropolitan areas contained over 60 percent of the population. The growth of the inner cities has, however, slowed considerably. In the ten years between 1960 and 1970, the census reflects that central cities grew by only about 1 percent. In contrast the

**416**

suburban rings around the cities grew by a phenomenal 25 percent during that same period. This was caused in part by the fact that the inner cities already contained as many people as they could hold. Virtually every square inch of land had a building on it, many of them very high, and the transportation and roads and other services were already strained beyond capacity. Those who wanted or needed to live near the city settled as close to it as they could, thus creating vast suburbs. In addition, there were various urban crises and pressures that caused some people to move out of the cities into the suburbs, but these movements were balanced by the apparently endless flow of people who moved into the cities from outside. Thus we now have extremely densely populated inner cities surrounded by an ever-growing ring of suburbs which together contain the great majority of our people.

The situation in Canada, despite its agricultural heritage and relatively small population, is remarkably similar. It is the second largest country in the world yet has a population of only 21 million—roughly the same as California. Over 70 percent of this small population lives in urban areas, with 40 percent of it being concentrated in only seven metropolitan areas. Thus despite its vast territory and small population, Canada is even more urbanized than the United States.

The other western industrialized countries are also chiefly urban: France is 63 percent urban; West Germany 79 percent; Israel 82 percent; Japan 70 percent; New Zealand 64 percent; the Soviet Union 55 percent; Sweden 77 percent; and the United Kingdom 75 percent. The contrast with the so-called underdeveloped or less industrialized countries is striking. Burma and India are 80 percent rural; Ceylon is 82 percent rural; China 80 percent; Egypt 62 percent; Haiti 88 percent; Iran 69 percent; and Kenya 84 percent. As these countries become more industrialized and developed, they too are showing a strong tendency to become more urban.

**POPULATION DENSITY**   Thus most of the people who live in the highly industrialized countries and more and more of those in the rest of the world live in or around cities. The immediate implication of this is that a great many people are concentrated in a very small area. If all of the people in the world were spread evenly over the available land, every single person could have ten acres all for himself. The average population density would be roughly 60 people per square mile. The average density in the United States is just about the world average—56 people per square mile. Obviously no one would feel cramped or experience a sense of crowding with this much space around them. The extreme concentration of people in urban centers changes the situation entirely. Even a small town will have several hundred people per square mile and larger cities tend to have population densities in the thousands. And, of course, some cities have extremely high densities running into the tens of thousands—the island of Manhattan in New York City tops them all at a full 70 thousand people per square mile. Furthermore, the cities are even more densely populated than these figures would suggest. People who live in the suburbs tend to work in the cities, swelling the daytime population enormously. It has been estimated that the major business and shopping areas of Manhattan may have as many as four or five hundred thousand people per square mile on a weekday. (Anyone who has tried to drive cross-town or simply walk along the streets in those areas will find this very easy to believe.) Working, shopping, driving, and generally living under conditions of very high population density is a fact of modern life. Our question is how this affects people.

### Crowding and Animals

There is a considerable amount of research on other animals that suggests that living under conditions of high population density may have severe negative effects. In a classic study, Calhoun (1962) put a number of rats in an enclosed area, gave them all the food and water they needed, kept the cage clean, and simply let the rats do what they would. Rats are prolific breeders and that is one of the things they did with great success. The population of the colony grew rapidly under these more or less ideal conditions. However, at a certain point the situation changed dramatically—the population declined sharply. This pattern—a gradual increase in population and then a sharp drop—is consistent under these circumstances. It has been demonstrated in the laboratory with rats, mice, voles, and various other creatures (Christian, 1963; Southwick, 1955; Snyder, 1968; etc.). The same phenomenon has been observed in natural settings when a large group of animals is confined to a small area. A group of deer stranded on an island was seen to go through the same population fluctuations (Christian, Flyger, and Davis, 1960). The most famous example of this phenomenon is the march of the lemmings in Norway. These mouselike creatures live on the frozen tundra and their population goes through this kind of cycle with considerable regularity. The colony thrives for a while growing steadily until there is a vast number of lemmings and then declines sharply with some of the remaining lemmings actually ending up falling into the sea.

Observations of the rats in Calhoun's experiment and the mice in Snyder's work tell us something of what goes on when the cages get very crowded. Ordinarily these animals manage to live together fairly peacefully. Each male builds a nest, finds one or more females to mate with, the females give birth, the young are raised, and so on. As long as there is enough food and water, relatively little fighting goes on; the nests are considered private property, and the females build comfortable quarters for their young who are taken good care of. Under conditions of very high density, there is a great deal of fighting, nests are invaded, females do not build adequate nests, and the young are not given sufficient care.

The immediate cause of the sharp decline in population is an increase in infant mortality. The number of pregnancies is about normal, there are somewhat fewer live births than usual, but the major change is that very few of the young survive to adulthood. Apparently the cause of this is that the nests and care are simply inadequate to keep the young alive. They cannot nurse, they are trampled under foot, they are exposed too young, and occasionally they are even eaten. At the same time many of the males in the colony become unusually aggressive, fight a lot, mate indiscriminately, and in general suffer a breakdown in their normal behavior.

These dramatic effects of living under high-density conditions have sometimes been interpreted as evidence for a so-called territorial instinct (Ardrey, 1966; etc.). According to this notion, animals require a certain amount of space around them and when this territory is invaded by other animals of their species, it triggers an instinctive aggressive response— the animal automatically fights to defend his territory by driving off the intruder. When a great many animals are crowded together, presumably all of their territorial instincts are triggered, everyone fights everyone else, and the colony breaks down.

It seems clear that this is an oversimplification even for lower animals. Anyone who has ever seen a cage of ten rats or mice knows that these animals do not require a certain amount of space around them. The animals do not space themselves evenly around the cage trying to keep as much area as possible to themselves. On the contrary all ten rats will probably sleep in a big pile at one end of the cage. There may be an occasional fight during the day, but rats obviously do not avoid close physical contact nor do they drive off another animal that comes too close to them. Under some special circumstances there may be a territorial or self-protective instinct triggered by having too many animals too close to them, but the animals do not have a simple need for a given amount of space.

Another explanation of the effects of high-density living is that the presence of the other animal is extremely stressful and causes a hormonal change. According to this theory, the animals in high-density conditions are under great tension which causes increased adrenal activity. When the adrenal gland is overactive, there is a tendency for the reproductive glands to become underactive. At the extreme, this would cause reduced fertility in the animals, result in fewer births, and obviously cause a decrease in population. Even though there seems to be little evidence that fewer than normal pregnancies occur, it might be that the animals who are born are less healthy because of some hormonal imbalance. Although there is no question that the presence of a great many other animals does cause stress, it seems unlikely that the mere increase in adrenal activity is enough to account for the dramatic increase in infant mortality and social breakdown.

Whatever the explanation of these phenomena turns out to be, these observations do suggest that living under high density conditions may have negative effects. Yet generalizing from the results of work on other animals to humans is always both difficult and questionable. This is particularly true when complicated social factors and interpersonal relations are involved.

As the noted biologist René Dubos has said:

> The readiness with which man adapts to potentially dangerous situations makes it unwise to apply directly to human life the results of experiments designed to test the acute effects of crowding on animals (1970, p. 207).

Thus although this work on other animals is suggestive, we must look at research on humans to discover how they respond to crowding.

### Crowding and Humans

The answer is that crowding does not generally have a negative effect on people. At the moment, the best guess is that the effects of crowding are very complicated and depend largely on other factors in the situation. High density seems to intensify social interactions and make them more important. But it does not necessarily make them more negative. On the contrary, high density seems to magnify the typical reaction whether that reaction be positive or negative. In other words, if in the given situation the person would ordinarily respond negatively, he will respond more negatively when crowded; if he would ordinarily respond positively, he will respond more positively under conditions of high density. There is still too little research to be certain of this formulation, but it is consistent with all of the available research and is our best guess right now.

Let us look at some of the research that has been done. To begin with, various people have looked at the relationship between density and pathology in natural settings. In particular they have concentrated on major cities in the United States. One such study looked at the largest metropolitan areas in the country. The measure of density was the number of people per square mile. In other words, this type of study was concerned simply with how many people lived within the boundaries of the city relative to the size of the city. These measures of density were then correlated with measures of the amount of crime committed in the cities. It was found (Freedman, Heshka, and Levy, 1973; Pressman and Carol, 1971) that there was a small but significant correlation between density and crime when only those two factors were considered (r = about .35). Of course density tends to be highly correlated with other factors such as income, and it in turn is also highly correlated with crime rate. It is therefore impossible to tell from the simple correlation whether density causes crime or whether some other factor, such as income, leads to both higher density and higher crime rates. In order to assess this it is necessary to control for income and other social factors and then look at the remaining relationship between density and crime. When this is done by the use of partial correlations or multiple regressions, the relationship between density and crime disappears. Across the major metropolitan areas in the country, once income is controlled there seems to be little relationship between density and crime rate. For example, Los Angeles has one of the lowest densities but has the highest crime rate.

In addition there have been studies of individual cities along much the same lines. Honolulu, Chicago, and New York have all been investigated to see whether density is associated with juvenile delinquency, mental illness, or any other kind of pathology. Although the results are not perfectly consistent, by and large they show the same patterns found across the metropolitan areas. In Honolulu (Schmitt, 1955, 1961), Chicago (Winsborough, 1965; Galle et al., 1972), and New York (Freedman, Heshka, and Levy, 1973) there were strong simple correlations between population density and various measures of pathology. In these studies density was measured not only by population per acre but also by the number of rooms per person in their dwellings. Thus they were measuring not only the number of people that lived in a particular area, but also how much space people had in their own homes. However, no matter how density was measured, once income and other social factors were controlled, the relationships between density and pathology tended to disappear. The one exception was in Honolulu where they remained substantial; but in all of the other studies the partial correlations were essentially zero. Thus, it appears that in the real world there is little relationship between population density and obvious signs of pathology.

Although these kinds of correlational studies are very useful, they are always somewhat difficult to interpret. So many factors are involved, and so many different variables are uncontrolled that the conclusion can never be definitive. Perhaps density does have very strong effects which are obscured for some reason that we do not understand; perhaps our measures are bad; perhaps we are looking at the wrong variables; perhaps density only operates under special circumstances. All we can say at the moment is that there is no indication of an overall general negative effect of density in our cities. Remember, of course, that we are talking about the psychological effects of density as separate from economic and social effects of concomitants of density such as poor transportation, lack of jobs, poverty, and so on. Overpopulation and high density cause other logistic problems which should not be blamed on density itself. What we are asking here is whether humans have a psychological response to being in conditions of high density, not whether high density sometimes causes problems in the management of a city. Thus, although crowded cities may cause lots of frustrations and other kinds of difficulties, the evidence seems to be that the crowding itself is not the cause of any negative responses.

Since these correlational studies are difficult to interpret, it is useful to look at a number of experiments that have been conducted on the same problem. The basic design of all of this research is to put people in either high- or low-density situations and observe their behavior. Naturally the period of time spent in the situation is relatively short, usually no more than a few hours although sometimes as much as twenty days. Nevertheless the evidence from these studies is helpful in determining how people respond to crowding.

The results indicate that high density is not an aversive situation nor does it operate as a simple stressor such as pain or hunger might. In a series of studies (Freedman, Klavansky, and Ehrlich, 1967), people under high- or low-density conditions performed a number of tasks ranging from very simple ones, such as crossing out all of the sevens on a page of random numbers, to much more complicated problems such as solving anagrams. If crowding were a stressor, it would be expected that it would have familiar effects on these kinds of tasks. It should improve performance on simple tasks and interfere with performance on more complicated tasks. Or if the stress were great enough, it might be expected to hurt all of the tasks. None of this happened. Instead there was absolutely no effect of density on performance. Subjects did as well under high-density conditions as they did under low-density on all of the tasks used. This held for several different subject populations and for many different tasks, strongly suggesting that high density is not a stressful situation in the normal sense of the word.

Other studies have shown that density does have complicated effects on emotional and social behavior. With interest in air-raid shelters, submarines, and spaceships, Smith and Haythorn (1971) confined men for periods of up to twenty days in either very small or considerably larger isolation chambers. There were either two or three men in each group. They report that there was actually less hostility and aggressiveness between the participants in the small than in the large room. In other words, in this instance, high density seemed to have positive effects. Perhaps the most interesting result of a long series of studies on isolation done by these experimenters is that in general men adapt very well to those conditions. They can live in very small quarters totally cut off from the outside world for fairly long periods of time without showing any negative effects. They continue to perform complicated tasks extremely well, their health is good, and their mental and psychological functions seemed fine. Although the situation may not be entirely pleasant, even the combination of isolation and high density does not produce particularly negative effects.

Other experiments have demonstrated that high density seems to intensify typical responses. In two experiments (Freedman et al., 1972), all-male or all-female groups were put in high- or low-density conditions and various measures were taken of their competitiveness and the severity of sentencing they gave in a mock jury situation. It was found that men tended to respond more competitively and to give more severe sentences in the high-density condition than they did in the low-density condition; while women were actually less competitive and gave milder sentences under conditions of high density. In addition the men in the group liked each other less under conditions of high than low density; and the women liked each other more under conditions of high density. A second series of studies, however, showed that this was not due to a difference in how the sexes respond to crowding, but rather a difference in how they responded to the social situation. Apparently the men saw the situation as threatening whereas the women saw it as fairly friendly. Since crowding seems to exaggerate the typical response, the men were more negative under crowded conditions but the women were more positive.

In a later study (Freedman, Heshka, and Levy, 1973) the pleasantness of the situation was explicitly varied. For some subjects the group interaction was inherently pleasant while for other subjects it was inherently unpleasant. Under these circumstances it was found that for all-male groups, all-female groups, and mixed sex groups the same pattern held—when the situation was pleasant, it was more pleasant under high-density conditions; when it was unpleasant, it was more unpleasant under high-density conditions. This would appear to be strong support for the notion that density serves as an intensifier of the typical social response rather than as a negative or positive factor itself.

There is as yet relatively little work done on this problem. Therefore although the statements we have made are based on all of the available research, they are still tentative. The main importance of this work is that it does begin to explore the response to one of the most important factors in modern civilization—the presence of vast numbers of other people. In addition the research seems to cast doubt on the generally held assumption that crowding is necessarily a negative factor. It is one more illustration of how important it is to base conclusions on careful observations and research rather than simply on intuition or experience, which can often be misleading.

## Personal Space

Closely related to the question of how crowding affects people is how people use and relate to the amount of space between them. Work by Hall (1959, etc.), Sommer (1969, etc.), and others has dealt with what Hall termed "personal space." You have probably noticed that when you are talking to somebody it is immediately apparent if he is standing "too close to you." If he is, you will probably back up to make the distance correct, and then you will feel more comfortable. Similarly, if you are standing "too far apart," you will move a little closer to make the distance correct. The appropriate distance between people varies according to the situation, the relationship between the people, what they are doing, and also for different ethnic groups. For any given set of conditions, however, there is one correct distance and anything further away or closer will make the person feel uncomfortable and he will do what he can to correct it.

The most consistent findings are that the closer the relationship and the friendlier the people feel, the closer they tend to stand. Friends, spouses, relatives, and lovers stand only a few feet or less from each other, while a typical distance for slight acquaintances might be three or four feet. An interesting implication of this relationship is that standing close to somebody tends to be an invitation to intimacy. At a cocktail party, a man will stand closer than usual to a woman to whom he is attracted, thus intentionally or perhaps unintentionally signalling that he would like to become more intimate with her. And if she is not interested in him, she may back up a few steps, thus increasing the distance to one that is more normal for casual acquaintances. On entering a room of strangers, one can often tell who is friendly with whom by noticing how far apart they stand. Assuming there is enough space in the room, the closer people stand, the closer their relationship or at least the closer they would like their relationship to be.

Standing too close to somebody can also be a threatening gesture. It can imply intimacy but also aggressiveness. Standing within the closest range of personal space violates the individual's safety zone and constitutes a threat. Verbal arguments that get out of hand sometimes end up with the two people standing face-to-face and yelling at each other. Even if they are talking softly, that position has strong elements of aggressiveness in it.

Naturally, the particular behavior and situation also affect the distance that people keep from each other. Informal or friendly surroundings tend to make people stand closer together than do formal, cold conditions. Similarly, a friendly, intimate conversation brings people closer together physically than a discussion involving business, asking directions, or any other less personal topic. A businessman who sits on one side of a desk and offers you a chair on the other side is maintaining a distance both physical and social between you and him. If he pulls his chair around to your side of the desk he is being warmer and more friendly. Much of this kind of behavior is not conscious or deliberate even though its implications are usually quite straightforward.

Perhaps the most interesting aspect of the use of personal space is that different nationalities have quite different preferences. Americans stand extremely far apart compared to most of the rest of the world. Europeans stand closer and South Americans closer still. This often produces misunderstandings and embarrassments. When an American and a Brazilian talk, the American feels that his toes are being stood on, that the Brazilian is constantly crowding too close to him—he feels threatened, perceives the Brazilian as being overly aggressive and forcing intimacy. In contrast, the Brazilian feels that the American is always backing away from him, that he is being unfriendly and cold. Thus, when they talk, they will tend to move slowly across the room, with the American always backing up, and the Brazilian always moving closer. This may have nothing to do with the warmth of their personalities, but simply with the meaning that is given to a particular distance in their respective cultures. What is considered too close for an American is considered just right for a Brazilian; and what is considered a cold, impersonal distance to a Brazilian is considered just right by an American. These kinds of differences in interpretation naturally occur in all sorts of behaviors by different ethnic groups, but the different use of personal space is particularly difficult to deal with because ordinarily it is an unconscious reaction to space with neither person being aware of exactly what is bothering him.

Research on personal space thus indicates that people do respond to the physical distance between them as an important stimulus in the social situation. Unfortunately, some authors have gone way beyond this and used the concept of personal space to explain responses to crowding, overpopulation, and even as evidence for innate feelings of territoriality. As we saw in the work on crowding, there is little evidence for any of that. The important point of the work on personal space is that all aspects of the social situation are attended to by the people involved, and something as simple as physical space can often be an important determinant of people's reactions and emotional responses. In addition, personal space can serve as a cue to another person of the individual's feelings about him and can be used to communicate desires for intimacy, aggressive feelings, and other personal reactions.

## NOISE

Just as it is the nature of a city to have a lot of people, it is impossible to imagine a city that is not noisy. Almost by definition a city creates a great deal of noise. The people, the cars, the machines all produce noise, and there are of course a great many of them. When a city is quiet, as it sometimes is very early in the morning when no one is up yet, it has an eerie almost unreal quality. The city is asleep; it is not functioning because when it does there is noise. And the noise levels can be exceedingly high. A quiet room might have 30 or 40 decibels of noise; a noisy room might have 50 or 60; whereas the noise level on the streets of New York or Tokyo is 80, 90, or even 100 decibels, with peaks reaching much higher than that. On some of the noisy corners in Tokyo and Kyoto there are meters that tell the noise level in large electric lights. As one watches they indicate that the cars, trains, and pedestrians are creating an average noise level well above 90 decibels. To give some idea of how loud that is, if you are walking next to somebody it is extremely difficult to hear what he is saying unless he practically shouts at you. Around Columbia University, trucks rumble by on Amsterdam Avenue. Pedestrians have grown accustomed to interrupting their conversations until the truck passes because it is literally impossible to hear what the other person is saying unless he shouts in your ear. And of course we must not forget that classic instance of urbanization, the New York subway. There are those who would say that the screeching of the wheels is even more unpleasant than the heat and crowding that one experiences during rush hour. Clearly cities have noise and lots of it, but what effect does it have on the people living there?

Although, as we shall see, the answer is somewhat complicated, the most striking result of research on this problem is that people cope remarkably well with noise just as they do with crowding. Human beings appear to have almost endless capacity to adapt to various kinds of stress in the environment. People will tell you that loud noises are unpleasant and irritating; they will choose to be in a quiet environment rather than a noisy one; and yet when they are exposed to loud noise, it has relatively little effect on their behavior.

Initially, there are both physiological and behavioral effects of loud noise: galvanic skin response and other measures indicate that people do respond more to loud than soft noises. Similarly performance on various kinds of tasks is interfered with by very loud noise. But the important finding is that these effects are transitory. They appear at the beginning of exposure to the noise and quickly disappear. People adapt to the noise and, at least on these measures, it no longer bothers them. Their performance goes back to normal as does their physiological response. In a study by Glass and Singer (1972), subjects were exposed to 108-decibel noise at the rate of nine seconds per minute for 23 minutes. This is an extremely loud noise—not quite physically painful but approaching that level. After a little more than three minutes of noise spread over the 23-minute period, the physiological response of subjects receiving the noise was virtually identical to those who heard no noise at all. Adaptation was almost perfect even to this level of noise.

Although people are remarkably good at dealing with and adapting to noise, this does not mean that they are totally unaffected by loud noises. Performance on certain types of tasks is interfered with by extremely loud noise. Once they have adapted to the noise, people can perform simple tasks just as well as they can when there is no noise present. For example they can do simple problems in addition; they can compare pairs of numbers (e.g., 45126 and 45326) and decide whether they are the same or different; they can look through a list of words and pick out all of those containing a's; and so on. It also seems that even quite complex tasks such as reading difficult material, performing complicated problems in mathematics, solving anagrams, etc., are not affected by loud noise.

In contrast, tasks that require constant, careful monitoring are. If someone is put in front of a series of dials, told to watch all of them and report whenever one gets above a certain level, loud noise interferes with his performance. This may seem like a somewhat strange task, but actually it is similar to that performed by pilots, engineers, and other people who control complicated machinery. In addition, someone who is trying to perform two tasks at once finds that loud noise interferes with performance. For example, in a study by Finkelman and Glass (1970) subjects were given the primary task of tracking a line by moving a steering wheel. A secondary task on which less emphasis was placed involved repeating digits that they had heard. The primary task was totally unaffected by the level of noise, but the secondary task was performed less well when there was loud noise. Thus even though people are extremely adaptable to noise and are affected much less than we might have expected, certain kinds of performance are impaired by very high levels of noise.

**The Costs of Adaptation.** A series of studies by Glass and Singer (1972) has revealed that the story is even more complicated. They found, as have many others, that people adapt easily to loud noises. However, they did not stop there. They further questioned whether there were any effects of this adaptation process. Yes, people can adapt to noise, but what does this do to them? In a fascinating series of experiments they found that costs may be involved in adaptation—it may require effort or energy which under some circumstances seems to produce a decrement in performance after the noise ceases. Even when subjects adapt well to the noise and perform perfectly, once the noise is no longer present they seem to do less well on tasks than they would have if they had not been exposed to noise in the first place.

In one study subjects were exposed to extremely loud noise (108 decibels), moderate noise, or no noise at all. As might be expected the participants rated the loud noise as more irritating, more unpleasant, and more distracting. Despite this their performance was equally good whether there was loud noise, moderate noise, or no noise at all. Afterwards they were given two other tasks—one involving graphic puzzles that were either difficult or impossible to solve, and the other involving proofreading. On these tasks those subjects who had been exposed to loud noise did less well than those who had heard either moderate or no noise. This result appears to be highly consistent and seems to indicate that exposure to very loud noise does in some way exhaust the subject so that he is less able to work later on. During the noise he can gather his energy and manage to perform successfully, but once the need for concentration is removed, his tiredness shows up in terms of impaired performance.

**Predictability and Control.**   Glass and Singer also found that loud noise had these negative effects only under certain circumstances. When the noise occurred at unpredictable times and was not in any way under the control of the subject, the performance decrements occurred. However if the subject knew when the noise was going to occur or felt in any way that he could control the noise, he performed just as well as if there were no noise at all.

The predictability and control over the noise were varied in a number of different ways. In some experiments subjects heard either nine-second noise bursts that occurred exactly a minute apart for 23 minutes or noise bursts of varying lengths that occurred at random times during the 23 minutes. The same total amount of noise was heard by all of the subjects. Although the physiological responses and performance during the noise were the same for the predictable and unpredictable conditions, only the unpredictable noise produced a decrement in performance on tasks that were given after the noise periods. difference in the effect occurred despite the fact that subjects rated the predictable and unpredictable noises equally irritating, distracting, and unpleasant. In other words, the subjects did not perceive the predictable noise as causing less discomfort or disruption, but it did in fact interfere with performance less than the unpredictable noise. In other studies the noise was signalled by a light in some conditions and not signalled in others, with the performance decrement occurring only when the noise was unsignalled.

Perceived control over the noise also seems to eliminate its negative effects. Subjects were given a button which they were told would stop the noise if it was pressed. In another study subjects were told that their partner had such a button and they could signal him if they wanted him to press it and stop the noise. Even when the subjects did not press the button or signal their partner, simply having available the possibility of controlling the noise prevented the performance decrement.

This body of research thus has produced three major findings: (1) Noise has surprisingly little effect on people's behavior. Their physiological responses adapt very quickly and performance on most tasks is unaffected. There is some decrement in performance on tasks requiring constant vigilance and on secondary tasks when a subject is paying primary attention to another task. (2) Although performance during the noise is relatively unaffected, having experienced the noise does seem to interfere with tasks given after the noise is terminated. Subjects appear to be less able to perform these tasks than they would have been if they had not been exposed to noise in the first place. (3) But this decrement in performance occurs only when the noise is unpredictable and uncontrollable. If the subject knows when the noise is going to occur or can control it himself, no such decrements occur. This suggests that people are exceedingly adaptable, that they can endure seemingly stressful situations without being negatively affected, and that what negative effects do occur seem to be dependent on psychological factors such as perceived control more than on the actual intensity of the aversive stimulus.

All of this does not mean that we can ignore the noise in the cities. Most people still experience it as unpleasant and would prefer a quieter environment. The loud noise is stressful and can interfere with some kinds of behaviors. More to the point, most of the loud noise is unpredictable (you never know when a car is going to backfire or a truck is going to rumble by) and largely out of our control. Therefore urban noise meets the criteria for producing the maximum negative effects. However, this research does indicate that the negative effects will be relatively mild compared to what we might have expected. People do adapt extremely well to loud noise and much of the time probably do not even notice that they are living in a noisy environment. Obviously people are able to perform very complex jobs despite the noise—otherwise the cities would long since have perished. Thus we should not be surprised that people in the city do continue to function reasonably well despite the exceedingly high levels of noise and, as described earlier, despite the very high levels of population density. The effects of these variables may under some circumstances be negative but, by and large, the adaptability of human beings overcomes even severely aversive stimulation. This is not to say that people are unaffected by their environment, but only that the psychological factors are probably more important than the actual physical situation.

## CHAPTER REVIEW

1. Population pressures and urban society.
2. Density distinguished from population.
3. No overall negative effects of high density.
4. Density as an intensifier.
5. "Correct" distances.
6. Ethnic differences in personal space.
7. Adaptation to noise.
8. Predictability and control as key factors.

### APPLICATIONS AND SPECULATIONS

1. If crowding does not have generally negative effects on people, what does this suggest for planning new housing in urban areas? Does it mean we should encourage as high densities as possible, or are there other considerations?
2. Density seems to intensify typical reactions. Can you think of examples of high density situations that are more positive than they might be if the density were lower? Can you think of counter-examples in which the social interactions are positive but are made less so by high density.
3. If noise has such slight negative effects, why does every one complain about it? Does this say anything about the usefulness of self-reports?

### SUGGESTIONS FOR ADDITIONAL READING

#### Articles

Calhoun, J. B. Population density and social pathology. *Scientific American*, 1962, *206*, 139–48.

Freedman, J. L., Levy, A. S., Buchanan, R. W., and Price, J. Crowding and human aggressiveness. *Journal of Experimental Social Psychology*, 1972, *8*, 528–48.

Winsborough, H. H. The social consequences of high population density. *Law and Contemporary Problems*, 1965, *30*, 120–26.

*Books and Longer Discussions*

Freedman, J. L. The effects of population density on humans. In J. Fawcett (Ed.), *Psychological Perspectives on Population*. New York: Basic Books, 1973. Pp. 209–38.

Glass, D. C. and Singer, J. E. *Urban Stress*. New York: Academic ress, 1972.

Jacobs, J. *The death and life of great American cities*. New York: Random House, 1961.

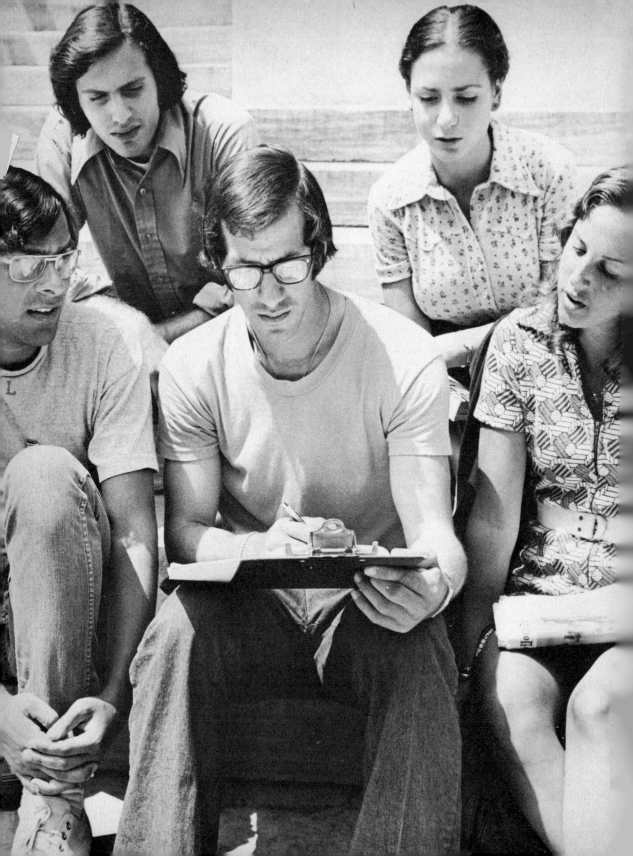

# fourteen

# methodology

In many respects research methods in social psychology are similar to those in any other field of science. However, just as in other fields, research in social psychology poses certain problems and involves certain procedures that are more or less unique to it. In this chapter, we shall first discuss general aspects of methodology and then shall concentrate on problems that are particularly important in social psychology.

**TYPES OF RESEARCH**

All research begins with a question. A scientist is interested in a problem and tries to answer it. Since the questions that are asked differ in their relationship to a theory and in their specificity, there are essentially three types of research: research testing a specific hypothesis from a theory, research testing a specific hypothesis not related to an organized theory, and research not testing a specific hypothesis. The first type begins with a formal theory from which hypotheses are derived, and the research is designed to see if the hypothesis is correct and to test the theory. For example, Festinger and Carlsmith (1959) deduced from the theory of cognitive dissonance the hypothesis that the larger the incentive for performing a discrepant act, the less the dissonance and the less attitude change that should occur. In contrast, a specific hypothesis may not be tied to a particular theory—it may be suggested by previous research, observations, or just intuition. Schachter (1959) was interested in affiliation, read studies on isolation, thought about the problem, and formulated the hypothesis that high fear increases affiliation. Although he had some rationale for this idea, it was not derived from a theory.

Other research does not begin with a specific hypothesis but with broader, less specific questions: What factors affect affiliation? What differences in persuasibility are attributable to personality? What is the effect of bringing whites and blacks into closer contact? The investigator knows what he is interested in, but he has no clear idea what he is going to find out. Rather than being designed to test a particular hypoth-

434

esis, this type of research is designed to collect as much information as possible about the variable or variables involved. It is usually called *empirical,* as opposed to *hypothesis-testing, research.*

The three approaches are all valuable, but differ somewhat in their aims. The major goal of theory-related research is to evaluate the theory —to determine whether it makes accurate predictions, whether it has limitations, whether it is correct. The prediction in the Festinger and Carlsmith study was that paying subjects $20 would result in less attitude change than paying them $1. If the results were in line with this prediction, the theory would be supported and we would be that much more confident that it is correct. If the results showed the opposite effect or no difference between the two conditions, the theory would not be supported and we would question its accuracy.

The second type of research is similar in form and purpose to theory-related research. It involves a specific hypothesis whose validity we want to test. Positive results confirm it; negative results do not. The major difference is that the findings are not relevant to a broad theoretical framework.

Empirical research is quite different. Instead of asking a specific question, the experimenter is interested in a variable, such as fear, or a particular phenomenon, such as persuasibility. He usually has no clear hypothesis as to the effect of the variable or the specific factors that affect the phenomenon. Empirical research, therefore, is not designed to see if a specific hypothesis is correct but rather to gather information about the variable or phenomenon in question. The major difference between empirical and hypothesis-testing research is that empirical work tends to deal with many variables at once and to have many dependent measures in order to collect more data on the general problem. For example, an experiment designed to study the factors that affect persuasibility would have the subjects take a comprehensive personality test; would obtain information on demographic characteristics such as age, sex, and birth order; and might also vary the level of fear and the sex of the communicator. Then, the experimenter would examine all the data to see if any relationships appeared. Of course, the variables are not selected entirely at random. The experimenter has some ideas about what might be important—for example, he could assume that age, sex, and self-esteem were more likely to be related to persuasibility than blood type or the number of vowels in a subject's last name. He would study some variables and not others, but he would try to collect as much information as he could.

A major difference between theoretical and the other two types of research is in the likelihood of finding positive results, that is, a relationship between the variables or an effect of the experimental conditions. A study testing a deduction from a theory is relatively likely to produce such results. All theories are explanations of an organized body of data. This means that predictions from a theory are based in part on previous findings. Of course, the better established the theory, the more probable it is that its predictions will be supported. Nontheoretical research varies in the extent to which it is based on other research, but it tends to be less so than theoretical research. It is based, not on a theory, but on someone's hunch or intuition and is therefore less likely to produce positive results. On the other hand, when it does, there is a big payoff—it may discover unexpected new relationships that open up important new areas of study.

Another difference between the types of research is the significance of negative results (the lack of difference between conditions or lack of relationship between variables). In theoretical research, negative results (e.g., the amount of payment for performing a discrepant act has no effect on the amount of attitude change) are very important. Since the theory predicts a difference, the lack of one constitutes nonsupport for the theory. In nontheoretical research—hypothesis-testing or empirical —negative results have relatively little meaning. They do not tell us anything about an existing body of facts. The study was based on someone's hunch, so all that negative results tell us is that one person was wrong or that a particular variable is not related to some other variable in this particular situation. Thus, theoretical research has a high likelihood of payoff, because positive results are probable and even negative ones are useful and the payoff is primarily in terms of supporting or not supporting an existing theory. In contrast, nontheoretical research has a relatively low chance of payoff, because positive results are less likely and negative ones have little meaning; but when there is a payoff, it is often a big one because it may constitute a discovery.

In general, hypothesis testing (theory-related or otherwise) is most effective when a body of information is already available on a subject, and the empirical approach is most effective when the area is one about which very little is known. Testing hypotheses is a systematic way of adding to the available knowledge and validating the theories that tie it together; empirical research is a way of collecting a lot of information quickly but in a relatively unsystematic way that does not lend itself to efficient theory building. Both approaches have their place in social psychology, although there seems to be a feeling in the field (not shared by the present authors) that empirical research is somehow less worthy than hypothesis testing.

Another major difference between types of research is the extent to which the experimenter is interestd in a particular concrete situation. Both theoretical and empirical research may or may not be focused on a situation that actually exists in the real world. For example, the effect of fear arousal on attitude change can be investigated from a theoretical point of view (e.g., learning theory) or without any theory. Regardless of the theoretical position or lack of it, the research can deal with a specific issue or can be concerned only with the general question. An experimenter in this field may concentrate all his work on the question of whether high fear increases the effect of antismoking campaigns. He is interested in the effects of fear on attitude change, but he is focusing on attitudes toward smoking. Perhaps arousing fear will have different effects on other kinds of attitudes, or perhaps the levels of fear aroused will work differently with other issues. For the moment, he wants to find out how to change attitudes toward smoking. The research may have applications to the general question of how fear affects attitude change, but that is not his primary concern.

In contrast, the investigator may not be interested in any particular attitude, but only in the general question of how fear affects attitude change. With this starting point, he will use many different issues and situations in order to make his finding as general as possible. His results may not be especially applicable to attitudes toward smoking except in the broadest sense. That is, his most general findings will of course apply to all attitudes, but he will probably not be able to specify the exact levels of fear that will produce the most change in attitudes toward smoking.

Work that focuses on a particular situation has usually been referred to as applied research while the other has been called basic research. Unfortunately, "applied" research has acquired somewhat negative connotations in the United States. For many years most of the prestige and status went to those who conducted basic research and were, by and large, uninterested in specific problems. This was not only unfair, but also tended to make an unrealistic distinction between the two approaches. Actually, basic research usually grows out of a concern with existing problems and must necessarily deal with particular issues. Thus, the fear arousal literature has tended to focus on issues related to health even though at least some of the experimenters chose these for convenience rather than because they were interested in these particular questions.

Since some kind of issue must be chosen, it seems reasonable to expect an experimenter to choose issues of general concern whenever possible. When studying the effects of fear arousal, it would be desirable for the experimenter to pick an issue with which society is concerned— smoking or cancer or safe driving—rather than issues of little importance such as whether teeth should be brushed up and down or sideways. Naturally the basic researcher will want to pick issues that fit his research design as well as possible, but with that one restriction, he should try to pick issues that are important in their own right. Similarly, the person who is going to focus his research on a particular issue, such as smoking, can try to design his experiments so that the findings will have as general an application as possible. He should try to relate the research to previous work, and whenever possible design the study so that it will test propositions that have been suggested by other results. In this way, basic and applied psychologists can complement each other, working back and forth between specific issues and more general propositions and, hopefully, progress in the field can be accelerated.

**METHODS OF RESEARCH** Regardless of how research begins, the next step is to decide what method is to be used. There are two basic varieties—correlational and experimental—each of which has advantages and disadvantages. As we shall see, which type is preferable depends largely on the problem being studied and the goals of the experimenter.

### Correlation Research

Correlational research consists of observing the relationship between two or more variables. It asks the question, when variable A is high, is B also high (a positive correlation), is B low (a negative correlation), or is B's value unrelated (no correlation)? For example, in studying fear and affiliation, one could look at some people who are afraid and some who are not afraid and see how much each group affiliates. One might compare people in wartime with people in peacetime, or Londoners during a bombing raid and afterward. One might observe people during an air raid and compare those who show a lot of fear with those who show very little. If it turned out that the people experiencing a lot of fear tended to affiliate more than those showing less fear, one could report that high fear was correlated with affiliation.

A correlational study is an efficient way of collecting a large amount of data about a problem area. For example, we could collect thirty personality variables about a large number of people and twenty different measures of behavior. Then we could see which personality factors correlate with which behaviors. In this way, we can discover a large number of relationships and interrelationships in a relatively short time. In contrast, it would take many experimental studies to investigate the effect of each personality factor on each behavior. For this reason correlational studies are often used in empirical research; they make possible the efficient collection of large amounts of data.

Correlational techniques also sometimes enable us to study problems to which experimental methods may not be applicable. For example, much of the research on the effects of crowding on people has involved correlations. It is impossible experimentally to place individuals in high density situations for very long periods of time. Since being in a crowded situation for ten years might produce very different effects from being in it for only four hours or even twenty days, the experimental work, although useful, is limited. Therefore investigators turned to statistics that had been collected in actual situations. Data on the population density of various cities and parts of cities were available, as were data on crime and mental illness committed in those areas. By correlating measures of density with measures of crime and mental illness, it was possible to get some indication of the relationship between density and pathology. Naturally this had all of the difficulties of correlational studies, particularly the problem of making causative statements and ruling out other variables such as income; but it had the great advantage of providing some evidence on the effects of density over much longer periods of time than would have been possible in an experimental design.

**Disadvantages.**    The major weakness of correlational studies is that they leave the cause and effect relationship ambiguous. If a  study indicates that people who are more afraid affiliate more than those who are less afraid, this does not necessarily mean that high fear leads to greater affiliation. It may be that affiliating increases fear rather than the other way around. Those who affiliate tend to get frightened; those who do not affiliate become less frightened; therefore we find a relationship between affiliation and fear. In other words, the direction of causality (does fear lead to affiliation or does affiliation lead to fear) is unknown.

This is not always a serious drawback in a correlational study. In many cases we can be fairly certain of the direction of causation. The science of astronomy is based virtually entirely on correlations and yet there is little doubt about most of the directions of causality. When the moon is in particular positions, there are high tides on earth. We assume that the moon is causing the high tides rather than the high tides causing the moon to be in that position. First borns who are anxious affiliate more than later borns. Obviously, if there is any causal relationship between these two factors, it must be birth order causing greater affiliation—not the other way around. No matter how much you affiliate as an adult, it cannot affect the order of your birth.

An even more serious ambiguity than the direction of causality is the possibility, in all correlational studies, that neither variable is directly affecting the other—rather that some other unspecified factor is affecting both of them. When we find that people who are very frightened affiliate more than those who are less frightened, there is always the chance that these two groups of people differ in more ways than their amount of fear. People who frighten easily may be weaker, more dependent, younger, less intelligent, or more other-directed than those who frighten less easily. If frightened people are generally weaker than those less frightened, this weakness could explain their greater affiliation. They are weak, need protection more, and therefore affiliate more in order to get protection.

Any of the other factors could also cause the greater affiliation in a high-fear subject, and we can never be certain. We have divided the subjects in terms of the amount of fear that they felt and then looked at their affiliation. We would like to say that the greater fear is producing the greater affiliation. Even if we are certain that the direction of causality is correct, however, we cannot be certain that it is the fear that is producing the effect. It might be weakness or some other factor that goes along with fear, rather than the fear itself. All that we have discovered is that fear and affiliation are related, that they go together, but we do not know if it is the fear that is important or some entirely different factor that is correlated with both fear and affiliation.

This problem of attributing causation is even more obvious in the research on the relationship between crowding and crime in the cities. As we mentioned, the finding is that there is a substantial correlation between the two—higher densities being associated with higher crime rates. But what does this mean? One possibility, of course, is that crowding causes crime. Another possibility—the opposite—is that crime causes high density. Choosing between these is not too difficult in this case. *If one causes the other,* it is more plausible that living under high density conditions makes people commit crimes than it is that people move into areas because there is a lot of crime there.

However, it is even more likely that neither relationship is correct and that some other factor is producing the correlation. Crowding is strongly associated with income level—poor people tend to live under more crowded conditions than do rich people. Crime is also strongly associated with income level, with poor people committing more crimes. Now we can see that the relationship between crowding and crime may be due entirely to the fact that both of them are associated with income level. Poor people live in high density areas and commit more crimes. Therefore despite the correlation between density and crime, density itself may have no effect on crime rate.

### Experimental Research

In the experimental method, conditions having different levels of a factor (the independent variable) are produced by the investigator or some external force, subjects are randomly assigned to the conditions, and some dependent variable is measured. If we are interested in factors that affect affiliation, we select one such factor and deliberately vary it in an experiment. Suppose we want to know whether fear increases affiliation. To study this, we want to have two groups of subjects who are identical in every respect except their amount of fear. If they differ in any other way, we cannot be certain the degree of affiliation is due to the different levels of fear—it might be due to other differences. As explained above, if one group is more afraid and also weaker, there is no way to be certain which factor is causing the increased affiliation. On the other hand, if the groups do not differ in anything except their level of fear, any difference must be attributed to greater fear.

A crucial problem, then, is to be sure that the subjects differ only in terms of the variable being studied. They must, as far as possible, be identical when they enter the experiment. This is accomplished by _randomly_ assigning the subjects to experimental conditions, by deciding entirely by chance which experimental condition to put them in. Random assignment can be achieved by flipping a coin, by cutting a deck of cards, or ideally, by using a random number table, which guarantees that the choice is entirely by chance.

The basic idea behind random assignment is that nothing the subject brings with him to the experimental situation should determine which group he is in. This determination is made by the experimenter, and he makes it purely on a chance basis. If the subjects were assigned to conditions on any basis other than this, the groups might differ in some way unrelated to the experimental procedures. For example, we might ask subjects to choose between high- and low-shock conditions and perhaps pay them enough extra for the high-shock condition so that some would choose it. If we did this, however, it is likely that subjects who chose high shock would be different from those who chose low shock. The former subjects would probably be less afraid of shocks, perhaps more concerned about money or whatever incentive was offered, and so on. They might also be more suggestible, since they were more willing to do what the experimenter wanted them to do. Any of these factors could, by itself, produce a difference in affiliation. Although no experimenter would use this assignment procedure, this kind of selection often occurs in natural situations and introduces ambiguity into correlational research. People who sky dive experience more fear than people whose favorite sport is tennis. We might observe how much these two groups affiliate in order to study the effect of fear on affiliation. But obviously people who choose to sky dive, who have selected a risky, frightening sport, are different from those who choose tennis. Thus, a correlational study comparing sky divers and tennis players in their amount of affiliation would have the disadvantage that the groups probably differ in ways other than fear. The experimental method avoids this through random assignment.

Similar problems occur if subjects are assigned to conditions on the basis of something they do or some attribute they have, even if they do not choose the condition themselves. We would not assign subjects who arrive early to one condition and those who arrive late to another, or even subjects who sign up on weekdays to one and weekend subjects to another. We do not know how these groups differ, but the possibility exists that they do—and any experimental results might be due to that difference.

As one more example of how not to assign subjects to conditions, it would be incorrect to put subjects who understand the instructions in one condition and those who do not understand them in another. This is a tempting method of assignment, because often one condition is more complicated than another and we would like to be certain that everyone understands the instructions. But obviously, the groups would then differ in intelligence or interest in the proceedings, and such differences might affect the results.

It can also happen that subjects are randomly assigned, but some subjects do not understand the instructions and must be eliminated from the study. If the instructions in one condition are more difficult and more subjects in that condition do not understand them and are therefore eliminated, there is no longer random assignment. There has been some self-selection—the less bright subjects in the difficult condition have decided (not intentionally, perhaps, but just as surely) not to participate. Thus, the other condition, in which even the less bright had no difficulty with the instructions, has on the average less bright subjects. Any time something a subject does or an attribute of his determines his condition in a study, random assignment has been lost.

One way of conceptualizing random assignment is that before an experiment begins, no one can specify any characteristic on which the subjects in one condition differ from those in another. They are, as far as anyone can tell, identical, except that some have been put in one condition and some in another. When assignment has been random, we can be certain within the confidence limits established by statistical tests that the two groups do not differ in any systematic way. Any differences between the two groups in, say, intelligence would be due entirely to chance. There is a possibility that one group would be more intelligent on the average than another group. But the likelihood of this happening has been well established by statisticians, and the statistical tests we conduct on the results obtained are based on the likelihood of differences occurring by chance, If, for example, we find that a high-fear group affiliates more than a low-fear group, we ask the question: What is the likelihood that this would have happened by chance? This means, what is the likelihood that we assigned more affiliative people to one group than another? We apply a statistical test to the difference so that we state exactly what that chance is. We might find that only one time in a hundred would the two groups have differed that much simply by chance. This makes us believe that the results are probably due to our experimental manipulation. Thus, as long as we are certain that the subjects have been randomly assigned to conditions and that the experimental manipulation differed only in the way we intended (e.g., one produced high fear and the other produced low fear), we can be confident that the differences that appear are due to the manipulation and not some unknown factor. This ability to specify the particular aspect of the situation that produced an effect is the major advantage of the experimental method.

The major limitations of experimental research derive from difficulties involving the independent variable. Experiments tend to involve a restricted range of a variable, because it is difficult to produce strong emotions or to expose subjects to extreme conditions. Some subjects can be made more afraid than others, but none of them will be terrified. We shall discuss the difficulties involved in the manipulation of the independent variable in more detail below. For the moment, the point is that we are restricted in the kinds of procedures we can use and, therefore, in the strength of a variable we can produce.

The experimental method is generally not applicable to a study of the effects of natural occurrences. Air raids, floods, surgery do not strike people entirely randomly, and therefore subjects are not assigned randomly to conditions. Sometimes there appears to be a high degree of chance in whom such occurrences affect and randomness might be approximated, but it is never perfect. Thus, any findings are correlational rather than experimental.

Finally, experiments are relatively inefficient for collecting large amounts of data on many variables. Since each factor must be produced by the experimenter, he is usually limited to one or two factors at a time. He could certainly not vary twenty factors at once as is often done in correlational studies.

Correlational and experimental work complement each other. There are many cases in which both methods are useful. In general, correlational studies are particularly effective in the collection of large amounts of data; they provide us with ideas and hypotheses, which can then be studied in more detail experimentally.

Since the experimental method allows us to conclude that a particular variable is the cause of a particular effect, it enables us to test a hypothesis about how one variable affects another. It is therefore useful primarily in testing such hypotheses, in pinning down and specifying in detail relationships between variables, and in providing us with explanations of such relationships. For example, during wartime, people tend to cluster together more than during peace. This might suggest that fear leads to affiliation. But the greater affiliation might be due to other factors. Note that the greatest clustering occurs in air raid shelters, which are naturally small and which people occupy, not to be together, but to be safe from bombs. The bombs make the people afraid, so they go to bomb shelters—which are invariably crowded. Perhaps they would prefer to be alone and safe rather than with others and safe, but since the shelters are crowded, they have no choice. The suggestion that fear leads to affiliation must accordingly be tested in more controlled situations—in an experiment in which two or more levels of fear are produced and affiliation measured. In other words, correlational work can produce data on which a hypothesis is founded, and experimental work can test the hypothesis.

## FIELD AND LABORATORY RESEARCH

The next step in the research is to decide where it should be done. Although most research in social psychology during the last ten or fifteen years has been conducted in the laboratory, there has always been some conducted in the field and the amount of field research now seems to be increasing. Both experimental and correlational research can be done in either the laboratory or the field and each setting has advantages and disadvantages.

### Field Research

**Advantages.** Research in the field tends to deal with real people in real situations, as opposed to experimental subjects in relatively unreal situations in the laboratory. Accordingly, field research tends to minimize suspicion, so the subjects' responses are more spontaneous and less susceptible to the kinds of bias that suspicion produces.

The researcher in the field can often collect data from types of people who cannot be attracted to an experimental laboratory. It has often been said that American social psychology is based on college sophomores, because they are the ones who are most available for experiments in laboratories. Field research can collect data from a wider variety of subjects and thus adds to the generality of the findings.

Another advantage of work in the field is that we are sometimes able to deal with extremely powerful variables and situations that could not be studied in the laboratory. This is particularly true of correlational work because experimental field work is limited by the same kinds of factors that limit it in the laboratory. But with correlational work, we can, as mentioned previously, observe people in extreme situations—when they are waiting to be operated on in a hospital or huddled together in an air raid shelter. This advantage sometimes applies to field experiments when the manipulation is done not by the experimenter but by some natural event that just happens to affect people randomly and therefore fits the criterion of an experiment.

**Disadvantages.** The major disadvantages of field research stem from the lack of control over the situation. It is generally extremely difficult to assign subjects to conditions randomly, to be certain that they are all experiencing the same thing, to get accurate measures on the dependent variable, and so on. A great many random events and conditions enter into a field study and often obscure the effects of the variables in which we are interested.

In particular, it is difficult to find pure manipulations of the independent variable and pure measures of the dependent variable. The experimenter must find or arrange circumstances that produce specific differences—and no others—between conditions. Even if he could find a situation that would, for example, produce two levels of fear, it is exceedingly difficult to be certain that the two conditions do not differ in other ways. In the laboratory he could design a pure procedure that would accomplish this; in the field it is much more difficult. If subjects have been randomly assigned to conditions, the experimenter can conclude that any difference in their behavior is due to the experimental manipulation. But if that manipulation is not pure (e.g., not just differences in fear), the interpretation of the effect is ambiguous. Yes, it is due to the manipulation, but does that mean it is due to fear or to some other variable? Similarly, measurement of the dependent variable is often elusive in the field. The experimenter must not only produce differences in fear, he must also obtain a measure of affiliation in the same setting. If he finds an ideal independent manipulation, it is highly unlikely that it would be accompanied by a convenient method of assessing its effect.

With sufficient ingenuity and hard work, it is sometimes possible to find or arrange appropriate situations, but they are few and far between. The world is generally not set up to facilitate the study of a specific problem that happens to occur to a psychologist. He may, therefore, find that field research does not lend itself to the problem in which he is interested.

### Laboratory Research

**Advantages.** The advantages and disadvantages of laboratory research are mirror images of those of field research. The major advantage of work in the laboratory is the control over the situation that it affords. The experimenter can be quite certain what is happening to each subject; if he is doing experimental work, he can randomly assign the subjects;

he can subject them to the exact experiences necessary to study the problem; he can minimize extraneous factors and go a long way to eliminate random variations in the procedure. Even when variations do occur, he can at least be reasonably certain that he knows exactly what happened. Similarly, he has great control over the dependent variable and can measure it in considerably more detail and in a more uniform manner than he generally could in the field. Therefore the laboratory is the ideal place in which to set up a situation that is designed to study a specific problem.

**Disadvantages.** The problems with laboratory work center around two aspects of the situation—the fact that the subject knows he is being studied and the limitations on the kinds of manipulations that can be used. Whenever someone knows he is a subject in an experiment, there is always the possibility that he is not behaving naturally or spontaneously, that he is trying to please or displease the experimenter, that he is behaving in the way he thinks he should, that he is not accepting the experimental manipulation because he is distrustful, and so on. Any of these effects could produce bias in the results or obscure relationships and effects that actually exist. Although there are ways of minimizing these problems, as we shall discuss in detail below, they always exist to some extent.

Limitations on the kinds of manipulations that can be used mean that laboratory research usually deals with low or moderate levels of variables. The subject cannot be terrified; he cannot be made terribly sad; he cannot be made hysterical with laughter. In most cases this simply means that the effects are less strong than they would be if the variables were more extreme but that the basic relationships are the same. However, it is a serious weakness when there is reason to believe that high levels of a variable would produce different effects from intermediate ones. In the work on the relationship between fear and attitude change, for example, it has been suggested that very high levels of fear would interfere with attitude change, whereas lower levels increase change. Since laboratory work never deals with extremely high levels of fear, this possibility has never been adequately tested. In most cases, however, the main problem created by this limitation is that it makes it more difficult to find the effect of a variable even though the effect exists.

A relatively minor disadvantage, which was mentioned previously, is that laboratory work tends to deal with a limited population of subjects. The vast majority of laboratory studies involve college students or perhaps students at a university nursery school. This problem is not inherent in the laboratory method. With sufficient ingenuity and a little hard work, it should be possible to attract a wide range of subjects to experimental laboratories, particularly if the laboratories are not located on college campuses. Perhaps anyone who agrees to take part in a psychological study is unrepresentative of the white population. But psychologists can, at least, try to employ a wide variety of subjects.

It is true that field and laboratory research tend to differ in the ways we have described, but to a large extent these differences have been exaggerated in discussions of the relative advantages of the two techniques. It is possible to obtain considerable control of variables outside the laboratory and it is possible to make laboratory situations extremely realistic. The study on the foot-in-the-door technique discussed in Chapter 12 demonstrates that under appropriate circumstances, field situations allow as much control as laboratory studies. In that study housewives were randomly assigned to conditions, an experimenter went from door to door manipulating the independent variable, and a second experimenter obtained a dependent measure. There was tight control over the manipulation, no haphazardness in the random assignment, and an unambiguous dependent measure. From the point of view of control, the study was as good as most studies conducted in the laboratory. It would probably have been set up differently in a laboratory, but that would not have provided any additional controls over either the independent or dependent variables.

Similarly, laboratory settings can often be exceedingly realistic. The subjects in the Carlsmith and Gross study, who delivered electric shocks to their partners and were then asked to work for the Save-the-Redwoods campaign, were in a realistic situation as far as they were concerned. True, they were in an experiment during the shock part of the study, but nevertheless they were delivering electric shocks and presumably feeling guilty because of it. Then, after the experiment was over (in their view), they were asked to do a favor for the person whom they had shocked. This request and the subsequent compliance were as realistic as anything that could take place in the field.

The basic issue is not where the experiment takes place but how realistic it is. If the subject knows he is in an experiment and thinks the request is part of the experiment, there tends to be a loss of realism. He would probably wonder why the request was being made and would worry about its significance. If, on the other hand, the request is made outside the experimental situation (regardless whether in the field or in the laboratory), the subjects should not be suspicious, the situation should be realistic for them, and the data obtained should not suffer from lack of naturalness on their part. Field studies tend to be more realistic and easier to make realistic than laboratory studies, but the distinction is one of degree. The important distinction is between realistic and nonrealistic studies, and realism can be produced either in the field or in the laboratory.

### Archive and Cross-Cultural Studies

Two other kinds of research might be mentioned, although they are in a sense special cases of the field and laboratory types. The first is the so-called archive study, in which the investigator does not collect the data himself but uses data that are already available in published records. In most cases this is actually a kind of field study with the main difference being that someone else has done the hard work. An example of the use of archives is the study, described in Chapter 4, on the relationship between cotton prices and lynchings in the South. The investigators started with the hypothesis that frustration leads to aggression and then argued that a drop in cotton prices would produce frustrations, which would, in turn, produce an increase in aggression in the form of lynchings. The data an cotton prices and on the number of lynchings were readily available in statistics collected by the United States government and others, and the investigators simply looked up these data and ran correlations between the two variables. Similarly, the studies of the relationship between population density and crime relied entirely on data that were already available.

Since there is rarely any random assignment of subjects to experimental conditions, archive work is almost always correlational—but it can be very informative. The major problem with using archives is the difficulty of finding data with which to test the hypothesis we are interested in. However, there is a vast amount of data collected for other purposes that can be fruitfully used to study a variety of problems. Included in this is all the work done by psychologists both within and outside the laboratory; the accumulated data are generally available to other psychologists. Thus, reanalysis of previous work is one way of conducting research.

Cross-cultural work can be done in the field, in laboratories, or even by the use of archives. The only requirement is that data be collected in more than one culture. This type of research has two purposes. First, it allows for greater generality of findings if they hold in more than one culture. There is always the suspicion that a particular relationship between, say, fear and affiliation may hold in the United States but not in Japan. If we want to consider this relationship a basic process in human social interaction, we naturally want it to hold for all kinds of populations. Cross-cultural work is one way of testing the limitations and generality of any particular finding.

Another, more sophisticated use of cross-cultural work is in studying the importance of variables that differ in two societies. One of the basic hypotheses we have discussed in this book is the relationship between frustration and aggression. This relationship could be tested by observing whether societies that are high in frustration exhibit more aggression than those low in frustration. Of course, observing only two societies would not be particularly useful, because they would differ on many variables beside frustration. Just as correlational studies on individuals need fairly large numbers to produce meaningful results, so do cross-cultural studies. The research must assess frustration and aggression in a large number of societies and see whether high levels of frustration generally tend to be associated with high levels of aggression. In this way, the extraneous, incidental factors present in each society become less important, and the relationship between frustration and aggression emerges.

Naturally, cross-cultural work can also tell us how societies differ. Any time different results are found in different cultures, we have discovered something about each culture. We have, for example, found that Norwegians conform more than the French in a particular situation. We may not know why they do, we may not know whether or not it is due to the particular situation, but we know that in that limited set of circumstances, there is more conformity in Norway than in France.

**RESEARCH ETHICS**

After an investigator has decided what kind of study to do and where to do it, he faces the most difficult decision—how to do it. In designing any research, and particularly any that involves humans, ethical considerations must be taken into account. The social psychologist wants to discover how people behave in social situations. To do so, he must expose subjects to certain conditions and observe how they respond. But he must be concerned about their privacy and about the conditions to which he exposes them.

An individual's right to privacy must be respected and cherished. As the president's panel on privacy and behavior research stated, every individual must be allowed to "decide for himself how much he will share with others his thoughts, his feelings, and the facts of his personal life." The social psychologist must guard the individual's privacy and at the same time pursue his research. Although this is a complex, personal matter, certain guidelines should be observed. The president's panel has listed several that are particularly important.

"Participation by subjects should be voluntary and based on informed consent to the extent that it is consistent with the objectives of the research." Ordinarily individuals should not be subjected to experimentation unless they have agreed to it, and, whenever possible, this agreement should be given after they have heard exactly what is going to take place during the course of the study. The experimenter has an obligation to tell a potential subject as much as possible about the study before asking him to participate.

Often, however, it is not possible to tell a subject everything about the study. This is typical of research in social psychology. Studies of impression formation, in which subjects are given a list of adjectives and asked to form an impression of the person, can be conducted with subjects who know all about the purposes and procedures of the work. But virtually all the other studies described in this book require concealment of certain aspects of the investigation. In some experiments, such as the balance studies involving Fenwick, only the purpose and specific hypotheses need be concealed. In others, such as the Asch conformity study, both purpose and details of procedure must be concealed. The experimenter must give as much information as he can, but the president's panel did not feel, nor do we, that research that requires concealment must cease. Instead, the panel added, "in the absence of full information, consent [should] be based on trust in the qualified investigator and the integrity of his institution." In other words, the individual may volunteer for a study without knowing everything about it because he trusts the investigator and the institution responsible. In essence, he is putting himself into their hands, because he believes they will do nothing to which he would object if he could be told. This is a legitimate and meaningful form of consent. However, it places a particularly heavy burden on the investigator to be worthy of that trust, and we shall return to this shortly.

"In some research, however, soliciting consent at all . . . destroys experimental purpose." An example of this type is the work on the foot-in-the-door effect, in which housewives were asked to post signs and were never told they were in a study. Sometimes this is the only feasible or by far the best way of investigating a problem, and with appropriate safeguards it is allowable. It should be used only when it is the sole way of conducting the research, when the work is important enough to warrant an invasion of privacy (no matter how slight that invasion is), and particularly when there is minimal possibility that the invasion of privacy will produce unpleasant consequences for the subject.

A distinction should be made between personal, private information about an individual and public information. Information about an individual's finances, sexual behavior, or even preferences for movies is personal. An individual's behavior when he is angry or frustrated is also quite personal. Research designed to obtain such information must carefully observe the guidelines on privacy. In contrast, whether someone crosses the street when the light is red, is willing to post a sign for safe driving, or smokes cigarettes is relatively public information. Almost anyone can obtain this information merely by watching the individual's behavior in public. Although an investigator should always be careful about the right to privacy, collecting public information of this sort need not be done under such strict guidelines.

In summary, the guidelines for the protection of privacy are to obtain informed consent if possible, to obtain consent based on trust if some concealment of purpose is necessary, and to conduct research without consent only when there is no other way to do it and there is minimal danger of causing distress.

Another ethical consideration perhaps even more complicated than that of privacy concerns the conditions to which the subject is to be exposed. The determination of what should be done rests largely with the individual investigator. This is as it should be, because ultimately it is his responsibility. However, all universities now have a special committee to provide some supervision for the experimenter. Certain guidelines apply to all research in social psychology.

It is obvious that nothing should be done to a subject that has any likelihood of causing lasting harm. It may seem somewhat foolish to mention this, but unfortunately, it is sometimes lost sight of. Medical research, for example, has often exposed willing or unwilling humans to drugs, viruses, and other agents that could conceivably cause great harm. There have been lawsuits over such practices, and they are better controlled today. But the researcher is in conflict; his goals are noteworthy—he wants to save lives, discover a cure for cancer, in social research perhaps discover how to prevent war—so he may think some risk of harm to a subject is justified. We feel that, at least in social psychology, this is not so. A subject, even with his permission, should not be exposed to potentially harmful conditions.

After this criterion is satisfied, the problem becomes subtle and more difficult. Is it allowable to cause subjects some pain or distress if it is not lasting or extreme? We feel that it is, but only if stringent criteria are met. The experimenter must consider all the ways of studying the problem that do not cause distress. Often the same problem can be studied without aversive conditions, and if so, they must be used. If this is not possible (e.g., the study involves reactions to pain or frustration), the experimenter must decide whether the importance of the problem warrants the use of procedures that will cause distress. Although we are talking about procedures that will not cause lasting pain or distress, there must be ample justification for exposing someone to an unpleasant experience. It is, of course, difficult to decide how important a problem is, but an attempt should be made to do so. Thus, a replication of earlier work, a small point in a larger problem, or a slight extension of a previous finding would be less justification than a test of an important theory, a possibility of discovering a new relationship, or a major extension of previous work. The greater the distress the procedure will cause, the more justification, in terms of the importance of the work, is needed to use it.

Assuming that no other procedure is possible and the problem seems important enough, the experimenter must next give careful attention to the procedure he will use and the setting in which he will use it. Two issues are involved: first, conditions produced in the laboratory that are similar to those the person is likely to encounter in his normal life are always preferable to unique conditions. Being threatened with an injection may be frightening, but it is a usual occurrence in the world—we all get injections. In contrast, being threatened with total isolation for five hours is also frightening, but it is not a usual occurrence—most people never face this threat. The advantage of the natural situation is that it is more likely to produce valid results that are comparable to behavior in the real world, and more important from an ethical point of view, it is less likely to cause distress that the individual cannot handle or that will produce a lasting impression on him. The ruling considerations should be that the experiment should not change the person's life in any meaningful way (except insofar as it teaches him something, which is always a possibility). If the experiment exposes him to a natural situation, it will probably not be an important event in his life; if the situation is unnatural, it is more likely to become an important and perhaps harmful event. Thus whenever possible, the conditions should be similar to ones that occur naturally. The details need not be similar, but the emotion they arouse and the general feelings should be.

Second, the subject should have volunteered to be in the study. As stated above, he need not necessarily be told everything that will happen during his participation, but he should know that he is in an experiment and should have freely given his permission. In other words, only someone who has given informed consent or consent based on trust should be exposed to distressing conditions. Subjects who have not given consent should be exposed only to conditions that have a minimal chance of causing distress.

Finally, in all experiments great care should be taken to guarantee, as much as possible, that the subject leaves feeling no more distress than when he arrived. This can be accomplished by extended explanations of the study, its purpose, significance, methods, etc., and by reassuring the subject in whatever way is appropriate. This so-called debriefing is an essential part of all research and is particularly important when the experimental procedures are likely to cause the subject distress.

These ethical considerations impose considerable restrictions on the social scientist, but they need not prevent him from doing legitimate research. With sufficient ingenuity and care, he can study virtually any problem and still safeguard the privacy and well-being of his subjects.

However, ethical considerations usually do prevent him from conducting experiments on the effect of very strong aversive conditions; this is one of the limitations of the experimental method in social psychology.

### Role-Playing Technique

Concern about the ethical problems of research and also the difficulty of doing experimental research, has caused some people in the field to suggest what they consider an alternative to the experimental method. This consists of substituting what is called "role-playing" studies for actual experiments. In the typical role-playing study, the investigator describes a situation to the subject, and asks the subject what he or some other person would do under those circumstances. For example, a subject reads a description of the Festinger and Carlsmith (1959) experiment. He is told that a subject performed a task which is described in detail, that he was then asked to tell the next subject that the task was very enjoyable and that he was offered money for doing this. He is then asked how much he thinks someone in that situation would say that he liked the task. Or he is asked how much he thinks he would say he would have liked the task in that situation. In this role-playing study, some subjects would be told that the individual was paid one dollar and some would be told he was paid twenty dollars, thus repeating the conditions of the original experiment. The data then are simply what the subject says he or the other person would do under these circumstances.

Obviously this way of doing research is extremely efficient and avoids many of the problems inherent in the experimental method. There are no ethical problems because the subject is not himself involved in any experimental situation nor in any deception. There is no great skill necessary in presenting the instructions to the subjects or designing the specific procedure, because everything can be written down on a piece of paper and there is no reason for the subject to feel any suspicion. The whole procedure can be very quick and can even be done in large groups. The temptations of using this method are evident.

Unfortunately, the data obtained from this kind of procedure are not very useful for psychologists. What a subject says he or another subject would do in a given situation may or may not be what the subject actually would do in that situation. You are asking the subject to guess what he would do if he found himself in those circumstances, and people are not very good at making those guesses. Typically, role-playing subjects will give the correct answers only when the results are obvious beforehand. In any situation where we are not certain what the behavior will be—that is, in almost all interesting situations—we could not count on the subjects' responses. Actually there is no more reason to trust the subjects' guesses than there is to trust your own. If the subject can guess what he would have done, presumably the experimenter could guess just as well—perhaps better if he is experienced. Therefore, there is little advantage to running a role-playing study over simply recording the experimenter's hunches. But the whole business of doing research is to test the experimenter's hunches, not to assume they are correct. We would not automatically accept an experimenter's hunches, and there is no more reason to accept the guesses of a large number of subjects. No matter how many subjects are asked, what they say is only guessing—not real behavior. In order to find out how subjects will behave in a real situation, it is necessary to put them in it.

In fact, the whole basis of psychology and social psychology as a science is that we do not trust anyone's intuitions about how people behave. This is the difference between the scientific and the nonscientific approach to the study of human behavior. As soon as we start trusting people's guesses as to how they or others would behave, we are no longer treating psychology as a science. No matter how realistic the role-playing situation is made, as long as a subject is playing the roles and not actually experiencing the situation himself, his responses will be only guesses and as such are not scientific data. They are, of course, interesting as indications of people's perceptions of themselves and of others. If this is what you are interested in, the role-playing technique could be very useful. But it must always be understood that subject's responses tell us something about how they perceive and how they guess, not how they would behave in that situation.

## DESIGNING THE STUDY

With these ethical considerations in mind, the investigator must design and conduct his study. As an example of this process, we shall now discuss in detail the design and execution of a laboratory experiment.

The investigator has a problem he wants to study. He must set up a situation in which one or more variables (the independent variables) are experimentally manipulated and in which subjects are randomly assigned to groups in such a way that the groups differ only in terms of these independent variables. Everything about the situation must be identical for the groups except the one variable in which he is interested. Then the experimenter must measure one or more responses (the dependent variables) in order to see what effect the independent variable has. He must take his measurements in such a way that he minimizes the subject's suspicion. Only then can he elicit responses that reflect, as much as possible, the way the subject would respond if he were in a similar situation that occurred naturally rather than in one produced by the experimenter.

### The Independent Variable

The first step in the process generally is to decide on the specific way to manipulate the independent variable. The psychologist starts with a variable that is defined on a conceptual level. For example, he hypothesizes that high fear leads to an increase in affiliation. He may or may not have a detailed definition of *fear* in his mind, but he must have a fairly clear picture of the variable. Let us say he defines *fear* as the internal feeling produced by the anticipation of negative reinforcement from a known source. This conceptual definition may sound impressive but is very general. The experimenter's big problem is deciding on the particular way in which he is going to arouse fear. According to his definition, he must set up a situation in which the subject is anticipating negative reinforcement from a known source, but the definition says nothing about the specific conditions under which this should be done.

There are several criteria for a good manipulation of this sort. Ideally, it should work on all subjects. The more uniformly the method works, the stronger is its effect and the more likely it is to produce significant and meaningful results. Therefore, the psychologist wants to use something that everyone or almost everyone is afraid of.

A second point is that social psychologists typically deal with several levels of a particular variable rather than simply its presence or absence. An affiliation study would probably involve high- and low-fear conditions rather than high- and no-fear conditions. There are two reasons for this.

First, and more important, is the necessity of making the conditions as similar as possible in all respects except the one that differentiates them in terms of fear. This is difficult to do unless we use almost identical terms when describing the situation to both groups of subjects. For example, if we told one group of subjects that they were going to be given electric shocks and did not mention this to the other, the two groups would differ in many ways. They might differ in terms of fear (the variable we are interested in), but they would also differ in feelings about the experiment and the experimenter, in how much they wondered what the study concerned, and so on. Also, we have talked longer to one group of subjects than to the other, and although we cannot be sure what effect this would have, it is potentially important. In contrast, we could tell both groups that they are going to be shocked but make it more frightening for one than the other by varying the description of the shocks—we could tell one group that the shocks will be severe and painful and the other group that they will be mild and not painful. This would make the conditions virtually identical except for the few words necessary to produce the difference in fear. Then, any differences in the behavior of the two groups would be attributable to fear level and not to extraneous variables.

The second reason for dealing with two levels of a variable rather than its presence and absence is that it is generally not possible to be certain that a particular internal state is entirely absent. Even if the external conditions would not ordinarily arouse fear, many subjects may be afraid simply because they are in an experiment or because they are people who are always somewhat frightened. Similarly, even someone who has just eaten may be slightly hungry, even someone who has just slept twelve hours may be tired, and so on. Thus, from a conceptual and practical point of view, it makes little sense to think in terms of the total absence of a variable—instead, we talk in terms of less and more.

Other considerations in choosing the experimental procedure revolve around its practicality, morality, legality, and so on. Obviously we want to choose something we are able and willing to do to a subject. Under most circumstances, we could not take him up in an airplane and suddenly tell him the engine has failed. Although this probably would make him afraid, most of us would feel it was highly unethical. Also we would not have the resources at our disposal necessary to carry it out. Thus we must choose a method that is feasible from a practical point of view and that will not harm the subject or do anything else we would consider unethical.

In choosing a manipulation, we must also take into account the necessity of collecting dependent measures. The manipulation of the independent variable that is chosen must be compatible with some acceptable dependent measures. Closely related to this is the necessity of finding a manipulation that is plausible, that would not arouse too much suspicion, and that, accordingly, would enable us to set up a situation in which the subject would respond as spontaneously as possible.

With all these considerations in mind, the experimenter eventually chooses a manipulation. He might decide to tell the subjects that they are going to be handling snakes. Many people are afraid of snakes and some snakes are dangerous, so this should arouse a considerable amount of fear. The problem with this manipulation is that many subjects are, in fact, not afraid of snakes as long as the snakes are not dangerous. Thus many subjects would not be at all afraid and the manipulation would not be successful. We could, of course, say they are poisonous snakes or perhaps giant anacondas. The few subjects who believed it might be terrified, but it would probably raise considerable skepticism among most subjects and they would feel no fear.

Another possibility might be to lock subjects in a room and simulate a fire that, presumably, would be threatening to engulf the building. If this were done convincingly, the subjects would probably be exceedingly frightened. However, in addition to obvious ethical problems there are several difficulties with this technique. First, many subjects probably would not believe there was a fire. To make the fire believable would require elaborate apparatus, shouting people, firemen breaking down doors, etc.—it probably is not worth the effort. But most important is the virtual impossibility of finding a comparable situation for the low-fear or control group. A small fire might be thought to arouse less fear than a large one, but if the fire is dangerous, the subjects will be afraid; and they will probably be just as afraid of burning to death in a small fire as in a large one. If there is no fire, the conditions are so different that it might be hard to compare them. Certainly any difference between the high-fear (fire) subjects and the low-fear (no fire) subjects would be difficult to attribute entirely to the amount of fear they felt.

Finally, this manipulation would make it extremely difficult to maintain good control over the situation and collect reliable measures of the dependent variable. In a study that used essentially this manipulation (French, 1944), uncontrollable events occurred. A group of subjects were put in a room at the top of an old building at Harvard, ostensibly to discuss a problem. Soon after the experimenter left, smoke began coming under a door in the room. The subjects soon discovered that all the doors were locked, and at this point they presumably should have been very frightened. Unfortunately (or perhaps fortunately) human beings do not usually take this kind of situation lying down. Several groups included varsity football players, and they broke down the door, terminating the experiment. Other groups managed to break into the closet from which the smoke was pouring and discovered the smoke machine. Still others convinced themselves that it was an experiment and calmly went about discussing the problem, ignoring the smoke that was beginning to fill the room. And so on. If the investigators had been studying responses to crisis situations, these would be interesting results. However, they were attempting to study a specific dependent variable (organization). When this is the aim of an experiment, crisis situations often make it difficult to exert sufficient control so that dependent measures can be collected.

There is one manipulation that has been widely used in social psychology experiments, has been found to arouse fear in most subjects, enables the experimenter to produce several levels of fear conveniently, and also minimizes the amount of suspicion the subjects might feel. This is the the anticipation of electric shocks. For most subjects electric shocks are particularly frightening, partly because they rarely experience them and partly because they know that electric shocks can be extremely painful. Thus almost all subjects are frightened by the threat of receiving them. Yet electric shocks are not so strange and unfamiliar that the subject is being exposed to a situation likely to harm him.

Moreover, it is extremely easy to manipulate the amount of fear shocks arouse by describing them in different terms for different conditions. All the subjects would presumably be somewhat afraid, but the more painful they expected the shocks to be, the more afraid they would be. In this way all the subjects could be given almost identical instructions and yet the intensity of the fear could be manipulated conveniently by changing a few words in the description of the shocks. The high-fear

condition could be told: "These shocks will hurt, they will be painful.
. . . It is necessary that our shocks be intense. . . . These shocks will be
quite painful, but of course, they will do no permanent damage." A low-
fear condition could be told: " . . . very mild electric shocks. . . . What
you will feel will not in any way be painful. They will resemble more a
tickle or tingle than anything unpleasant." If the instructions are delivered convincingly they should arouse relatively little suspicion, because
even sophisticated subjects know that psychologists often deal with
electric shocks. Also the experiment can be described as, say, a study on
responses to intense stimuli.

There are obviously many other ways of arousing fear that could
be adapted for this type of study. It is desirable to vary the independent
variable in more than one way in different studies so that we can be
more certain that we are dealing with fear and not some other emotion.
If the findings on fear and affiliation, for example, are based entirely on
the anticipation of electric shocks, someone might argue that they were
not the result of fear but something specific to electric shocks. By manipulating fear in many ways, all of which are consistent with our
original conceptual definition of fear (see p. 455), and finding the same
results, we increase confidence in our interpretation of the findings in
terms of fear rather than in terms of the specific manipulation. Sarnoff
and Zimbardo (1961), for example, demonstrated a difference between
fear and anxiety by using different procedures for arousing the emotions
(see pp. 14–17). This reinforced our belief that fear leads to affiliation
and also made the definition of fear more specific.

Another way of increasing confidence in the interpretation of the
independent variable is to provide some sort of independent check on
the manipulation. On the face of it, telling subjects they are about to be
shocked should arouse fear and the more severe the description, the
more fear it should arouse. The possibility always exists, however, that
the manipulation did not arouse fear, that for some reason the subjects
were not worried about electric shocks, or perhaps that the two groups
did not differ in the amount of fear they felt. If we know that there is
some response or behavior that is highly correlated with fear, by measuring it we can provide an independent verification of the presence of
fear. For example, we could take measures of the subject's blood pressure
and pulse rate. Although physiological measures are generally poor indicators of the presence of fear, they do tend to be correlated with it. The
greater the fear, the higher should be the blood pressure and pulse rate.
If we find that the subjects in the high-fear condition actually do have
higher pulse rates and blood pressure than those in the low-fear condition, our confidence in the effectiveness of the manipulation is increased.
We are not absolutely certain that it is fear we are producing, but we do
know that we have aroused some internal state differentially in the two

conditions and that fear is one of the likely possibilities. Another kind of check on the manipulation is a self-report from the subjects. We can ask the subjects how frightened they feel, how nervous, whether or not they are nauseated, and so on. If the high-fear subjects report that they are more afraid than the low-fear subjects and particularly if the two groups do not differ on irrelevant feelings such as nausea, it becomes highly probable that the manipulation really was affecting fear levels.

Thus there are two ways of pinning down the meaning of the experimental manipulation. One is to use many different kinds of fear manipulations, all derived from our conceptual definition of it. If the different manipulations produce the same effect on the dependent measure (for example, if in all cases the high-fear group affiliates more than the low-fear group) we can be quite confident that it is fear that is producing the effect. The other way is to provide a direct check on the manipulation, either by the use of self-reports or by some other variable that we know from previous research to be highly correlated with fear. Unfortunately neither of these approaches is particularly easy in most instances. A great deal of care is required to be certain of our interpretation of the manipulation, and much of the controversy in social psychology revolves around different interpretations of the same experimental manipulation.

### Dependent Variable

The original problem was to study the effects of fear on affiliation. We have decided how to manipulate fear; we must now decide how to measure affiliation. We want to do it in such a way that there is a minimum of ambiguity in the meaning of the dependent measure because we would like to be absolutely certain that it is affiliation we are studying. Also we must minimize the possibility of biasing the subject's responses. We do not want the subject to respond in a particular way because he thinks it is "correct" or because he thinks the experimenter wants him to respond that way or for any other extraneous reason. We want him to respond spontaneously, with his response being due to the experimental situation and the independent variable.

In the case of affiliation, our first criterion for a good dependent measure is not particularly difficult to meet. There are relatively few possibilities for measuring affiliation. They all are variations of allowing the subject a choice of affiliating or not affiliating and observing which he chooses. The particular way in which the choice is presented would depend in large part on making it fit in with the experimental manipulation of the independent variable and the whole setting of the study. But there is no great difficulty in assessing the desire to affiliate.

Dependent variables other than affiliation, however, are often more difficult to measure. In studying the effect of modeling on aggression, for example, the experimenter is faced with a considerable problem in finding a good dependent measure of aggression. He can observe whether the subject punches someone, draws a knife and stabs him, or performs other violent acts. These are clearly aggressive behaviors and would be excellent, unambiguous indications of aggressiveness. Fortunately for our society, but perhaps unfortunately for the experimenter, the likelihood of any subject committing a violent act such as these is virtually zero. Therefore, the investigator must depend on subtler indications of aggressiveness. He could ask a subject to make comments about another person and then code these comments in terms of their aggressive content. But many people would not consider it aggressive behavior to make negative comments about somebody else when asked to do so by an experimenter. Even delivering an electric shock to another person might not be considered aggressive if the experimenter has told them that this is part of the study. In other words, finding a dependent measure that fits the conceptual definition of aggression is feasible, is unequivocal, and is quite difficult. Considerable ingenuity is necessary to design such a measure. The same is true of many other variables that are important to social psychologists.

Often the social psychologist cannot find a perfect measure of the variable he is interested in. For practical or ethical reasons he is forced to resort to somewhat equivocal measures. Other interpretations of the measure are possible, and therefore the experimenter cannot be certain that his results reflect the variable he is investigating. One solution to this problem is to use many different measures of the same variable. If the measures all produce the same results and are all designed to tap the same variable, he can have increased confidence in the meaning of his findings. Any one measure of aggression might be interpreted in a variety of ways, but ten different measures of aggression that produce the same results, even if each of them separately could be interpreted in several ways, make it more likely that the variable measured is aggression.

Having many measures also reduces the possibility that the results are due to some characteristic peculiar to a given measure. For example, delivering electric shocks carries with it a variety of meanings and connotations, not all of which the experimenter can know. Therefore, results based only on giving electric shocks are to some extent confused with characteristics of that particular behavior. If, on the other hand, the same results are obtained from delivering electric shocks, making negative statements, taking money from another person, slapping someone across the face, and drawing nasty pictures of someone, it begins to appear that they are not due to any specific characteristics of any one measure. The results appear regardless of the measure of aggression, so we have considerably more confidence in them.

This does not mean that we always use more than one measure in an experiment or even that it is essential to have experiments that use different measures. Occasionally we find a measure that is very compelling, that has few alternative interpretations, and that just about everybody will accept as an adequate measure of a particular variable. But most of the time it is helpful to have a variety of measures of the same variable, if not in the same experiment, at least in different experiments. In this way we can increase both the generality of the results and our confidence that they are due to the variable in which we are interested.

This then is the basic procedure for conducting an experiment in social psychology. A hypothesis is formed, an independent variable is chosen, the manipulation is constructed, the experimental situation is designed, and a dependent measure is selected. Generally, a considerable amount of pretesting is necessary to work out the exact method of manipulating the independent variable, smooth out the procedure, and make as certain as possible that the dependent measure is appropriate to the situation. When the pretesting has been completed and the type of subjects selected, the experiment is ready to be run.

**EXPERI-MENTER BIAS**

Up to now we have been talking about aspects of the experimental method that are more or less general to all kinds of research. The choice of setting (laboratory or field) is not unique to social psychology, although it is more important in this area than in most others. The difficulty of manipulating the independent variable and of choosing a dependent measure is common to virtually all fields of science. In addition, there is one problem that, although not unique to social psychology, is particularly relevant and troublesome in this field—experimenter bias.

As we discussed in Chapter 12, subjects in a study are extremely susceptible to influence by the experimenter. They do virtually anything he asks. This is true even if he does not make any direct request. If he implies, consciously or otherwise, that he would like the subjects to respond in a certain way, there is a tendency for them to respond in that way. If, for example, the experimenter would like the subjects in one condition to be more aggressive and those in another condition to be less aggressive, subjects in the two conditions may differ in the way he expects simply because explicitly or implicitly he communicates his wishes. Moreover, the experimenter may not have made any deliberate attempt to influence the results. On the contrary, experimenters are aware of this problem and try to be as neutral and consistent as possible. But subtle cues tend to be picked up by the subjects and influence their behavior.

Many studies (e.g., Rosenthal, 1966) have shown powerful effects produced by the experimenter's expectations and desires. In school settings, students a teacher thinks are bright do better than students the teacher thinks are less bright—even though the students do not actually differ in intelligence. This is even true of rats in a simple learning situation with identical rats: if an experimenter is told the rats are smart, they do better than if he is told they are dumb. Perhaps experimenters tend to handle the "smart" rats somewhat more gently and to encourage them somewhat more than they do the "dumb" rats. If an experimenter's expectations can have an important effect on such fairly simple, noninteractive behavior as learning in rats, obviously they can have an even more dramatic effect on complex social processes.

There are two solutions to the problem of bias. One is to keep the experimenter ignorant as to the experimental condition of the subject. This is usually referred to as keeping the experimenter "blind." If he does not know which experimental condition he is dealing with, there is no way for him to affect the conditions differentially. Although he may behave differently from one experimental session to another and these differences may affect the way the subjects respond, he cannot systematically behave one way for one condition and another way for another. This guarantees that randomness still prevails, because the experimenter cannot make the variations in his procedure anything other than random. He can, of course, try to guess what condition a subject is in, and if he wants or expects one condition to produce more aggression than the other, he may behave in differential ways to subjects he thinks are in the two conditions. But since he does not know who is in what condition, his differential behavior cannot produce systematic differences. In other words, as long as the experimenter is totally blind (i.e., ignorant) as to the condition subjects are in, any differences in the way they are treated are randomly distributed between the various conditions. These differences may affect the way subjects behave and may increase the variance in their behavior but cannot produce overall differences between conditions.

In many experiments, however, it is impossible to keep the experimenter blind as to the subjects' condition. Typically, the experimenter himself must deliver the experimental manipulation in one way or another. He tells the subject to expect severe or mild shock, he brings the subject a Coke, he knows how many confederates are present in a conformity situation, and so on. The experimenter is the main source of instructions and manipulations, and his skill is generally necessary to make certain that the manipulation is effective. Even in these cases, some degree of blindness can be introduced into the experiment. For example, two experimenters can be used, with one of them delivering the experimental manipulation and the other collecting the dependent measure, thus keeping the person who collects the dependent measure blind to the experimental condition. This is a relatively simple procedure and was generally used in the compliance studies described above. One experimenter produced the guilt and another made the request. It is not quite as good as having an experimenter who is totally blind, because the first experimenter might communicate in some way what he wanted the subject to do later or might affect in some way the later behavior, but the procedure should substantially reduce bias.

A second solution to the problem of experimenter bias is to standardize the situation in every way possible. If everything is standardized and there are no differences between conditions other than those that are deliberate, there can be no bias. This is usually not easy to accomplish, but various procedures can maximize the amount of standardization between conditions. In the extreme case, a subject might appear for an experiment, find a written instruction on the door telling him to enter, have all instructions presented on tape, and complete the experiment entirely before he meets a live exprimenter. In this way, every factor in the situation would be absolutely standardized, and experimenter bias would be eliminated.

This degree of standardization is rarely feasible. Most manipulations require the presence of at least one live person. The experiments concerning guilt all depend on another person being hurt in some way, and that person's presence should make the arousal of guilt stronger. Tape recordings do not allow any procedural variations, which might be necessitated by variations among subjects. A live experimenter can repeat instructions if they have not been understood, emphasize aspects to which the subject seems to be responding, and, in general, increase the strength of the manipulation by these variations. In addition, most manipulations are more forceful when delivered by a live experimenter, simply because people respond to other people more strongly than they respond to impersonal tape recordings. This is not always true. Being told by a tape recording that he is going to be given severe electric shocks might be very frightening for a subject—even more so than hearing the same thing from a live experimenter. But this is a special instance. Generally, a live experimenter has more effect than a recorded or written message.

Another problem with taped instructions is that the situation becomes somewhat unreal. As we have already discussed, many experiments suffer from a lack of realism, and the careful experimenter exerts considerable effort to make the setting more realistic. Written or taped instructions tend to make the situation more unusual and magnify this already serious problem. The subject tends to be more suspicious and less spontaneous, and the results become less valid.

These drawbacks do not mean that written or taped instructions are impossible—on the contrary, they are often useful—but at least part of the manipulation usually has to be conducted by a live experimenter. Nevertheless, the more standardization that can be introduced, the more likely it is that experimental bias would be eliminated.

In actual practice, the solution to the problem of bias is usually a combination of the two procedures we have described. As much as possible, the experimenter is kept blind as to the subjects' experimental condition; also as much as possible, instructions are standardized by the use of tapes or written materials. It is often impossible to eliminate completely the possibility that some bias has crept into a study, but experimenters must take this into account and do whatever they can to minimize the likelihood that there is any.

An even subtler source of bias in a social psychology experiment is the subject's desire to give the "correct" response in the situation. When people know they are subjects in a psychological experiment, there is some pressure on them to think about what they are doing. Under these circumstances most subjects want to give the socially acceptable response, in part because they want to please or impress the experimenter. They feel that if they give the "correct" response, the experimenter would be more favorably impressed than if they give an inappropriate response. This feeling could be minimized somewhat by having the subject respond anonymously so that the experimenter would not know how he behaved in the situation. Unfortunately, this does not solve the problem entirely. Most subjects want to impress not only the experimenter but also themselvs. They want to think of themselves as good people and therefore do what they can to behave in the right way. As long as a subject is thinking about these considerations, it is virtually impossible to eliminate this kind of bias.

For example, if an experimenter were interested in the effects of frustration on aggression toward whites and blacks, he might frustrate a subject and then give him an opportunity to aggress against either a white or a black. If this were done in a straightforward manner, most subjects would be aware that the experimenter was interested at least in part in differential aggression toward whites and blacks. At this point, every subject would have some feelings about the appropriate or most acceptable behavior. Most white college students would probably think that it is wrong to be prejudiced and, in particular, that it is bad to aggress more against a black than against a white. These subjects live in a social environment in which bigotry, discrimination, and prejudice are considered wrong by most people. Clearly the socially acceptable and desirable response would be to treat the white and the black equally or even to bend over backward and aggress more against the former than against the latter. The problem is that if they acted this way the subjects might be responding the way they think they should respond, not necessarily the way they would respond in a natural situation. The responses would be influenced not by the subjects' natural tendencies but instead primarily by their assumptions about the correct way of responding. In fact, many white subjects may feel considerable prejudice against blacks and may have a tendency to aggress more against them than against other whites, but their knowledge about what is socially acceptable behavior interferes with this spontaneous behavior and causes them to respond differently.

This kind of bias is almost impossible to eliminate entirely but can be minimized in a variety of ways. The goal is to produce a situation in which the subject responds spontaneously without worrying about the correctness of his response. The basic tactic is to disguise the dependent measure or to distract the subject from its importance. One way of doing this is by not telling the subject that he is being observed. In field research, within the ethical limits described above, people sometimes are not told that they are subjects in an experiment. They are approached and their behavior may be measured, but nothing is said about a psychological study. For example, we could observe how white sales people in a store treat black and white customers on a particularly busy, hard day compared to an easy day. If frustration led to aggression, the salespeople should be nastier on the hard day; and even worse to blacks than to whites if that aggression is directed at people differentially.

In the laboratory, disguising the measure and distracting the subject are somewhat more difficult. As we discussed previously, experiments can be set up so that the crucial measure is taken after the subject thinks the experiment is over. In the Carlsmith and Gross study, for example, the manipulation of guilt occurred during what the subject thought was the experiment but the measure of compliance was obtained afterward. Another tactic is to make the subject think that he is an experimenter rather than a subject. This was done in the Festinger and Carlsmith study and many other experiments as well. The subject is told that he is to act as an observer or to assist the experimenter, but in the description of his role not much emphasis is placed on observing his behavior. This distracts him from the main emphasis of the experiment and tends to make him behave more spontaneously. A third tactic is using unobstrusive or so-called nonreactive measures, in which the subject does not know that a measure is being taken. We could count how many cigarettes he smokes or how often he blinks as measures of stress, or observe whether he chooses a task that requires sitting with other people, as an indication of his desire to affiliate. All these techniques reduce the possibility that the dependent measure is affected by the subject's view of what is socially desirable rather than by the subject's natural inclinations in the situation.

As a final note, we should emphasize that social psychology is, in general, a probabilistic science. Its findings and predictions are stated in probabilistic terms. We have said that high fear leads to greater affiliation than low fear. This does not mean that all people who are feeling high fear affiliate more than all people who are feeling low fear. It does

not even mean that all people affiliate more when they are afraic
when they are not afraid. In other words, it does not apply to
person nor to all situations. It does mean that greater fear *tends* to
people to affiliate more than low fear. More of the people who ar
ing high fear affiliate than do those who are feeling low fear. The
greater probability that a particular individual who is afraid aff
than that a particular individual who is not afraid does so. Simil
communication from a high-prestige communicator *tends* to p
more attitude change than one from a low-prestige communicatc
not everyone who reads the high-prestige communication changes
than everyone who reads the low-prestige communication. In ad
some people may actually change more as a result of a particula
prestige communication than a high-prestige communication.
variety of reasons, any given individual might be more influence
communication from a nursing student than by one from a Nobe
winner. But *most* people are influenced more by the high-prestig
munication. If all we know is that one person received a high-p
communication and another received a low-prestige communicatic
best prediction is that the former is influenced more. This is, how
probabilistic prediction and may not hold true in any given case.

A great deal of the variation in most situations has not beer
explained by social psychology. We have found that some percen
the variance in affiliation is due to the amount of fear the indivi
feeling. Many other factors, such as birth order and some we
know about yet, also affect the amount of affiliation. Therefore,
now say that high fear *tends* to produce an increase in affiliation.
cussing the factors that lead to liking, we said that proximity, sim
and rewardingness explain a considerable amount of the variance.
one who is close by, who is very similar to us, and who is rew
*tends* to be liked more than someone who does not have these qu
But someone who fits all these criteria is not necessarily going
friend. He tends to be and is more likely to be than someone wh
not have them, but the correspondence is not perfect. A group o
fear subjects affiliate more, on the average, than a group of lc
subjects, but any given member of the high-fear group may affili
than a particular member of the low-fear group.

This does not mean that the findings of social psychology a
or imprecise. It means that we have not yet specified all the factc
affect any given behavior and that the factors we have discovered
affect all individuals equally in all conditions. However, these
do affect behavior in the ways we have described, so we are able to
stand and predict behavior better because of the research.

1.  Theoretical, hypothesis-testing, and empirical research.
2.  Correlational versus experimental research.
3.  Research in the field or laboratory.
4.  Ethical considerations for social psychologists.
5.  Designing and conducting an experiment.
6.  Sources of bias and how to reduce them.

## APPLICATIONS AND SPECULATIONS

1.  If we accept strict ethical views about privacy and possible injury, how can we conduct research in social psychology?
2.  Some radicals claim that research in the behavioral sciences is necessarily in the service of the *status quo*. What do you think about that?
3.  It has been observed that the incidence of extreme political unrest in the form of riots is correlated with temperature—riots occur when it is hot. A simple conclusion would be that the heat causes the riot. Can you think of other interpretations involving additional variables?
4.  We discussed the difficulty of studying racist feelings in the laboratory. How might this problem be investigated?

## SUGGESTIONS FOR ADDITIONAL READING

### Books and Longer Discussions

Aronson, E., and Carlsmith, J. M. Experimentation in social psychology. In G. Lindzey and E. Aronson (Eds.), *Handbook of social psychology*. Reading, Mass.: Addison-Wesley, 1968.

Webb, E. J., Campbell, D. T., Schwartz, D., and Sechrest, L. *Unobtrusive measures: nonreactive research in the social sciences*. Chicago: Rand McNally, 1966.

# bibliography

Abelson, R. P., 1959. Modes of resolution of belief dilemmas. *Conflict Resolution, 3*, 343–52.

Abelson, R. P., Aronson, E., McGuire, W. J., Newcomb, T. M., Rosenberg, M. J., and Tannenbaum, P. H. (Eds.), 1968. *Theories of cognitive inconsistency: a sourcebook.* Chicago: Rand McNally.

Abelson, R. P., and Lesser, G. S., 1959. The measurement of persuasibility in children. In C. I. Hovland and I. L. Janis (Eds.), *Personality and persuasibility.* New Haven, Conn.: Yale. Pp. 141–66.

Abelson, R. P., and Rosenberg, M. J., 1958. Symbolic psycho-logic: a model of attitudinal cognition. *Behavioral Science, 3*, 1–13.

Adams, J. S., 1961. Reduction of cognitive dissonance by seeking consonant information. *Journal of Abnormal and Social Psychology, 62*, 74–78.

Adams, J. S., 1965. Injustice in social exchange. In L. Berkowitz (Ed.), *Advances in experimental social psychology.* Vol. 2. New York: Academic.

Aderman, D., 1969. Effects of anticipating future interaction on the preference for balanced states. *Journal of Personality and Social Psychology, 11*, 214–19.

Allee, W. C., and Masure, R. H., 1963. A comparison of maze behavior in paired and isolated shelf-parakeets (Melopsittacus undulatus Shaw) in a two-alley problem box. *Journal of Comparative Psychology, 22*, 131–55.

Allen, V. L., 1964. Uncertainty of outcome and post-decision dissonance reduction. In L. Festinger (Ed.), *Conflict, decision, and dissonance.* Stanford, Calif.: Stanford. Pp. 34–42.

Allen, V. L., and Levin, J. M., 1971. Social support and conformity: The role of independent assessment of reality. *Journal of Experimental Social Psychology, 7*, 48–58.

Allport, F. H., 1920. The influence of the group upon assoc and thought. *Journal of Experimental Psychology, 3,* 159–82.

Allport, F. H., 1924. *Social psychology.* Boston: Riverside Ed Houghton Mifflin.

Allport, G. W., 1935. Attitudes. In C. Murchison (Ed.), *Han of social psychology.* Worcester, Mass.: Clark University Press. Pp 884.

Allport, G. W., 1944. *ABC's of scapegoating.* Chicago: C YMCA College.

Allport, G. W., 1954. *The nature of prejudice.* Reading, I Addison-Wesley.

Allyn, J., and Festinger, L., 1961. The effectiveness of unantic persuasive communications. *Journal of Abnormal and Social Ps ogy, 62,* 35–40.

Anderson, N. H., 1965. Averaging versus adding as a stir combustion rule in impression formation. *Journal of Experimenta chology, 70,* 394–400.

Anderson, N. H., 1965. Primacy effects in personality impr formation using a generalized order effect paradigm. *Journal of P ality and Social Psychology, 2,* 1–9.

Anderson, N. H., 1968. Application of a linear-serial mode personality-impression task using special presentation. *Journal o sonality and Social Psychology, 10,* 354–62.

Anderson, N. H., 1968. Likableness ratings of 555 personalit words. *Journal of Personality and Social Psychology, 9,* 272–79.

Anderson, N. H., and Barrios, A. A., 1961. Primacy effects i sonality formation. *Journal of Abnormal and Social Psycholog* 346–50.

Anderson, N. H., and Norman, A., 1964. Order effects in i sion formation in four classes of stimuli. *Journal of Abnormal a cial Psychology, 69,* 467–71.

Apsler, R., and Sears, D. O., 1968. Warning, personal involv and attitude change. *Journal of Personality and Social Psycholo* 162–66.

Ardrey, R., 1966. *The territorial imperative.* New York: Athe

Aronson, E., and Carlsmith, J. M., 1963. The effect of the s of threat on the devaluation of forbidden behavior. *Journal of Ab and Social Psychology, 66,* 584–88.

Aronson, E., and Carlsmith, J. M., 1968. Experimentation ir psychology. In G. Lindzey and E. Aronson (Eds.), *Handbook of psychology.* Reading, Mass.: Addison-Wesley.

Aronson, E., and Linder, D., 1965. Gain and loss of esteem as determinants of interpersonal attractiveness. *Journal of Experimental Social Psychology, 1,* 156–71.

Aronson, E., and Mills, J., 1959. The effect of severity of initiation on liking for a group. *Journal of Abnormal and Social Psychology, 59,* 177–81.

Aronson, E., Turner J., and Carlsmith, J. M., 1963. Communicator credibility and communication discrepancy. *Journal of Abnormal and Social Psychology, 67,* 31–36.

Asch, S. E., 1946. Forming impressions of personality. *Journal of Abnormal and Social Psychology, 41,* 258–90.

Asch, S. E., 1951. Effects of group pressure upon the modification and distortion of judgments. In Harold Guetzkow (Ed.), *Groups, leadership and men.* Pittsburgh, Pa.: Carnegie Press. Pp. 177–90.

Ashmore, R. D., 1970. Prejudice: Causes and cures. In B. E. Collins (Ed.), *Social psychology.* Reading, Mass.: Addison-Wesley. Pp. 243–339.

Bales, R. F., 1950. *Interaction process analysis.* Reading, Mass.: Addison-Wesley.

Bales, R. F., 1950. A set of categories for the analysis of small group interaction. *American Sociological Review, 15,* 146–59.

Bales, R. F., 1958. Task roles and social roles in problem-solving groups. In E. Maccoby, T. M. Newcomb, and E. L. Hartley (Eds.), *Readings in social psychology* (3rd ed.). New York: Holt. Pp. 437–47.

Bandura, A., 1965. Vicarious processes: A case of no-trial learning. In L. Berkowitz (Ed.), *Advances in experimental social psychology,* Vol. 2. New York: Academic. Pp. 1–55.

Bandura, A., Ross, D., and Ross, S. A., 1961. Transmission of aggression through imitation of aggressive models. *Journal of Abnormal and Social Psychology, 63,* 575–82.

Bandura, A., Ross, D., and Ross, S. A., 1963. A comparative test of status envy, social power, and secondary reinforcement theories of identificatory learning. *Journal of Abnormal and Social Psychology, 67,* 527–34.

Bandura, A., and Walters, R. H., 1963. *Social learning and personality development.* New York: Holt.

Barker, R. G., Dembo, T., and Lewin, K., 1941. Frustration and regression: an experiment with young children. University of Iowa Studies in Child Welfare, *18,* No. 1.

Baron, R. A., 1971. Reducing the influence of an aggressive model: The restraining effects of discrepant modeling cues. *Journal of Personality and Social Psychology, 20,* 240–45.

Baron, R. A., and Kepner, C. R., 1970. Model's behavior a
traction toward the model as determinants of adult aggressive beł
*Journal of Personality and Social Psychology, 14,* 335–44.

Baron, R. S., Dion, K. L., Baron, P., and Miller, N., 1970.
norms, elicited values and risk-taking. Unpublished manuscript. L
sity of Minnesota.

Bartlett, F. C., 1932. *Remembering: a study in experiment
social psychology.* New York: Cambridge.

Bateson, N., 1966. Familiarization, group discussion, and
taking. *Journal of Experimental Social Psychology, 2,* 119–29.

Bavelas, A., Hastorf, A. H., Gross, A. E., and Kite, W. R.,
Experiments on the alteration of group structure. *Journal of Experi*
*Social Psychology, 1,* 55–70.

Becker, S. W., and Carrol, J., 1962. Ordinal position and coı
ity. *Journal of Abnormal and Social Psychology, 65,* 129–31.

Bem, D. J., 1965. An experimental analysis of self-persu
*Journal of Experimental Psychology, 1,* 199–218.

Bem, D. J., 1967. Self-perception: An alternative interpretaı
cognitive dissonance phenomena. *Psychological Review, 74,* 18

Bem, D. J., Wallach, M. A., and Kogan, N., 1965. Group dı
making under risk of aversive consequences. *Journal of Personali*
*Social Psychology, 1,* 453–60.

Bender, I. E., and Hastorf, A. H., 1950. The perception of pe
forecasting another person's responses on three personality scales
*nal of Abnormal and Social Psychology, 45,* 556–61.

Benham, T. W., 1965. Polling for a presidential candidate
observations of the 1964 campaign. *Public Opinion Quarterly, 29*
99.

Berelson, B. R., Lazarsfeld, P.F., and McPhee, W. N., 1954. V
*A study of opinion formation in a presidential election.* Chicago: l
sity of Chicago Press.

Berkowitz, L., 1954. Group standards, cohesiveness, and p
tivity. *Human Relations, 7,* 509–19.

Berkowitz, L., 1962. *Aggression: a social psychological aı*
New York: McGraw-Hill.

Berkowitz, L., 1968. Responsibility, reciprocity, and social d
in help-giving: an experimental investigation of English socia
differences. *Journal of Experimental Social Psychology, 4,* 46–63.

Berkowitz, L., and Cottingham, D. R., 1960. The interest val
relevance of fear-arousing communications. *Journal of Abnormal a*
*cial Psychology, 60,* 37–43.

Berkowitz, L., and Daniels, L. R., 1964. Responsibility and dependency. *Journal of Abnormal and Social Psychology, 66*, 427–36.

Berkowitz, L., and Geen, R. G., 1966. Film violence and the cue properties of available targets. *Journal of Personality and Social Psychology, 3*, 525–30.

Berkowitz, L., and Geen, R. G., 1967. Stimulus qualities of the target of aggression: A further study. *Journal of Personality and Social Psychology, 5*, 364–68..

Berkowitz, L., Green, J. A., and Macauley, J. R., 1962. Hostility catharsis as the reduction of emotional tension. *Psychiatry, 25*, 23–31.

Berkowitz, L., and Holmes, D. S., 1959. The generalization of hostility to disliked objects. *Journal of Personality, 27*, 565–77.

Berkowitz, L., and LePage, A., 1967. Weapons as aggression-eliciting stimuli. *Journal of Personality and Social Psychology, 7*, 202–7.

Berkowitz, L., and Rawlings, E., 1967. Effects of film violence on inhibitions against subsequent aggression. *Journal of Personality and Social Psychology, 5*, 368–72.

Berkowitz, W. R., 1970. Spectator responses at public war demonstrations. *Journal of Personality and Social Psychology, 14*, 305–11.

Berscheid, E., Dion, K., Walster, E., and Walster G. W., 1971. Physical attractiveness and dating choice: A test of the matching hypothesis. *Journal of Experimental Social Psychology, 7*, 173–89.

Berscheid, E., and Walster, E., 1967. When does a harm-doer compensate a victim? *Journal of Personality and Social Psychology, 6*, 435–41.

Bickman, L., 1971. The effect of another bystander's ability to help on bystander intervention in an emergency. *Journal of Experimental Social Psychology, 7*, 367–79.

Bickman, L., 1972. Social influence and diffusion of responsibility in an emergency. *Journal of Experimental Social Psychology, 8*, 438–45.

Blake, R. R., Helson, H., and Mouton, J. S., 1956. The generality of conformity behavior as a function of factual anchorage, difficulty of task, and amount of social pressure. *Journal of Personality, 25*, 294–305.

Blank, A., 1968. Effects of group and individual condition on choice behavior. *Journal of Personality and Social Psychology, 8*, 294–98.

Bochner, S., and Insko, C. A., 1966. Communicator discrepancy, source credibility, and opinion change. *Journal of Personality and Social Psychology, 4*, 614–21.

Boring, E. G., and Titchener, E. B., 1923. A model for the demonstration of facial expression. *American Journal of Psychology, 34*, 471–85.

Brehm, J. W., 1956. Post-decision changes in desirability of al
tives. *Journal of Abnormal and Social Psychology, 52,* 348–89.

Brehm, J. W., 1966. *A theory of psychological reactance*
York: Academic.

Brehm, J. W., and Cohen, A. R., 1959. Re-evaluation of cho
ternatives as a function of their number and qualitative sim
*Journal of Abnormal and Social Psychology, 58,* 373–78.

Brehm, J. W., and Cohen, A. R., 1962. *Explorations in co;
dissonance.* New York: Wiley.

Brehm, J. W., and Cole, A. H., 1966. Effect of a favor whi
duces freedom. *Journal of Personality and Social Psychology, 3,* 4

Brehm, J. W., and Jones, R. A., 1970. The effect on dissona
surprise consequences. *Journal of Experimental Social Psycholo*
420–31.

Brickman, P., Redfield, J., Harrison, A. A., and Crandall, R.,
Drive and predisposition as factors in the attitudinal effects of
exposure. *Journal of Experimental Social Psychology, 8,* 31–44.

Brock, T. C., 1965. Communicator-recipient similarity and de
change. *Journal of Personality and Social Psychology, 1,* 650–54.

Brock, T. C., and Becker, L. A., 1965. Ineffectiveness of
heard" counterpropaganda. *Journal of Personality and Social Ps
ogy, 2,* 654–60.

Brock, T. C., and Becker, L. A., 1966. "Debriefing" and su:
bility to subsequent experimental manipulations. *Journal of Experi
Social Psychology, 2,* 314–23.

Brodbeck, M., 1956. The role of small groups in mediatii
effects of propaganda. *Journal of Abnormal and Social Psycholog*
166–70.

Brophy, I. N., 1946. The luxury of anti-Negro prejudice.
*Opinion Quarterly, 9,* 456–66.

Brown, R., 1965. *Social psychology.* New York: Free Press

Bruner, J. S., Shapiro, D., and Tagiuri, R., 1958. The mean
traits in isolation and in combination. In R. Tagiuri and L. P
(Eds.), *Person perception and interpersonal behavior.* Stanford,
Stanford. Pp. 277–88.

Bruner, J. S., and Tagiuri, R., 1954. The perception of peo
G. Lindzey (Ed.), *Handbook of social psychology,* Vol. 2. Re
Mass.: Addison-Wesley. Pp. 634–54.

Bryan, J. H., and Test, N. A., 1967. Models and helping: N.
istic studies in aiding behavior. *Journal of Personality and Socia
chology, 6,* 400–407.

Burgess, T. D., and Sales, S. M., 1971. Attitudinal effects of mere exposure: A re-evaluation. *Journal of Experimental Social Psychology,* 7, 461–72.

Buss, A. H., 1961. *The psychology of aggression.* New York: Wiley.

Buss, A. H., Booker, A., and Buss, E., 1972. Firing a weapon and aggression. *Journal of Personality and Social Psychology,* 22, 296–302.

Byrne, D., 1961. Interpersonal attraction and attitude similarity. *Journal of Abnormal and Social Psychology,* 62, 713–15.

Byrne, D., and Blaylock, B., 1963. Similarity and assumed similarity of attitudes between husbands and wives. *Journal of Abnormal and Social Psychology,* 67, 636–40.

Byrne, D., and Nelson, D., 1964. Attraction as a function of attitude similarity-dissimilarity: the effect of topic importance. *Psychonomic Science,* 1, 93–94.

Byrne, D., and Wong, T. J., 1962. Racial prejudice, interpersonal attraction and assumed dissimilarity of attitudes. *Journal of Abnormal and Social Psychology,* 65, 246–53.

Calhoun, J. B., 1962. Population density and social pathology. *Scientific American,* 206, 139–48.

Campbell, A., Converse, P. E., Miller, W. E., and Stokes, D. E., 1960. *The American voter.* New York: Wiley.

Carlsmith, J. M., Collins, B. E., and Helmreich, R. L., 1966. Studies in forced compliance: I. The effect of pressure for compliance on attitude change produced by face-to-face role-playing and anonymous essay writing. *Journal of Personality and Social Psychology,* 4, 1–13.

Carlsmith, J. M., Ellsworth, P., and Whiteside, J., 1969. Guilt, confession and compliance. Unpublished manuscript, Stanford University.

Carlsmith, J. M., and Freedman, J. L., 1968. Bad decisions and dissonance: Nobody's perfect. In R. Abelson et al. (Eds.), *Theories of cognitive consistency.* Chicago: Rand McNally. Pp. 485–90.

Carlsmith, J. M., and Gross, A. E., 1969. Some effects of guilt on compliance. *Journal of Personality and Social Psychology,* 11, 232–39.

Carlsmith, J. M., Lepper, M., and Landauer, T. K., 1969. Two processes in children's obedience to adult requests. Unpublished manuscript, Stanford University.

Castore, C. H., 1972. Group discussion and prediscussion assessment of preferences in the risky shift. *Journal of Experimental Social Psychology,* 8, 161–67.

Chen, S. C., 1937. Social modification of the activity of ants in nest-bulding. *Physiological Zoology,* 10, 420–36.

Christian, J. J., 1968. Endocrine adaptive mechanisms and the

physiologic regulation of population growth. In Mayer and Van (
(Eds.), *Physiological mammology*. New York: Academic. Pp. 18&#x298;

Christian, J. J., Flyger, V., and Davis, D., 1960. Factors in the
mortality of a herd of sika deer *carvus nippon*. *Chesapeake Scie*r
79–95.

Clark, R. D. III, and Word, L. E., 1971. A case where the bys&#x2738;
did help. Paper presented at the meeting of the Eastern Psycho&#x2758;
Association, New York.

Cline, V. B., 1964. Interpersonal perception. In B. A. Maher
*Progress in experimental personality research*. Vol. 1. New York.
demic. Pp. 221–84.

Cohen, A. R., 1957. Need for cognition and order of comm
tion as determinants of opinion change. In C. I. Hovland (Ed.)&#x2758;
*order of presentation in persuasion*. New Haven, Conn.: Yale. Pp. &#x2758;

Cohen, A. R., 1959. Some implications of self-esteem for soc
fluence. In C. I. Hovland and I. L. Janis (Eds.), *Personality and per*
*bility*. New Haven, Conn.: Yale. Pp. 102–20.

Cohen, A. R., 1962. An experiment on small rewards for disc&#x2738;
compliance and attitude change. In J. W. Brehm and A. R. Cohen &#x2738;
*Explorations in cognitive dissonance*. New York: Wiley. Pp. 73–78.

Cohen, A. R., 1964. *Attitude change and social influence*.
York: Basic Books, Inc., Publishers.

Cohen, D., Whitmyre, J. W., and Funk, W. H., 1960. Eff
group cohesiveness and training upon creative thinking. *Journal c*
*plied Psychology, 44*, 319–22.

Coleman, J. C., 1949. Facial expressions of emotions. *Psyc*&#x298;
*Monograph, 63*, (1, Whole No. 296).

Coleman, J. F., Blake, R.R., and Mouton, J. S., 1958. Task dif&#x2738;
and conformity pressures. *Journal of Abnormal and Social Psych*
*57*, 120–22.

Converse, P. E., 1964. The nature of belief systems in mass p&#x2738;
In D. E. Apter (Ed.), *Ideology and discontent*. New York: Free
Pp. 206–61.

Converse, P. E., 1970. Attitudes and non-attitudes: Contin&#x2738;
of a dialogue. In E. R. Tufte (Ed.), *The quantitative analysis of*
*problems*. Reading, Mass.: Addison-Wesley. Pp. 168–89.

Converse, P. E., Clausen, A. R., and Miller, W. E., 1965. El&#x25b;
myth and reality: the 1964 election. *American Political Science R*&#x2738;
*49*, 321–36.

Cook, S. W., 1970. Motives in a conceptual analysis of at&#x2738;
related behavior. *Nebraska Symposium on Motivation, 18*, 179–231

Cooper, J., 1971. Personal responsibility and dissonance: The role of foreseen consequences. *Journal of Personality and Social Psychology, 18*, 354–63.

Cooper, J., and Brehm, J. W., 1971. Prechoice awareness of relative deprivation as a determinant of cognitive dissonance. *Journal of Experimental Social Psychology, 7*, 571–81.

Cooper, J., and Jones, R. A., 1970. Self-esteem and consistency as determinants of anticipatory opinion change. *Journal of Personality and Social Psychology, 14*, 312–20.

Costanzo, P. R., 1970. Conformity development as a function of self-blame. *Journal of Personality and Social Psychology, 14*, 366–74

Cottrell, N. B., Rittle, R. H., and Wack, D. L., 1967. Presence of an audience and list type (competitional or noncompetitional) as joint determinants of performance in paired-associates learning. *Journal of Personality, 35*, 425–34.

Cottrell, N. B., Wack, D. L., Sekerak, G. J., and Rittle, R. H., 1968. Social facilitation of dominant responses by the presence of an audience and the mere presence of others. *Journal of Personality and Social Psychology, 9*, 245–50.

Dabbs, J. M., Jr., and Leventhal, H., 1966. Effects of varying the recommendations in a fear-arousing communication. *Journal of Personality and Social Psychology, 4* (5), 525–31.

Darley, J. M., and Berscheid, E., 1967. Increased liking caused by the anticipation of personal contact. *Human Relations, 20*, 29–40.

Darley, J. M., and Latané, B., 1968. Bystander intervention in emergencies: diffusion of responsibility. *Journal of Personality and Social Psychology, 8*, 377–83.

Darwin, C., 1872. *The expression of the emotions in man and animals.* London: J. Murray.

Dashiell, J. F., 1930. An experimental analysis of some group effects. *Journal of Abnormal and Social Psychology, 25*, 190–99.

Davis, K. E., and Jones, E. E., 1960. Changes in interpersonal perception as a means of reducing cognitive dissonance. *Journal of Abnormal and Social Psychology, 61*, 402–10.

Davis, R. C., 1934. The specificity of facial expressions. *Journal of General Psychology, 10*, 42–58.

Davitz, J. R. (Ed.), 1964. *The communication of emotional meaning.* New York: McGraw-Hill.

Dean, R. B., Austin, J. A., and Watts, W. A., 1971. Forewarning effects in persuasion: Field and classroom experiments. *Journal of Personality and Social Psychology, 18*, 210–21.

478

Deutsch, M., 1960. The effect of motivational orientation upor and suspicion. *Human Relations, 13,* 122–39.

Deutsch, M., and Collins, M. E., 1951. *Interracial housing: ι chological evaluation of a social experiment.* Minneapolis: Univers Minnesota Press.

Deutsch, M., and Gerard, H. B., 1955. A study of normativ informational social influences upon individual judgment. *Journal c normal and Social Psychology, 51,* 629–36.

Deutsch, M., and Krauss, R. M., 1960. The effect of threat on personal bargaining. *Journal of Abnormal and Social Psycholog; 181–89.

Deutsch, M., and Solomon, L., 1959. Reactions to evaluatio others as influenced by self-evaluations. *Sociometry, 22,* 93–112.

De Wolfe, A. S., and Governale, C. N., 1964. Fear and at change. *Journal of Abnormal and Social Psychology, 69,* 119–23.

Dienstbier, R. A., and Munter, P. O., 1971. Cheating as a fu of labeling of natural arousal. *Journal of Personality and Social Ps; ogy, 17,* 208–13.

Dion, K. L., Baron, R. S., and Miller, N., 1970. Why do g make riskier decisions than individuals? In L. Berkowitz (Ed.), *Adι in experimental social psychology,* Vol. 5. New York: Academi 305–77.

Dion, K., Berscheid, E., and Walster, E., 1972. What is bea is good. *Journal of Personality and Social Psychology, 24,* 285–90.

Dittes, J. E., and Kelley, H. H., 1956. Effects of different conc of acceptance on conformity to group norms. *Journal of Abnormι Social Psychology, 53,* 100–107.

Dollard, J., Doob, L., Miller, N., Mowrer, O., and Sears, R., *Frustration and aggression.* New Haven, Conn.: Yale.

Doob, A. N., 1967. Some determinants of aggression. Unpub doctoral dissertation, Stanford University.

Doob, A. N., Carlsmith, J. M., Freedman, J. L., Landauer, T. K Tom, S., Jr., 1969. Effect of initial selling price on subsequent *Journal of Personality and Social Psychology, 11,* 345–50.

Doob, A. N., and Climie, R. J., 1972. Delay of measuremer the effects of film violence. *Journal of Experimental Social Psych 8,* 136–42.

Doob, A. N., and Wood, L. E., 1972. Catharsis and aggre Effects of annoyance and retaliation on aggressive behavior. *Jour Personality and Social Psychology, 22,* 156–62.

Doob, L., 1947. The behavior of attitudes. *Psychological Review, 54*, 135–56.

Dorfman, D. D., Keeve, S., and Saslow, C., 1971. Ethnic identification: A signal detection analysis. *Journal of Personality and Social Psychology, 18*, 373–79.

Dornbusch, S. M., Hastorf, A. H., Richardson, S. A., Muzzy, R. E., and Vreeland, R. S., 1965. The perceiver and the perceived: their relative influence on the categories of interpersonal cognition. *Journal of Personality and Social Psychology, 1*, 434–40.

Dunlap, K., 1927. The role of eye-muscles and mouth-muscles in the expression of the emotions. *Genetics Psychology Monographs, 2* (3), 199–233.

Dunnette, M. D., Campbell, J., and Jaastad, K., 1963. The effect of group participation on brainstorming effectiveness for two industrial samples. *Journal of Applied Psychology, 47*, 30–37.

Eagly, A. H., and Telaak, K., 1972. Width of the latitude of acceptance as a determinant of attitude change. *Journal of Personality and Social Psychology, 23*, 388–97.

Ehrlich, D., Guttman, I., Schonbach, P., and Mills, J., 1957. Post-decision exposure to relevant information. *Journal of Abnormal and Social Psychology, 54*, 98–102.

Ekman, P., and Friesen, W. V., 1971. Constants across cultures in the face and emotion. *Journal of Personality and Social Psychology, 17*, 124–29.

Ekman, P., Sorenson, E. R., and Friesen, W. V., 1969. Pan-cultural elements in facial displays of emotions. *Science, 164*, 86–88.

Elliot, D. N., and Wittenberg, B. H., 1955. Accuracy of identification of Jewish and non-Jewish photographs. *Journal of Abnormal and Social Psychology, 51*, 339–31.

Evans, R. I., Rozelle, R. M., Lasater, T. M., Dembroski, T. M., and Allen, B. P., 1970. Fear arousal, persuasion, and actual versus implied behavioral change: New perspective utilizing a real-life dental hygiene program. *Journal of Personality and Social Psychology, 16*, 220–27.

Feather, N. T., 1963. Cognitive dissonance, sensivity, and evaluation. *Journal of Abnormal and Social Psychology, 66*, 157–63.

Fensterheim, H., and Tresselt, M. E., 1953. The influence of value systems on the perceptions of people. *Journal of Abnormal and Social Psychology, 48*, 93–98.

Feshbach, S., 1955. The drive-reducing function of fantasy behavior. *Journal of Abnormal and Social Psychology, 50*, 3–12.

Feshbach, S., 1956. The catharsis hypothesis and some conseq»
of interaction with aggressive and neutral play objects. *Journal o*
*sonality, 24, 44–62.*

Feshbach, S., 1961. The stimulating versus cathartic effects
vicarious aggressive activity. *Journal of Abnormal and Social Psych*
*63, 381–85.*

Feshbach, S., and Singer, R. D., 1957. The effects of fear a
and suppression of fear upon social perception. *Journal of Abr*
*and Social Psychology, 55, 283–89.*

Feshbach, S., and Singer, R. D., 1970. *Television and aggre*
San Francisco: Jossey-Bass.

Festinger, L., 1954. A theory of social comparison processes
*man Relations, 7, 117–40.*

Festinger, L., 1957. *A theory of cognitive dissonance.* Sta
Calif.: Stanford.

Festinger, L., 1964. *Conflict, decision and dissonance.* Sta
Calif.: Stanford.

Festinger, L., and Carlsmith, J., 1959. Cognitive consequen
forced compliance. *Journal of Abnormal and Social Psychology, 58*
10.

Festinger, L., and Maccoby, N., 1964. On resistance to pers
communications. *Journal of Abnormal and Social Psychology, 68,*
66.

Festinger, L., Pepitone, A., and Newcomb, T., 1952. Some «
quences of de-individuation in a group. *Journal of Abnormal and*
*Psychology, 47, 382–89.*

Festinger, L., Riecken, H. W., and Schachter, S., 1956. *When ｪ*
*ecy fails.* Minneapolis: University of Minnesota Press.

Festinger, L., Schachter, S., and Back, K., 1950. *Social pressu*
*informal groups: a study of human factors in housing.* New
Harper & Row.

Fiedler, F. E., 1954. Assumed similarity measures as prec
of team effectiveness. *Journal of Abnormal and Social Psycholog*
381–88.

Fiedler, F. E., 1958. *Leader attributes and group effectivenes*
bana: University of Illinois Press.

Fiedler, F. E., 1964. A contingency model of leadership eff«
ness. In L. Berkowitz (Ed.), *Advances in experimental social psych*
Vol. 1. New York: Academic. Pp. 150–90.

Finkelman, J. M., and Glass, D. C., 1970. Reappraisal of th«

tionship between noise and human performance by means of a subsidiary task measure. *Journal of Applied Psychology, 54,* 211–13.

Fishbein, M., 1972. The prediction of behavior from attitudinal variables. In K. K. Sereno and C. C. Mortensen (Eds.), *Advances in communication research.* New York: Harper & Row.

Fishbein, M., and Hunter, R., 1964. Summation versus balance in attitude organization and change. *Journal of Abnormal and Social Psychology, 69,* 505–10.

Fisher, S., and Lubin, A., 1958. Distance as a determinant of influence in a two-person serial interaction situation. *Journal of Abnormal and Social Psychology, 56,* 230–38.

Fitch, G., 1970. Effects of self-esteem, perceived performance and choice on causal attributions. *Journal of Personality and Social Psychology, 16,* 311–15.

Flanders, J. P., and Thistlewaite, D. L., 1967. Effects of familiarization and group discussion upon risk-taking. *Journal of Personality and Social Psychology, 5,* 91–97.

Frager, R., 1970. Conformity and anticonformity in Japan. *Journal of Personality and Social Psychology, 15,* 203–10.

Freedman, J. L., 1963. Attitudinal effects of inadequate justification. *Journal of Personality, 31,* 371–85.

Freedman, J. L., 1964. Involvement, discrepancy, and change. *Journal of Abnormal and Social Psychology, 64,* 290–95.

Freedman, J. L., 1965. Long-term behavioral effects of cognitive dissonance. *Journal of Experimental Social Psychology, 1,* 145–55.

Freedman, J. L., 1965. Preference for dissonance information. *Journal of Personality and Social Psychology, 2,* 287–89.

Freedman, J. L., Carlsmith, J. M., and Suomi, S., 1969. The effect of familiarity on liking. Unpublished paper, Stanford, Calif.: Stanford.

Freedman, J. L., and Doob, A. N., 1968. *Deviancy.* New York: Academic.

Freedman, J. L., and Fraser, S. C., 1966. Compliance without pressure: the foot-in-the-door technique. *Journal of Personality and Social Psychology, 4,* 195–202.

Freedman, J. L., Heshka, S., and Levy, A., 1973. Population density and pathology: Is there a relationship? Unpublished manuscript.

Freedman, J. L., Klevansky, S., and Ehrlich, P., 1971. The effect of crowding on human task performance. *Journal of Applied Social Psychology, 1,* 7–25.

Freedman, J. L., Levy, A. S., Buchanan, R. W., and Price, J., 1972.

Crowding and human aggressiveness. *Journal of Experimental Psychology, 8*, 528–48.

Freedman, J. L., and Sears, D. O., 1965. Selective exposure. Berkowitz (Ed.), *Advances in experimental social psychology.* V New York: Academic.

Freedman, J. L., and Sears, D. O., 1965. Warning, distractio resistance to influence. *Journal of Personality and Social Psycholo* 262–65.

Freedman, J. L., and Steinbruner, J. D., 1964. Perceived choic resistance to persuasion. *Journal of Abnormal and Social Psycholog* 678–81.

Freedman, J. L., Wallington, S., and Bless, E., 1967. Comp without pressure: the effect of guilt. *Journal of Personality and Psychology, 7*, 117–24.

French, J. R. P., Jr., 1944. Organized and unorganized grou der fear and frustration. *University of Iowa studies: studies in welfare.* Iowa City: University of Iowa.

Freud, A., 1946. The ego and the mechanisms of defense (tra C. Baines). New York: International Universities Press.

Frieze, I., and Weiner, B., 1973. Cue utilization and attribu judgments for success and failure. *Journal of Personality.* In press.

Frois-Wittmann, J., 1930. The judgment of facial expre *Journal of Experimental Psychology, 13*, 113–51.

Funkenstetin, D., King, S. H., and Drolette, M., 1954. The dir of anger during a laboratory stress-inducing situation. *Psychos* *Medicine, 16*, 404–13.

Gage, N. L., 1952. Judging interests from expressive bet *Psychology Monographs, 66*, (18, Whole No. 350).

Galle, O. R., Gove, W. R., and McPherson, J. M., 1972. Popu density and pathology: What are the relations for man. *Science* 23–30.

Gallo, P. S., 1966. Effects of increased incentives upon the threat in bargaining. *Journal of Personality and Social Psycholo* 14–20.

Gallo, P.S., and Sheposh, J., 1971. Effects of incentive mag on cooperation in the prisoner's dilemma game: A reply to Gu Deutsch, and Epstein. *Journal of Personality and Social Psycholog* 42–46.

Gates, M. F., and Allee, W. C., 1933. Conditioned behavior lated and grouped cockroaches on a simple maze. *Journal of Con* *tive Psychology, 15*, 331–58.

Geen, R. G., and Berkowitz, L., 1966. Name-mediated aggressive cue properties. *Journal of Personality, 34,* 456–65.

Geen, R. G., and O'Neal, E. C., 1969. Activation of cue-elicited aggression by general arousal. *Journal of Personality and Social Psychology, 11,* 289–92.

Geer, J. H., Davison, G. C., and Gatchel, R. I., 1970. Reduction of stress in humans through nonvertical perceived control of aversive stimulation. *Journal of Personality and Social Psychology, 16,* 731–38.

Gentry, W. D., 1970. Effects of frustration, attack, and prior aggressive training on overt aggression and vascular processes. *Journal of Personality and Social Psychology, 16,* 718–25.

Gerard, H. B., 1954. The anchorage of opinions in face-to-face groups. *Human Relations, 7,* 313–26.

Gerard, H. B., 1963. Emotional uncertainty and social comparison. *Journal of Abnormal and Social Psychology, 66,* 568–73.

Gerard, H. B., and Mathewson, G. C., 1966. The effects of severity of initiation on liking for a group: a replication. *Journal of Experimental Social Psychology, 2,* 278–87.

Gerard, H. B., and Rabbie, J. M., 1961. Fear and social comparison. *Journal of Abnormal and Social Psychology, 62,* 586–92.

Gerard, H. B., Wilhelmy, R. A., and Connolley, E. S., 1968. Conformity and group size. *Journal of Personality and Social Psychology, 8,* 79–82.

Gilchrist, J. C., Shaw, M. E., and Walter, L. C., 1954. Some effects of unequal distribution of information in a wheel group structure. *Journal of Abnormal and Social Psychology, 49,* 554–46.

Glass, D. C., and Singer, J. E., 1972. *Urban stress.* New York: Academic.

Goldberg, S. C., 1954. Three situational determinants of conformity to social norms. *Journal of Abnormal and Social Psychology, 49,* 325–29.

Goldsen, R. K., Rosenberg, M., Williams, R. M., and Suchman, E. A., 1960. *What college students think.* Princeton, N.J.: Van Nostrand.

Goranson, R. E., and Berkowitz, L., 1966. Reciprocity and responsibility reactions to prior help. *Journal of Personality and Social Psychology, 3,* 227–32.

Greenberg, M. S., and Frisch, D. M., 1972. Effect of intentionality on willingness to reciprocate a favor. *Journal of Experimental Social Psychology, 8,* 99–111.

Greenwald, A. G., and Sakumura, J. S., 1967. Attitude and selective learning: Where are the phenomena of yesteryear? *Journal of Personality and Social Psychology, 7,* 387–97.

Grusec, J. E., and Skubiski, S. L., 1970. Model nurturance, d« characteristics of the modeling experiment, and altruism. *Jour Personality and Social Psychology, 14*, 352–59.

Guetzkow, H., 1960. Differentiation of roles in task-oriented g In D. Cartwright and A. Zander (Eds.), *Group dynamics: researc theory* (2nd ed.). New York: Harper & Row. Pp. 683–704.

Guetzkow, H., and Simon, H. A., 1955. The impact of certair munication nets upon organization and performance in task-or groups. *Management Science, 1*, 233–50.

Guilford, J. P., 1929. An experiment in learning to read fac pression. *Journal of Abnormal and Social Pspchology, 24*, 191–202.

Gullahorn, J. T., 1952. Distance and friendship as factors gross interaction matrix. *Sociometry, 15*, 123–34.

Gumpert, P., Deutsch, M., and Epstein, Y., 1969. Effect of inc magnitude on cooperation in the prisoner's dilemma game. *Jour Personality and Social Psychology, 11*, 66–69.

Gumpert, P., and Festinger, L. Affective reactions toward who violate rules. Unpublished manuscript.

Gundlach, R. H., 1956. Effects of the on-the-job experience Negroes upon racial attitudes of white workers in union shops. *Ps logical Review, 2*, 67–77.

Guyer, M., and Rapoport, A., 1970. Threat in a two-person *Journal of Experimental Social Psychology, 6*, 11–25.

Haas, R. G., and Linder, D. E., 1972. Counterargument avail and the effect of message structure on persuasion. *Journal of Persc and Social Psychology, 23*, 219–33.

Haefner, D. P., 1964. The use of fear arousal in dental healt» cation. Paper presented at the meeting of the American Public ▶ Association, October 7.

Hall, E. T., 1959. *The Silent Language.* Garden City, N.Y.: D day.

Hamilton, D. L., and Huffman, L. J., 1971. Generality of impre formation processes for evaluative and nonevaluative judgments. *nal of Personality and Social Psychology, 20*, 200–207.

Harding, J., and Hogrefe, R., 1952. Attitudes of white depa» store employees toward Negro co-workers. *Journal of Social Iss» 18–28.

Harris, V. A., and Jellison, J. M., 1971. Fear-arousing comm» tions, false physiological feedback, and the acceptance of recomm tions. *Journal of Experimental Social Psychology, 7*, 269–79.

Hartmann, D. P., 1969. Influence of symbolically modeled i

mental aggression and pain cues on aggressive behavior. *Journal of Personality and Social Psychology, 11*, 280–88.

Harvey, O. J., and Consalvi, C., 1960. Status and conformity to pressures in informal groups. *Journal of Abnormal and Social Psychology, 60*, 182–87.

Hastorf, A. H., Kite, W. R., Gross, A. E., and Wolfe, L. J., 1965. The perception and evaluation of behavior change. *Sociometry, 48*, 400–410.

Heider, F., 1958. *The psychology of interpersonal relations.* New York: Wiley.

Heise, G. A., and Miller, G. A., 1951. Problem-solving by small groups using various communications nets. *Journal of Abnormal and Social Psychology, 46*, 327–35.

Henchy, T., and Glass, D. C., 1968. Evaluation apprehension and the social facilitation of dominant and subordinate responses. *Journal of Personality and Social Psychology, 10*, 446–54.

Hendrick, C., Bixenstine, V. E., and Hawkins, G., 1971. Race versus belief similarity as determinants of attraction: A search for a fair test. *Journal of Personality and Social Psychology, 17*, 250–58.

Hendrick, C., and Taylor, S. P., 1971. Effects of belief similarity and aggression on attraction and counteraggression. *Journal of Personality and Social Psychology, 17*, 342–49.

Heslin, R., and Amo, M. F., 1972. Detailed test of the reinforcement-dissonance controversy in the counterattitudinal advocacy situation. *Journal of Personality and Social Psychology, 23*, 234–42.

Hess, R. D., and Torney, J., 1967. *The development of political attitudes in children.* London: Aldine.

Hewgill, M. A., and Miller, G. R., 1965. Source credibility and response to fear-arousing communication. *Speech Monograph, 32*, 95–101.

Higbee, K. L., 1969. Fifteen years of fear arousal: Research on threat appeals 1953–1968. *Psychological Bulletin, 72*, 426–44.

Hochbaum, G. H., 1954. The relation between group members' self-confidence and their reactions to group pressures to uniformity. *American Sociological Review, 19*, 678–87.

Hoffman, L. R., and Maier, N. R. F., 1961. Quality and acceptance of problem solutions by members of homogeneous and heterogeneous groups. *Journal of Abnormal and Social Psychology, 62*, 401–7.

Hokanson, J. E., 1961. The effects of frustration and anxiety on overt aggression. *Journal of Abnormal and Social Psychology, 62*, 346–51.

Hokanson, J. E., 1961. Vascular and psychogalvanic effects of experimentally aroused anger. *Journal of Personality, 29*, 30–39.

Hokanson, J. E., and Burgess, M., 1962. The effects of three of aggression on vascular processes. *Journal of Abnormal and Psychology, 64*, 446–49.

Hokanson, J. E., and Gordon, J. E., 1958. The expression a hibition of hostility in imaginative and overt behavior. *Journal c normal and Social Psychology, 57*, 327–33.

Hokanson, J. E., and Shetler, S., 1961. The effect of overt a sion on physiological tension level. *Journal of Abnormal and Socic chology, 63*, 446–48.

Hollander, E. P., 1960. Competence and conformity in the a ance of influence. *Journal of Abnormal and Social Psychology, 61* 69.

Holmes, D. S., 1972. Aggression, displacement and guilt. *J of Personality and Social Psychology, 21*, 296–301.

Homans, G. C., 1961. *Social behavior: its elementary forms* York: Harcourt Brace.

Homans, G. C., 1965. Group factors in worker productivity. Proshansky and L. Seidenberg (Eds.), *Basic studies in social psych* New York: Holt. Pp. 592–604.

Horowitz, I. A., and Rothschild, B. H., 1970. Conformity as a tion of deception and role playing. *Journal of Personality and Psychology, 14*, 224–26.

Houston, B. K., 1972. Control over stress, locus of contro response to stress. *Journal of Personality and Social Psychology, 21* 55.

Hovland, C. I. (Ed.), 1957. *The order of presentation in persu* New Haven, Conn.: Yale.

Hovland, C. I., 1959. Reconciling conflicting results derived experimental and survey studies of attitude change. *American Ps ogist, 14*, 8–17.

Hovland, C. I., Harvey, O. J., and Sherif, M., 1957. Assim and contrast effects in reactions to communication and attitude c *Journal of Abnormal and Social Psychology, 55*, 224–52.

Hovland, C. I., and Janis, I. L. (Eds.), 1959. *Personality an suasibility.* New Haven, Conn.: Yale.

Hovland, C. I., Janis, I. L., and Kelley, H. H., 1953. *Com cation and persuasion.* New Haven, Conn.: Yale.

Hovland, C. I., and Mandell, W., 1952. An experimental cor son of conclusion-drawing by the communicator and by the auc *Journal of Abnormal and Social Psychology, 47*, 581–88.

Hovland, C. I., and Pritzker, H. A., 1957. Extent of opinion change as a function of amount of change advocated. *Journal of Abnormal and Social Psychology, 54*, 257–61.

Hovland, C. I., and Sears, R. R., 1940. Minor studies in aggression: VI. Correlation of lynchings with economic indices. *Journal of Personality, 9*, 301–10.

Hovland, C. I., and Weiss, W., 1952. The influence of course credibility on communication effectiveness. *Public Opinion Quarterly, 15*, 635–50.

Hoyt, M., Henley, M. D., and Collins, B. E., 1972. Studies in forced compliance: Confluence of choice and consequence on attitude change. *Journal of Personality and Social Psychology, 23*, 205–10.

Hunt, P. J., and Hillery, J. M., 1972. Social facilitation at different stages in learning. Paper read at the Midwestern Psychological Association Meetings, Cleveland, Ohio.

Husband, R. W., 1940. Cooperative versus solitary problem solution. *Journal of Social Psychology, 11*, 405–9.

Insko, C. A., 1962. One-sided versus two-sided communications and countercommunications. *Journal of Abnormal and Social Psychology, 65*, 203–6.

Insko, C. A., 1964. Primacy versus recency in persuasion as a function of the timing of arguments and measures. *Journal of Abnormal and Social Psychology, 69*, 381–91.

Insko, C. A., 1967. *Theories of attitude change.* New York: Appleton-Century-Crofts.

Insko, C. A., Arkoff, A., and Insko, V. M., 1965. Effects of high and low fear arousing communications upon opinions toward smoking. *Journal of Experimental Social Psychology, 1*, 256–66.

Insko, C. A., Blake, R. R., Cialdini, R. B., 1970. Attitude toward birth control and cognitive consistency: Theoretical and practical implications of survey data. *Journal of Personality and Social Psychology, 16*, 228–37.

Insko, C. A., and Robinson, J. E., 1967. Belief similarity versus race as determinants of reactions to Negroes by southern white adolescents: a further test of Rokeach's theory. *Journal of Personality and Social Psychology, 7*, 216–21.

Isen, A. M., and Levin, P. F., 1972. Effect of feeling good on helping: Cookies and kindness. *Journal of Personality and Social Psychology, 21*, 384–88.

Jahoda, M., and West, P., 1951. Race relations in public housing. *Journal of Social Issues, 7*, 132–39.

Janis, I. L., 1954. Personality correlates of susceptibility to p‹ sion. *Journal of Personality, 22,* 504–18.

Janis, I. L., 1955. Anxiety of indices related to susceptibility t suasion. *Journal of Abnormal and Social Psychology, 51,* 663–67.

Janis, I. L., and Dabbs, J. M., 1965. Why does eating while re facilitate opinion change?–an experimental inquiry. *Journal of E mental Social Psychology, 1,* 133–44.

Janis, I. L., and Feshbach, S., 1953. Effects of fear-arousing munications. *Journal of Abnormal and Social Psychology, 48,* 78–92

Janis, I. L., and Field, P. B., 1956. A behavioral assessment o suasibility: consistency of individual differences. *Sociometry, 19, 24*

Janis, I. L., and Field, P.B., 1959. Sex differences in personalit tors related to persuasibility. In C. I. Hovland et al. (Eds.), *Comm tion and persuasion.* New Haven, Conn.: Yale. Pp. 55–68.

Janis, I. L., Hovland, C. I., Field, P. B., Linton, H., Graha Cohen, A. R., Rife, D., Abelson, R. P., Lesser, G. S., and King, 1959. *Personality and persuasibility.* New Haven, Conn.: Yale.

Janis, I. L., Kaye, D., and Kirschner, P., 1965. Facilitating eff‹ "eating-while-reading" on responsiveness to persuasive communic‹ *Journal of Personality and Social Psychology, 1,* 181–86.

Janis, I. L., and Mann, L., 1965. Effectiveness of emotional playing in modifying smoking habits and attitudes. *Journal of E mental Research in Personality, 1,* 84–90.

Janis, I. L., and Rausch, C. N., 1970. Selective interest in com cations that could arouse decisional conflict: A field study of partic: in the draft-resistance movement. *Journal of Personality and Socia chology, 14,* 46–54.

Janis, I. L., and Terwilliger, R. F., 1962. An experimental stu psychological resistances to fear-arousing communications. *Jourr Abnormal and Social Psychology, 65,* 403–10.

Jecker, J. D., 1964. The cognitive effects of conflict and disso› In L. Festinger (Ed.), *Conflict, decision and dissonance.* Stanford, ‹ Stanford. Pp. 65–82.

Jellison, J. M., Riskind, J., and Broll, L., 1972. Attribution of ‹ to others on skill and chance tasks as a function of level of risk. *J‹ of Personality and Social Psychology, 22,* 135–38.

Jennings, M. K., and Niemi, R. G., 1968. The transmission ‹ litical values from parent to child. *American Political Science R‹ 62,* 169–84.

Johnson, D. W., and Johnson, S., 1972. The effects of attitud‹ ilarity, expectation of goal facilitation, and actual goal facilitati‹

interpersonal attraction. *Journal of Experimental Social Psychology, 8,* 197–206.

Jones, E. E., 1964. *Ingratiation.* New York: Appleton-Century-Crofts.

Jones, E. E., and deCharms, R., 1957. Changes in social perception as a function of the personal relevance of behavior. *Sociometry, 20,* 75–85.

Jones, E. E., Gergen, K. J., Gumpert, P., and Thibaut, J. W., 1965. Some conditions affecting the use of ingratiation to influence performance evaluation. *Journal of Personality and Social Psychology, 1,* 613–26.

Jones, E. E., and Harris, V. A., 1967. The attribution of attitudes. *Journal of Experimental Social Psychology, 3,* 1–24.

Jones, S. C., and Panitch, D., 1971. The self-fulfilling prophecy and interpersonal attraction. *Journal of Experimental Social Psychology, 7,* 356–66.

Julian, J. W., Regula, C. R., and Hollander, E. P., 1967. *Effects of prior agreement from others on task confidence and conformity.* Technical Report 9, ONR Contract 4679. Buffalo, N. Y.: State University of New York.

Julian, J. W., Ryckman, R. M., and Hollander, E. P., 1966. *Effects of prior group support on conformity: an extension.* Technical Report 4, ONR Contract 4679. Buffalo, N.Y.: State University of New York.

Kahn, M., 1960. A polygraph study of the catharsis of aggression. Unpublished doctoral dissertation, Harvard University.

Kaplan, M. F., 1971. Context effects in impression formation: The weighted average versus the meaning-change formulation. *Journal of Personality and Social Psychology, 19,* 92–99.

Katz, D., 1960. The functional approach to the study of attitudes. *Public Opinion Quarterly, 24,* 163–204.

Katz, D., McClintock, C. G., and Sarnoff, I., 1957. Measurement of ego-defense related to attitude change. *Journal of Personality, 25,* 465–74.

Katz, D., Sarnoff, I., and McClintock, C. G., 1956. Ego-defense and attitude change. *Human Relations, 9,* 27–46.

Katz, E., 1957. The two-step flow of communication: an up-to-date report on an hypothesis. *Public Opinion Quarterly, 21,* 61–68.

Kelley, H. H., 1950. The warm-cold variable in the first impressions of persons. *Journal of Personality, 18,* 431–39.

Kelley, H. H., 1955. Salience of membership and resistance to change of group-anchored attitudes. *Human Relations, 8,* 275–89.

Kelley, H. H., 1967. Attribution theory in social psychology. *Nebraska Symposium on Motivation, 14,* 192–241.

Kelley, H. H., Condry, J. C., Dahlke, A. E., and Hill, A. H., Collective behavior in a simulated panic situation. *Journal of Exper* *tal Social Psychology, 1, 20–54.*

Kelley, H. H., Hovland, C. I., Schwartz, M., and Abelson, 1955. The influence of judges' attitudes in three methods of s« *Journal of Social Psychology, 42, 147–58.*

Kelley, H. H., and Lamb, T. W., 1957. Certainty of judgmer resistance to social influence. *Journal of Abnormal and Social Ps* *ogy, 55, 137–39.*

Kelley, H. H., and Shapiro, M. M., 1954. An experiment i» formity to group norms where conformity is detrimental to achievement. *American Sociological Review, 19, 667–77.*

Kelley, H. H., Shure, G. H., Deutsch, M., Faucheux, C., La» J. T., Moscovici, S., Nuttin, J. M., Rabbie, J. M., and Thibaut, 1970. A comparative experimental study of negotiation behavior. *nal of Personality and Social Psychology, 16, 411–38.*

Kelley, H. H., and Stahelski, A. J., 1970. Errors in percept intentions in a mixed-motive game. *Journal of Experimental Socia* *chology, 6, 379–400.*

Kelley, H. H., and Volkart, E. H., 1952. The resistance to c of group-anchored attitudes. *American Sociological Review, 17, 4.*

Kelley, H. H., and Woodruff, C., 1956. Members' reactions parent group approval of a counter-norm communication. *Jour* *Abnormal and Social Psychology, 52, 67–74.*

Kelman, H. C., 1961. Process of opinion change. *Public O* *Quarterly, 25, 57–78.*

Kelman, H. C., and Hovland, C. I., 1953. "Reinstatement" communicator in delayed measurement of opinion change. *Jour* *Abnormal and Social Psychology, 48, 327–35.*

Kephart, W. M., 1957. *Racial factors and urban law enforc«* Philadelphia: University of Pennsylvania Press.

Kerckhogg, A., and Davis, K. A., 1962. Value consensus an« complementarity in mate selection. *American Sociological Revie«* 295–303.

Kiesler, C. A., 1963. Attraction to the group and conform» group norms. *Journal of Personality, 31, 559–69.*

Kiesler, C. A., Collins, B. E., and Miller, N., 1969. *Attitude c*l *a critical analysis of theoretical approaches.* New York: Wiley.

Kipnis, D., and Vanderveer, R., 1971. Ingratiation and the power. *Journal of Personality and Social Psychology, 17, 280–86.*

Klapper, J. T., 1960. *The effects of mass communications.* New York: Free Press.

Klopfer, P. H., 1958. Influence of social interaction on learning rates in birds. *Science, 128,* 903–4.

Knox, R. E., and Douglas, R. L., 1971. Trivial incentives, marginal comprehension, and dubious generalizations from prisoner's dilemma studies. *Journal of Personality and Social Psychology, 20,* 160–65.

Kogan, N., and Carlson, J., 1968. Group risk-taking under competitive and noncompetitive conditions in adults and children. *Journal of Educational Psychology, 60,* 158–67.

Kogan, N., and Doise, W., 1969. Effects of anticipated delegate status on level of risk-taking in small decision-making groups. *Acta Psychologica, 29,* 228–43.

Kogan, N., and Wallach, M. A., 1967. Risk taking as a function of the situation, the person, and the group. In G. Mandler (Ed.), *New directions in psychology.* Vol. III. New York: Holt.

Konečni, V. J., 1972. Some effects of guilt on compliance: A field replication. *Journal of Personality and Social Psychology, 23,* 30–32.

Konečni, V. J., and Doob, A. N., 1972. Catharsis through displacement of aggression. *Journal of Personality and Social Psychology, 23,* 379–87.

Kramer, B. M., 1950. Residential contact as a determinant of attitudes toward Negroes. Unpublished doctoral dissertation, Harvard University.

Krech, D., Crutchfield, R. S., and Ballachey, E. L., 1962. *Individual in society.* New York: McGraw-Hill.

Lamm, H., and Kogan, N., 1970. Risk-taking in the context of intergroup negotiation. *Journal of Experimental Social Psychology, 6,* 351–63.

Landy, D., 1972. The effects of an overheard audience's reaction and attractiveness on opinion change. *Journal of Experimental Social Psychology, 8,* 276–88.

Lane, I. M., and Messé, L. A., 1971. Equity and the distribution of rewards. *Journal of Personality and Social Psychology, 20,* 1–17.

Lane, I. M., and Messé, L. A., 1972. Distribution of insufficient, sufficient, and oversufficient rewards: A clarification of equity theory. *Journal of Personality and Social Psychology, 21,* 228–33.

Lane, R. E., and Sears, D. O., 1964. *Public Opinion.* Englewood Cliffs, N.J.: Prentice-Hall.

Langfeld, H. S., 1918. The judgment of emotions from facial expressions. *Journal of Abnormal and Social Psychology, 13,* 162–84.

LaPiere, R. T., 1934. Attitudes versus actions. *Social Force* 230–37.

Larsson, K., 1956. *Conditioning and sexual behavior in the albino rat.* Stockholm: Almqvist & Wiksell.

Latané, B. (Ed.), 1966. *Studies in social comparison.* New Academic.

Latané, B., and Darley, J. M., 1968. Group inhibition of bys intervention in emergencies. *Journal of Personality and Social Ps ogy, 10,* 215–21.

Latané, B., and Rodin, J., 1969. A lady in distress: inhibiting of friends and strangers on bystander intervention. *Journal of I mental and Social Psychology, 5,* 189–202.

Lazarsfeld, P. F., Berelson, B., and Gaudet, H., 1948. *The p choice* (2nd ed.). New York: Columbia.

Leavitt, H. J., 1951. Some effects of certain communication p on group performance. *Journal of Abnormal and Social Psycholo,* 38–50.

Leavitt, H. J., and Knight, K. E., 1963. Most "efficient" so to communication networks: empirical versus analytical search ometry, 26,* 260–67.

Le Bon, G., 1896. *The crowd.* London: Benn.

Lepper, M. R., 1970. Anxiety and experimenter valence as minants of social reinforcer effectiveness. *Journal of Personality a cial Psychology, 16,* 704–9.

Lepper, M. R., Zanna, M. P., and Abelson, R. P., 1970. Co irreversibility in a dissonance-reduction situation. *Journal of I ality and Social Psychology, 16,* 191–98.

Lerner, M. J., 1971. Observer's evaluation of a victim: j guilt, and veridical perception. *Journal of Personality and Socie chology, 20,* 127–35.

Lerner, M. J., and Matthews, G., 1967. Reactions to the su of others under conditions of indirect responsibility. *Journal of I ality and Social Psychology, 5,* 319–25.

Leventhal, G. S., and Anderson, D., 1970. Self-interest a maintenance of equity. *Journal of Personality and Social Psyc* 15,* 57–62.

Leventhal, G. S., and Lane, D. W., 1970. Sex, age and equ havior. *Journal of Personality and Social Psychology, 15,* 312–16.

Leventhal, G. S., Michaels, J. W., and Sanford, G., 1972. Ir and interpersonal conflict: Reward allocation and secrecy about as methods of preventing conflict. *Journal of Personality and Social Psychology, 23*, 88–102.

Leventhal, H., Jones, S., and Trembly, G., 1966. Sex differences in attitude and behavior change under conditions of fear and specific instructions. *Journal of Experimental and Social Psychology, 2* (4), 387–99.

Leventhal, H., and Niles, P., 1964. A field experiment on fear-arousal with data on the validity of questionnaire measures. *Journal of Personality, 32*, 459–79.

Leventhal, H., and Niles, P., 1965. Persistence of influence for varying durations of exposure to threat stimuli. *Psychological Reports, 16* (1), 223–33.

Leventhal, H., and Singer, R. P., 1966. Affect arousal and positioning of recommendations in persuasive communication. *Journal of Personality and Social Psychology, 4*, 137–46.

Leventhal, H., Singer, R. P., and Jones, S., 1965. Effects of fear and specificity of recommendation upon attitudes and behavior. *Journal of Personality and Social Psychology, 2* (1), 20–29.

Leventhal, H., and Watts, J. C., 1966. Sources of resistance to fear-arousing communications on smoking and lung cancer. *Journal of Personality, 34* (2), 155–75.

Leventhal, H., Watts, J. C., and Pagano, F., 1967. Effects of fear and instructions on how to cope with danger. *Journal of Personality and Social Psychology, 6*, 313–21.

Levinger, G., and Schneider, D. J., 1969. Test of the "Risk is a value" hypothesis. *Journal of Personality and Social Psychology, 11*, 165–70.

Lewin, K., 1951. *Field theory in social science.* New York: Harper & Row.

Linde, T. F., 1964. Influence of orthopedic disability on conformity behavior. *Journal of Abnormal and Social Psychology, 68*, 115–18.

Linder, D. E., Cooper, J., and Jones, E. E., 1967. Decision freedom as a determinant of the role of incentive magnitude in attitude change. *Journal of Personality and Social Psychology, 6* (3), 245–54.

Linder, D. E., and Worchel, S., 1970. Opinion change as a result of effortfully drawing a counterattitudinal conclusion. *Journal of Experimental Social Psychology, 6*, 432–48.

Lindzey, G., 1950. An experimental examination of the scapegoat theory of prejudice. *Journal of Abnormal and Social Psychology, 45*, 296–309.

Lindzey, G., and Rogolsky, S. J., 1950. Prejudice and identification of minority group membership. *Journal of Abnormal and Social Ps* *ogy, 45,* 37–53.

Lippit, R., and White, R. K., 1943. The "social climate" o dren's groups. In R. G. Barker, J. S. Kounin, and H. F. Wright *Child behavior and development.* New York: McGraw-Hill. Pp. 48

Lorenz, K., 1966. *On aggression.* New York: Harcourt, Brace

Lorge, I., and Solomon, H., 1959. Individual performanc group performance in problem solving related to group size and pr exposure to the problem. *Journal of Psychology, 48,* 107–14.

Lumsdaine, A. A., and Janis, I. L., 1953. Resistance to "cc propaganda" produced by one-sided and two-sided "propaganda" p tations. *Public Opinion Quarterly, 17,* 311–18.

Maas, H. S., 1950. Personal and group factors in leaders' soci ception. *Journal of Abnormal and Social Psychology, 45,* 54–63.

Macaulay, J. R., and Berkowitz, L. (Eds.), 1970. *Altruism and ing behavior.* New York: Academic.

MacDonald, R. A. P. Jr., 1970. Anxiety, affiliation and socia tion. *Developmental Psychology, 3,* 242–54.

McGuire, W. J., 1961. The effectiveness of supportive and tional defenses in immunizing and restoring beliefs against pers *Sociometry, 24,* 184–97.

McGuire, W. J., 1961. Resistance to persuasion conferred by and passive prior refutation of the same and alternative counte ments. *Journal of Abnormal and Social Psychology, 63,* 326–32.

McGuire, W. J., 1969. The nature of attitudes and attitude c In G. Lindzey and E. Aronson (Eds.), *The handbook of social p ogy,* Vol. 3 (2nd. ed.). Reading, Mass.: Addison-Wesley. Pp. 13

McGuire, W. J., and Papageorgis, D., 1961. The relative e of various types of prior belief-defense in producing immunity persuasion. *Journal of Abnormal and Social Psychology, 62,* 327–3

MacKenzie, Barbara K., 1948. The importance of contact termining attitudes toward Negroes. *Journal of Abnormal and Psychology, 43,* 417–41.

McMillen, D. L., 1971. Transgression, self-image, and cor behavior. *Journal of Personality and Social Psychology, 20,* 176–79

Macy, J., Christie, L., and Luce, D., 1953. Coding noise in oriented group. *Journal of Abnormal and Social Psychology, 48,*

Madaras, G. R., and Bem, D. J., 1968. Risk and conserva group decision making. *Journal of Experimental Social Psycho.* 350–66.

Mallick, S. K., and McCandless, B. R., 1966. A study of catharsis of aggression. *Journal of Personality and Social Psychology, 4*, 591–96.

Malof, M., and Lott, A. J., 1962. Ethnocentrism and the acceptance of Negro support in a group pressure situation. *Journal of Abnormal and Social Psychology, 65*, 254–58.

Mann, J. H., 1959. The effect of interracial contact on sociometric choices and perceptions. *Journal of Social Psychology, 50*, 143–52.

Mann, L., and Janis, I. L., 1968. A follow-up study on the long-term effects of emotional role-playing. *Journal of Personality and Social Psychology, 8*, 339–42.

Marquis, D. G., 1962. Individual responsibility and group decisions involving risk. *Industrial Management Review, 3*, 8–23.

Martens, R., 1969. Effect of an audience on learning and performance of a complex motor skill. *Journal of Personality and Social Psychology, 12*, 252–60.

Mausner, B., 1954. The effect of prior reinforcement on the interaction of observer pairs. *Journal of Abnormal Social Psychology, 49*, 65–68.

Mayo, C., and Crockett, W. H., 1964. Cognitive complexity and primacy-recency effects in impression formation. *Journal of Abnormal and Social Psychology, 68*, 335–38.

Merei, F., 1949. Group leadership and institutionalization. *Human Relations, 2*, 23–29.

Mettee, D. R., 1971. Changes in liking as a function of the magnitude and effect of sequential evaluations. *Journal of Experimental Social Psychology, 7*, 157–72.

Mettee, D. R., 1971. The true discerner as a potent source of positive affect. *Journal of Experimental Social Psychology, 7*, 292–303.

Meyer, T. P., 1972. Effects of viewing justified and unjustified real film violence on aggressive behavior. *Journal of Personality and Social Psychology, 23*, 21–29.

Milgram, S., 1961. Nationality and conformity. *Scientific American, 205* (5), 45–51.

Milgram, S., 1963. Behavioral study of obedience. *Journal of Abnormal and Social Psychology, 67*, 371–78.

Milgram, S., 1965. Some conditions of obedience and disobedience to authority. *Human Relations, 18*, 57–76.

Milgram, S., Bickman, L., and Berkowitz, L., 1969. Note on the drawing power of crowds of different size. *Journal of Personality and Social Psychology, 13*, 79–82.

Miller, N., and Campbell, D. T., 1959. Recency and prim persuasion as a function of the timing of speeches and measure *Journal of Abnormal and Social Psychology, 59,* 1–9.

Mills, J., and Aronson, E., 1965. Opinion change as a func communicator's attractiveness and desire to influence. *Journal of P ality and Social Psychology, 1,* 173–77.

Mills, J., Aronson, E., and Robinson, H., 1959. Selectivity posure to information. *Journal of Abnormal and Social Psycholo* 250–53.

Mills, J., and Harvey, J., 1972. Opinion change as a funct when information about the communicator is received and whet is attractive or expert. *Journal of Personality and Social Psycholo* 52–55.

Mills, J., and Jellison, J. M., 1968. Effect on opinion change ( ilarity between the communicator and the audience he addressed *nal of Personality and Social Psychology, 9,* 153–56.

Mills, J., and Mintz, P. M., 1972. Effect of unexplained arou affiliation. *Journal of Personality and Social Psychology, 24,* 11–13.

Minard, R. D., 1952. Race relationships in the Pocahonta field. *Journal of Social Issues, 8* (1), 29–44.

Minas, J. S., Scodel, A., Marlowe, D., and Rawson, H., 1960 descriptive aspects of two-person non-zero-sum games, II. *Jour Conflict Resolution, 4,* 193–97.

Mintz, A., 1946. A re-examination of correlations between ings and economic indices. *Journal of Abnormal and Social Psyc* 41, 154–60.

Mintz, A., 1951. Non-adaptive group behavior. *Journal of . mal and Social Psychology, 46,* 150–59.

Mintz, P. M., and Mills, J., 1971. Effects of arousal and in tion about its source upon attitude change. *Journal of Experimen cial Psychology, 7,* 561–70.

Mirels, H., and Mills, J., 1964. Perception of the pleasantne competence of a partner. *Journal of Abnormal and Social Psyc* 68, 456–60.

Morrissette, J. O., Switzer, S. A., and Crannel, C. W., 1965. performance as a function of size, structure and task difficulty. *of Personality and Social Psychology, 2,* 451–55.

Mouton, J., Blake, R. R., and Olmstead, J. A., 1956. The re ship between frequency of yielding and the disclosure of personal i *Journal of Personality, 24,* 339–47.

Munn, N. L., 1940. The effect of knowledge of the situation upon judgment of emotion from facial expressions. *Journal of Abnormal and Social Psychology, 35*, 324–38.

Murray, H. A., 1933. The effect of fear upon estimates of the maliciousness of other personalities. *Journal of Social Psychology, 4*, 310–29.

Murstein, B. L., 1961. The complementary need hypothesis in newlyweds and middle-aged married couples. *Journal of Abnormal and Social Psychology, 63*, 194–97.

Newcomb, T. M., 1943, *Personality and social change.* New York: Holt.

Newcomb, T. M., 1961. *The acquaintance process.* New York: Holt.

Newcomb, T. M., 1963. Persistence and regression of changed attitudes: long range studies. *Journal of Social Issues, 19*, 3–14.

Newcomb, T. M., Koenig, K. E., Flacks, R., and Warwick, D. P., 1967. *Persistence and change: Bennington College and its students after 25 years.* New York: Wiley.

Nisbett, R. E., and Gordon, A., 1967. Self-esteem and susceptibility to social influence. *Journal of Personality and Social Psychology, 5*, 268–76.

Nisbett, R. E., and Schachter, S., 1966. Cognitive manipulation of pain. *Journal of Experimental Social Psychology, 2*, 227–36.

Nordhøy, F., 1962. Group interaction in decision-making under risk. Unpublished master's thesis, School of Industrial Management, Massachusetts Institute of Technology.

Orne, M. T., and Evans, F. J., 1965. Social control in the psychological experiment: antisocial behavior and hypnosis. *Journal of Personality and Social Psychology, 1*, 189–200.

Osborn, A. F., 1957. *Applied imagination.* New York: Scribner.

Osgood, C. E., 1952. The nature and measurement of meaning. *Psychological Bulletin, 49*, 197–237.

Osgood, C. E., Suci, G. J., and Tannenbaum, P. H., 1957. *The measurement of meaning.* Urbana: University of Illinois Press.

Osgood, C. E., and Tannenbaum, P. H., 1955. The principle of congruity in the prediction of attitude change. *Psychology Review, 62*, 42–55.

Oskamp, S., and Kleinke, C., 1970. Amount of reward as a variable in the prisoner's dilemma game. *Journal of Personality and Social Psychology, 16*, 133–40.

Osterhouse, R. A., and Brock, T. C., 1970. Distraction in yielding to propaganda by inhibiting counterarguing. *Journal* sonality and Social Psychology, 15, 344–58.

Page, B. I., and Wolfinger, R. E., 1970. Party identification. I Wolfinger (Ed.), *Readings in American political behavior* (2nc Englewood Cliffs, N.J.: Prentice-Hall. Pp. 289–99.

Page, M. M., and Scheidt, R. J., 1971. The elusive weapons Demand awareness, evaluation apprehension, and slightly sophis subjects. *Journal of Personality and Social Psychology*, 20, 304–18.

Pallak, M. S., 1970. Effects of expected shock and relevan relevant dissonance on incidental retention. *Journal of Personali Social Psychology*, 14, 271–80.

Pallak, M. S., and Pittman, T. S., 1972. General motivatio fects of dissonance arousal. *Journal of Personality and Social P ogy*, 21, 349–58.

Palmore, E. B., 1955. The introduction of Negroes into wh partments. *Human Organization*, 14, 27–28.

Pastore, N., 1960. Attributed characteristics of liked and ( persons. *Journal of Social Psychology*, 52, 157–63.

Patel, A. S., and Gordon, J. E., 1960. Some personal and situ determinants of yielding to influence. *Journal of Abnormal and Psychology*, 61, 411–18.

Paulus, P. B., and Murdoch, P., 1971. Anticipated evaluati audience presence in the enhancement of dominant responses. *of Experimental Social Psychology*, 7, 280–91.

Pessin, J., 1933. The comparative effects of social and mec stimulation on memorizing. *American Journal of Psychology*, 45, 2

Pettigrew, T. F., 1969. Racially separate or together? *Journa cial Issues*, 25, 43–69.

Piliavin, I. M., Robin, J., and Piliavan, J. A., 1959. Good Sam ism: An underground phenomenon? *Journal of Personality and Psychology*, 13, 289–99.

Pilkonis, P. A., and Zanna, M. P., 1969. The choice-shift p enon in groups. Replication and extension. Unpublished manuscri University.

Pliner, P., Hart, H., Kohl, J., and Saari, D., 1973. Complianc out pressure: Some further data on the foot-in-the-door techniqu nal of Experimental Social Psychology. In press.

Pressman, I., and Carol, A., 1969. Crime as a diseconomy c Talk delivered at the Operations Research Society of America C tion.

Proshansky, H., and Murphy, G., 1942. The effects of reward and punishment on perception. *Journal of Psychology, 13,* 295–305.

Prothro, J. W., and Grigg, C. W., 1960. Fundamental principles of democracy: Bases of agreement and disagreement. *Journal of Politics, 22,* 276–94.

Rabbie, J. M., 1964. Differential preference for companionship under threat. *Journal of Abnormal and Social Psychology, 67,* 643–48.

Rabow, J., Fowler, F. J., Jr., Bradford, D. L., Hofeller, M. A., and Shibuya, Y., 1966. The role of social norms and leadership in risk-taking. *Sociometry, 29,* 16–27.

Raven, B. H., 1959. Social influence on opinions and the communication of related content. *Journal of Abnormal and Social Psychology, 58,* 119–28.

Raven, B. H., and French, J. R. P., Jr., 1958. Group support, legitimate power, and social influence. *Journal of Personality, 26,* 400–409.

Regan, D. T., 1971. Effects of a favor and liking on compliance. *Journal of Experimental Social Psychology, 7,* 627–39.

Regan, D. T., Williams, M., and Sparling, S., 1972. Voluntary expiation of guilt: A field experiment. *Journal of Personality and Social Psychology, 24,* 42–45.

Regan, J. W., 1971. Guilt, perceived injustice, and altruistic behavior. *Journal of Personal and Social Psychology, 18,* 124–32.

Rhine, R. J., 1958. A concept-formation approach to attitude acquisition. *Psychology Review, 65,* 362–70.

Rhine, R. J., and Severance, L. J., 1970. Ego-involvement, discrepancy, source credibility, and attitude change. *Journal of Personality and Social Psychology, 16,* 175–90.

Richardson, H. M., 1939. Studies of mental resemblance between husbands and wives and between friends. *Psychological Bulletin, 36,* 104–20.

Richardson, H. M., 1940. Community of values as a factor in friendships of college and adult women. *Journal of Social Psychology, 11,* 303–12.

Riecken, H. W., 1958. The effect of talkativeness on ability to influence group solutions of problems. *Sociometry, 21,* 309–21.

Rim, Y., 1963. Risk-taking and need for achievement. *Acta Psychologica, 21,* 108–15.

Rim, Y., 1964. Interpersonal values and risk-taking. Paper presented at the First International Congress of Psychiatry, London.

Rogers, R. W., and Thistlewaite, D. L., 1970. Effects of fear arousal and reassurance on attitude change. *Journal of Personali Social Psychology, 15,* 227–33.

Rokeach, M., and Mezei, L., 1966. Race and shared belief as in social choice. *Science, 151,* 167–72.

Rosen, S., 1961. Postdecision affinity for incompatible inforr *Journal of Abnormal and Social Psychology, 63,* 188–90.

Rosenberg, M. J., 1960. Cognitive reorganization in response hypnotic reversal of attitudinal affect. *Journal of Personality, 28,*

Rosenberg, S., and Olshan, K., 1970. Evaluative and descrip pects in personality perception. *Journal of Personality and Soci chology, 16,* 619–26.

Rosenthal, R., 1963. On the social psychology of the psychc experiment: the experimenter's hypothesis as unintended determi experimenter results. *American Scientists, 51,* 268–83.

Rosenthal, R., 1964. Experimental outcome-orientation and sults the psychological experiment. *Psychological Bulletin, 61,* 4

Rosenthal, R., 1966. *Experimenter effects in behavioral re* New York: Appleton-Century-Crofts.

Rosnow, R. L., Holz, R. F., and Levin, J., 1966. Differential of complementary and competing variables in primacy-recency. *of Social Psychology, 69,* 135–47.

Ross, A. S., 1971. Effect of increased responsibility on by: intervention: The presence of children. *Journal of Personality ana Psychology, 19,* 306–10.

Rothbart, M., 1970. Assessing the likelihood of a threatening English Canadians' evaluation of the Quebec separatist mov *Journal of Personality and Social Psychology, 15,* 109–17.

Ruckmick, C. A., 1921. A preliminary study of the emotion *chological Monographs, 12* (3, Whole No. 136), 30–35.

Saegert, S., Swamp, W., and Zajonc, R. B., 1973. Exposure, c and interpersonal attraction. *Journal of Personality and Social P ogy, 25,* 234–42.

Saenger, G., and Gilbert, E., 1950. Customer reactions to tr gration of Negro sales personnel. *International Journal of Opini Attitude Research, 4,* 57–76.

Sarnoff, I., 1960. Reaction formation and cynicism. *Journal sonality, 28,* 129–43.

Sarnoff, I., and Corwin, S., 1959. Castration anxiety and t of death. *Journal of Personality, 27,* 374–85.

Sarnoff, I., and Katz, D., 1954. The motivational bases of  change. *Journal of Abnormal and Social Psychology, 49,* 115–24.

Sarnoff, I., and Zimbardo, P. G., 1961. Anxiety, fear and social affiliation. *Journal of Abnormal and Social Psychology, 62,* 356–63.

Schachter, S., 1951. Deviation, rejection and communication. *Journal of Abnormal and Social Psychology, 46,* 190–208.

Schachter, S., 1959. *The psychology of affiliation.* Stanford, Calif.: Stanford.

Schachter, S., Ellertson, N., McBride, D., and Gregory, D., 1951. An experimental study of cohesiveness and productivity. *Human Relations, 4,* 229–38.

Schachter, S., and Singer, J. E., 1962. Cognitive, social and physiological determinants of emotional state. *Psychological Review, 69,* 379–99.

Schachter, S., and Wheeler, L., 1962. Epinephrine, chlorpromazine, and amusement. *Journal of Abnormal and Social Psychology, 65,* 121–28.

Schaps, E., 1972. Cost, dependency, and helping. *Journal of Personality and Social Psychology, 21,* 74–78.

Schein, E. H., 1951. *Coercive persuasion.* New York: Norton.

Schein, E. H., 1956. The Chinese indoctrination program for prisoners of war. *Psychiatry, 19,* 149–72.

Schellenberg, J. A., and Bee, L. S., 1960. A re-examination of the theory of complementary needs in mate selection. *Marriage and Family Living, 22,* 227–32.

Schlosberg, H., 1952. The descriptions of facial expressions in terms of two dimensions. *Journal of Experimental Psychology, 44,* 229–37.

Schmitt, D. R., and Marwell, G., 1972. Withdrawal and reward reallocation as responses to inequity. *Journal of Experimental Social Psychology, 8,* 207–21.

Schmitt, R. C., 1957. Density, delinquency and crime in Honolulu. *Sociology and Social Research, 41,* 274–76.

Schmitt, R. C., 1966. Density, health and social disorganization. *Journal of American Institute of Planners, 32,* 38–40.

Schneider, F. W., 1970. Conforming behavior of black and white children. *Journal of Personality and Social Psychology, 16,* 466–71.

Schopler, J., and Compere, J. S., 1971. Effects of being kind or harsh to another on liking. *Journal of Personality and Social Psychology, 20,* 155–59.

Schwartz, S. H., and Clausen, G. T., 1970. Responsibility, norms, and helping in an emergency. *Journal of Personality and Social Psychology, 16,* 299–310.

Scodel, A., and Austrin, H., 1957. The perception of Jewish photographs by non-Jews and Jews. *Journal of Abnormal and Social Psychology, 54,* 278–80.

Sears, D. O., 1966. Opinion formation and information prefe[r]
in an adversary situation. *Journal of Experimental Social Psychol*[ogy]
130–42.

Sears, D. O., 1967. Social anxiety, opinion structure, and o[pinion]
change. *Journal of Personality and Social Psychology, 7,* 142–51.

Sears, D. O., 1968. The paradox of defacto selective exposure[:]
out preference for supportive information. In R. P. Abelson et al.
*Theories of cognitive consistency.* Chicago: Rand McNally. Pp. 7[ ]

Sears, D. O., 1969. Political behavior. In G. Lindzey and E. [Aaron]
son (Eds.), *Handbook of social psychology.* Vol. V. Reading, Mass[. A]
dison-Wesley. Pp. 315–458.

Sears, D. O., and Freedman, J. L., 1963. Commitment, infor[mation]
utility, and selective exposure. ONR report No. 12, under grant[ ]
233 (54).

Sears, D. O., and Freedman, J. L., 1965. Effects of expect[ed fa]
miliarity of arguments upon opinion change and selective ex[posure.]
*Journal of Personality and Social Psychology, 2,* 420–25.

Sears, D. O., and Freedman, J. L., 1967. Selective exposure[ and]
formation: a critical review. *Public Opinion Quarterly, 31,* 194–21[3]

Sears, D. O., Freedman, J. L., and O'Connor, E. F., Jr., 196[4. The]
effects of anticipated debate and commitment on the polarization[ of au]
dience opinion. *Public Opinion Quarterly, 28,* 615–27.

Sears, D. O., and McConahay, J. B., 1973. *The politics of vi*[olence:]
*The new urban blacks and the Watts riot.* Boston: Houghton-Miffli[n.]

Sears, D. O., and Whitney, R. E., 1972. Political persuasio[n. In I.]
DeS. Pool, et al. (Eds.), *Handbook of communication.* Chicago[: Rand]
McNally.

Sears, D. O., and Whitney, R. E., 1973. *Political persuasion.* [Morris]
town, N.J.: General Learning Press.

Sears, R. R., 1961. Relations of early socialization experie[nce to]
aggression in middle childhood. *Journal of Abnormal and Soci*[al Psy]
chology, 63, 466–93.

Sears, R. R., Whiting, J. W. M., Nowlis, V., and Sears, P. S.[, 1953.]
Some child-rearing antecedents of aggression and dependency in [young]
children. *Genetic Psychological Monographs, 47,* 135–236.

Secord, P. F., and Berscheid, E. S., 1963. Stereotyping and t[he gen]
erality of implicit personality theory. *Journal of Personality, 31,* [ ]

Shaffer, D. R., and Hendrick, C., 1971. Effects of actual eff[ort and]
anticipated effort on task enhancement. *Journal of Experimental* [Social]
*Psychology, 7,* 435–47.

Shaw, M. E., 1954. Group structure and the behavior of individuals in small groups. *Journal of Personality, 38*, 139–49.

Shaw, M. E., 1954. Some effects of problem complexity upon problem solution efficiency in different communication nets. *Journal of Experimental Psychology, 48*, 211–17.

Shaw, M. E., 1954. Some effects of unequal distribution of information upon group performance in various communication nets. *Journal of Abnormal and Social Psychology, 49*, 547–53.

Shaw, M. E., 1955. A comparison of two types of leadership in various communication nets. *Journal of Abnormal and Social Psychology, 50*, 127–34.

Sherif, M., 1935. A study of some social factors in perception. *Archives of Psychology*, No. 187.

Sherman, M., 1927. The differentiation of emotional responses from motion picture views and from actual observations. *Journal of Comparative Psychology, 7*, 265–84.

Sherman, S. J., 1970 (a). Effects of choice and incentive on attitude change in a discrepant behavior situation. *Journal of Personality and Social Psychology, 15*, 245–52.

Sherman, S. J., 1970 (b). Attitudinal effects of unforeseen consequences. *Journal of Personality and Social Psychology, 16*, 510–20.

Singer, J. E., Brush, C., and Lublin, S. D., 1965. Some aspects of deindividuation: identification and conformity. *Journal of Experimental Social Psychology, 1*, 356–78.

Singer, R. P., 1965. The effects of fear-arousing communications on attitude change and behavior. Unpublished doctoral dissertation, University of Connecticut.

Sistrunk, F., and McDavid, J. W., 1971. Sex variable in conforming behavior. *Journal of Personality and Social Psychology, 17*, 200–207.

Skolnick, P., 1971. Reactions to personal evaluations: A failure to replicate. *Journal of Personality and Social Psychology, 18*, 62–67.

Smith, F. T., 1943. An experiment in modifying attitudes toward the Negro. *Teachers College Contributions to Education*, No. 887.

Smith, K. H., 1961. Ego strength and perceived competence as conformity variables. *Journal of Abnormal Psychology, 62*, 169–71.

Smith, M. B., Bruner, J. S., and White, R. W., 1956. *Opinions and Personality*. New York: Wiley.

Smith, R. E., Smythe, L., and Lien, D., 1972. Inhibition of helping behavior by a similar or dissimilar nonreactive fellow bystander. *Journal of Personality and Social Psychology, 23*, 414–19.

Smith, S., and Haythorne, W. W., 1972. Effects of compat crowding, group size, and leadership seniority on stress, anxiety tility and annoyance in isolated groups. *Journal of Personality and Psychology, 22*, 67–69.

Smith, S. S., and Jamieson, B. D., 1972. Effects of attitude a involvement on the learning and retention of controversial m *Journal of Personality and Social Psychology, 22*, 303–10.

Snyder, A., et al., 1960. Value, information, and conform havior. *Journal of Personality, 28*, 333–41.

Snyder, R. L., 1968. Reproduction and population pressu E. Stellar, and J. M. Sprague (Eds.). New York: Academic. Pp. 1

Sommer, R., 1969. *Personal space: the behavioral basis of* Englewood Cliffs, N.J.: Prentice-Hall.

Staats, A. W., and Staats, C. K., 1958. Attitudes establish classical conditioning. *Journal of Abnormal and Social Psycholo* 37–40.

Star, S. A., Williams, R. M., Jr., and Stouffer, S. A., 1958. infantry platoons in white companies. In E. E. Maccoby, T. M. New and E. L. Hartley (Eds.), *Readings in social psychology* (3rd ed. York: Holt. Pp. 596–601.

Starkweather, J. A., 1956. The communication value of c free speech. *American Journal of Psychology, 69*, 121–23.

Staub, E., 1970. A child in distress: the influence of age and ber of witnesses on children's attempts to help. *Journal of Pers and Social Psychology, 14*, 130–40.

Staub, E., 1971. Helping a person in distress: the influence plicit and explicit "rules" of conduct on children and adults. *Jou Personality and Social Psychology, 17*, 137–44.

Stein, D. D., Hardyck, J. A., and Smith, M. B., 1965. Race a lief: an open and shut case. *Journal of Personality and Social P. ogy, 1*, 281–89.

Stoner, J. A. F., 1961. A comparison of individual and grou sions involving risk. Unpublished master's thesis, School of Inc Management.

Storms, M. D., and Nisbett, R. E., 1970. Insomnia and the a tion process. *Journal of Personality and Social Psychology, 16*, 3

Stouffer, S. A., 1955. *Communism, Conformity, and Civil ties.* Garden City, N.Y.: Doubleday.

Stouffer, S. A., Lumsdaine, A. A., Lumsdaine, M. H., Willia M., Jr., Smith, M. B., Janis, I. L., Star, S. A., and Cottrell, L. S., Jr

Combat and its aftermath. In *Studies in social psychology in World War II*. Vol. 1, *The American soldier*. Princeton, N.J.: Princeton.

Stouffer, S. A., Suchman, E. A., DeVinney, L. C., Star, S. A., and Williams, R. M., Jr., 1949. Adjustment during army life. In *Studies in social psychology in World War II*. Vol. 1, *The American soldier*. Princeton, N.J.: Princeton.

Stricker, L. J., Messick, S., and Jackson, D. N., 1970. Conformity, anticonformity and independence: Their dimensionality and generality. *Journal of Personality and Social Psychology, 16*, 494–507.

Strodtbeck, F. L., James, R. M., and Hawkins, C., 1958. Social status in jury deliberations. In E. Maccoby, T. Newcomb, and E. Hartley (Eds.), *Readings in social psychology*. New York: Holt. Pp. 379–87.

Stroebe, W., Insko, C. A., Thompson, V. D., and Layton, B. D., 1971. Effects of physical attractiveness, attitude similarity, and sex on various aspects of interpersonal attraction. *Journal of Personality and Social Psychology, 18*, 79–91.

Swingle, P. G., 1970. Exploitative behavior in non-zero sum games. *Journal of Personality and Social Psychology, 16*, 121–32.

Tagiuri, R., Blake, R. R., and Bruner, J. S., 1953. Some determinants of the perception of positive and negative feelings in others. *Journal of Abnormal and Social Psychology, 48*, 585–92.

Tagiuri, R., and Petrullo, L., 1958. *Person perception and interpersonal behavior*. Stanford, Calif.: Stanford.

Taylor, D. W., Berry, P. C., and Block, C. H., 1958. Does group participation when using brainstorming facilitate or inhibit creative thinking? *Administrative Science Quarterly, 2*, 23–47.

Taylor, D. W., and Faust, W. L., 1958. Twenty questions: efficiency in problem solving as a function of size of group. *Journal of Experimental Psychology, 44*, 360–68.

Taylor, S. E., and Mettee, D. R., 1971. When similarity breeds contempt. *Journal of Personality and Social Psychology, 20*, 75–81.

Teger, A. I., and Pruitt, D. G., 1967. Components of group risk-taking. *Journal of Experimental Social Psychology, 3*, 189–205.

Teger, A. I., Pruitt, D. G., St. Jean, R., and Haaland, G. A., 1970. A reexamination of the familiarization hypothesis in group risk taking. *Journal of Experimental Social Psychology, 6*, 346–50.

Thibaut, J. W., and Kelley, H. H., 1959. *The social psychology of groups*. New York: Wiley.

Thibaut, J. W., and Riecken, H. W., 1955. Some determinants and

506

consequences of the perception of social causality. *Journal of Perso* 24, 113–33.

Thistlewaite, D. L., de Haan, H., and Kamenetsky, J., 195! effects of "directive" and "nondirective" communication procedu attitudes. *Journal of Abnormal and Social Psychology, 51,* 107–13.

Thistlewaite, D. L., and Kamenetsky, J., 1955. Attitude ( through refutation and elaboration of audience counterarguments *nal of Abnormal and Social Psychology, 51,* 3–9.

Thompson, D. F., and Meltzer, L., 1964. Communication of tional intent by facial expression. *Journal of Abnormal and Socia chology, 68,* 129–35.

Tilker, H. A., 1970. Socially responsible behavior as a func▪ observer responsibility and victim feedback. *Journal of Personali Social Psychology, 14,* 95–100.

Tinbergen, N., 1951. *The study of instinct.* Fair Lawn, N.J.: ( University Press.

Tittle, C. R., and Hill, R. J., 1967. Attitude measurement an diction of behavior: An evaluation of conditions and measuremen niques. *Sociometry, 30,* 199–213.

Torrance, E. P., 1955. Some consequences of power differen decision making in permanent and temporary three-man groups. Ir Hare, E. F. Borgatta, and R. F. Bales (Eds.), *Small groups: studies ir interaction.* New York: Knopf. Pp. 482–91.

Travis, L. E., 1925. The effect of a small audience upon ey▪ coordination. *Journal of Abnormal and Social Psychology, 20,* 142–

Valins, S., 1966. Cognitive effects of false heart-rate feec *Journal of Personality and Social Psychology, 4,* 400–408.

Verba, S. R., Brody, A., Parker, E. B., Nie, N. H., Polsby, ▪ Ekman, P., and Black, G. S., 1967. Public opinion and the war ir nam. *American Political Science Review, 61,* 317–33.

Vernon, P. E., 1933. Some characteristics of the good judge ▪ sonality. *Journal of Social Psychology, 4,* 42–58.

Wallace, J., and Sadalla, E., 1966. Behavioral consequences of gression: I. the effects of social recognition. *Journal of Experimen search Personality, 1,* 187–94.

Wallach, M. A., and Kogan, N., 1965. The roles of informatic cussion, and consensus in group risk taking. *Journal of Experimen cial Psychology, 1,* 1–19.

Wallach, M. A., Kogan, N., and Bem, D. J., 1962. Group in on individual risk taking. *Journal of Abnormal and Social Psyc* 65, 75–87.

Wallach, M. A., Kogan, N., and Bem, D. J., 1964. Diffusion of responsibility and level of risk taking in groups. *Journal of Abnormal and Social Psychology, 68,* 263–74.

Wallach, M. A., Kogan, N., and Burt, R. B., 1965. Can group members recognize the effects of group discussion upon risk taking? *Journal of Experimental Social Psychology, 1,* 379–95.

Wallach, M. A., and Malbi, J., 1970. Information versus conformity in the effects of groups discussion on risk taking. *Journal of Personality and Social Psychology, 14,* 149–56.

Walster, E., 1964. The temporal sequence of post-decision processes. In L. Festinger (Ed.), *Conflict, decision and dissonance.* Stanford, Calif.: Stanford. Pp. 112–28.

Walster, E., 1970. The effect of self-esteem on liking for dates of various desirabilities. *Journal of Experimental Social Psychology, 6,* 248–53.

Walster, E., Aronson, E., and Abrahams, D., 1966. On increasing the persuasiveness of a low prestige communicator. *Journal of Experimental Social Psychology, 2,* 325–42.

Walster, E., Aronson, V., Abrahams, D., and Rottmann, L., 1966. Importance of physical attractiveness in dating behavior. *Journal of Personality and Social Psychology, 4,* 508–16.

Walster, E., and Berscheid, E., 1967. When does a harm-doer compensate a victim? *Journal of Personality and Social Psychology, 6,* 435–41.

Walster, E., and Festinger, L., 1962. The effectiveness of "overheard" persuasive communications. *Journal of Abnormal and Social Psychology, 65,* 395–402.

Waterman, C. K., 1969. The facilitating and interfering effects of cognitive dissonance on simple and complex paired-associate learning tasks. *Journal of Experimental Social Psychology, 5,* 31–42.

Weiss, W. A., 1953. A "sleeper" effect in opinion change. *Journal of Abnormal and Social Psychology, 48,* 173–80.

Weiss, W. A., and Fine, B. J., 1956. The effect of induced aggressiveness on opinion change. *Journal of Abnormal and Social Psychology, 52,* 109–14.

White, G. M., 1972. Immediate and deferred effects of model observation and guided and unguided rehearsal on donating and stealing. *Journal of Personality and Social Psychology, 21,* 139–48.

Whiting, J. W. M., and Child, I. L., 1953. *Child training and personality: a cross-cultural study.* New Haven, Conn.: Yale.

Whyte, W. F., 1943. *Street corner society: the social structu*
*an Italian slum*. Chicago: University of Chicago Press.

Whyte, W. H., Jr., 1956. *The organization man*. New York: ?
and Schuster.

Wichman, H., 1970. Effects of isolation and communication c
operation in a two-person game. *Journal of Personality and Socia*
*chology, 16*, 114–20.

Wicker, A. W., 1969. Attitudes versus action: The relationsl
verbal and overt behavior responses to attitude objects. *Journal c*
*cial Issues, 25* (4), 41–78.

Wicker, A. W., 1971. An examination of the "other variable
planation of attitude-behavior inconsistency. *Journal of Personalit*
*Social Psychology, 19*, 18–30.

Wilke, H., and Lanzetta, J. T., 1970. The obligation to hel
effects of amount of prior help on subsequent helping behavior. *Jc*
*of Experimental Social Psychology, 6*, 488–93.

Williams, R. M., Jr., 1947. *The reduction of intergroup ten*
New York: Social Science Research Council Bulletin 57, 71.

Williams, R. M., Jr., 1964. *Strangers next door: ethnic relatio*
*American communities*. Englewood Cliffs, N.J.: Prentice-Hall.

Wilner, D. M., Walkley, R. P., and Cook, S. W., 1952. Resid
proximity and intergroup relations in public housing projects. *Jc*
*of Social Issues, 8*, 45–69.

Wilner, D. M., Walkley, R. P., and Cook, S. W., 1955. *Hum*
*lations in interracial housing: a study of the contact hypothesis*. N
apolis: University of Minnesota Press.

Winder, A. E., 1955. White attitudes towards Negro-white
action in an area of changing racial composition. *Journal of Socia*
*chology, 41*, 85–102.

Winsborough, H. H., 1965. The social consequences of high
lation density. *Law and Contemporary Problems, 30*, 120–26.

Wishner, J., 1960. Reanalysis of "impressions of personality."
*chological Review, 67*, 96–112.

Wolf, R., and Murray, H. A., 1937. An experiment in judgin
sonalities. *Journal of Psychology, 3*, 345–65.

Wolosin, R., Sherman, S. J., and Mynatt, C. R., 1972. Per
social influence in a conformity situation. *Journal of Personality ar*
*cial Psychology, 23*, 184–91.

Woodworth, R. S., 1938. *Experimental psychology*. New
Holt.

Worchel, S., and Brehm, J. W., 1971. Direct and implied social restoration of freedom. *Journal of Personality and Social Psychology, 18,* 294–304.

Works, E., 1961. The prejudice-interaction hypothesis from the point of view of the Negro minority group. *American Journal of Sociology, 67,* 47–52.

Wrightsman, L. S., 1960. Effects of waiting with others on changes in level of felt anxiety. *Journal of Abnormal and Social Psychology, 61,* 216–22.

Zajonc, R. B., 1965. Social facilitation. *Science, 149,* 269–74.

Zajonc, R. B., 1968. Attitudinal effects of mere exposure. *Journal of Personality and Social Psychology, 8.* Monograph, 1–29.

Zajonc, R. B., Heingartner, A., and Herman, E. M., 1969. Social enhancement and impairment of performance in the cockroach. *Journal of Personality and Social Psychology, 13,* 83–92.

Zajonc, R. B., and Sales, S. M., 1966. Social facilitation of dominant and subordinate responses. *Journal of Experimental Social Psychology, 2,* 160–68.

Zajonc, R. B., Wolosin, R. J., and Wolosin, M. A., 1972. Group risk-taking under various group decision schemes. *Journal of Experimental Social Psychology, 8,* 16–30.

Zajonc, R. B., Wolosin, R. J., Wolosin, M. A., and Loh, W. D., 1970. Social facilitation and imitation in group risk-taking. *Journal of Experimental Social Psychology, 6,* 26–46.

Zellman, G. L., and Sears, D. O., 1971. Childhood origins of tolerances for dissent. *Journal of Social Issues, 27,* 109–36.

Zellner, M., 1970. Self-esteem, reception, and influenceability. *Journal of Personality and Social Psychology, 15,* 87–93.

Zilman, D., 1971. Excitation transfer in communication-mediated aggressive behavior. *Journal of Experimental Social Psychology, 7,* 419–34.

Zilman, D., 1972. Rhetorical elicitation of agreement in persuasion. *Journal of Personality and Social Psychology, 21,* 159–65.

Zilman, D., Katcher, A. H., and Milavsky, B., 1972. Excitation transfer from physical exercise to subsequent aggressive behavior. *Journal of Experimental Social Psychology, 8,* 247–59.

Zimbardo, P. G., 1960. Involvement and communication discrepancy as determinants of opinion conformity. *Journal of Abnormal and Social Psychology, 60,* 86–94.

Zimbardo, P. G., and Ebbesen, E. B., 1970. Experimental modifica-

tion of the relationship between effort, attitude, and behavior. J《
of Personality and Social Psychology, 16, 207–13.

Zimbardo, P. G., and Formica, R., 1963. Emotional comparisc
self-esteem as determinants of affiliation. Journal of Personality, 31
62.

Zimbardo, P. G., Snyder, M., Thomas, J., Gold, A., and Gurw
1970. Modifying the impact of persuasive communications with ex
distraction. Journal of Personality and Social Psychology, 16, 669–8

Zimbardo, P. G., Weisenberg, M., Firestone, I., and Levy, B.,
Communicator effectiveness in producing public conformity and p
attitude change. Journal of Personality, 33, 233–56.

Zimbardo, P. G., Weisenberg, M., Firestone, I., and Levy, B.,
Changing appetites for eating fried grasshopper. In P. Zimbardo
The cognitive control of motivation. Chicago: Scott. Foresman. Pp. 4

# A

Abelson, R. P., 253, 270–71, 303, 314r, 339r
Abrahams, D., 275
Adams, J. S., 402
Adams, Sherman, 153
Aderman, D., 47
Allee, W. C., 172
Allen, V. L., 222, 240r, 352
Allport, F. H., 171, 172
Allport, G. W., 245–46
Anderson, D., 404
Anderson, N. H., 35–36, 59r, 76, 249, 250
Apsler, R., 307
Ardrey, R., 419
Aristotle, 49, 123
Arkoff, A., 293
Aronson, E., 79, 83, 98r, 263r, 273, 275, 276, 285, 314r, 315r, 329, 339r, 354, 364–65, 467r
Asch, S. E., 33, 213, 215, 221, 222, 224, 225, 450
Ashmore, R. D., 336, 339r
Austin, J. A., 305

# B

Back, K., 64, 98r
Bacon, Francis, 5
Bales, R. F., 146–47
Bandura, A., 113, 129, 135r, 219
Barker, R. G., 107
Baron, R. A., 114, 129
Baron, R. S., 204, 205r
Bartlett, F. C., 41
Bateson, N., 201
Bavelas, A., 144, 150, 167r

Beach, F., 62
Becker, L. A., 275
Bem, D. J., 54, 202, 204, 205r, 37̇ 374–75, 380r
Berkowitz, L., 109–10, 128, 130, 167r, 194, 205r, 293, 308, ̇ 404, 406, 413r
Berry, P. C., 189
Berscheid, E., 41, 46, 69, 78, 401,
Bickman, L., 410
Blake, R. R., 229, 231
Blank, A., 201, 202
Bless, E., 398
Block, C. H., 189
Bochner, S., 285, 286
Booker, A., 110
Boring, E. G., 37
Bradley, E., 408
Brehm, J. W., 349–50, 358–59, 38̇ 393, 394, 413r
Brock, T. C., 275, 309
Brophy, I. N., 75
Brown, E., 327
Bruner, J. S., 42, 43, 253
Brush, C., 197
Bryan, J. H., 386
Buchanan, R. W., 431r
Burgess, T. D., 72
Burt, R. B., 201
Buss, A. H., 110, 130, 135r
Buss, E., 110
Byrne, D., 87, 251

# C

Calhoun, J. B., 418, 430r
Campbell, A., 332
Campbell, D. T., 467r

512

514

# ubject index

# A